WHAT PEOPLE ARE SAYING

WHEN I WAS SMALL

"This is a really cute book. Great little story, encouraging the making of memories. The artwork paired very well with the story."

"I would recommend this book to anyone with a family to share it with. My daughter loved the illustrations and we enjoyed it very much!"

A BLESSED LIFE: ONE WORLD WAR II SEABEE'S STORY

"Tamra McAnally Bolton uncovers the long-buried war-time memories of her 96-year-old father over coffee and raisin pie at the kitchen table of the long-time family home near Jacksonville, Texas. This surprisingly gentle story of an East Texas farm boy going to fight for his country wraps around the reader like a homemade quilt. You're not going to want to put this book down, so make your pot of coffee ahead of time."

Brad Maule, actor and singer best known for his role as General Hospital's Dr. Tony Jones, Acting/Directing and Filmmaking professor Stephen F. Austin State University in Nacogdoches, Texas.

"You don't have to be a veteran to enjoy this easily read account of her Dad's Seabee service centered on his WWII service on Iwo Jima. Get a

copy. It's really good! Also involves a wonderfully descriptive account of "every family" Small town country life in East Texas which could be "any small town USA."

J. Hawkins

"Couldn't put this one down. Tamra shares the stories of her dad's WWII experiences in spellbinding short tales. I have never heard first hand experiences of WWII in such detail. I cried, I laughed and I loved it. I highly recommend this book."

E. Edom

"To page through this book was like spending a quiet day at the old farm. Tamra's descriptive writing draws you to the back sun room where you can taste the coffee and listen to the amazing stories that shaped her father's life and in turn, her own. Best read in a long time."

R. Hall

His 100TH Year

TAMRA M. BOLTON
with
SHERRY L. BRYANT, MELANIE E. ROOS,
AND SHAUN M. MCANALLY

Cover photo: © 2023 Tamra McAnally Bolton
Cover, interior design and ebook adaptation: Deena Rae; eBookBuilders
Author Photo: Calie Anne Photography

Poverty Ridge Press
1090 CR 3905
Jacksonville, TX 75766
Email: povertyridgepress47@gmail.com

File version 202311049.019

This book is dedicated to all caregivers who labor tirelessly and unselfishly for those in their charge.

ALSO BY TAMRA

When I Was Small

A Blessed Life: One World War II Seabee's Story

The Art of Story Keeping

ACKNOWLEDGMENTS

One of the things I've learned this past year is it takes many people to bring a book to life. Not only did my sisters contribute an incredible amount of time and energy to this collaborative project, but they infused it with love as well.

I am deeply grateful to my sister Sherry, for her beautiful job of editing mounds of material and also for the idea of adding the takeaway thoughts to the end of each month.

Also thanks to Deena Rae of E-BookBuilders, who is indispensable at both book design and layout.

Most of all, I am thankful to my Lord and Saviour Jesus Christ for giving me the idea for a book about our dear parents and this incredibly precious journey we are on as they travel to their forever home.

CONTENTS

McANALLY FAMILY TREE

OUR PARENTS:

STUART – DAD, DADDY, POP, PAWPAW
HILDA – MOM, MAMA, NANNIE

THEIR CHILDREN:

MELANIE – MEL MARRIED TO PHILIP (DECEASED 2016)
CHILDREN: ANDY, ANGELA, AND JOANNA
Spouses and grandchildren:
Andy married to Kara (Mary Grace and Garrett),
Angela married to Austin (Wyatt, Valerie, and Kolt),
JoAnna married to Rex (Ethan, Jared, Brandon, and Hannah Jo)

SHERRY – MARRIED TO BILL
CHILDREN: BEN AND STUART (STU)
Spouses and grandchildren:
Ben married to Shelley (Cooper and Parker),
Stuart married to Ashley (Knoxlynn)

TAMRA – MARRIED TO MARC
CHILDREN: RACHEL, CALEB, AND RITA
Spouses and grandchildren:
Rachel married to Rob (Gus and Addie),
Caleb (Emelia),
Rita married to Jason (Athena, Raylan, and coming in January 2024, Hilda Mae)

JOSHUA – JOSH (DECEASED 1986)

SHAUN
CHILDREN: CHRISTOPHER

FOREWORD

Writing a book is usually a pretty solitary venture until the final copy when editing and other necessary helps are included. This book, however, is very different in that it has four authors – three who did the actual writing and one who contributed in other sometimes intangible ways. When I approached my siblings with the idea of recording our journey with Mom and Dad over the course of the next year, they agreed, albeit somewhat reluctantly. It would take all of us, encouraging and prompting one another to finish what was at times, an overwhelming task.

While my sister Sherry and I, being writers, found the task mostly enjoyable and natural, my sister Melanie had trepidations about her contributions, but quickly got on board in a big way and was glad to be a part of the process. My brother Shaun and his thoughts are woven into our own written contributions, along with the occasional quote from him, including the accompanying photos for each month.

To more easily understand our family connections, a simplified family tree is included in the front of the book to serve as a reference.

This is not meant to be a literary work, but rather a simple record of our daily life on our farm as we become the caregivers for our parents. Neither is it a standard by which to measure others' caregiving, for there is no such measure. It is simply our way of extending a hand of encouragement and hope for those who find themselves on this path. Some of the entries you might find tedious, even boring, but that is part of life too. We also hope you find humor, an occasional chuckle, a tearful reminder of wonderful memories, and even a glimmer of hope beyond the task at hand.

Our hope for you as a caregiver, or someone who loves and supports them, is that you will realize you are not alone, others have been where you are or will be, and we are all just doing the best we can at one of the toughest jobs in the world.

The takeaways at the end of each month are designed to give you a thought to ponder or a helpful idea to carry with you on your own journey.

May God bless your efforts as you travel the path before you and may He give you strength and courage for each day.

If you would like to see videos and more photos and follow us through our experiences, you can go to: his100thyear.book on Instagram.

His 100TH Year

99

AUGUST

August in Texas is often unbearably hot and dry, and seems extremely long. The only salvation for August is that it's Dad's birthday month. Occasionally, we get a break in the weather via an early cool front or some much-needed rain which helps alleviate the dog days. Dad usually plans to work the cows during this time, so we always pray for cooler weather around the end of August. We usually have quite the crowd for his birthday, and Dad can't stand for "all that good help to go to waste." He also utilizes spring break and other handy times when the grands and great-grands are around to help. Since my siblings and I now all qualify as "senior citizens," we tend to agree with Dad on this scheduling more than we used to.

This time was a little different because of a change in circumstances. A dear friend of the family had passed and her funeral was planned for the same day as Dad's birthday get-together. We didn't want to miss her service, so we persuaded him to do all the vaccinating, spraying, hauling to the sale, etc. the weekend before his planned celebration. He was all for it. The extra help wasn't here, but we managed to get it all done, without any major injuries or problems. It was like old times… We also moved the other herd from down at the Homeplace back to the farm for the coming winter. Thank goodness Dad likes to get an early start; we were finished before the temps climbed into the 90s that day.

We only had a couple of scares while working the cattle – a belligerent mama cow charged us and we had to take to the fence. Of course we know

Dad can't get out of the way and that's the kind of thing that scares the stuffing out of all of us, except Dad. He can't move fast enough to escape, but he still insists on getting into the working pens "to supervise." Another problem is Dad is getting so deaf that we can't yell loud enough to warn him anyway, so a certain amount of serious praying and furious arm-waving goes on while we are in the pens sorting cattle.

Dad has a certain way he likes to do things and while we try to do it his way, sometimes the cattle don't cooperate and we have to make split-second decisions that Dad doesn't always appreciate. But, if the job gets done and no one gets hurt too bad (bruises and minor cuts don't count), Dad is always grateful and thanks us each time for our help and tells us what a good job we did. We still enjoy working together as a family, even after half a century. It is more challenging than it used to be, but we can usually do more than we think we can – we all moved pretty fast when that cow charged us – well, all of us except Dad!

The following Saturday, we were certainly grateful that the festivities didn't involve nerve-wracking, sweaty, dirty, and stinky a.m. activities. We all arrived for his party that morning in clean clothes and mostly chipper spirits.

Turning 99 is a pretty big deal, but Dad, as usual, didn't make too much of it. He went along with all the fuss and "ta-do" as he calls it and seemed to enjoy the day, eating, visiting, and posing for pictures. I think Dad is amused, but sometimes a bit irritated by all our "carrying on." He lets us know when we've pushed too far by gently reminding us "I've lived all this time without a keeper…I don't think I need one now." He knows how much we love him and that we only want to do what is best. To show he's not really upset about it, he'll give us a familiar look of half-concealed amusement and we are relieved. We don't want him to feel crowded and inept, because he is more capable than we are in some things – we are just trying our best to keep our Daddy as long as we can. Even though we know we can't hold onto him forever, we are going to give it a whirl anyway.

Sherry

FRIDAY, AUGUST 19TH, 2022

What a day! Busy from 5:30 AM on… feeding and watering the calf with Pop, watering flowers and the little trees up on the hill and around the house – seems as if the whole world needs watering. We surely need some rain. Fixed breakfast for Pop and me (with vitamin chasers) then the same for Mom.

Dad got a kick out of us trying to get his picture on his 99th birthday. He thought we made quite a fuss about his special day.

Tomorrow is Pop's birthday, so I started making the pineapple cake – his favorite. Since I'm a messy cook, the counter was littered with dirty mixing bowls, measuring cups, spoons, and spatulas. Popped the layers in the oven, then cleaned up the wreckage. Started fixing "lunch" – I still can't get used to eating the noon meal at 2:00. And Mom usually doesn't want hers until 3:00, so the day is chopped into little pieces of time, making it difficult to launch into a project … like this cake! Finally got the filling made; then stacked and filled the layers while also sweeping and cleaning for the gathering tomorrow.

In the thick of cleaning, Shaun called and asked if I could take him to Tyler to get his truck. That gave us some time to visit; you'd think we'd have plenty of time to talk, but he is a busy guy with his painting business, and I'm usually cooking or cleaning when he comes over to see Mom and Dad.

The drive to Tyler usually only takes about 25 minutes, but it was the 5:30 getting-off-work time and traffic was nuts! After dropping Shaun off, I stopped by a store to get a few more items for tomorrow, then drove home and fixed a snack for Pop. Took Mom her yogurt and evening meds and vitamins. Shoved more water at Pop – a constant struggle to get him to stay hydrated. Took Mom her 9:00 coffee ice cream cone. Made coleslaw for tomorrow. Rounded up tablecloths, plates, forks, and cups – oh my!

SATURDAY, AUGUST 20TH

A blur of activity as we greeted folks and got all the food items ready for the meal. A special highlight was when Pop revealed the gender of my son and daughter-in-law's baby who will arrive in March. We had arranged it all with Pop ahead of time. When everyone gathered for the blessing on the food, Stu stepped forward and said that he and Ashley wanted to give his Pawpaw a present, but part of it was delayed … it wouldn't arrive for several months. Pop opened the bag and pulled out a pink baby outfit and announced, "It's a girl!" Everyone applauded and cheered! I so very much hope Mom and Dad will be able to enjoy this latest addition to their legacy.

After lunch as I snapped the photo of Pop standing behind his cake in that familiar pose – hands on his hips – I spotted that twinkle in his eyes … a twinkle that is rarer these days than it used to be. Suddenly I remembered a photo taken around 40 years ago. He'd dug out his WWII Navy uniform to see if it still fit. It did, a bit snug, but he got it on! He had stood exactly the same way, hands on his hips, grinning, and looking to the side with that twinkle in his eyes. Standing straight is harder now – the weight of 99 years bears down. But with an effort, like now with the family gathered all around, he can command that spine to straighten up, and he stands tall and proud, surrounded by those who admire and love him for the wonderful man he is.

Those big, gold, glittering numbers on his cake are beautiful, but they carry an unspoken question: How many more cakes and candles and Happy Birthday songs? Every special occasion now carries the weight of How Many More? Impatiently shaking those thoughts out of my head, if not my heart, I joined in the laughter and fun. And later, when the blessed rain began like a benediction on the day, I said "Thank you" to the One who has loved my Pop all his life.

WEDNESDAY, AUGUST 24TH

Pop is officially 99 today! I called early to wish him a happy day. I know lunch will be a happy time because Melanie is making his favorite meal:

chicken and dressing, yeast rolls, candied sweet potatoes, and so forth. She's a trooper! Apparently Pop celebrated his birthday by loading and hauling some limbs that Bill had cut up for him. Pop loves to get stuff done every day. He likes the saying we heard awhile back: To be happy, people need three things – someone to love, something useful to do, and something to look forward to. That's a pretty true statement.

SATURDAY, AUGUST 27TH

Headed to Jacksonville early. Tam has a press trip to Door County, Wisconsin, and will leave very early tomorrow morning, so she needs to pack and get things lined out at home. Melanie has been here all week and needs to get to her home, so I came and will stay until next Saturday. Melanie called while I was driving to tell me that Tam had lost her cell phone, which has her boarding pass on it and is also what she uses to take photos on trips. When I arrived, Caleb, Tam's son, had thought of one more place it might be – in the truck they'd had to have towed to the repair shop last night. It was there! Tam was so relieved. For just a little while today, all three of us sisters were together. With our divided schedule of staying with the folks, this doesn't happen very often. I miss it.

MONDAY, AUGUST 29TH

Early eye appointment in Tyler for Pop, so got Mom's breakfast even earlier than usual. She would rather eat around 9:00 or later since she stays up late watching her movies, but on days like this, I have to roust her out amid the groans of "It's too early!"

The technicians checked Pop's vision before his eye shot. I was hoping his vision might be better, but it was about the same. For just five minutes, I wish I could see what *HE* sees; then maybe I could figure out ways to help him with tasks that frustrate him. Sometimes he can see something that surprises us, like a bird swooping across the sky, but then he sometimes can't tell who a person is until they get really close or say something.

As we checked out and made his next appointment, the young lady noticed his birth date and wished him a belated Happy Birthday. When I told her we'd just had his 99th birthday party, she did a double take of his records and said, "Oh my goodness! 99!" That tickled Pop. She asked him what his secret was, and he said, "I just keep staggering along," and grinned. Our dad is a funny guy!

WEDNESDAY, AUGUST 31ST

Woke Pop up at 6:30 – he doesn't like to sleep late. He says if you do that, you waste the best part of the day. Neither of us felt very peppy, though … I was tired. Took care of a few chores, one of which was to call the surveyor. He can't meet with us until next Tuesday – that will be on Melanie's week, so I had to tell her and write a note on the calendar. Keeping each other informed of upcoming events and appointments and medication changes, and so forth can be challenging. That teapot calendar hanging by the rotary phone in the kitchen is our daily planner. We write notes on it and clip appointment cards on the edges; sometimes it's so cluttered that it hangs crooked.

Heard from Tam – she is stuck on a plane in Chicago because of flooding in Dallas. It will be the wee hours before she gets back here!

Melanie

AUGUST 20TH - 27TH

We had Papa's 99th birthday ahead of the date of August 24th. That date fell in the middle of the week. Tam was to leave on her first press trip in over a year. We did not want to have this very special celebration without our little sister; so, we chose the weekend before. Unfortunately, Andy, Kara, Garrett, and Mary Grace were unable to attend. Conflicts will happen. I tried to be generous about it. Mostly, I tried to not think about it. That helped. A precious friend had passed away, so we began Daddy's celebration day with a celebration of another kind. My brother, Shaun, was a pallbearer. My sisters, Papa, & I were there. It was a touching commemoration of her life.

Back at the house, the crowd was gathering. My twin daughters were there with their kids. My grandson, Brandon, joined us via phone from the naval base at Goose Creek, South Carolina. I was so thankful that Rex brought over his refurbished 1935 Ford flatbed truck for Papa to see. Papa certainly enjoyed it. He said he had one like it back in his sawmill days. Sherry's son, Stuart, named after Papa, let Daddy reveal the gender of his and Ashley's first child. It would be Papa's and Mama's 16th great-grandchild. Daddy and Mama had big smiles.

Sherry had made a three-layer pineapple cake, Papa's favorite. After a lunch of brisket and fixins, Papa blew out candles, and looked so handsome for any age much less almost a century! Lovely day, grandchildren talking, great grands running and playing up at the barn on the hay rolls, sisters, brother, and I with reflective looks. Is there another candle left to enjoy? God willing, Papa will march right on into that 100th year!

Mom and Dad posing with Rex's old truck...just like they used to.

During Papa's birthday week, God sent abundance of rain. Papa was so joyful, and it saved the summer from ending in flaming drought! Another unusual sight this birthday week was a small flock of wood storks that enjoyed the pond. The old oak in the pasture, up the hill from the pond, made a great nighttime roost.

On Papa's actual birthday, August 24th, I asked what special meal he would like. His favorite is a Thanksgiving meal: chicken & dressing, homemade yeast rolls, candied sweet potatoes, cantaloupe, cranberry sauce, and corn. Yum!

Tamra

Since my time with Mom and Dad is over the weekend – Saturday morning until Monday morning – I don't have the same experiences and schedules my sisters have during their Monday through Friday routine. I am grateful to them for allowing me a smaller piece of the scheduling pie because honestly, I don't know if I could do more. Taking care of one of my toddler grandchildren every Thursday night and Friday, homeschooling my fourteen-year old granddaughter Tuesdays and Thursdays, doing most of the chores, shopping, paying bills, cooking, and pet care at my house since my husband is disabled, leaves me little wiggle room. He has also been in the hospital – ICU, rehab, back to hospital for more surgery and then back to rehab – since June 21st. So, on top of everything else, I have been making sixty mile round trips every few days to see him, and we still don't know when he'll get to come home. Trying to get any of my writing work done in between all of this is a real challenge some days! Thank goodness I have understanding siblings, and somehow it all works out.

Dad can still give the cows shots, which is tricky when it is subcutaneous (under the skin).

I look forward to being with Mom and Dad and I pop in often during the week to check on them, sometimes bring groceries or medicine from town or bring over a bit of something yummy, but not as often as I used to…since things have gotten so busy. Melanie says it is nice just knowing I am on the next hill, so she can call on me, if she needs me. Usually, it is to borrow some flour, Crisco, butter, eggs or some other item. Dad calls my pantry "the country store." It is used pretty often, but I am glad I have what is needed since the nearest store is eight miles away.

The worst thing about staying with Mom and Dad this time of year is the thermostat – or rather the setting of it. Dad keeps it on 80 degrees, but I can't stand it, so I'm constantly turning it down to at least 77 or 78. I have a fan and a ceiling fan in Josh's old room where we stay, but even that doesn't help enough some days. Dad will say "I'm cold!" and go out on the front porch where it's 110 degrees "to warm up." Mom will complain sometimes, but not as much as Dad… at least about the temperature of the house. She does her complaining mostly about how fast or slow we are to answer her calls for assistance, which sometimes amount to "Has the mailman run?" when we think she is having a coronary the way she is yelling.

We all manage to keep our sense of humor most of the time. I try to put myself in their place when I feel myself getting irritated and that helps. Calling and talking to Melanie or Sherry helps to blow off steam, as we commiserate and encourage one another. We are so glad to be doing what we are doing, but it is not easy and we are only human. We get tired and sometimes let things bother us that normally wouldn't in different circumstances. Recognizing those times has become easier, but dealing with them is growing increasingly more difficult.

We have been doing this for over two years now…staying 24/7 with Mom and Dad, since Mom's fall on July 4, 2020 when she broke her shoulder. In a way it seems like yesterday and in some ways, it seems like it has been forever. We all know it will come to an end someday, but I think we try to push that to the back of our mind most of the time. I know I am grateful for every minute I spend with them…sweating or not!

Dad and Mom's routine on Saturdays and Sundays is pretty predictable, except when special celebrations or activities are scheduled, like Dad's 99th birthday, which we celebrated on Saturday the 20th. I was so glad we had Rex to fix the BBQ and beans for the party; they are always so delicious. Sherry outdid herself on the pineapple cake for Dad, and Mel's rolls are always a hit at every family gathering. I bring a dessert, casserole, or salad, nothing special, but whatever it is usually disappears.

Watching Dad enjoy his day and seeing everyone interact with him, especially the great-grands, was a treat. He gets such a kick out of watching the little ones run and play and have fun. Emelia, the three-year-old, knows Dad is hard of hearing so she practically yells at him when she addresses him, which is hilarious! Dad thinks it's pretty funny too.

All in all, I believe Dad had a pretty good time. I asked him later what his favorite part of the day was and he said, "I guess it was just everyone being together and visiting." I know he misses his brothers and sisters; they were always getting together and having coffee and sharing the latest news. Now, he is the only one left and I'm sure that is a lonely feeling…even surrounded by others, it is not the same. Several times during the day, I caught a glimpse of sadness crossing his face – I wonder if he was thinking about them.

Getting Dad's picture with his cake is always a big deal and we must have looked like the worst case of paparazzi descending on him in the Big

Room, as he and Mom call it. We had set up the table with the cake in front of the fireplace so the light would be better and it gave us all elbow room to man our phones for the event. I wish now I had taken a picture from the back – of all of us leaning, straining, and jockeying for the best picture position!

Mom loves for Mel to braid her hair...except Mom calls it plaiting.

Straightening up for his moment in the spotlight, Dad looked thirty years younger…he got that grin on his face he reserves for when he's really tickled about something…I think it was the comical show we were giving him that put that twinkle in his eye. Or…maybe he was just thinking how blessed he was to be so important to this bunch of slightly touched folks.

EVERYONE'S *Journey*
IS DIFFERENT, BUT
THE *Destination* IS THE SAME.

SEPTEMBER

Another September already! Growing up, it meant back to school, early morning bus rides, Big Chief tablets, fat pencils, the last of the hay baling, and Mama canning pear preserves. Thinking back on those simpler times, I sometimes wish I could go back and appreciate them the way I do now. Our latest routines are a far cry from those long ago days. Today, we are constantly juggling our own households and responsibilities with Mom and Dad's schedule of pills and doctor's appointments, all the while trying to keep up with Dad and his projects. That alone is a full time job.

We exhaust ourselves trying to motivate Mom to get up and move and at the same time we run after Dad as he goes from one thing to another like his life depends on it...and maybe it does. They are so different in temperament, habits, likes and dislikes; it is a miracle they have lived together and loved one another for over seventy-five years. She is a night owl, Dad is a morning lark. Mom loves movies and puzzles. Dad enjoys being outdoors more than anything. Their differences have become even more magnified since they have reached their nineties. Mom is happiest when she is at home in her own space where nothing changes. Dad likes to be home too, but he also enjoys getting out and about, going to town, visiting, and going to church. He was a paint contractor for over sixty-five years in our small town and knew just about everyone. Now, my brother, Shaun, is the contractor and he tries to keep Dad informed on what's happening. Almost every day, Shaun drops by and fills Dad in on his work day and who he saw around town. It helps Dad feel like he is still a part of things. He gave up driving at ninety-eight, so that loss of independence has been a little hard on him.

Mom hasn't driven in over twelve years and her world has shrunk accordingly. When she was still going strong, she spent time every Tuesday visiting the shut-ins and nursing homes. Sometimes, Mom was the only person, outside of the staff, that those poor souls ever saw. I am sure Mom earned plenty of crowns for her years of visiting. Her kindness wasn't the only thing she was known for; her driving skills were legendary. She was a force on our small country roads in her big four-door Cadillac. People pulled over when they saw that big yellow chariot coming and I'm pretty sure closed their eyes till she passed. We loved to kid her, but she was a good driver, even if she did have a lead foot.

While Dad gave up driving on the road, he can still handle the tractor and drive the truck around the farm. Sometimes, when he has a close call with a tree or post, we would like for him to give it up, but we realize that would take away the last bit of freedom Dad has and none of us are willing to take that step.

It is hard to keep our own emotions in check when Dad is using his chainsaw, tractor, or splitting firewood, but we also know that doing those things is probably what keeps him going. I am sure he gets some amusement out of our "hovering" over him and spying on him with binoculars from the house, but he knows we mean well. At least, I hope he does.

September makes us think of the coming holidays, hopefully cooler weather, and looking forward to slipping into a more restful routine. We look forward to the changes in the weather, me especially. Cooler weather also means less time outside for Dad, which equals less danger and less stress for all of us. I know it sounds selfish and maybe it is, but there is a collective sigh of relief when the cold rainy weather keeps Dad in his chair by the fire…where the only tool in his hand is his Kindle and his biggest decision is when to add more wood to the fire or clean out the ashes. Frankly…Dad just wears us out!

Sherry

THURSDAY, SEPTEMBER 1ST

SO done with August! Every year when I flip the calendar page from August to September, I do a happy dance! The weather outside may be exactly the same on September 1stas it was on August 31st, but I can almost feel that promise of fall in the air … sometime this month, we'll have our first actual cool down after the dog days of summer, and the dog days of summer in Texas are snarly, snappy ones!

Around here, calendar flipping takes a bit longer than in most houses, I'm guessing. Mom loves calendars and has specific ones for certain places. There are two in the kitchen: one on the wall between the refrigerator and the cabinets, and one at the other end of the kitchen next to the rotary phone. One goes in the hall bathroom and one in Mom's bathroom. Then there is the dining room calendar and the one in the sunroom for Pop to enjoy. One hangs next to Pop's bed and another on his west wall. Mom always has an extra calendar, so we hang it in the library room.

We call it the library room instead of the library because it wasn't built as a library such as rich folks would have. It was built as a bedroom for Melanie and me in 1954 when Pop added the kitchen and bathroom to the two original rooms he and Mom started out with in 1949. (Until he added that part, he and Mom only had a kitchen/dining room and a bedroom – all four of us were in there!) After it was no longer needed as a bedroom, bookcases were added and added. Mom loves reading. We started calling it the library room; just saying "the library" sounded a bit pretentious for its modest size.

Anyhow, flipping all the calendar pages takes several minutes, but I enjoy it – it's like having a clean slate every 30 or so days. Younger people keep track of their upcoming events on their phones, but I love the tactile experience of an actual paper calendar, just as I prefer the touch of a real book rather than an e-reader, and photo albums instead of photos in "the cloud." Nothing wrong with either way … I'm just old school, I guess.

Unexpectedly, Tam came over at 8:00! I figured she'd be worn to a nub and want to hibernate after her very late arrival, but she brought us great souvenirs from Door County, showed us some photos, and shared the highlights of her trip. Remembering Pop's liking for apple cider doughnuts, she brought several of those and we all got to sample them

After Tam left, Pop wanted to check the water level at the Homeplace – a farm where he grew up and now owns, only a few miles away. He puts cows there for part of the year, and the creek is their source of water, but the weather has been pretty dry. We found that the creek still had quite a bit of water in it, mainly because a beaver had built a dam that kept the water from flowing out. Beavers are bad news for trees near creeks, but this one time old busy beaver did Pop a favor by keeping that water hemmed in.

Dad and Shaun working together on his shop room. Shaun says, "I couldn't have built it without Dad. He answered a lot of my questions and kept me from making mistakes. It is easy to work with Dad because he usually understands what I am trying to do."

There's a great pear tree at the Homeplace, too, so Pop and I picked a big bucket of pears. He and I like pear cobbler better than apple pie. My niece Rita and her two kids Athena and Raylan came out to visit a bit. When we were ready to leave, Pop asked Raylan to lead him out to the truck, so Raylan grabbed Pop's big hand in his little one and headed out. That tickled Pop.

Late in the afternoon, Shaun came over and visited awhile. Then Pop and I sat on the front porch and watched a glorious rain. The hummingbird battles were entertaining as well – one little fighter was trying to defend both feeders at opposite ends of the porch. No brotherly love among those little buzz bombs.

FRIDAY, SEPTEMBER 2ND

Pop and I headed to town to pay bills and get a few items at Walmart. After we got back home, Tam brought her little granddaughter Emelia over. She's nearly three and so much fun to watch. Pop especially enjoys seeing the liveliness of the little ones and listening to their jabbering even though he can't hear well enough to understand what they're saying. When he hears little ones just at the babbling stage, he says, "They haven't picked out a language yet."

After Tam took Emelia home for lunch and a nap, I started fixing ours and cleaning up the kitchen because Emelia and I are going to make pear tarts later – she wants to fix one for her daddy. I hope my granddaughter will enjoy baking with me someday … SO much fun making the pear tarts. We pretty much got flour and pear juice everywhere, but it was worth it. She was as proud as if she'd won a trophy, and I know her daddy will make her feel as if she has!

I made a regular sized cobbler, and Pop and I dove into it as soon as decency allowed … sweet pear slices swimming in a bubbly, buttery ooze and wrapped in a flaky crust. Oh. My. We do try to watch Pop's sugar intake somewhat, but part of the joy of life is eating good food, and at 99, if he can't enjoy an occasional treat, what's the point? Overall, he had a pretty healthy diet – he loves salad and many vegetables (with some notable exceptions). Mom, on the other hand, is the junk food queen, and her sugar level is fine … go figure.

While Pop watched a college football game, I grabbed the big clippers and cut the wisteria back and a few briars that were climbing into some trees. Green briar is one of Satan's plants. When the game was over, Pop and I strolled down the road. I try to encourage him to move as much as possible, especially now that fall and winter are looming in the not too distant future. After it gets cold, Pop will want to stay by the fireside. Then I helped Mom with her jigsaw puzzle. Mom mainly walks between her room and the big room, but we can usually get her to make a few rounds in the big room before she retires to her movie watching. Sometimes we feel like the exercise police or the water nags, but we have to keep them moving and hydrated. Drink and move! Drink and move!

MONDAY, SEPTEMBER 12TH

Getting off to the folks' is never just get up and go – I have to leave things at my house in reasonably good order so I don't come back to a mess. The pretty drive up there is enjoyable and helps me mentally shift gears from my house to theirs. Hauled my stuff inside, then had to jump in their car to take Pop to his eye shot appointment in Tyler. He's more comfortable in their Mercury than in my Jeep.

Back home and started lunch. The a/c guy came and fixed their unit – it was just stopped up, so it wasn't very expensive. Glad that's off Pop's mind. As he's gotten older, things bother him more than they used to. A problem will stay on his mind until it's taken care of. Neither he nor Mom shake things off now as well as they once did. I don't know if it's the heavy footsteps of time they hear behind them, or the fact that they have less to occupy their minds other than the problems that need attention.

Tam came over to show Pop that he had gotten some drought relief money! That was good news. He has lost some cattle this year and with the price of feed, fertilizer, and just about everything cattle-related going up (except the price he gets when he sells a few), he needs any break he can get.

Now Pop is watching Monday Night Football, and Mom is watching her movies. I need to stay up until the game is over so I can put drops in Pop's eyes. This is one role reversal that is still so odd to me – being the last one up at night. For years and years, when I'd come back to visit and stay overnight, I'd hear Mom's footsteps back and forth while I lay under the cozy covers. The dining room is one of the two rooms built in 1949 and still has the original wooden floors; they squeak and creak a little when someone walks over them. I'd hear Mom go back and forth from the big room, through the dining room, into the kitchen, and back. It always made me feel like a kid again, even when I was in my 50s and early 60s, because my mama was still up, taking care of things.

After she got shingles in 2010 all that changed. I became the one up late. Even after she recovered somewhat from that, it was forever different – she never drove after that. Her world began shrinking a little more each year. But when she fell and broke her shoulder on July 4, 2020, that was the start of another level of care … one of us girls needed to be with her and Pop all the time. It has worked out pretty well, but we do have long days. So here I am, walking the same path through the house Mom used to walk, hearing the same floors creak. I wonder if Mom can hear it, and if she can, does it make her feel safe and loved the way her steps used to make me feel?

TUESDAY, SEPTEMBER 13TH

Sprang up to turn off my phone alarm at 5:45 … took me a few seconds to realize which house I was in – such is my fractured life. Ah, I'm in my "country" home – Mom and Dad's. Some folks have a summer home up north and a winter one in the south; I have a country home fifty miles away from my neighborhood home! Often I'll open a kitchen drawer or yank open a cabinet at *their* house that is in the same spot as one at mine, but they contain different items from mine. Then when I go back home, I do the same thing there.

One constant for both places, though, is going out on the patio as soon as the coffee is ready and having a cup as the sun rises. That's my quiet time when I talk to the Lord and share my concerns for the day and gratitude for the joy of being able to help my parents stay in their home with all their familiar things around them. Still pretty dark out this morning, or would be if the nearly-full moon wasn't still above the western horizon. Had to wrap up - 56° out here – Yay Fall! Pop didn't come out until about 6:45. He had "Old Blackie" on, a light coat he bought years ago to take on a trip; it's now his "go to" jacket for cool days. I got a blanket to put over his legs after he sat down. He gets colder in his old age than he used to … a lot colder. He told me that back in his house-painting days, 56° was t-shirt weather for him! As Pop and I sip our coffee and gaze out past the barn he built over 70 years ago, out to the pastures and ponds and grazing cows, peace settles over me like a warm blanket. Right here, right now, life is good …

All too soon, that little break was over …time to fix breakfast and start the daily routine (as routine as it ever is around here). We headed to the lake to meet the main surveyor and look over the preliminary copy. Pop wanted to get the entire perimeter of their place surveyed as well as the parts he and Mom intend to pass along to us kids … a huge "loose end" he didn't want to put off any longer. I can't imagine what it must feel like for him to know that the place he worked for and added to over the years will someday be broken back up into smaller parcels. If only there was another way.

After the survey business, I fixed lunch and cleaned the kitchen while Mom and Dad talked on the front porch, then went to the sunroom to talk to Melanie. When Pop and Shaun joined me, I put my phone on speaker so she could "be here" too. Then Tam showed up, and all of us siblings had a good visit. We all got tickled at Shaun. He'd been sitting in one of the white wicker rockers, and when he got up, he said he had "wicker butt."

That evening, Pop and I had a nice walk down the road almost to the ranch gate near the corner, a relaxing end to a busy day.

WEDNESDAY, SEPTEMBER 14TH

Well, nothing quite like lifting your 99 year-old Pop high in the tractor bucket so he can tie a strap around a tree! This dead pine on the hill west of the pond has been bothering him for some time. He can see it from the patio as he's drinking his morning coffee, and he wants its dead self out of sight. So, we headed out after breakfast, Pop on the John Deere and me in the truck. Of course the cows associate both vehicles with a handout of some sort, so they all came bawling up the slope. We parked, and Pop sized up the tree by getting right against it and looking up to see where the main weight was and how it leaned … reminded me of a coon hound treeing something.

"These trees get bigger the closer you get to 'em,"he observed. Grabbing the battery powered saw, he cut a pie slice out of the side where he wanted the tree to fall, but since he can't see as well as he used to, the slice cuts didn't exactly meet in the middle, and it wouldn't come out. We tried to dig it out with the claw part of the hammer, but that didn't work, so Pop decided to drive the truck back to the shop and get some wedges and a sledgehammer.

While he was gone, I walked over to the family cemetery and watered the flowers. When Pop drove back, I flagged him down and suggested that we let the cows in the pasture surrounding the cemetery enclosure since they hadn't been in there in a few weeks. They would love the fresh grass, and that would get them out of our way. He said he'd been thinking that very thing, so we opened the gate. They didn't need much coaxing since the rest of the pastures were getting pretty short in this drought.

After the cows started through the gate, we went back to our project. That's when I found out about the bucket thing. I told him I would get in the bucket, but nothing doing. He showed me how to use the "joy stick" to move the bucket up and down and tilt it to dump it … as in "Don't do that!" After he climbed into the bucket, I timidly moved the stick just a little at a time until he signaled to stop. Fortunately, he was really close to the tree and could hold onto it a little as he tossed the end of the strap around the tree and tried to catch it on the other side. After a couple or three tries, he caught the strap and tied it securely. Those Navy knots from WWII come in handy. What a relief to get him safely back on the ground! Then we had to attach two chains to the strap and the tractor so we'd have enough length to keep the falling tree from bashing into the tractor "lid."

After cutting into the tree on the opposite side from the missing slice, he put in wedges to encourage it to fall in the proper direction. Next he climbed on the tractor and drove far enough to put tension on the strap and chains; I kept pounding the wedges farther in, watching the top of the tree for movement and listening for the telltale pops. When they finally came, I yelled and Pop stomped on the gas! Kaboom! Whew, such a relief to get that big tree down with nobody bleeding or missing any parts.

Unfortunately, the butt end of the tree was still on top of the stump; I suggested we call it a day once we got the tree flat on the ground, and I *thought* he agreed. He fastened the chain around the end of the tree, climbed back on the tractor, and tried several times to yank it off. Nothing doing. I suggested going around to the other side which was downhill anyway, and that worked. But instead of stopping, he and that John Deere kept right on going ... dragging that entire tree over the hill and out of sight. I knew he was heading for a ditch to push the tree into, so I ran the whole way there so I could get the chain off and save Pop from having to climb off and back on the tractor. That's really hard on his knees and hips. When I got on the tractor to ride back up the hill with him, I could tell he was proud to still be able to do some work. It made me proud, too, even if I did have to hoof it for two hundred yards.

THURSDAY, SEPTEMBER 15TH

Headed outside while the moon was still shining and the stars were out ... needed my jacket, a throw over my legs, and hot coffee to be warm enough. Pop didn't sleep well at all - his swollen foot bothered him. He wondered if he had phlebitis, but when I looked it up, the symptoms didn't seem to match. After breakfast, Pop wanted to cut a half dead sweetgum tree between the barn north of the house and the pond beyond it, so he climbed on the tractor and I drove the truck with the chainsaw and other tools. One side of the tree had a big crack in the bark, so Pop decided that would be a good starting point. Just a minute or two after he started cutting, Shaun drove up in his side-by-side. I was glad to see him because I could hear that tree start to crack. Shaun told Pop to get back, and the tree fell – right where Pop wanted it to.

We put a chain around the butt of the tree to drag it off, but a big jagged piece at that end dug into the dirt so hard that the tractor couldn't budge it. Shaun cut the tree in two pieces and wrapped the chain around one of them. When Pop started forward with the tractor, a long limb whirled over and whopped the lid of the tractor, right over where Pop was sitting. If that solid top hadn't been over him, that limb would have knocked him to kingdom come! That's one of the tough things about trying to take care of Pop – all the things he wants to do involve chainsaws, tractors, fire, axes and other sharp objects. We want him to be able to do what he loves, but it is nerve wracking at best. Sometimes we get hurt ourselves trying to keep *him* from getting hurt.

After Pop got that piece hauled down the hill, Shaun got on the tractor and we rounded up all the other limbs. Later, I called Melanie and told her that I would swap some days with her so she could visit more with Brandon before he heads back to his Navy duties; she appreciated that. We have to juggle our schedules for the important things in our own families. I feel for people who have to care for elderly parents with little to no help – that has to be so very difficult.

FRIDAY, SEPTEMBER 16TH

Just the highlights: proofread article for Tam, helped Pop cut up and move part of a huge white oak limb (warm with 58% humidity … sweaty work), got some needed signatures on the surveys, trip to Walmart, cooked lunch, estate sale with Tam, bought birthday gifts for Athena and Raylan, made pear cobbler, usual dispensing of meds and washing dishes … tired!

MONDAY, SEPTEMBER 26TH

Didn't get on the road to Mom and Dad's until after 10:00. Tam had already gone to her house, but came back to help me tote my stuff inside and fill me in on Mom's UTI medicine and what food is already prepared … the "changing of the guard" involves a lot of information.

Later, Shaun showed me some of the new shop he had built and how to drive his side-by-side. He's going on a vacation and is leaving his little ride at Mom's and Dad's so we can tool around in it instead of using the farm truck.

TUESDAY, SEPTEMBER 27TH

A very busy day … back and forth with the doctor's office about Mom's upcoming pacemaker replacement, meds and food prep, dishes, bills, a trip to the "village" (as Dad calls it) to drop off the Power of Attorney papers at the bank. It feels so odd to be doing that … I hate it, but it's necessary, just in case. Picked up Mom's prescription at the pharmacy and dropped by Farm and Ranch so Pop could get cattle salt and calf creep. Back home for lunch. After a short rest, Pop and I went up to the barn to fill the calf's water bucket, unload the salt and feed, put salt and mineral out for the big cows, then drove down to the cemetery.

By then the afternoon sun was casting long shadows across the hills and distant trees. While Pop sat on the bench swing under the pine, watching the cows trekking up to the mineral trough, I watered the cemetery flowers. So quiet with just the sound of the trickling water, the breeze in the trees, and the occasional bawl of a calf. I watched Pop and wondered what he was thinking about as he looked out over the land he's worked for so many years. Is he thinking of how it used to look over 70 years ago when John Jolly told him this place was known as the poorest farm around? Now the once bare hilltop has two fine barns and a cattle working area; the rest of the land is fenced and planted with grass, two ponds glitter in the late afternoon sunshine, and seal-fat cows lie under the shade of scattered trees. So much work for so many years. Is he wondering about what will happen to it after he and Mom are gone? Me too, Pop, me too.

"Dad had to help me hold things in place…I enjoyed working with Dad again. He was my boss for many years and I learned my painting trade from him."

WEDNESDAY, SEPTEMBER 28TH

After the usual morning activities, Pop and I went back up to work on that big white oak; three tree-sized limbs had fallen off it during storms. One was pretty rotten, but the other two were sound enough for firewood, and each one branched into limbs the size of trees. I don't see how those limbs stuck on the tree as long as they did! Dad wasn't about to let good wood go to waste, so he started cutting up one of the limbs for firewood. I tossed/rolled/heaved the cut pieces into the tractor bucket – some were hosses! Hope I didn't hurt my back. Guess I'll find out tomorrow morning when I try to get out of bed.

Back to the house to charge the chain saw batteries and check on Mom. Called the cardiologist to ask when to stop Mom's blood thinner before the pacemaker battery surgery. They said for her to skip it Sunday, Monday, and Tuesday. Then I had to call the home health folks to ask Nurse C. to check Mom's INR the day before her surgery to make sure she's good to go. Then someone at the cardiology office called again about when to stop the blood thinner. I just said okay as if I was hearing it for the first time. Then Melanie called and said that the clinic had called me twice, but I was on the phone with the other folks, so they were going to call Mom and Dad's house phone. It rang while I was still talking to Melanie. Ran to get it, and the person on the phone was also telling me when to stop Mom's blood thinner! At least we aren't suffering from lack of information.

After lunch Mom and Dad relaxed while I washed dishes – a *lot* of dishes. A short while later Pop had revived and was ready to tackle the sawing again. That's one thing that makes for long hard days up here … while Pop is resting, I'm either cleaning the kitchen, fixing food for Mom, or some other chore. Then he's ready to go again and I'm still pooped!

THURSDAY, SEPTEMBER 29TH

Most of this day was spent at the trustee meeting in town. Pop's truck was gone when I got back … I knew what *that* meant! Quickly changed into my work clothes and walked up the hill and down to that oak we've been working on. Some large pieces were up at the woodpile waiting to be split, but a herd of long skinny limbs were scattered all around our work area. Pop was on the tractor, shoving those into a low spot nearby, using the tractor bucket as a combination battering ram and shovel. "Mad Mac Beyond Thunderdome," I thought as I watched Pop fearlessly attack the mass of limbs, pushing them into a pile taller than the tractor lid. He's loving this – for a little while he feels young again, and strong. Roll on, Pop, roll on! Just try not to damage the tractor too much … remember that big stump hidden in the weeds a few years back… and the tree that bent one of the hay forks … and getting stuck in the pond …

FRIDAY, SEPTEMBER 30TH

49° this morning! Too cold for coffee on the patio, so Pop and I had a cup in the sunroom. Did a few chores and enjoyed a nice "buggy" ride in Shaun's side by side, so Pop could see the cows and enjoy the first fall color in the trees. When we got back, I drove to Tam's house to get some photos of her three little grandkids as they celebrated their birthdays, which are really close together. Tam had made each of them a cake and let them decorate them however they wanted. They were so proud! And that was the end of the relaxing part of the day!

When Pop says he's just going up on the hill to see if the wood splitter will start, the translation is, "I'm going to split firewood." So here we go. The first step is to move all the stuff that got put around it since last year. Then we could see that the tires on it were pancake flat. I backed up the truck and we attached to the splitter. I slowly pulled around to the wood pile while Pop held the back of the splitter down so it wouldn't nose dive into the dirt. Those tires looked really sad. But, when Pop pulled on the starter, it fired right up – of course. I really don't mind splitting wood, but some of those log sections were really big, at least two feet thick. We had to roll them over to the splitter platform, then heave them upright and split and rotate all around the edge until we could get the whole thing in pieces.

We had remembered to bring his folding chair so he could rest every little while. Often, I would announce "water break" so he could rest and I could get him to drink more water than he would have on his own. He's like a camel, going long distances without water. He could get away with that in his younger days, but not now. After we had split most of the wood, he said, "Let's call it a day." That sounded good to me. When he said something about not being any good anymore, I exclaimed, "Pop, you are 99 and out here splitting and stacking firewood! How many people your age in the whole world are able to do that? You need to be grateful or the Lord might get peeved at you!" He smiled … he does realize how blessed he is, but every now and then, he needs a reminder. We all do.

Melanie

SEPTEMBER 5TH - 10TH

This is the month of the goat weed roundup. Papa loves to mow the pastures leaving them clear of weeds for a beautiful winter setting. He would mow for three or four hours in the morning. If it wasn't too hot, he mowed for two or three hours in the evening. He finished mowing 50 acres during my week.

One incident that stood out to me as I watched with binoculars and bated breath the path of the tractor back and forth, up and down steep hills, around deep ditches was when Papa was out of sight behind the north pond. I heard a horrible racket like Papa had hit a stump or was off in a ditch! I grabbed my phone, the truck keys, opened the gate, and drove over the rough ground, bouncing high in the seat, but rushing on despite the rough terrain! Finally, I crossed the dirt covered culvert, up and over the hill where I could scan the creek bottom. My heart was beating painfully and suddenly, there he was, working his way back and forth across the field. I drove to the shade of the pines surrounding Tam's cabin and just sat calming my fears. My earthly father had been safe in our heavenly Father's hands. I fight a constant battle with fears and where to draw the line between my fears and Papa's independence. I keep reminding

Sherry often brings Mom the roses from her garden and Melanie shares her flowers too. I am content to just admire them.

myself that I control nothing. God's love and mercy has protected Daddy for 99 years. He never stops caring, loving, and guarding. "Oh, ye of little faith" - trust and take joy in each moment that Papa can do the things he loves. These things give meaning to life and, as Papa says, "justify his existence." Papa is happiest when things get done and he is in the middle of it. He is a Seabee (WWII) whose motto is "can do!" He inspires me to do more, not complain, and enjoy life. Simple hard work, the beauty of a sunrise, autumn fog, the smell of wet soil after many days of dry heat, checking the herd, finding a new calf, getting in the hay crop; all are wrapped in my heart by the slightly bent figure outlined against the hills of home.

Toward the end of the week, we watched the burial of Queen Elizabeth, the longest reigning monarch of the UK. Papa said she was a real lady. She loved her place in Scotland where she died. She was 97.

SEPTEMBER 19TH - 23RD

The next week I was here was the week that Dad spent helping Shaun build his inner 12 foot square room in his new shop. Every morning, all week, Papa would look, with anticipation, for Shaun to show up and take him down to his house. Shaun used 2" X 12" X 12' boards, which made for an extremely heavy wall. They used the tractor to lift the walls in place and bolt them down. Papa shared his years of knowledge, and wisdom, which helped in many ways that my brother could see and appreciate. We ate lunch together for 5 days that week. It was a sweet time of fellowship and sharing.

Tamra

The month of September is half over and I am still running behind. At the end of August (28th - 31st) I was gone on a press trip to Door County, Wisconsin. I had a great time and enjoyed catching up with some of my fellow writers/photographers. The day before I left, however, was a disaster and I spent a good deal of the flight to Wisconsin trying to decompress. Marc, my husband, was still in the hospital, my son had borrowed his truck, because his car was on the fritz, and then, Marc's truck quit. I had to call AAA and arrange to get it towed to the mechanic, pick up my son and his daughter and take them to get his car fixed, lost my phone, had to check in for my flight, pack my bags, etc. Thank goodness, my son located my phone in his dad's truck at the mechanic's shop before I went to town and got a new one. My sweet sisters covered for me while I was gone and made sure Mom and Dad were well-cared for. They understand what I do, but I think Mom and Dad are still confused and a bit suspicious of my flying all over the place and wandering around the country.

After I returned from Wisconsin, I kept my three-year-old granddaughter, Emelia, that next night and all day Friday, September 2nd, then from 11:00 till 3:00 on Saturday the 3rd. No time to rest and recover because I was at Mom and Dad's Saturday, Sunday, and Monday morning till Melanie got there about mid-morning. Addie, my fourteen-year-old grand was coming that evening to spend the night, all day Tuesday, Tuesday night, and part of the day on Wednesday, so we would be busy with her homeschooling, WMA Bible study meeting, getting groceries, etc. and the rehab center called and said they were discharging Marc on the 7th! I had to get everything ready for him, cleaning and totally changing just about everything in the bedroom and bathroom for safety and mobility. Thank goodness Sherry came over and helped me move the heavier furniture and clean or I would have hurt my back for sure. It was a crazy week, but I managed to get everything ready **and** write my column **and** a story on the Door County trip. Someday, when I look back on this time in my life, I will probably be amazed at how much I've managed to do, but right now, I'm just taking it one day at a time and dreaming of spending an entire day alone, just reading and drinking coffee.

Getting my husband Marc home, September 7th, from rehab was an ordeal. He couldn't straighten his leg, so squeezing a six-foot, five-inch 450 pound man into a pickup cab was no easy task. He finally wedged himself in at an angle and we made the twenty-five minute ride home. To say he was glad to be back home would be a gross understatement. To say I was one-hundred percent happy about it would be a lie. On top of all my other duties, I now had another person to wait on. It's not that I wasn't glad for him; I was just feeling overwhelmed. I do the best I can to stay positive, keep moving forward, and take care of things within my power. The Good Lord will have to handle the rest.

SATURDAY, SEPTEMBER 17TH

Last Sunday morning I got a laugh out of Mom; she is NOT an early riser. I went in to wake her for breakfast, opening her blinds, and saying, "Wakey! Wakey! Eggs and bakey!" Mom groaned and said, "Sounds like you're talking to a small child or an idiot." After a pause, she said, "Maybe I'm a little bit of both." We laughed. Sunday is usually my favorite day with them because it has a comfortable feel to it. We have time to talk out on the patio before Shaun comes up to take Dad on a ride around the place to check the cows and feed the heifers. Then we all watch David Jeremiah's latest sermon on television before we get ready for church. It is a busy time for me, writing Dad's check for the offering, making sure Mom gets her breakfast and meds before we leave, getting ready myself, putting Dad's hearing aid in, and making sure I have my things for Sunday school. Shaun always stops by on his way to preaching to check on Mom. I know that means a lot to her.

It is a rare treat when Mom comes to the table to eat with us. On Sundays, Shaun often drops in for lunch after church.

I love the drive to church every Sunday. If the weather is nice, we might see our community road-runner, red-tailed hawk or other familiar creature on the winding backroads to our little country church. Walking with Dad into church every week makes me smile. He will stop in the foyer, ask me if his 'hair looks alright,' especially if it is windy, and then he'll stroll back to his Sunday School class, lightly touching the pews as he passes. I wonder sometimes if he's not remembering all the souls that have gone on to glory as he walks the aisle. He enjoys catching up on the news in his class, but sometimes complains that all they want to talk about is their latest ailments. Which I think is hilarious, since Dad is twenty years or older than everyone else in there! He is not one to complain or waste time discussing physical problems. Like the Energizer bunny, he just keeps going and expects other people to do the same, without telling the whole world their woes.

WEDNESDAY, SEPTEMBER 21ST

Mom and Dad got a visit from a dear friend, Bobby Ray, this past week. He brought a bucket of pears and a handmade gift for Dad's birthday. He said he had been out of town for a while and was just now getting it to him. It was a red, white, and blue painted board with some wise words. I could tell Dad appreciated it.

This last week or so has been a blur of running to the pharmacy and follow-up doctor's visits for Marc and Dad, and Mom's appointments – one day, the 20th, I had Mom's appointment in the morning, Addie's piano lesson early afternoon (drop off and pick up), Marc's appointment at the hospital that afternoon, and I had to pick up meds, get groceries, go by the bank, and feed store, and try to find my sanity. Add to that, homeschooling, writing, doing chores at Mom and Dad's and at my house, keeping Emelia, etc., my weeks feel like months sometimes. I am so thankful for my brother and sisters and all they do. I can't even imagine trying to do everything for Mom and Dad by myself…I just couldn't do it.

Today is the last official day of summer and good riddance, I say. This summer has been dry and hot. The past few mornings have hinted at cooler days to come and I am looking forward to fall, now more than ever. I usually love to decorate for the seasons, but I am so mentally and physically exhausted, I just don't have the heart for it. I did find one small white paper-mache pumpkin that my granddaughter Addie had stuck in an overflow junk basket on my counter. Picking it out of the tangle of old charger cords, rubber bands, and batteries, I brushed it off, took it into the family room and plopped it on a side table, next to a deer-sculpted bowl and thought, "Yep…that looks like fall. I think that will do." My decorating was done. I took a picture and sent it to Addie. She texted me back, "Mammy, that is the most pitiful thing I have ever seen!" I laughed. Yes, it is, but that is my life right now.

Mom and Dad's air-conditioning unit went on the fritz last week and I had to call the repairman. They managed to get it fixed and it didn't cost much, thank goodness. I'm just glad it didn't quit on one of those ninety-eight degree days. My grandson, Raylan, turned three on the 18th. He has the sweetest disposition and the curliest blonde hair. Dad loves it when Raylan tries to tell him something; he puts his whole self into his story.

Emelia, my granddaughter turns three on October 2nd, and Athena, another granddaughter turns six on October 13th, so I gave them a combined birthday party on September 30th at my house. It is difficult to coordinate getting them all in one place, so I was glad this worked out. I made individual cakes for each of them to ice and decorate as they pleased. It was huge mess, loud and noisy, but fun. Sherry came over for a few minutes to give them their gifts. We enjoyed watching as much as they did opening. Later, when they went home, it took me awhile to clean up after the mayhem, but I was smiling the entire time. What a sweet memory!

Even though there were some happy moments this last week, it has been a tough one. An old friend passed away, our truck quit again, Marc's teeth started falling apart, one of my teeth lost a filling, and several personal crises were thrown in for good measure. In spite of it all, I found joy in helping Dad put out the salt and mineral for the cows and feed the heifers. In the midst of chaos, it is always nice to slow down, get outside and do something normal. Those are some of the moments I want to remember – just me and Dad enjoying a beautiful autumn afternoon – because after all, that's one of the few things that matter.

EVERYTHING IS A *Trade Off*
YOU CAN'T BE TWO PLACES AT ONCE, SO DETERMINE TO BE
"*Where Your Feet Are.*"

OCTOBER

Dad and Mama both favor October – Dad for the changes in nature and the rhythm of days, Mama because it's her birthday month and that means gifts and attention, two things she adores. Mama's celebrations are somewhat low-key compared to Dad's summertime wing-dings, not by choice as much as the time of year. Everyone is in school and working, busy with football, competitions, etc. making it difficult to squeeze in one more thing. Because she doesn't have as big a gathering as Dad's birthday, we usually try to make hers extra special. Sometimes we pull it off…sometimes not.

Growing up, October around the farm was a wonderful time for us kids. It seemed like the month lasted forever and we reveled in every minute. We looked forward to Mama's delicious pear cobblers, made with the last of the fall pears, and the bounty of canned pickles and other goodies from our summer garden. It was a time of slowing down. The hay was all safely stacked in the barns for winter, the lawn mower was quiet, and we enjoyed more time together in the lengthening evenings. We looked forward to piling brush after Dad came home from work, then as the night settled over the woods and pasture, Dad set the piles afire. We would stand there and watch as the orange and yellow sparks flew up to meet the stars as they came out, one by one. Lingering by the fire and warming our hands, Dad would tell us stories about the "old days" and teach us to recognize the night creatures – the spooky warble of a screech owl, the deep throaty whooo-

whooo of a great-horned owl, the lonesome sound of a whippoorwill, and the sharp bark of a red fox.

All of these happy memories help sustain us as we travel through this uncharted territory of old age with our parents. We are grateful to Mama and Dad for giving us a blessed childhood and such a rich heritage. We had no idea of the long journey life would take us on one day and how much we would need to rely on that solid foundation they both laid so many years ago.

Sherry

TUESDAY, OCTOBER 4TH

Even though it isn't my week, I headed to J'ville to take Mom and Pop to doctor visits. Driving to unfamiliar places stresses Melanie out; plus, I want to hear firsthand whatever the doctors say. Pop's appointment was this morning – tests on the blood vessels in his feet and legs to check the blood flow. Last spring, Dr. J was able to open up Mom's arteries and save her right foot which had looked awful, almost like a dead foot. Pop's doesn't look exactly the same – his right foot and ankle have big splotches of dark red with raised areas that look like blood blisters, as if someone could just poke a hole in each one and drain the junk out. His whole lower leg is swollen, and there are dark red raised bumps behind his knee, some about the size of a pencil eraser. His left leg looks pretty normal… it's odd that one looks so much worse than the other. Pop doesn't run to doctors – he usually has to have a major push; he kept thinking that maybe it would all get better if he kept his leg elevated as much as possible, but that's not happening.

We got in for the test pretty quickly. Pop had to put on shorts for the test which is kind of funny because he never wears Bermuda shorts, and his legs, except for the swollen parts, are like stork legs. I took a picture and sent it to Tam, Melanie, and Shaun. Pop was smiling – he's a real trooper! The room was not brightly lit, and he didn't wear his hearing aids, so he pretty much dozed off during the test.

When we spoke to Dr. J, the news was a mixed bag. Pop has blockages in both legs - veins and arteries, so a different situation from Mom's. We had been worried about how Pop would do with surgery at 99, so no surgery right now was sort of a relief. Doc said he could prescribe something to increase the blood flow. Compression socks might help, but the two different ones we've tried made his big toe throb so much that it kept him awake. Maybe this medicine will help.

After we got home, Pop and Shaun left to haul in the few bales from the highway meadow… twelve measly bales, and one, according to Shaun, about the size of a grizzly – a little one. This drought has really cut into what that meadow should have baled. Pop felt well enough to drive the tractor back with the little bale on the front forks and a big bale on the back. We loved seeing him come over the hill at the wheel of that John Deere!

WEDNESDAY, OCTOBER 5TH

Slept in the Big Room so I wouldn't wake Melanie up with my snoring. (I have been told I do that.) Usually, Mom's late movie watching keeps me awake until after midnight, but she turned in earlier than usual because of her pace maker change-out procedure in the morning. However, the grandfather clock chimes every fifteen minutes and tolls the hour, making sleep hard to come by anyway; so, I didn't get a lot. Found out later that Melanie had been awake since 3:30. Pop got up early also … good thing because Rick Webb knocked on the door at 6:00 – he had come over to have coffee with Pop and watch the sunrise … a treat for both of them!

Dad said Mom was "still the prettiest girl around," even at 95! We agreed.

Mom and I arrived at the cardiac place early. She wasn't feeling very well and had lain in the back seat on the drive there. When we got inside, we met Dr. I and found out that Mom's cardiologist is his daughter. They got Mom all ready and wheeled her back to surgery. She wanted me to pray for her beforehand, and I did. Then I sent my sisters and brother word that they had started. It isn't a risky surgery, but at nearly 95, any surgery is a big deal. Before long, though, she was back and very relieved to have that over! She wanted to sit up front on the drive home so she could see the autumn leaves; not too many are changing around here yet, but some are.

When we got back, Mom changed into her comfortable gown and relaxed. Then Pop came in to check on her; he worries when she isn't doing well. She's the love of his life, and the only one left who remembers the same things he does – how Jacksonville looked in the 30s and 40s, the folks from back then, what life was like during the Depression and the war years. It's a special thing to be able to turn to someone and say, "Remember when … ?" And they do.

SATURDAY, OCTOBER 8TH

Drove to J'ville for Mom's 95th birthday party … seems like I was just there. Wait, I was – on Tuesday and Wednesday, Ha! Melanie made a pecan pie for Mom's "cake" since she prefers pie. A bit more difficult to put candles in a pecan pie, but we managed. Set up her party table in front of the fireplace and put her pie, flowers, cards, and so forth on it. Mom looked so pretty standing behind the table. No one would believe for one minute that she's 95, not even 85. I'll bet there's not one other lady her age in the country or in the world who looks as good as she does.

Most of her gifts were jigsaw puzzles; she really enjoys those. While she was reading her birthday cards, her great-grandson Brandon called from his Navy station to wish her a Happy Birthday. After just a few minutes, she said, "Well, I'm glad you called …" which signaled that she was about done. It made me think of a Pickles comic strip I'd recently seen. The old couple are sitting on the sofa with their dog. The lady is knitting, and the man is reading when their daughter calls. The old lady answers and says, "Oh hi, dear. Here's your dad," and hands him the phone. He says, "Hi there, thanks for calling" and hangs up, leaving the daughter looking at her phone, saying, "Wait, What?" I told my niece Joanna about that comic strip and how it was like Mom when Brandon called. We both cracked up. Mom asked what we were laughing about, and I said, "Oh, just something I recently saw about old folks." I have to be careful, though; in a lot of places, I already qualify as old folks!

MONDAY, OCTOBER 10TH

Before leaving for J'ville, I had my quiet time on the patio; watched several deer run through our back yard and a doe getting a drink from the birdbath. Hummingbirds are still coming through on their way south, so I put food out for them.

Also I ordered some Velcro-fastening shoes for Pop that I hope will fit his "fat" foot and not fall off the other one. When I got to the house, Pop was spraying around the house for termites, ants, and so forth. The gallon container was a little heavy, so he would spray awhile and rest awhile.

After I toted all my stuff inside, he and I rode in Shaun's buggy up to the barn and sprayed around the firewood shed and the big barn. I helped do that because Pop got a bit dizzy. That always worries us. After we drove back to the house, he got in his recliner to rest, Mom worked on her puzzle, and I read my Sunday School lesson. Later, we had a visit from Shaun, then Monday Night Football for Pop, and a movie (or two) for Mom. Thank you, Lord, for a fairly ordinary day!

TUESDAY, OCTOBER 11TH

Got my coffee and went out on the patio while it was still pretty dark. Pop came out later and we enjoyed looking at the early sun streaking over the hill and glittering on the ponds. Went in to get Mom's meds for her – groans and moans of not sleeping a wink. For the 37th time, I pointed out that if she naps most of the day, she will not sleep at night. The only solution is for me to keep waking her up during the day so her "clock" will reset. Letting her sleep during the day to catch up is not a solution … sigh.

Pop and I fed the orphan heifer, then cleaned up his shop a little. Dead dirt daubers, leaves, and dirt on the floor, tools here and there instead of hanging on the proper hooks, buckets and cans and so forth scattered across the floor – trip hazards for Pop. We also tried to air up the wheelbarrow tire – moderate success. The air compressor worked, but the size connection we needed wasn't there.

After lunch, Pop told me that earlier when he had looked out the sunroom windows at the leaves, they suddenly all looked brown. (They are still mostly green.) He said the color gradually changed back to normal, but it happened again in just a short while, except it didn't last as long the second time. He's afraid it might be a side effect of the new blood thinner Dr. J prescribed, so he doesn't want to take it anymore. I know that pill is important to help his leg and foot, so I called "Dr. Tam" as we call her and told her what Pop had decided. She called Dr. B who said he'd do an eye exam next Monday in addition to Pop's regularly scheduled eye shot. That way we'll know if something new is going on. Until then, we'll leave off the pill. Mom's and Dad's health is like a dam that constantly springs leaks … we plug one hole, but another pops open.

Later, I realized that we were totally out of eggs, so I called Marc and Tam – the "Country Pantry" on the next hill. They have chickens. When Marc answered, I announced in my best Forrest Gump voice, "We don't have no eggs, Lieutenant Dan." He got a laugh out of that. I told Pop I was walking over there to get some eggs and he said he'd walk over with me, but I might have to carry him back up the hill. Funny guy. I can barely carry myself up that steep hill!

WEDNESDAY, OCTOBER 12TH

After our usual morning routine, I called the courthouse to check on something for Pop – he wondered if we could just stall where we are on the survey stuff and not file it until after he and Mom have gone on to Glory, but no. The main sticking point is the family cemetery; we're allowed to have one, but the county commissioners' court must approve it … mainly to preserve future access to it.

Later, Tam came over and I rode with her to Whitehouse to get some pumpkins. She and Marc always hide some pumpkins in the woods for their grandkids to find; then they decorate some of them for Halloween. Decorating instead of carving works better around here because the weather can still be really warm. Jack O'Lanterns would look pretty sad around here by the 31st … like that melting Salvador Dali clock. Tam bought several, mostly little ones the kids can pick up easily. I got a BIG one! Pop said it was a perfect pumpkin and admired it so much I decided to leave it at their house and get another one later for myself. I think he showed that pumpkin to everyone who came in the house.

THURSDAY, OCTOBER 13TH

More cutting up on the hill. When the batteries gave out, we went back to the house so Pop could rest while they charged again. I love that battery powered saw because the saw batteries aren't the only ones that need charging! While Pop rested, I washed Mom's gowns … not a simple prospect since there are multiple "Mom instructions" on how to wash (wet spots, then squirt them with Spray and Wash, use the gentle cycle) and dry (only 3 minutes on delicate) then hang them up to finish drying so they won't shrink – a strict gown-washing protocol. Sigh.

Back up on the hill to continue cutting. We were getting to the end of that long log, and I told Pop he needed to be careful on the next few cuts because it looked to me as if the log would roll toward him. He didn't think so. Since I was on the same side he was, I moved back and over a bit. Sure enough, the log rolled his way! Fortunately he was back far enough also. "I was wrong on that one," he admitted.

After a quick trip to Nacogdoches for the "grandparents" sonogram for my new granddaughter, I headed back to the folks. Shaun called to ask where I was. He'd stopped by the house and found the door unlocked, Mom asleep, Pop and the truck missing. I told him I knew exactly where Pop was – up on the hill cutting up wood by himself. Shaun went up there and found him. The batteries had given out, along with Pop. When I got back to their house, Pop had had time to rest awhile, so he and I walked down the road with Hobo the cat leading the way. She is definitely a "people" cat. She wants to be wherever we are. An eventful day, but good.

FRIDAY, OCTOBER 14TH

I'm nearly too tired to write. Hard day. 45° this morning, but warmed up to 85° or so this afternoon. After a "worker's" breakfast for Pop and me and getting Mom all fixed up, we went back up on the hill to cut up the rest of that big limb. By the time we got that done, the batteries needed charging again, so back to the house. I burst in on Mom and urged her to get up and work on a jigsaw puzzle – she has been staying in her recliner too much. She didn't like that and said I was "bullying" her! Oh My Goodness! If she doesn't move, she'll get to where she can't. Then she will wish that she had done differently, but "If wishes were horses, then beggars would ride."

After the batteries charged up and we had rested a bit, back to the hill where Pop got one of his iron wedges stuck, trying to force two log sections apart; then it fell out and got buried by the tractor tires. We'll need a magnet to find it. After he moved all the chunks up to the wood splitter, back to the house where I tried to find a birthday card for Mom to send to Aunt Aline. What a mess! Cards were scattered everywhere: ones Mom has been given, those sent to her with pleas for charitable donations, some she has picked out for specific people, and then forgotten to send. Mom is not exactly a hoarder, but she is definitely a *keeper*. I spent over an hour sorting and trying to organize that stuff. Then Pop came looking for me, ready to split more wood.

After just a few chunks, the splitter ran out of gas. While it cooled off, Pop and I went looking for a calf that had been limping for a day or two. We located her near the little pond under the pine trees. We could see that her back right leg was swollen below the knee and decided that we'd try to get her into the pen this evening and give her a penicillin shot. Back to the woodpile, splitting, then stacking, ending up with the "big hoss" as he called it. It weighed at least 200 pounds, probably more. It was all we could do to wrestle it onto the splitter platform.

After that battle, we rested, then got in Shaun's "buggy" and found that calf in about the same spot as before. Pop drove the buggy while I slowly herded the calf over to the corral. Then we moved her into the smaller pen that opens into the working chute. Down to the house to get the penicillin, then back to the barn to fix the needle and try to get her into the chute. Pop insisted on getting in the chute behind her so he could give the shot. It was beginning to get dark by then, and we were both tired. I should have insisted that we wait until daylight when we'd be fresher. That calf was able to turn around and get past Pop twice. After that, I said, "Pop, let's give it up until tomorrow." He was tired and said he thought that was a good idea. We had a snack back at the house and turned in pretty quickly after that. Long day.

SATURDAY, OCTOBER 15TH

Well, Pop told me this morning that the calf had stepped on his foot as he ran past… his bad foot! I should never have let Pop get in that chute. Shaun came over and could tell that something was wrong, Tam too, when she came to take over. I get really quiet when I'm upset. Anyway, after a while, I packed and headed home, berating myself the whole way. Bill and I sat on the rock patio under the sweetgum tree, and I told him about the long week and what all had happened and how hard it is to keep putting out fires and trying to keep Mom and Pop going with no light at the end of the tunnel. I just sat and cried about it.

People say dealing with aging parents is like raising kids, but it isn't. Your kids will grow up and become more independent and have better and better days, your parents won't. There's no prom to plan for, no graduation to look forward to, no first job and no wedding… just doctor visits, hospital stays, a steady decline, and a funeral at the end. Yes, Heaven is on the other side, and I'm SO grateful for that, but we kids will be left behind, trying to figure out how to face the future without the ones who have been here for us our whole lives; for me, that's nearly three quarters of a century. Heavenly Father, please give us all strength to face whatever each day brings, and the grace to forgive ourselves when we make mistakes.

MONDAY, OCTOBER 17TH

Had a big day cleaning out my half of one of our sheds, dirty work but so worth it. I heard from Tam that when Dr. B checked Pop's eyes, they were not affected by the blood thinner, so he's back on that. He also said that dehydration could have caused that weird color change of the leaves when Pop looked outside. We have been battling Pop's low water intake for years. Looks like the water nags were right on target!

TUESDAY, OCTOBER 18TH

I had to call about Mom's appointment to get the staples out from her pacemaker surgery. Brian will be taking care of that – he's the guy who checks her pacemaker function periodically. He also said that Mom is getting a new remote battery checking device, so when Melanie takes Mom to that appointment, she will need to take the old one so he can return it. Called Melanie and told her all this. We keep the phone lines hot trying to get information to each other.

MONDAY, OCTOBER 24TH

A ton of stuff to pack for Mom's and Dad's, plus some last minute chores, then headed northwest. Talked to Tam on the way – she has a crazy week coming up – getting suitcases to take to Rachel in Dallas, dropping Addie off to join Rachel on a trip, picking Rob up to bring him back home, keeping Emelia, and so forth. She told me she would leave the garage door open so I could park in there next to Mom's car – a ripsnorter of a cold front is coming in late tonight.

Arrived and took the bouquet of roses from my yard inside to show Pop. He enjoys seeing pretty flowers, especially the ones with a good smell. I peeked in on Mom, but she was still asleep. Tam and I checked on the limping heifer and she gave it another shot; we put it and the orphan calf in the hay enclosure so they will have a shelter from the blast of cold air. We try to do as many of these chores as possible so that Pop doesn't have to, especially in bad weather.

Later in the day the weather was still comfortable, so Pop and I took a stroll down the road with Hobo leading the way, her tail straight up like a baton. Pop says it's as if she feels that she needs to be out front so we won't get lost. After that, football for Pop, movies for Mom, snacks and meds for both … then the storm blew in with a flash and a rumble!

TUESDAY, OCTOBER 25TH

The wind was still howling this morning, so Pop and I had coffee in the sunroom. Definitely an inside day, at least until tonight when Shaun takes Pop to the hay show and dinner. Found out about Bobby B's passing. He sang at Bill's and my wedding over 40 years ago. Such a fine couple. Then I talked to my daughter-in-law's mom about all the business items she and her husband have had to take care of since her mother's passing: finalizing bills, closing accounts, selling the house, and so forth. I haven't been where she is now, but I know it's coming. That busyness keeps some of the sorrow at bay for a while, but once everything is done, those emotions move front and center.

Tonight, Pop seemed to be taking a really long time in the shower. I stood outside his bathroom door and listened, but the shower wasn't running. I'm always concerned about his passing out in there and hitting his head – he does have dizzy spells from time to time and has passed out before. Finally, I asked him through the door if he was okay. He said he was, but something in his voice told me otherwise, so I said, "Pop, I can tell in your voice that's something's wrong. What is it?"

He told me that he'd used the wash rag a little too vigorously on the back of his knee and tore one of those blood bumps sticking out, and it wouldn't stop bleeding! I asked him if he was decent, and he said he had his boxers on, so I told him I was coming in. Blood on the towel, blood on the wash rag, blood on the floor mat and running down the back of his leg! Heavenly days! I grabbed the wash rag and could tell that he'd used hot water on it.

"Pop, you need to use cold water to help the bleeding stop." I got it cold and told him to keep it pressed against that place. He hadn't ripped the top of that bump completely off, just tore the bottom half loose. I raced into the kitchen, looking for band aids, then ran back and cleaned the blood off the back of his leg while he kept pressure on that spot. I unwrapped several band aids and had them ready to go on so I could get them on fast … I must have used four or five. Then I wrapped a long towel around his knee and taped it to add a little more pressure. After he got in the bed, I gathered all the bloody towels and stuff and put them on to wash. Lord, watch over Pop, stop that bleeding, and give him a good night's rest, please.

WEDNESDAY, OCTOBER 26

Pop had to take some Tylenol last night, but he did get some rest. Even though the towel fell off during the night, he didn't bleed out of the band aids. I changed those carefully, but didn't put his new pressure socks on. So glad that I got those zip up socks with open toes – Pop can tolerate those very well, just not today. I took care of the heifers and went to town for several items and checked on Shaun's job – a 1950s house, complete with one green bathroom and a pink one. The owners are keeping the retro look, which is smart.

Late in the day, Pop and I went on a walk, Hobo leading the way, of course. Pop's blood pressure reading before the walk was 200/85, and I hoped that the walk would help, and it did. Those high pressures scare us to death, but the blood pressure pill he took for a while had side effects he didn't like, so we're trying some natural products. We are doing the best we can to keep the folks stapled, glued, and taped together.

THURSDAY, OCTOBER 27

I had to call the hospital's business office. Whoever I spoke with said I wasn't on Mom's Hippa form. I knew that I was. After several more calls, I got someone who "found" me in the system and answered my questions. Dealing with the business side of the medical profession is another difficult aspect of helping Mom and Pop

Pop and I got ready to head to the courthouse to file the survey he got done for future inheritance purposes. This has been a huge hurdle and unpleasant to think about, but we want to do all we can to avoid the kind of family squabbles that often occur. The more "cut and dried" that Mom and Dad leave things, the fewer issues will arise. I don't think that would happen with us, but I've lived long enough to know that people will surprise you. Some folks would have a fist fight over a cracked teapot.

On our way up the courthouse steps, Pop tripped and had to grab the side railing – I'm thankful it was there! He sat in the hallway while I checked on the steps to follow to file the survey. First was paying the county taxes. Found out we had to go across the street to the appraisal office for a form showing the taxes had been paid before we could submit the survey, so I walked across while Pop sat on a bench outside the courthouse; he preferred to enjoy people watching on this fine autumn day.

The lady in that office said he'd also have to pay the school taxes in order to get the form. Pop usually waits until January to pay those since he doesn't get a discount for paying early, so I walked back across the street and asked him about it. I don't want to make decisions for him as long as he is able to do it. That's disrespectful. He said to go ahead, so back to the appraisal office and paid the school taxes, plus a fee for a paper stating that the taxes had been paid.

Back across to the courthouse to turn all the survey copies in, but the county clerk said we had to give them to the county surveyor whose office was just down the street. The guy we needed was heading out the door for another appointment, but he kindly stayed long enough to get us all taken care of. I really appreciated that, and Pop was so glad to get such a huge item off his plate.

While we were taking care of all the survey paperwork, I started feeling bad. Of course, the first thing I thought of was Covid – that persistent ogre of 2020. After we got home, I headed to the clinic and got the test, but it was negative. Thank you, Lord! Pop and I got in the buggy and went to the barn to feed the heifers. That injured calf does NOT look good… she had a foamy spittle on her lower lip. Something is wrong with her far beyond a hurt foot.

We rode all around the pastures, across the pond dam, and behind Shaun's house. Back at the house I finished washing the dishes, then Pop and I got ready to go to Bobby B's visitation. Pop said he'd take his cane, grinned, and added, "If I catch one of them funeral guys follering me around with a tape measure, I'll whack him with my cane." I nearly fell over laughing! Pop has a unique sense of humor. The funeral home was really crowded when we arrived. So many people there to celebrate this fine man and support his sweet wife, a tribute to a life well lived.

FRIDAY, OCTOBER 28

Rainy day … I went up to check on the heifer – she won't make it through the day, poor thing. Mel came today for a visit after going to Bobby B's funeral. I told her about Pop's bleeding episode and what I did for it in case it happens again during her week. Pop seems a bit down today, I don't know why. It could be the combination of his foot, the funeral, the poor heifer, and maybe the rain, rain, rain that's keeping him hemmed up inside. I'm so glad he has the Kindle to read; maybe I can encourage him to start a new book today.

Melanie

OCTOBER 3-8

This month we found out about Papa's legs. Both veins and arteries are not functioning properly. Recommendation is medicine to open more blood flow to his legs and feet. Now, Papa takes more pills than ever in his life. Most are natural products to aid in his blood pressure issues, blood sugar, and boost his immune system. Tam (we call her Dr. Tam) is a great researcher of natural products that help, and not hurt the body. The ones Papa takes seem to be working very well. Hope the addition of this traditional medicine works also.

Mama has always taken supplements. We have a large pill holder for 7 days – morning meds and evening meds. Tam usually fills it up on the weekends. Mama is 95, so they must be helping her as well.

Getting the hay off of the highway meadow was on Papa's mind. Papa and Shaun loaded the trailer and Daddy drove the last 2 rolls in on the tractor. It was so special to see Daddy come over the hill of our country road bringing in that hay – one more time.

Sherry came up to take Papa to the doctor and spent the night. It afforded us some sister time. We don't get that much anymore. We try to snatch a day here and there, but it is usually the special occasions of birthdays, Thanksgiving, and Christmas. It is a blessing to care for Papa and Mama, but it is a drastic change that limits our interaction with each other, our children, and grandchildren. Tam has a blessing and a "curse." She is ever present (she lives on the next hill to Papa and Mama) and can be with her husband and family, but she's on call 24/7. Sherry and I live 50 and 80 miles away respectively. I have missed many special events – games, banquets, celebrations, and the day to day just being there for my children and grandchildren.

One thing necessary for my emotional and spiritual well-being is being "all in" whether at home or at Papa's and Mama's. Divided attention leads to more disappointment, resentment, and a sense of loss. Keeping my focus on the folks while I'm with them is the recipe for a good week. My nephew Stu has a saying I like to remember: "Keep your mind where your feet are!" I embraced that. Don't look ahead or behind; just live in the now with joy in what you are doing.

Papa is using his cane more now. We take short walks up to the corner of the road. Neighbors stop occasionally and visit for a while. Porch sitting, as the sun sets, is a beautiful time of day. A few hummingbirds still sip at the feeders. Wind gently sweeps the chimes, and is a sweet sound among the crickets and other late evening insects. We wait for the coyotes to call. Earlier in the summer it was whippoorwills. I always have hope that they will be loud enough and close enough for Papa to hear. On the back patio, in late evening, we can hear a Great Horned owl off in the creek bottom. His voice is a lower tone and Papa can always hear him.

Mel took Mom and Dad to the downtown pumpkin patch to have their picture made...good idea Sis!

Mama is a moon watcher. She loves to see the full moon of each month. She knows what each month's full moon is called. I make a special effort to get her out on the front porch to see it each month.

October was eventful. Mama's birthday and her only sister's birthday are in this month. Aunt Aline lives in Iowa. Mama is 95 and Aunt Aline is 92. All their brothers and sisters have gone on to glory. There were 11 of them. We celebrated Mama's birthday on Saturday the 8th this year.

When I got home after my first week in October, there was no water! When my son Andy checked, he found a broken pipe. Things happen when you are gone a week at a time. You just fix it and carry on.

OCTOBER 17TH-22ND

Mama had her pacemaker battery taken out and replaced earlier this month. I took her this week to have the 12 staples removed and the incision checked. Mama has a very low threshold of pain. As each staple came out, her face crumpled, and she made a little moaning sound. I was scrunched up and felt so sorry for her.

We had an early freeze on the 19th of this month. When we were growing up, Papa always came to wake us up for school. When the first frost happened, he would come in with the announcement: "It's white in the bottom, boys!" (Even though most of us were girls.) Loved hearing that! So, on this occasion, I called Tam and Sherry so they could hear Papa say those iconic words, again.

Tamra

SATURDAY, OCTOBER 1ST

I came over to Mom and Dad's early today so I could catch Sherry before she headed home. I wanted to give her half of that yummy blueberry muffin she brought me on Thursday, it was huge! She gave it to me as a thank you for going over to Mom and Dad's and fixing their dinner on my day "off." Poor thing was stuck in an interminable board meeting, and while I was perturbed at first because Mel called and asked me, instead of her, I thought about it and I knew she would never interrupt a meeting by leaving, even for a minute…she's too polite. She also knew that Melanie **always** has her phone at hand while I am sometimes hard to reach, so it made sense she would text her first. Good thing I'm not on that board, I would have stood up and said, "Let's get this thing wrapped up. I've got things to do!" Haha. When I got Mel's call, I was in the middle of Addie's grammar lesson, which, next to math, is the hardest thing for her to grasp. I guess that had something to do with my aggravation.

I went over to Mom and Dad's, but there was nothing to fix, so I came back over to the house and got some sandwich stuff I had picked up in town earlier that morning before my dental appointment. They seemed satisfied with that and the potato salad I found in the fridge. I slowed down long enough to sit and listen to Daddy say the blessing over the sparse offering – and that made the entire episode worthwhile. I realized I was no longer frustrated and in the hurry I was before. I also realized (again) what a blessing it is to be able to enjoy Mom and Dad being here.

Back to this morning…when I got here, I could tell something was wrong. Sister was too quiet, and when I went to put my things in Josh's room for my stay, everything was topsy-turvy. It was a sign of a difficult week for Sister. She is always as neat as a pin and usually leaves things in perfect order. Her demeanor when I arrived was definitely on the down side. It was not like her at all. I knew it had been a busy week from the amount of activity I observed from the vantage point on my hill, and that was just what I was aware of. After she filled me in about Dad hurting his bad foot, I tried to help her feel better by pointing out that it is usually Dad's relentless push to get things done – no matter what – that usually results in him getting hurt. But, I could do little to assuage her feelings of guilt. But really, trying to doctor a three-hundred pound plus calf in the dark, by puny flashlight is not a good idea, no matter your age – much less after working all day splitting firewood.

Poor Sister had already taken Dad to town this morning to fill up his truck and the gas cans for the saw and wood splitter, plus she had vacuumed most of the house, and no telling what else. Mom was still in her room, but Dad was already up at the wood shed, splitting wood, at 9:00 a.m. when I arrived. Sherry filled me in on the leftovers, what was needed at the grocery store, and Mom's meds that needed picking up at the pharmacy. I visited with Sister a minute before she left for home and I headed to town. She has a full plate when she gets home and is coming back on Tuesday to take Dad to his appointment with Dr. J. We have been concerned about his feet and legs for a while, but it has taken him a long time to make up his mind to go to the doctor. I think Mom's successful surgery on her legs earlier this year prompted him to finally see what the doctor could do about his problem. I really hope they can do something to help his foot; it is becoming worse by the day.

Sherry is also spending the night on Tuesday and taking Mom to get her pacemaker battery replaced on Wednesday. I told her that I am perfectly capable of taking them to their appointments, but I know she wants to hear what Dr. J has to say about Dad's foot for herself. I will be taking Dad to his eye appointment at 9:00 a.m. Monday. I don't want Mel to tear her toenails off trying to get here so early. I don't mind those drives with Dad; it gives us a chance to talk and enjoy the scenery. We like to check out what has changed since last month, etc. Dad is usually quiet on the return trip; his eyes bother him after the shots, at least for the day.

Autumn is a good time to catch up on all those little chores around the farm. Dad is working on the feed troughs for the heifers he plans to wean.

Got to town and picked up Mom's meds, a few groceries and then got stuck at the train tracks that run east/west through town. It took almost ten minutes for that long thing to pass! Of course, it always happens when I am in a hurry. Talked to Sherry a bit on the phone while she was driving home…I hope she feels better about what happened; it wasn't her fault. I don't like to call her or Mel at home because I know how it is to have such a short time to try and do things at home and feel **at** home. Sometimes, I get confused about where I am, reaching for the soap on the wrong side of the cabinet, looking for the flour in the wrong place, sometimes, I want to rearrange the cabinets and drawers like mine at home are, but then, it would be just as confusing for Sisters, so I just fumble through.

Stripped the beds when I got back from town and put them on to wash while I finished the vacuuming Sherry had started and mostly done. The house is quiet now, except for the pooka-pooka-pooka of the washing machine as it agitates. I have also filled Mom's pill holder for the upcoming week and endured the moans and complaints as I split some of her pills. Every little noise seems to bother Mom if she's not asleep. She claims to be a light sleeper (she used to be), but now, as Sherry says, Mom can sleep the "sleep of the dead." Of course, if we say anything, Mom argues with us. To prove my point that she really does sleep through a lot, I took a video with my phone of me trying to wake her up. I pulled on her toes, shook her foot, all the while saying, "Mom! Mom!" It was a full minute before she finally woke up. It was so funny. I showed it to her and she said, "Why didn't you let me sleep?" Hello…

In the meantime, Dad had come in from stacking firewood and had gone to sleep in his chair in the Big Room. I sat at the kitchen table, listening to the washing machine, jotting down some notes for an article and my column, and waited for him to wake up so we could split and stack the rest of the wood.

I fixed Mom and Dad a hodge-podge lunch from the leftovers that Sherry pointed out before she left. I wasn't hungry, so I just drank some tea while they ate. Mom actually came to the table to eat with Dad, something she doesn't do that often, Dad enjoys having her company. I don't blame him…Mom is entertaining. I try to encourage her to come to the table, even if she doesn't feel like eating right then. It seems to perk her up too, although she would never admit it.

Dad rested a bit after lunch while I worked on my notes, then we headed back to the barn to finish with the wood.

It was a warm day, but not too hot. We worked splitting and stacking for a couple of hours. Dad had to rest several times, but I kept right on splitting and stacking because I knew he wouldn't want to quit until it was done, and I still had to put the sheets back on the beds, wash dishes, and go to my house and take care of my critters before dark. When we were done, Dad and I sat in the shade of the woodshed and talked awhile. I have learned not to be in a hurry on the outside when I'm with Dad, even if I feel hurried on the inside. Usually, if I do, my insides eventually settle down and I enjoy the moment. These are the times I want to remember – the everyday, routine tasks that makes up our life on the farm.

SUNDAY, OCTOBER 2ND

Shaun and Ricky are still gone on their trip to Nashville and the truck show. It is weird not having him here on Sunday mornings. I took Dad for a ride in Shaun's buggy today, something Shaun usually does…again, it feels weird. I know Dad has missed him and his daily visits, but Shaun has called and checked on Dad and Mom often. They are supposed to be back sometime today. I am looking forward to hearing about their adventures…I know Dad is too. I made soup and cornbread for lunch today. Dad and I went to church this morning, but he didn't feel like going tonight, so I went alone.

Mom was so funny today. She can act just like a little kid sometimes. I put out a puzzle that was 500 pieces, instead of her preferred 300. She balked and let me know that she would put it up if I didn't help her with it. I told her she needed to challenge herself to try a more difficult puzzle, but she just gave me "the look" and repeated, "I'll put it up!" like it was a threat or something. I laughed and told her, of course, I would help her. Then later when I was reading, she wandered into the Big Room to see what I was doing. Her hair was a fright! She asked me if I would comb and fix it for her. Of course, I always do, if she asks. Most of the time, she remembers to say thank you, but when she forgets, I say it for her. That gets me "the look" too.

WEEKEND OF MOM'S BIRTHDAY, OCTOBER 8TH & 9TH

This evening is the Full Hunter's Moon. I sat out on the front porch waiting for it to peek over the big oaks east of the house. Mom has always been a moon watcher; she loves looking at the full moon throughout the year and rarely misses one. She knows all their names too. Sometimes, it is too hot or cold or cloudy for moon watching, but this evening is perfect. Cool, but not cold, a slight northeasterly breeze is keeping the lingering summer mosquitoes at bay as I rock and wait. Listening to the slowed cadence of the crickets, I hear the distant tremulous call of a screech owl, and I am carried back to an earlier time when we spent evenings out on our old screened-in porch, listening to night sounds as the moon rose. Dad's voice blended in with the night music as he told us stories of his boyhood days during the Depression, his dad's adventures hunting and trapping in the Big Thicket, and the time his dad spent living among the Cherokee Indians in Oklahoma. We had television, but Dad always won out over anything on that black and white RCA set. Sometimes Dad would lapse into silence and we would wait, just enjoying being at home and together as a family. We learned contentment on that old familiar porch.

Finally, Old Man Moon made his appearance, drawing my thoughts back to the present and Mom. I sighed, hesitant to leave the comfort of that porch rocker and my memories. But knowing Mom would want to see the moon before it got too late, I went inside to pull her away from *Little*

Dorritt blaring from her TV. She has to listen to it at a decibel level I am sure is banned in most countries. Thank goodness Mom and Dad live out in the sticks and it doesn't bother anyone…except me. I opened her door and waved my hand for her to lower the volume and then showed her for the umpteenth time how to hit the pause on the remote for the VCR…yes, she still has a VCR and watches VHS tapes regularly.

Slowly, we made our way from her bedroom out to the front porch where she could see her birthday moon, the Hunter's Moon. Her birthday is tomorrow, the 9th. Shuffling all the way to the end of the porch with her walker, she stopped and looked up to admire its beauty. The smile on her face and wonder in her voice made me forget the snippiness of her earlier comments. I also pointed out Jupiter to her, a bonus treat for the night. After looking at the stars coming out and one last look at the moon, we made our way back inside.

Back in her room, I gave her the nightly meds, and after a trip to the bathroom, she went back to her movie – once I showed her, again, how to find the play button on her remote.

It was a long day and we are all tired. Dad went to check on the cows before night fell, but I knew it was just his way of getting alone for a while. Even in a good day you need a little space.

Now he is watching some college football, Kansas State vs. Iowa State. His volume is even louder than Mom's. I am sitting in the kitchen, and it is nearly 9:00 p.m., time for Mom's nightly coffee ice cream cone. I am caught between blaring British dialogue and two overly excited sportscasters trying to make a game seem more interesting than it is. As soon as I deliver Mom's appropriately towering ice cream cone, I am retreating to Josh's room to unwind, read a bit, and hopefully get at least five hours of sleep before Dad is up and going again.

SATURDAY, OCTOBER 15TH

Mom has her days and nights mixed up. Not that she doesn't know which is which, although she does get confused sometimes, but she has acquired the habit of watching movies all night, then sleeping most of the day. This throws off her meds schedule and makes getting her to eat a meal on time with the rest of us even harder. It is one thing to have a baby with a mixed up schedule, but it is another thing altogether when it is a 95 year old. If you wake a baby, you can usually soothe them by rocking or feeding them, but when we wake Mom up, she moans and groans, saying, "It's too early! Why are you waking me up?" like we are trying to kill her instead of take care of her. She doesn't always fall back to sleep, but she does often enough that we are back and forth checking to see if she took her meds, etc. Her bladder is our best ally, because when we can't get her up and going, it usually does.

Some days, she is up and going fairly early, usually on the days she has a doctor's appointment. She wants to make sure she has plenty of time to "fix up" as she calls it, so she "won't look like ole Mard Crump" a poor long-passed soul who apparently was rather unkempt. Vanity is another ally we can employ if needed. Mom never wants to be seen in her "natural state" except by immediate family members, so when we need to get her up and moving, we arrange for company to "pop in." It is rather underhanded I suppose, but it works, and some days, I'll try anything to motivate her. I have had her balk on me a few times. She will give me "the look" and shut her door in my face. Which I think is pretty funny; it reminds me of my kids when they were about three or four. But, you can't put your 95 year-old Mom in time out…even if it is tempting.

WEDNESDAY, OCTOBER 19TH

First freeze/frost of the season, about a month earlier than normal. 28 degrees this morning. I waited for Dad to call with his usual proclamation "It's white in the bottom this mornin' boys!" but I knew he couldn't see to dial the phone like he always has, so I texted Mel "Dad hasn't called me…first frost." In just a few minutes, the phone rang and Dad's young sounding voice boomed out the familiar phrase. It made my day! It may not seem like much, but I have heard Dad say that phrase at the first frost for as long as I can remember. Even after I married and moved over on the next hill, he has still called every fall at the first frost. It is our special tradition. It is one consistent thing from my childhood days and I treasure it. I am so thankful he is still here to officially announce the new season. The tradition actually started with his dad, my grandpa Robartus who said the same thing every year to Dad and his siblings growing up, just like Dad did for us. I kept up the tradition with my own kids too. I hope they pass along the story and the fun to their kids.

SUNDAY, OCTOBER 23RD

Church service was good. Dad and I really enjoy Brother Dale and his sermons. Karen and Aunt Shirley playing the piano and organ make our music service extra special. After church and a bite to eat, I took Dad down to see Darryl and look at his newest chestnut crop. Darryl was glad to see us and he showed Dad his big cooler where he keeps the nuts until he ships them, then we took a ride in his buggy around the place, a parcel of the original Homeplace where Dad grew up, and Dad really enjoyed seeing how his nephew is taking care of the land and using it to grow things. I wonder as he looked at the familiar hills and woods, if he was recalling boyhood memories and exploits with his brothers. The spring is still there and running strong that he used to haul water from and I know he was happy to see it once again. He admired the towering cypress trees that Darryl had planted in the once tangled thicket of the bottomland near the creek. Dad is also intrigued with the chestnut trees Darryl has successfully nurtured and wished him well in his future crops. I know Dad is pleased that the tradition of caring for the land continues.

Dad enjoyed seeing the improvements his nephew Darryl has made to his part of the old Homeplace

SATURDAY, OCTOBER 29TH

Busy all morning trying to get everything done and Mom and Dad settled before I went home and got ready for the Princess Tea this afternoon. Rita, Athena, and I had a wonderful time. I finally got to visit with my friend Tiffany and even had our picture made together. Her choir did a great job with their annual fund-raising Tea. Athena was a bit shy at first, but when one of the high school girls dressed as Elsa talked to her, she warmed right up and started participating in the activities. I had let Athena borrow one of my Pulpwood Queen Book Club tiaras and she wore a long blue fluttery dress…she looked the part of a little princess! Rita and I dressed up too, and I even brought my OZ scepter that Addie had made for one of my Pulpwood Queen Big Hair Ball outfits. It was fun to once again play dress up for a day.

SUNDAY, OCTOBER 30TH

The temptation to stay inside and take a much needed nap was almost stronger than my need for a bit of alone time, but not quite. Even though the temperatures are in the 60s, a hefty breeze out of the west/southwest made it seem cooler. The cloudy rainy days on Friday and Saturday brought much needed rain and left the air feeling clean and fresh, just like fall should be. The old hickory down towards the pond is beginning to show tinges of gold on its canopy. Hopefully, the winds won't blow the leaves away before they make it to the show-off stage. Some years, its color rivals that of the yellow golds you see in New England; others, its full beauty is stripped off by the howling northers that often visit us in November. Fall is late here most years, with colorful foliage sometimes evident well after Thanksgiving. But sometimes, we see the first stages of the autumn leaves, then a freeze hits and they all drip off like late March icicles and are gone in a day. We never know what we are going to get, so each morning, we look out at first light to see any changes. Dad has always consulted nature and relied on his internal barometer and sense of what was coming; he has been more reliable than our local weatherman on most occasions. It has been six months since I have been down to my cabin, other than to do a quick check and some wishful thinking. Today, I set aside a couple of hours to recharge. Mom and Dad are fed, reading and working puzzles, so I felt I could steal away for a bit.

Dad used to take walks in the woods to clear his head. He mentioned that today as I headed for my cabin. I know he misses being able to get away for some quiet time. With a big family to feed, farm to run, and a business, I am sure he had little time for himself. I remember finding him one day leaning back against a huge red oak tree down in the pasture overlooking the ponds. I was about nine or ten, but I could tell from his faraway gaze that he was seeing something I couldn't see. Feeling like an intruder, I quietly backed away and left him to his thoughts. I don't know if he ever knew I was there. I understood, even then, that sometimes people need space and alone time.

When I'm at Mom and Dad's I try to be one hundred per cent there, but because of the close proximity to my own home, my mind is often divided. It is a challenge I don't feel I am always up to. I sometimes wonder if my sisters think I have it easier, living so close to Mom and Dad, but for me, it is not. I am never *away* and can't put things out of my mind, even for a little while, unless I am on a press trip. Even then, I have moments when worry invades my thoughts, and I have to remember my sisters are there and everything is all right. None of us, including Mom and Dad, have ever journeyed this path before. Just like the early explorers, we trudge on day after day figuring out how to circumvent obstacles, back-tracking when we find our way blocked, and renewing our faith in the purpose of the journey we began over two years ago. The destination we all know and yet it is unknown – the paradox of care-giving to the terminal. We are all terminal – some just know they are closer to the station, but no one knows the arrival time. We don't often talk about it, but when we do, we are all in agreement. We want what Mom and Dad want…to go in their own way, when God sees fit. Even though, as their children, we don't want to let go at all…ever.

This weekend I changed Dad's sheets as usual, but today, I put on his flannel sheets for the fall and winter. I thought back to May when I finally took them off for the summer. I remember praying that I would be able to put them back on for another winter. God answered that prayer today. I couldn't help but smile as I plumped his sad little flat pillows and turned down the covers.

We all do the *Best* we can...
Don't expect *Perfection* from
Yourself or other *Caregivers*.

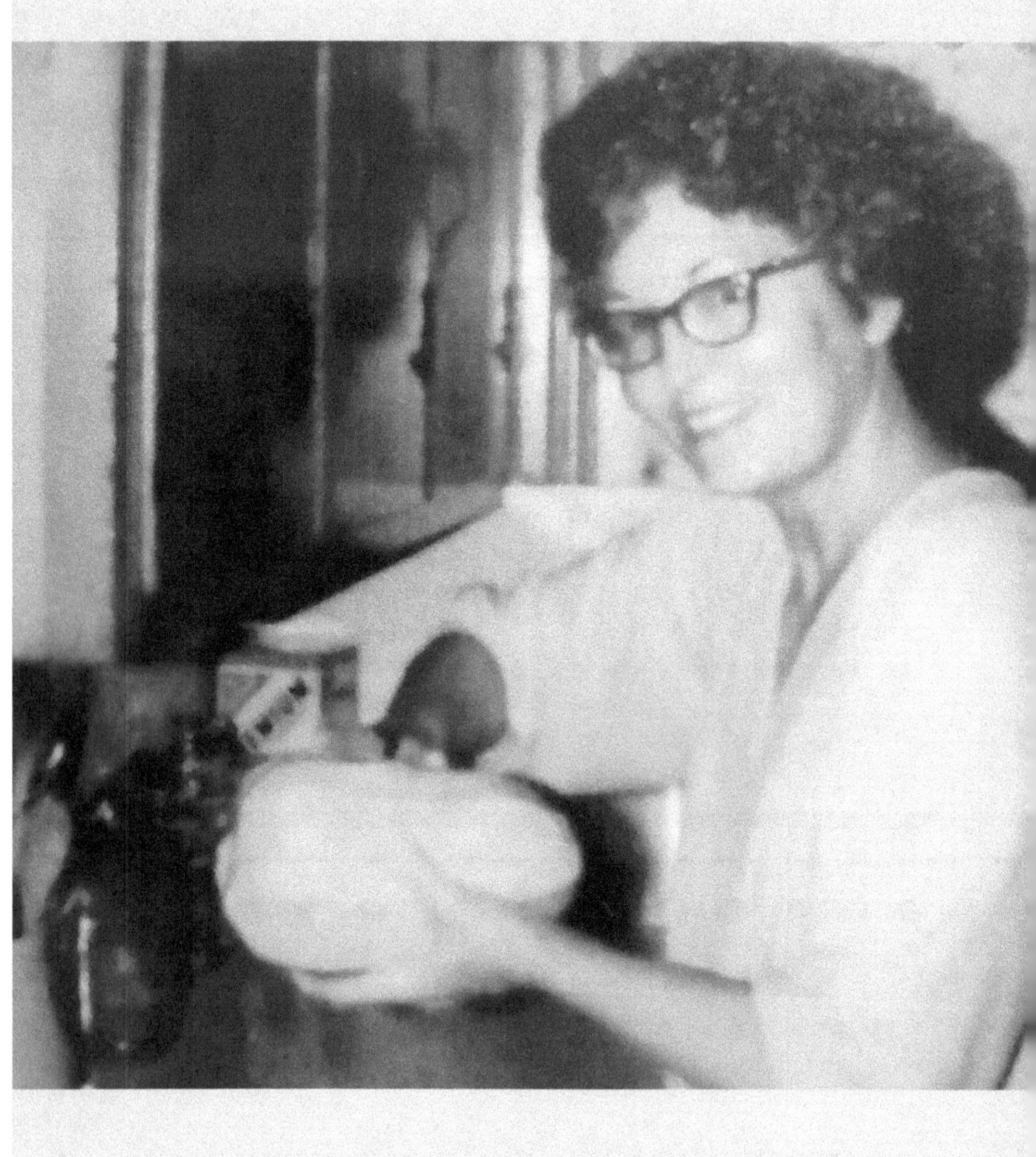

NOVEMBER

The most exciting part of November is the anticipation leading up to the first frost and Thanksgiving. This year, the first frost came early, so it made for a lengthier fall which suits me fine. The weather is the most talked about topic with most rural folks and we are no exception. Coordinating the daily feeding and haying of the cows is one of the main subjects of conversation as a cold front approaches, especially if it involves below normal temperatures and snow or ice. A blue norther, as we call it, can create as much excitement in our house as a carnival coming to town. This year, we were caught off guard with that early cold snap and Dad was glad he had decided, at my brother's prompting, to put up that late cutting of hay – looks like we are going to need it.

This time of year brings to mind past holidays and fond memories of my childhood. We always had a big crowd at my grandmother's house for Thanksgiving. Her small white house would be bursting with aunts, uncles, cousins, and various hangers-on. Every available surface was heavy with pretty homemade fruit and pumpkin pies, towering carrot and Italian cream cakes, fat hams with orange glaze prickling with cloves, enormous juicy turkeys, and every imaginable vegetable and casserole dish. It was a gorgeous time of sharing food, laughter and story-telling.

Those days are long gone along with all of Dad's brothers and sisters and a good many of our cousins. Dad is the only one left that remembers his childhood and what it was like growing up in that large boisterous family of eleven kids during the Great Depression. Mom remembers some of that time, but even now, her memory is fading. I imagine Dad's mind travels back to those earlier, happier times during this season, even as he looks forward to our own family gathering this year.

Because of illness and conflicting schedules, we had a smaller crowd than usual this year at Mom and Dad's, but even that couldn't put a damper on Dad's enjoyment of his favorite holiday. He gave the prayer before the meal, something we all look forward to and then he spent the day eating and catching up on all the family news.

Mom enjoyed the company, but by night fall, she was so tired that she fell asleep during her first movie of the evening.

At every special occasion, the thought crosses my mind, as I'm sure it does everyone else's…will this be the last one? It makes me sad to consider it, but on the other hand, it makes me more mindful to be in the moment. Taking mental pictures of everyone laughing, talking, and enjoying the day helps me to treasure the time I am in. None of us is promised another birthday, Thanksgiving or Christmas, and by appreciating what we have right now and who we are with, we realize those are the things that are the most important – things Mom and Dad are still teaching us every day.

Sherry

FRIDAY, NOVEMBER 4TH

Meanwhile, back at the ranch ... my days at my house are always packed since I need to catch up on projects I can't do from fifty miles away, or take care of extra chores so that Bill doesn't have to do them in addition to his regular job. Not too many husbands would be so willing to spend half of their time being "single," but he's good about it, except for the occasional wisecrack. He's still working, so any home repairs or replacement situations that come up need to be scheduled when I'm home. So, here I am, waiting for the guy who is going to replace the 40+ year-old linoleum in the laundry room with Luxury Vinyl Planks – which sounds more highfaluting than it is.

We also had foundation problems, so I had to arrange for an estimate on that. Since they can't get to the repair this week, it will have to wait until the next time I'm home, not great timing with Ben and his family coming for the holidays.

MONDAY, NOVEMBER 7TH

It may not take a village, but at times, taking care of Mom and Dad takes all three of us sisters. Pop had an early eye appointment today, so Tam took him to that while Melanie stayed with Mom until I could get there to take over. She would normally have gone home last Saturday morning, but Tam was gone over the weekend on a press trip to Green Bay, Wisconsin. She didn't get back until the wee hours this morning – she's probably running on fumes. Melanie helped me carry my stuff in and filled me in on Mom – she's not feeling well and not wanting to eat. I'll have to do my best on that.

Melanie left, then Tam and Pop got back. The eye people prepped the wrong eye for the shot, realized the error, and prepped the other eye. Poor Pop, with both eyes dilated, he'll be in his recliner all day. Mom went to sleep, too, so I cleaned some of the floors and set up Mom's new Medtronic device that automatically sends her pacemaker info to the cardiologist. Called my insurance people about the slab work – it isn't covered. No surprise there. Fixed us all lunch and cleaned up the kitchen.

Tam came back over to show me some photos from her press trip. Later, Pop and I fed the heifers. Shaun came by for a few minutes after he got off work. He makes it a point to go in and see Mom every time, even if she's already watching her movies. He's the baby of the family – 53 tomorrow! Pop's eyes had cleared up enough for him to watch Monday Night Football later.

TUESDAY, NOVEMBER 8TH

Good Grief! Those acorns falling onto the metal roof sound like golf balls! I need to put some earplugs in tonight. There's a new scattering of them on the patio every morning … makes for an uncomfortable walk out there to have our coffee. Town trip, then Pop needed to go vote – Tam took him for that civic duty. Then ranch chores and lunch.

Another very full day, but the main thing is that it's Shaun's birthday, and for the first time, Mom didn't make his birthday cake. That Duncan Hines yellow cake mix with homemade chocolate frosting has been in Shaun's birthday pictures for decades, but not this time. Mom just wasn't up to doing that, even with help. I was very surprised. Even when she doesn't feel well, she makes an extra effort when Shaun comes over, and has always insisted on making his cake, long after she stopped cooking anything else.

I could have made it myself, but that was Mom's thing, and it wouldn't have been the same. So, I made blueberry muffins. Shaun loves blueberry anything. I put a candle in one of the muffins and we all sang "Happy Birthday." Then he opened his cards. It was fun, just not the same … one of the many changes that are inevitable as we go along this path.

WEDNESDAY, NOVEMBER 9TH

Had my quiet time on the patio – cloudy, but the full moon peeped through a couple of times. There was a total lunar eclipse last night, but it happened without my help – slept right through it. Pop joined me after a while – we had to sit under the carport to keep from getting beaned by those acorns.

After breakfast, Pop wanted to fill in some holes up at the big barn where we'd had the temporary enclosure for the orphan calves. I helped him switch the tractor hay forks to the bucket so he could get a load of dirt to use. Also, an armadillo had dug under the north side of the barn, so I used a shovel to fill that one in. Next, Pop wanted to drive the tractor down in the bottom and round up scattered limbs from that huge dead pin oak that had fallen over. After opening the gate for him, I fixed Mom's breakfast, then grabbed some bottles of water and snacks and drove the truck to where Pop was working. We wound up with two piles, but one was too close to the neighbor's fence to burn. The other pile had a lot of dirt mixed in, but we finally coaxed it to burn. I'd brought a chair for Pop; we rested, had our snacks, and watched the fire. After a bit, we headed to the house, but stopped on the way to see if we could light up an old hickory log, but a no-go on that one. Lots of hickory nuts on the ground from a couple of younger trees. I might get some later, but they'll be a royal pain to crack!

Mom seems a bit better today, Yay! I helped her change into a cooler gown – hot and humid today: 80° and 65% humidity … air you can wear. Combed and braided Mom's hair, then she went to the sunroom to talk with Dad while I cooked the meal. After lunch, I walked way up on the knob with the binoculars so I could check on the fire – it was about out. We've had more than our share of wild experiences with fires getting out, so I try to keep an eye on them.

THURSDAY, NOVEMBER 10TH

A day of pluses and minuses … like most days, I suppose. A minus – Pop's foot bothered him during the night. A plus – we still got a lot done: fed and watered the heifers, cut up more firewood, cleaned up some outside, rounded up fallen limbs and so forth. When we returned to the house from the wood pile the second time, Mom was in the sunroom, sitting in Pop's recliner – not usual for her, but I was glad to see her there instead of staying in her room. Pop was, too. They sat and visited for a good while … a plus.

While they visited, I cleaned off the little porch outside the sunroom and scrubbed the birdbath. Went to town by way of Rita and Jason's so I could get Pop's cant hook he had lent Jason. We needed it for extra "oomp" to heave those wood chunks onto the splitter. Got Chick-fil-A for lunch. (Sometimes picking up lunch just makes sense.)

Later on, I braided Mom's hair, then she worked on a jigsaw puzzle until Nurse C arrived. After the checkup was done, Mom came looking for Pop. He was outside on the patio, and I knew the sunshine would do Mom good, so I coaxed her outside, after blowing all the acorns off the concrete – she goes barefoot 95% of the time!

Dad disappears on us when he can...but usually we can track him down. Caught 'cha Dad!

The nurse was right behind Mom and motioned that she wanted to talk to me. She said she'd noticed some things that we need to be aware of … Mom's wanting to spend more time with Dad, talking about wanting to "go on" and so forth. Not that her passing is imminent, but it's out there, and we need to be ready, as ready as anyone can ever be for that. I'd label that as a minus except that the Lord is calling the shots here, and He knows best. I love the saying I heard once: God gives us the same answer we would give ourselves if we knew what He knows. Good one to remember.

FRIDAY, NOVEMBER 11TH

Mom felt bad this morning and said she thought she was dying, but when I asked if she was hurting, she said, "No, I just feel bad all over." I explained that even a doctor couldn't do anything with that, and asked if maybe she had gas or was constipated. Sometimes either of those can lead to a lot of discomfort. After a while, she said she felt a little better. Pop worries when Mom feels really bad, and **his** blood pressure goes up. So for Mom's sake *and* Pop's, we try to figure out a solution, but sometimes we don't have a clue what to do.

He went in to see her and took her hands in his and said, "These little hands have done a lot of work." He loves her so much. I don't know how one would do without the other … they are the only two left who have most of the same memories. Pop has outlived all his siblings, and Mom has one sister left in Iowa. We kids can listen to stories of the old days in the 30s and 40s, but that isn't the same as being able to talk about it because you lived it. They would probably like to pass on at the same time, but that would kill us kids! Pop told me one time that he suggested to Mom (jokingly, of course) that they could just go out on a high bridge over a river, hold hands, and jump off. Mom said, "That won't work – I'm afraid of the water." Pop laughed and laughed over that one.

WEDNESDAY, NOVEMBER 16TH

I never put Christmas decorations up until at least Thanksgiving weekend, unlike my son Ben and his family who start celebrating Christmas right after Halloween. When I lament the poor orphan status of Thanksgiving, he says, "We're thankful … thankful for Christmas." Ha! This year, however, I have to break my rule. Ben and his family will be here for three days starting December 17. Since I am in Jacksonville every other week, that only leaves me two weeks here to get everything ready … so, up the decorations go. Which also involves dusting first – not my favorite chore. It's one of those jobs that only last a short while, like a Facebook post I saw: "I dusted once, and it came back … not falling for **that** again!"

Got the tree up – mine is tall and very fat, so it takes a while to assemble. I strung the lights on it, then put the fake greenery over the windows and set other doodads here and there. What a weird word – doodads. Who came up with that?

MONDAY, NOVEMBER 21ST

Managed to leave my house by 9:00. Melanie called shortly before I got to Mom's and Dad's, and we discussed the Thanksgiving weather forecast – it isn't looking too promising. Most of the time we can get out in the huge side yard and set up games for everyone: washers, corn hole, horseshoes, and even a badminton net, and most people eat outside at the picnic tables. At some point in the afternoon, the kids trek up to the hay barn and play on the hay bales. Not this year … a very rainy forecast, so we'll have to set up tables in the garage and all over the house to get everyone settled. Usually we can figure on at least thirty people, in some years, closer to forty. We'll make it work.

Toted my stuff inside, and then sat by the fire to visit the folks. I remember the days when we had an even, lively exchange of activities and future plans, but now it's more one-sided. Mom doesn't get out much except to doctors' offices; her main activities are jigsaw puzzles, word search books, reading, and watching movies, so she doesn't have much to add to the conversation. Since Pop retired from painting, his focus is mostly the ranch and church on Sundays, but he also enjoys social occasions. He's a people person; Mom has always treasured her alone time.

Later I started lunch, but when I grabbed a carton of chicken broth out of the pantry and, out of habit, checked the date, it had expired in 2018! We probably need to do a check of everything in there and in the refrigerator. It's easy to let stuff get shoved to the back, and use what's right in front. As Pop says, "You have to rotate your stock."

Finally got the turkey sausage soup done, and only then thought about the turnip greens in it. Mom and Pop are both on blood thinners, so they don't need turnip greens … sigh. It's so hard to cook food they enjoy and still control salt, sugar, fat, and green stuff. There's not a lot of green in each bowl, so maybe it will be okay today – I'll fix something different tomorrow.

After we ate, we all relaxed in front of the fire, then played Mexican Train, a domino game we all enjoy. Mom won the first game – always a good thing – she does not handle losing very well! When Pop's eyesight began to fail, he had to stop playing because he had trouble seeing the colored dots on the dominos. Then Tam found a set with big numbers instead, and he was able to play again. We try to find ways to compensate for losses so they can still enjoy as many activities as possible.

TUESDAY, NOVEMBER 22ND

Niece Rita came over to ask about taking Pop's planer apart, to see if she could fix it. She's a handy girl with tools, but that planer was as stubborn as a mule. She couldn't get it to budge, even using every trick she'd seen on the "University of YouTube."

While Rita and I were talking, Pop decided to get his coveralls on and go up on the hill to feed and water the heifers. Out of the corner of my eye, I noticed Pop struggling to get the coveralls on. He said something wasn't right, and when I looked, He'd turned them sideways and had gotten his leg in the sleeve! Of course, it was his "fat" foot, not the skinny one. Thought I'd never get his foot backed out of there! As I wrestled with it, Pop said, "Ain't that something? That's the kind of thing you don't need to tell people about … they'll be coming after me to go to the big house." I was laughing so hard I thought we might have to get the scissors and cut him out of those coveralls! We finally got him out and back in, with the right extremities in their customary places.

After he left to feed and Rita went planer shopping, Athena, Raylan, and I took a long walk up in the pasture, played "I Spy," and ate some snacks. Such a good time with those precious children!

Rita had gotten back by then and was watching Pop chop some kindling. He seemed pretty weak, and when I checked his blood pressure, the top number was 77! Grabbed some potato chips, one of his favorite snacks, and checked his BP again after he ate those. The top number had come up to 129. I asked him, "Are you alive now?" That reminded him of when our cousin's husband Stanley had a really low BP. His wife Rhonda said, "Boy, you'd better lie down – you're dead!" Dad always gets a laugh out of that.

WEDNESDAY, NOVEMBER 23RD

Had my coffee and fed Hobo – she sits on a chair outside the side porch windows until she sees the kitchen light come on; then she stands on the chair arm and stretches up with her front paws on the window screen as high as she can reach, letting me know that she is quite ready for her breakfast, thank you very much! I made a fire and kept checking on Pop to make sure he was still breathing – normally he would have already been up. Finally I walked in and said, "Pop!" and startled him. He didn't think it was all that late.

At breakfast, he told me he had had an upset "lower region" as he puts it, since last Saturday! Ever since he was on Iwo Jima in World War II, he has had regular bouts of bowel trouble. While on the island, he lost a lot of weight, going from 202 pounds to 160. I think he picked up some parasite or bug over there. I hope he feels like eating his favorite meal tomorrow.

I scurried around straightening up, doing some laundry, and helping Mom get a shower. Her bathroom has a very small hot water heater just for her, and she ran out of hot water before she got all rinsed off. I had to grab some plastic pitchers, run to the hall bathroom, fill them up, hustle back and pour them over her. It's a pretty good distance, too. After she got dressed, she sat on the front porch for awhile – very warm today ahead of the rain due tomorrow.

Pop fed the calf, blew the acorns off the patio and upper driveway, and cut down some dead plants in front of the little barn. Melanie arrived around 4:00 with all her items for our feast, plus a Christmas tree she's giving to Mom and Dad (Theirs has gotten a little Charlie Brown-ish.) and the corn hole game we're setting up in the garage. It won't be as much of a challenge with the shorter distance, but, oh well …

Melanie and I got the tables ready in the dining room and on the side porch, and prepped for the chicken and dressing and candied sweet potatoes. Rex arrived around 8:00 … he brought his huge smoker over so he could get an early start on the turkeys. I can taste it already! Time to hit the hay and sleep fast.

THURSDAY, NOVEMBER 24TH

Thanksgiving Day is always such a whirl, even though we do some prep ahead of time. Melanie spends the early morning on the centerpiece of the feast: chicken and dressing and homemade yeast rolls. We couldn't have Thanksgiving without those. From 5:45 A.M. on, we were cooking, washing pots/pans/bowls, setting out paper plates/napkins/forks/cups, and greeting folks as they arrived, taking photos, and getting food set out.

Sure enough, the weather did NOT cooperate – rainy and cold. Everyone had to be inside the whole time. Good thing Mom and Dad have a sprawling house. Also, our crowd wasn't as big this year. Several folks were sick and stayed home, so we only had around 28 people. Still, it was a wonderful time. We thanked God for our blessings and enjoyed a fine meal and great fellowship with family.

Stu and Ashley ate with her parents in Nacogdoches, but then came to our gathering for their family baby shower at 3:00, hosted by Melanie, Tam, and my niece Rachel. Cute baby elephant cake, lots of sweet gifts, and laughs when Stu held up some diapers and asked, "So how many of these will we use in a day … 5? 6?" This is their first child, so they have a lot to learn.

Gradually, folks said their goodbyes and headed for home and their own beds. (The older I get, the more I understand the appeal of one's own bed!) As Tam's son-in-law passed her neighbor's house, he spotted Tam's lost dog in their yard and called to tell her – she was so relieved! She really wanted a good dog, and this one seemed to be ideal. That was a Thanksgiving bonus!

Melanie and I cleaned, put away, and straightened up for about two hours. Then Mom (who had not come out of her room until around 1:30 because she didn't feel well) got her second wind and wanted to play Mexican Train. Poor Melanie was nearly comatose by then because she didn't get much sleep last night, but she gamely played several rounds before we announced that we were done and headed to bed.

FRIDAY, NOVEMBER 25TH

Poor Melanie got zero sleep … it was just one of those nights for her. After breakfast, she and I put the Thanksgiving decorations away, then decorated the fireplace mantel for Christmas. When Tam came over, we all put up the new tree and strung lights on it. I'm glad we can do that for the folks – they love looking at it but just aren't up to doing all that themselves. There may come a day when I won't be able to decorate for the holidays – that will be a sad day. After both my sisters left, I put the ornaments on the tree – Mom likes to watch and let me know where there's a bare spot that needs filling. Some ornaments never see the light of day – ones Mom doesn't want "anything to happen to." If you don't enjoy them, what's the point?

Every time I put ornaments on their tree, I think about a couple of years ago when Hobo quietly followed Pop into the Big Room. He had learned that the door into the house didn't always close completely, and took every opportunity to slip in and find a cozy spot. The Big Room with its cheery fireplace definitely qualified as cozy. Pop had gotten in his recliner and closed his eyes, so he had no clue he had company. There stood the Christmas tree, and cats climb, so up Hobo went. A few minutes later, Mom came in and asked, "Why are all these ornaments on the carpet?" Pop got up to investigate and found himself eyeball to eyeball with Hobo at the top of the tree. When he grabbed her front part, she held onto the tree with her back paws. Pop said she stretched out about a yard before letting go!

Melanie

November is the month of the "thunder of acorns." We have a very fine post oak tree that shelters the house. During summer's heat that shade is a relief. In spite of a drought, latter day rains produced a bumper crop of very fat acorns. As November dawned, those fat, very fine acorns fell from many branches onto the metal roof producing startlingly loud sounds. As Papa and I sit in the late afternoon warmth of these early days of November, we literally jump at the sudden sound! Hobo, the cat, has a particular reflex reaction as well. We sit under the eve of the metal carport because these little natural missiles can collide with considerable force and pain

NOVEMBER 1ST- 5TH

Projects keep Papa agile and happy. This month we have mended a feeding trough and cut up large limbs that have fallen from oaks killed by the deep freeze of February, 2020. A hickory snag fell during a recent storm and Papa and I worked on that. He has transitioned from a big, heavy chain saw to an Easy Start chain saw Sherry and I got him to this battery powered one, from Shaun. We rejoice in that for two reasons: one, it is slightly lighter in weight; two, when it runs out of "juice" Papa has to sit down and rest. Papa reminisced that the slope used to be covered in majestic hickory trees and is now reduced to one very large mature tree and one snag that is bent very far over and will eventually succumb to wind and gravity. On top of the hill, ablaze in golden yellow foliage, is a next generation hickory that blesses Papa's heart as he enjoys its rich color. Things change; yet, if we chose to look, the beauty of change can lift the spirit. I admire Papa's optimism that has been the hallmark of his life.

Working the cattle this month is an event fraught with uncertainty. Checking the supplies is necessary; checking on the "help" is vital. Shaun, myself, Andy, and Garrett round out Papa's crew. We know a fall storm is coming Friday night, but Papa decided to go ahead. Although it was a "wild and stormy night," morning dawned clear and beautiful. Papa and Shaun had put the cattle in the corral except for the big bull, 3 or 4 cows and a couple of calves. Andy had to encourage the bull into the corral with the hot shot, but finally got him in. The older bull was still in a challenging mood. The younger ones tested him by tying up in a head butting and shoving match from one end of the pen to the other. They even bounced into the heavy metal fence and shook it! I ended up on top of that fence ready to drop down on the other side. This 73-year-old grandmother still has some moves!

Finally, we were able to get them all separated and start working them through the chute for semi-annual shots and pour-on worm meds. This year Papa had a chair on the inside of the small pen where I was loading the needles. He sat there basking in the sunshine, enjoying the day, and giving, from his storehouse of wisdom, advice on how and when to do things. Loved seeing his joy in the day and contentment to let the next generation work together and learn from his long accumulation of knowledge.

Mama does not want to eat. We have to cajole and make modifications to her diet. Boost with extra protein and two scoops of Blue Bell Homemade ice cream is a combination she can tolerate. For the most part, the joy in eating is gone for Mama. She forces herself to eat simply for the calories. She mentions, frequently, that she would rather go on to heaven. Her world is closing in on her. She feels bad a lot of the time. I have noticed that she is making more of an effort to come to the table and eat with Papa and me. I encourage her and tell her how glad we are that she has chosen to join us. Usually, Mama sits in her room and we bring her meals. Amazing as it seems, Mama looks forward to 9:00 pm and her Blue Bell coffee ice cream cone. I love seeing her big smile when I open her door and come in with it. She watches movies at night, works on her word search puzzles during the day and then moves to her jigsaw puzzle table by midafternoon. Lately, I hear her walker coming through the library room out to the sunroom for a change of scenery. Its bank of windows looks out to the old barn that Papa built when I was a baby.

Time to break out the Mexican Train dominoes…evenings by the fire are sweet times, unless Mom starts to lose!

From the sunroom we can also see both ponds and a tall hill we call the "nob." Papa built this room addition when he was in his 70's. As Mom settles into one of the wicker rockers, I leave them to talk of old times, people of their past, and how things used to be. I go find something to do as they share together. They need that togetherness. One morning Mama got to the sunroom before Papa. When he came in, he took Mama's hand and asked how she was doing. She wasn't feeling very well, she said. He kissed her hand and gently held it for a while. What a touching moment it was.

NOVEMBER 14TH - 19TH

This is my second week this month with the folks. As I come up over the hill for the first glimpse of my childhood home, I see smoke rising from the chimney, a sure sign that winter has begun. I can already visualize the cozy warmth of the coming winter days by that familiar fireplace.

Later, as we sit and sip, Papa with his coffee and me with my hot tea, Papa's thoughts turn down past trails of life and change over the last century. He talked of Harper's Mule Barn and Auction that was in operation downtown until after World War II. When Papa was about 10 or 11 years old, his Dad bought an L.C. Smith double-barreled shotgun there. He talked about the newer auction built on the highway, a locker plant that used to be next door and how he and Uncle Holly had ordered new freezers from Sears & Roebuck in 1958 or '59.

NOVEMBER 23RD - 25TH

My week home was Thanksgiving week. I crammed all my home things to do into two and a half days, since I will spend part of Wednesday, Thanksgiving Day, and part of the day after with the folks.

This is Papa's favorite holiday. No mostly unnecessary gifts to clutter up life and drain your wallet. Thanksgiving involves a gathering of family, many thanks for the year to date and hope for the future. Sherry, Tam, and I cook, and our girls help. In the afternoon, there is a shower for Sherry's daughter-in-law, Ashley, and son, Stu. They are expecting their first child, a girl. Papa always prays before our meals. This year was no exception. Love his prayers, so humble and genuine. He made sure to thank the Lord for Rex driving such a long way to be here early to smoke 2 turkeys for our feast.

We don't all get to be together very often. Some live far away and can't be here for every holiday, and sometimes illness prevents folks from coming. We three sisters were especially blessed to be together for several hours, instead of just a few minutes as we "come on duty." I do miss our sister time!

Tamra

WEDNESDAY, NOVEMBER 2ND

Got my bags packed for Green Bay, Wisconsin press trip and checked in for my early morning flight. I am looking forward to seeing the new additions to the GB Packers complex since I was last there in 2014. I went on a walk today with Eula Mae and the cats. Those silly cats, Wynken, Blynken, and Nod, think are dogs, following me wherever I go. By the time we got back to the house, their tongues were hanging out. Eula Mae, being a puppy, was still ready to go, but I had to get some house chores done and cook some things for Marc to eat while I was gone on my trip, so one walk was all I had time for. Set my alarm for 3:30 am and did a last minute check of my bags and flight times – I guess I am ready.

MONDAY, NOVEMBER 7TH

Had a wonderful trip to Green Bay, but was glad, as always, to be back in East Texas. Finally got home about 1:30 am. I promised Sherry I would take Dad to his eye appointment this morning; I didn't want her to "tear her toenails off" getting up here for the early appointment. Mel was pooped after staying an extra two days, and I wanted her to be able to go on home this morning.

I noticed the sassafras trees around Mom and Dads' are turning bright red this year. I love them; they are one of our prettiest trees in the fall. When I got to Mom and Dad's about 7:15, Dad was ready to go, but I visited with him and Mel a bit before we left. This was supposed to be our first visit to Dr. B's new offices, but they called and said it would be several more weeks before they got everything moved, so back we went to that tiny place with no parking. We were in and out of there in just over forty-five minutes and got back home just after Sherry got there. Dad was glad we didn't have to wait – me too.

He made a cup of coffee and headed back to the sunroom to rest his eyes. I wondered why he had that orangey stuff around both eyes and Dad said they prepped the wrong eye, realized their mistake, thank goodness, and prepped the correct one. Stuff like that happens, but I believe that is the first time since he's been going to Dr. B. Glad they caught it. I visited with Sherry a bit, checked on Mom, and headed home to unpack and see what needed doing at my house.

TUESDAY, NOVEMBER 8TH

Today is Shaun's birthday. He is 53 years old…my baby brother…53! I was hoping Mom would make his cake like she always has, but she said she just wasn't up to it. Sherry and I both volunteered to help her make it, but she refused. She has never missed a birthday cake in all of Shaun's 53 years; it makes me sad to think that he won't have his cake for his special day. I never thought she would give that one thing up, but she has, a sure sign that she is slowly giving up. Sherry made him some blueberry muffins instead. He loves anything blueberry. We sang Happy Birthday and gave him his cards. Dad told us a funny story about having Shaun. He said he told somebody about having a baby and they said, "You must have a new wife!" Dad said, "No, it's the same old one." (Mom was 42 when Shaun was born.)

Today is also Election Day, and so I took Dad to vote. He doesn't miss an election of any sort, even though for the last few years I have had to sign the form so I can read and mark the ballot for him; he can't see to read or mark it himself. We enjoyed our ride over to the polling place, a local Baptist church. Not our usual polling place just down the road at another church, but our county commissioners voted to change things up. I don't think I like that, we've been at the same place for over fifty years… why change it now?

SATURDAY, NOVEMBER 12TH

Dad built the first fire in the fireplace today. He enjoys that chore, sometimes too much. If it drops below 60 degrees, he will build a fire, leaving the rest of us in a sweat. But today, it was in the 40s, so a fire felt good. He enjoys sitting back in his recliner and watching the flames, a restful pursuit … until the white oak he used to build the fire started a tremendous popping and sputtering. Just when we would relax and Dad would drift off, the explosions roused him up. I thought it was pretty entertaining, Mom said it was annoying. Ha!

I love this time of year when the room is once again enveloped in the familiar warmth and smell of the fireplace. The faint odor of pine rosin and wood smoke reminds me of the upcoming holidays and lazy nights of reading by the fire or playing Mexican train with Mom and Dad. I look forward to the longer nights and the brisk days ahead. Every winter is different and I don't know how this one will play out, but I am hopeful that it will be a mostly good one for us all – only time will tell.

Mom was pretty pitiful this morning, but after Dad got the fire built, she ventured into the Big Room to sit with Dad. She asked me to fix her hair and after I braided it, she worked on her puzzle some. She hasn't shown much interest lately, so I was glad to see her working on it again. Although she intermittently complained about the popping firewood and the fire being too hot and fanning herself, Dad just smiled and stared at the flames. They crack me up sometimes.

There will be a hard freeze tonight so I pick a big bouquet of the remaining bush morning glory flowers and put them into a vase. It made for a cheerful sight on the side table in the kitchen.

It is evening now; the earlier sunset makes for a long stretch till bedtime. Time drags sometimes when I am over here because it is hard for me to concentrate on work or read with Mom's TV so loud. I want to stay in the Big Room and enjoy the fire, but the noise of *Murder She Wrote* blasting through Mom's door makes it almost impossible to think. I find myself rereading or rewriting entire paragraphs. I glance over at Dad and there he sits, perfectly comfortable, engrossed in his latest Kindle book, not bothered in the least by the constant chatter of Angela Lansbury's delightful accent. Like Dad has said before "being partially deaf can be a blessing in some circumstances." I am glad he enjoys reading; it is one of the few things he can do during the cold winter months to help pass the time.

I decided to check my email on my phone, since I am unable to read. After about an hour, I glance over to see Dad's hand poised over the lighted Kindle, but not moving. The fire has worked its magic and Dad's eyes are slammed shut, his mouth twitching slightly, and I know that any minute he will start snoring. I hesitate to disturb him, but it is too early to go to bed, not quite 8:00 pm and he hasn't taken his shower yet. I will have to wake him to take his medicine…ah, he just woke up and started reading again. I get up to give him his meds before he drifts off again and check to see if Mom has taken hers. From Mom's room I hear the clever conclusion of the murder mystery episode, and the loud "Oh Me!" as Mom rouses from her own slumbering episode. She claims she doesn't fall asleep, but some nights she misses most of the show she is trying to watch.

SUNDAY, NOVEMBER 13TH

This morning during the service, Pastor Dale recognized the veterans. Dad was the only WW II veteran there. We used to have half a dozen, but they are all gone. I am thankful that people still honor our veterans, it is the least we can do.

Driving home alone after the evening service, in the dark, I am overwhelmed by sadness and feelings of disappointment and hopelessness. I want to keep driving…right past Mom and Dad's and just keep going. I don't really even want to stop at my house, not even to hide, because I've figured out – there is no place to hide. I cannot hide from my children's bad decisions, my own poor judgement when I try to help them, and I can't hide from the fractured relationships all around me and the fall-out I am forced to confront daily. Somehow, I still manage to function. I want to cry, but the tears won't come. I feel like I am drowning and there is no life raft…at least not for me.

I chide myself for thinking the thoughts that are streaming through my head, but I feel powerless to stop them. I need to pray, but the words won't form. Sighing, I notice the beginnings of a headache, I turn into their drive, glancing at the brightly lit porch and wonder at how empty and uninviting it can appear at night.

Pulling under the patio cover, I turn off the engine and sit staring at the darkness beyond the pool of light cast by the kitchen window. Knowing I have to go in, I gather my things, hesitate briefly, and then head for the door.

Turning the key, I remember the sheets I forgot to put in the dryer, so I stop at the Little Room and throw the sheets in so I can put them on before Dad goes to bed tonight. In the kitchen, I am faced with a sink of dirty silverware that I didn't have time to finish this afternoon. Maybe I could have, but I was so tired – after fixing dinner, cleaning, setting out another puzzle for Mom, making cookies, going over to check on Marc and see if he had lunch, feeding the animals, etc. I have been going at breakneck speed all week and didn't get a chance to have any recovery time from my GB trip. It was a great trip, but traveling is always tiring and it usually takes me a couple of days to feel like I've gotten enough rest. I thought I was doing ok, but now I realize I was pushing myself too hard. The flashes are getting more insistent now, refusing to be ignored. A migraine is coming on, but I have too much to do before I let it take over, so I push through.

Mom wants her fingernails trimmed, Mom and Dad both need their meds, the towels and Dad's clothes need folding. Mom's TV remote won't work, so I search for more batteries, digging through the overstuffed drawers and scraping the corners for three AAAs, but no luck. So, I have to manually adjust the volume for her – to stadium-popping level – my head is starting to pound, but I will stay on duty until I deliver Mom's nightly coffee ice cream cone, extra glass of water, adjust her heater and say goodnight.

Took Dad to Love's Lookout to see the fall foliage. It was one of the prettiest years we can recall.

Dad just jumped up to put another log on the fire and knocked over his full glass of water. As I retrieved a towel from the kitchen to soak up the spill, I thought of how many times Mom and Dad had cleaned up my messes when I was growing up, so when I was on my hands and knees cleaning up, I told Dad cheerily, "This part of the carpet really needed cleaning anyway!" That is what I tell my grandkids when they accidentally spill something at my house, "It's ok, that part of the floor really needed cleaning anyway." I remember what it was like to be embarrassed and scared because I didn't want to get in trouble or disappoint my parents. When Dad apologized for making a mess and me having to clean up after him, I told him it was ok, then teasing him, I said, "Now that doesn't count as part of your water intake for the day – you still have to drink a glass!" He chuckled at that as he poked the fire, replaced the tool, and warmed his hands.

When I got up and headed back to the kitchen for another glass, I felt my load lighten and my spirits lift. It is almost nine o'clock, ice cream cone time, thank goodness. The flashes and now floaters are getting worse. I swat at them, thinking they are gnats. Hope they won't last long, but now, I think I can make it.

WEDNESDAY, NOVEMBER 16TH

Lying in the semi-darkness of early morning, I enjoy the warmth of my comfy bed and listening to the quiet house. Thankful for this one day a week that I don't have someone coming over or somewhere I have to be. I am home and for this one day I have time to think, write, read, clean, go on a walk – it is my day – to do what I would like to do instead of doing and being there for everyone else. I am aware that I may not always have this time, so I treasure it all the more. At any moment, I know the phone could ring or a knock come at the door and everything can change. But, for now, I will lean into my day with a spirit of hopefulness and thankfulness. I plan to enjoy a pot of coffee, some homemade biscuits with bacon, read in my devotional books, and spend time with the Master Planner. For now, that is enough.

It lasted all of three hours. Then, I remembered I had promised Mom I would take a picture of the museum sign board so she could see it. They had a uranium glass exhibit and Rita was in charge of putting it together. Mom had lent several pieces for the exhibit and Rita had collected uranium glass from all over town making an impressive display. Today was the last day it would be up, and she hadn't gotten to see it. So, off to town I went to take photos to show Mom. Rita had taken some pictures of the display, but didn't think about the sign.

Today, Shaun and Dad came by in his buggy while I was on a walk with Eula Mae, my puppy, out in the pasture. Dad commented that she sure was a pretty pup. Dad enjoys dogs, but now that he is older, Hobo is more his speed. Of course, Hobo follows Dad around like a dog, but doesn't bark, which is a plus in Dad's book. All in all, it wasn't a bad "me day," just not exactly what I was hoping for.

FRIDAY, NOVEMBER 18TH

Emelia stayed with me last night. I will have her till tomorrow when her Dad can pick her up after work. I love keeping her, but it is hard sometimes. She woke up at 5:00 am, had two accidents (she is potty-training), one on my wool rug, spilled her water, and countless other things all before 9:00 am. I was exhausted. She had a horrible cough and was sneezing like crazy on top of everything and all I could think is "I can't get sick and take it over to Mom and Dad." Later, my washing machine flooded the pantry, I burned my toast, and I got some depressing news to round out the morning. Can I take a time out…for about a month?

SATURDAY, NOVEMBER 19TH

Today would be Aunt Babe's birthday. I remember how much I looked forward to going to her house, bringing her a little gift or a card and spending an hour or so drinking coffee and visiting. I really miss those days. After Caleb picked Emelia up, I headed over to Mom and Dad's. Mel brought me up to speed on the food, any changes in meds, etc. She also told me she was going to finish the quilt Mom was going to make for me but never did. Mel is the quilter in our family, like Mom. Me? I can't sew a button on, much less quilt.

Mel also mixed up the cornbread fixings, so all I had to do was add the egg, oil, and buttermilk. I appreciated that, making cornbread is not my forte either. She had made a yummy beef stew to go with it, so Dad was set for dinner today. After Mel left, Dad and I went up to feed the heifers and get a load of firewood. It was cold today, never getting above 40 degrees. The wind was blowing and the humidity was high, so it felt like 25 degrees. I tolerate cold very well, but heat, not so much. Dad is the opposite, go figure.

Hobo likes to try to get inside when the thermometer dips, but she has a warm and cozy house full of hay that Dad built for her, so she usually retreats there, with nothing but her face sticking out. Shaun came by about 4:00. I went with him up to the barn to check the inner gates. The heifers had been pushing some of them shut and then couldn't get to the water trough.

Later when we were in the Big Room, I looked around and Mom and Dad were both half-asleep. I said, "We need to do something! It's only 6:00…we can't just sleep and stare at the fire till bedtime. Let's play Mexican Train. Mom asked me if Dad was going to play, even though he was sitting right next to her…lol. I looked at Dad, "What about it? Are you up for a game?" He said, "I'll try. It's been awhile, you might have to refresh my memory." It has been months since we played, but they picked it right up and we played three hands – I won one, Mom won one, and one was a draw. Felt like old times, I enjoyed it and I think they did too. Hopefully, we can enjoy playing for one more season.

SUNDAY, NOVEMBER 20TH

The house is quiet this morning. The only sounds are the popping and sizzling of the fire in the fireplace and the early morning train rumbling through Tecula in the distance. It is the lull before the storm of activity that always surrounds our Thanksgiving celebration. It is Dad's favorite holiday, mine too. I like it because it is all about being together, visiting, eating, with no expectations, no angst about gifts, etc. Sherry has once again decorated the mantle with pumpkin and leaf decorations. She always makes every season look special for Mom and Dad by decorating the house. I appreciate it too, but it is sad when she changes them out, because the time seems so short. In just a week, these will come down to make way for the Christmas decorations…where did this year go? I am not ready.

While Dad was shaving this morning, I noticed he had a piece of loose skin on his cheek. I pulled it off and Dad quipped, "Fallin' apart!"

THANKSGIVING DAY, NOVEMBER 2022

I remember a time when Thanksgiving got a certain amount of respect and certainly received its due as an important holiday. The merchants back in the day had the decency to wait until after the turkey leftovers had been refrigerated before trotting out the Christmas decorations. There was an anticipation and specialness in those few weeks of December, but now we collectively groan in dismay when we see the red and green start appearing as early as August (or earlier) in some stores. By the time Halloween is over, we can't get excited about something we've been staring at for weeks. I wish we could hold back and just thoroughly enjoy Thanksgiving before we are hit with a barrage of Santas and snowmen. As Rodney Dangerfield would say, 'Turkeys don't get no respect!'

On Wednesday, I made several desserts to take to Mom and Dad's, plus a corn casserole. As usual, Mel is making the chicken and dressing and the rolls. Sherry usually brings a salad and a couple of side dishes. Rachel made a special cake for the occasion, a towering wonder called a PieCaken. She saw this one in New York and determined to create one for our festivities. Everyone was excited to try it, especially Shaun. He loves cooking shows and watches Molly Yeh all the time.

We had a smaller crowd than usual, but we enjoyed visiting, playing a few games inside, and of course, eating all that wonderfully delicious food.

Rachel's PieCaken was a hit! Since it was really chilly, Dad could keep a fire going in the fireplace all day; that made him happy. He had invited some friends from church to join us since they would not be with family; I think they had a good time. I know Dad enjoyed visiting with them. Mel's rolls were perfect, as was the dressing, and we all ate way more than we should have, but what's Thanksgiving for? The baby shower was such fun – we are all so happy for Stu and Ashley!

FRIDAY, NOVEMBER 25TH

Mel brought Mom and Dad her Christmas tree…thank goodness! Their tree is so scraggly, it looks like it was pulled out of a dumpster, but Mom doesn't like change, so we have been putting that poor pitiful tree up year after year. This one is full and so green, it is quite a contrast. I helped Mel and Sherry put it up and got the lights on it. Sherry will probably decorate it when she comes back over. She always does a good job, taking her time and being very meticulous about it. They don't want me to help because I just dump out the ornaments, start putting on hooks, and slapping them on the tree. Heck, I let my grandkids decorate mine. It is somewhat heavy around the bottom, but I'm sure it looks good from their angle…lol. I am just not that worried about how it looks, maybe I should be a bit more concerned – Naah.

SATURDAY, NOVEMBER 26TH

After everyone went home and it was just me, Mom, and Dad, I took a walk around the farm to take pictures of the trees and clouds. The sky was full of dark rolling clouds which provided the perfect backdrop for the brilliant gold and orange foliage. Dad remarked he had 'never seen the oaks as pretty as they are this year,' I agreed. Shaun was busy working on part of his shop, so I stopped down there on my walk to say hello and see his progress. I got back to Mom and Dad's just as the sun was setting. There was a break in the dark blue and purple horizon, turning the entire sky a glowing fiery red. It was one of the most spectacular sunsets I'd seen in a while. I called Mom and Dad out on the front porch so they could see it before it faded. After the hustle and bustle of Thanksgiving, it was so nice to take a quiet walk alone and soak up the beauty of autumn. Dad and Shaun fed the heifers before dark, and then we all had a quiet evening around the fire. I think we were all still recovering from Thanksgiving.

SUNDAY, NOVEMBER 27TH

Today dawned sunny and bright, but still cold. We went to church, after watching Charles Stanley and David Jeremiah with Shaun in Dad's room. That has been our routine on Sunday mornings for over a year now. We all look forward to it. Of course, I have to tote Mom's pillows in, fix her chair and footstool, adjust the ceiling fan, shutters, etc. and reposition the rolling fireplace before she is ready. I don't mind, I am just glad she still wants to make the trek back to Dad's room and watch the preaching.

After church, Dad and I went up to feed the heifers and get another load of firewood. We enjoyed the afternoon, talking about the weekend events and reading. I pulled out some more of the Christmas decorations for Sherry to put up. The manger was my thing though, I wanted to put it up, so I got out the old sack full of wrapped figures, more than half a century old, and the wooden stable. The sack of "hay" is at least that old and some of the newspapers were from the 1960s. I had more fun reading the newspapers they were wrapped in than I did putting up the scene…until I had a brilliant idea. I would hide a figure in the manger scene and see how long it would be before someone noticed. Hee Hee, I love doing stuff like that. It had to be small enough and not that noticeable. Bingo! When I went over to feed my critters and check on Marc, I took the tiny Bigfoot Addie and I had bought last year for a diorama she was working on. It was perfect. I nestled the miniature Sasquatch in between Mary and Joseph overlooking the baby Jesus in the manger. Some would call it sacrilegious; I call it just having fun. I hope I'm never so stuffy I can't laugh about absurdities.

Even though Mom didn't make Shaun's birthday cake this year, she had a card for him and they enjoyed celebrating.

Earlier, before I left to check my critters this evening, I had put a tin of old stale cookies on the table to take to my chickens. I forgot my coat, so I went back to Josh's room to retrieve it and before I could get back, Dad had opened the tin and gotten one of those months' old cookies out to eat. I told him it was some Mom had gotten **last** Christmas and I found them while straightening her room. They are chicken feed, not fit for human consumption. I think Dad thought I just didn't want him to have a cookie. I promised him I would make him some good cookies this next week.

Tonight, we watched football, which is an exercise in patience when watching with Dad. He has to have it blasting loud to hear it, but he can't see well enough to mute it when the commercials come on, so they nearly blow you over. I painted the mute button a bright yellow, but it still takes him a minute to find it, and sometimes, he doesn't mute it at all. I love watching the game, but I need ear plugs.

MONDAY, NOVEMBER 28TH

This morning Dad and I get ready and head to his eye appointment. We are looking forward to seeing the new building…and parking lot. We were surprised to see how huge and modern the new place is and how big the parking lot is…no more hunting a place to park, what a relief. We were in and out pretty quickly. Dad doesn't like getting the shots; it knocks him out of doing anything for the rest of the day. To lift his spirits, I asked him if he would like to go up to the local lookout park to see the fall foliage tomorrow. It's a short drive and you can see for miles and miles. He said he'd think about it.

TUESDAY, NOVEMBER 29TH

Dad and I make the drive up to the overlook and enjoy the gorgeous view. The brilliant foliage stretches as far as you can see and Dad got a good look at it through his binoculars. The weather was glorious and we stood there enjoying the view for quite a spell. Sherry got the tree decorated and it looks perfect! Mom is very pleased. Dad said it feels like Christmastime. I have to admit that their tree looks way better than mine, *but* mine has a plastic toy grenade, a hand-made gopher skin ornament, and a Bobba Fett figure. I think variety and weirdness should count for something.

DON'T EXPECT A *Medal*; YOU WON'T ALWAYS GET A PAT ON THE BACK FOR YOUR *Sacrifices*.

DECEMBER

There is something about Christmas that brings out the kid in Dad. Even now, anticipating his 100th Christmas, he has that gleam in his eye and a smile on his face when he talks about his many Christmas celebrations – the lean and the abundant – Dad appreciates them all. We still have a touch of melancholy mixed in with our joy when we remember those wonderful times we had years ago and the people we miss, but Dad is quick to count his blessings and express his gratitude to the "Good Lord for taking care of us all these years." His upbeat attitude rubs off on everyone around him and helps us siblings keep our own spirits up. Mom was an important part of our holiday traditions and celebrations too. She would always enjoy picking out gifts, wrapping paper, and bows. After wrapping gifts for years, she finally handed over most of that job to my sister Sherry who learned to wrap gifts as part of her job at a local five and dime store when she was a teenager. She would make our gifts look professional. Mom also baked the Christmas ham with her own orange and honey sauce, putting a jillion whole cloves all over it to give it that festive look and flavor. Candied sweet potatoes were always on the menu too, no one could make them like Mom. She also made sure that my brother Josh and I got to buy gifts for everyone, taking us to town and patiently following us around every store downtown until we were sure we had the perfect gifts. Christmas wouldn't have been nearly as meaningful or as much fun if it weren't for Mom and her contributions.

Reflecting on our Christmases growing up and how much fun we had is an important part of our holiday tradition, especially now. I wrote about Dad and some of our holiday memories in a piece I did for Parade.com several years ago. Here is an excerpt: "Dad loves Thanksgiving and Christmas. He manages to make the holidays magical through the traditions he has kept through the years. He always cuts some holly and hangs it over the doorway in the kitchen signaling the beginning of the Christmas celebration. When we were kids, he planned the Christmas tree hunt. Every year, he would drive to a place in our woods where he had spied some likely candidates and then we'd spend several hours tromping around, comparing the virtues of different trees until we decided, by vote, the winner. Never in a hurry, Dad would stroll along with his axe on his shoulder, relishing the adventure." After choosing the tree and bringing it home, we looked forward to decorating the tree together and afterwards we would sit, admire the lights, and a job well done.

We also looked forward to visiting our grandmother's house on Christmas Eve for a big extended family dinner and gifts around the tree. It was much the same as Thanksgiving with her little house barely able to hold all the uncles, aunts, cousins, and visiting friends that gathered there every year, but we didn't mind being crowded, it's all we knew. The tiny living room corner where the icicle-laden tree stood held a towering stack of gifts spilling over into the center of the room. We would spend several hours passing out gifts, while mounds of crumpled paper and colorful bows threatened to bury the smaller children in the chaos. Remembering the squeals of delight from us kids and the raucous laughter as the adults opened the inevitable gag gifts is a memory that always brings a smile to my face. I miss those happy days; we all do, especially now that all of Dad's brothers and sisters are gone. Aunt Shirley is the only sister-in-law left. Sometimes, it seems like I can almost hear the laughter and the clatter of platters and plates in that small plain kitchen, but I know it's only wishful thinking. Time moves on whether we are ready for it or not. I tend to be nostalgic to a fault and sometimes would rather live in those long ago days, but Dad's positive manner and his still keen enjoyment of each day encourages me to plant my feet in the present.

Mom is slowly fading into the past, with little to tempt her to stay in the present. I can see a change in her these last few months, even though we are trying hard to buoy her spirits. It is difficult to lift someone else up when you are feeling down yourself, so I try to stay positive. I am normally a very optimistic person, but the daily drain on my mind and spirit, my concern for Mom and Dad and my siblings, is making it hard to be the Pollyanna I have always been.

Sherry

THURSDAY, DECEMBER 1ST

I **hate** waking up too early, and 3:15 AM is definitely too early! Couldn't go back to sleep, so I finally threw in the towel, turned my light on, and studied my Sunday School lesson. Good to get *something* accomplished. The floor guy is coming today to put in my laundry room floor; it will be **so** nice to clear all that laundry room stuff out of the guest room where it has been sitting for weeks, and have those boxes of LVP disappear from the living room. Ben and family will be here in a couple of weeks, and I need to have the house shipshape by then. Next week I'll be back in Jacksonville, so this week is IT as far as getting "company ready."

MONDAY, DECEMBER 5TH

Didn't get to the folks' until around 10:30. Fixed them a late breakfast, then paid bills for Pop. We walked to the mailbox to drop them in. Very warm for December – mid 70s. Time to feed the heifers, so we got in the truck and headed up to the barn. On the way, Pop said, "You know, I have a wild idea." (Red Alert, Red Alert!) "What about getting that splitter out and splitting some of that oak and hauling it down? That wood rack is nearly empty." So here we went. The wind was blowing my hair all in my face, so I looked for an emergency tie. Grabbed some hay bale webbing first, but that didn't work too well, so when we poured up the feed, I found the end of a feed sack – the thick paper strip with the stitching that rips off to open the sack. That worked pretty well … country girl scrunchie!

Split a lot of wood, loaded it on the truck, then headed to the house and stacked it on the wood rack in the garage. While Pop rested, I fixed lunch, but since I got a late start, we didn't eat until 3:30. When I'm here, the way I eat is completely different from the way I eat at home; that can't be good for my system, but I don't know what to do about it. At least we **all** rested after we ate. Sometimes Pop rests while I cook and rests again after we eat while I'm cleaning up the kitchen. Then we're off to the races again. Days like that are pretty tough, but today was not one of those. After a nice rest, we played Mexican Train with Mom, then Pop watched Monday Night Football, while Mom watched her movies. I bounced between both of them with snacks and meds while getting ready for bed myself.

TUESDAY, DECEMBER 6TH

A fire in the fireplace … 64 degrees outside … Yikes! Mom got hot and wanted to change into a lighter gown. Pop thought the fire was wonderful. How are we going to manage their opposite thermostats this winter? Filled Mom's pill holder for the week, washed dishes, and cleaned the top of our domino table and even washed the dominos – they had been sticking to the table when we tried to shuffle them. We'll know tonight if it helped or not.

I had to go to town for several items, then fix the meal afterwards, so another late lunch. Pop wanted to split more wood, but when we got up on the hill, I could tell that he'd already split more while I was in town … pretty slick. He knows we don't like for him to do stuff like that by himself just in case he gets dizzy. I think he gets a kick out of seeing our reaction when he's pulled a fast one on us. Anyhow, we got the rest done except for a monster chunk and some misshapen pieces that kept popping out of the splitter sideways – a good way to get hurt.

Getting dark by then and still in the 70s – this isn't right for December! The flies are loving it, though – we've been battling them all day. I wonder if they're coming down the chimney when we don't have a fire? While we were playing dominos, Shaun called to tell us that he got called onstage at one of the Branson shows. A pretty girl sang "Santa Baby" to him. He sent a photo of it, and he was grinning from ear to ear!

WEDNESDAY, DECEMBER 7TH

Pearl Harbor Day and not one of our better days. Took Mom her Boost shake so she could take her meds, and here came the "Lord have mercy," "It's too early," moans and groans. She stays up late watching movies and is never ready for morning reveille. Pop didn't have a good night either;

his foot bothered him, plus he was coughing. After several chores, I took Mom her breakfast. She didn't want it yet, but I told her she needed to go ahead and eat. If not, every meal would get later and later until I would be bringing her the coffee ice cream cone at midnight instead of 9:00. I can't stay up late with her, then pop up early with Dad – I'll collapse. Then she said she felt bad. "Where?" "All over." That usually means that she has what I call the Morning Mullygrubs. I told her she needed to gird her loins because I had to wash her hair today. After I shut her door, I heard her say, "Why do I **have** to wash my hair? It's MY hair!"

Pop announced that he wanted to get the car and truck inspected and registered today, and the oil changed. That would require two trips since he can't drive in town anymore – just around the farm. (We keep calling it the farm, but it's a ranch now. Pop hasn't had a big garden for years and years, just beef cows. Habit, I guess.) Considering the time those trips would take, I knew we had to eat first, so I fixed the meal and washed some dishes, too. The dish drying towel was pretty damp by then, so I draped it over the back of the stove so the heat from the oven would dry it. This would prove to be a mistake.

Dad likes to shop, but wears a jacket because the stores are always too cold for him.

Pop and I ate; Mom always wants to eat later, so we headed out for the first trip to town. Got the truck inspected, but their price for the oil change was too rich for Pop's Depression-era raising, so we deferred the oil change and went back for the car. Mom needed to eat by then, so I hurried to heat her food: crispy squash in the air fryer, meat in the microwave, and carrots on the stove. I'd just turned toward the refrigerator to grab something out of it when Pop calmly observed, "There's something on fire on the stove."

Whirling around, I saw that the towel I had draped over the stove had caught fire when I turned the burner on under the carrots! I grabbed the towel and threw it into the sink, but a burning piece of it fell on the floor – the floor Pop had put down in 1954. Fortunately, no damage to it.

There was, however, a light brown scorch mark on the back of the (fairly new) white stove. I scrubbed and scrubbed, but it didn't come off. I felt **so** dumb.

After I took Mom her food, we headed back to town with the car and got the oil change and inspection at a different place. We saw a man there Pop has known for years, but Pop couldn't see well enough to tell who he was. After we left, he asked who it was, and when I told him it was Ricky R, he was upset with himself for not knowing so that he could ask how Ricky's wife was doing. We made it to the tax office for both registrations before they closed, and lo and behold, Ricky came in too! When he saw us, he joked to the clerk, "You need to call the sheriff – those people are following me." So Dad got the chance to ask about his wife after all.

Drove home and worked on the stove again; it looks better, but not perfect. Mom asked if we were going to play the game, and I told her that since she had not felt well all day, Pop and I had decided to watch a Christmas movie. She got mad and flounced into the library room where she has some DVDs and got an armload to watch. Of course she couldn't carry them and handle her walker too, so she asked me to carry them. As she passed by Pop in the big room, she exclaimed, "The girls think I can control feeling bad, but I can't!" As one of "the girls" I just reminded her that all I said was that since she had felt bad earlier, we had made other plans. Anyhow, it was a very long day. We didn't watch a movie after all.

THURSDAY, DECEMBER 8TH

Wow… thought today might be a light running one – a big negatory on that. Pop and I decided we should get rid of the thick layer of oak leaves and twigs on the east and north side of the house. Pop used the leaf blower while I grabbed a rake and an old plastic shower curtain to pile the leaves on. Melanie came up with that idea a couple of years ago, and it works great! We just pile the leaves on the curtain, grab two corners, and drag the load downhill to the fence and flop the leaves off. (And by "we" I mean me – that would be too hard for Pop. He runs the blower.)

A lot of leaves, twigs, and junk had collected in the roof valley by the sunroom, so I got a ladder and climbed up to rake that off while Pop was on the phone, giving Melanie a report on our activities for the day. Fortunately, the roof is metal, so they slid off pretty well even if they were sort of wet. Stopped for lunch, then back at it, but decided to blow or rake the rest of the leaves into the dirt road in front of the barn and burn them there instead of making the longer trek to the fence.

Later I darted inside to get Mom's lunch, and when I came out, I could see the cows giving us "the look." I told Pop they were likely to mug us if we didn't give them some hay, so we got on our pasture footgear and headed out. I fed the heifers while Pop started the tractor and speared a couple of hay bales. Climbing off and back on the tractor is tough on Pop, so I hustled to open the gate for him. After feeding the cows, we headed back to the house and fed ourselves some cake and coffee, but our breaks are brief when Dad has a chore on his mind.

Back out to finish the leaf blowing and burning. Tam drove up to visit a bit and gave me two walnut brownies – Bless her heart! Maybe I can burn off the calories while burning leaves. When all those leaves were just piles of ashes, we went inside, and I decorated the dining room for Christmas. Then Mom asked the inevitable question: "Are we going to play the game?" Of course Pop and I had been hard at it all day, and I knew he was tired. But he's a trooper and said he'd play a few. We played four games and Mom didn't win any of them.

With each loss, the comments of "I just don't have any luck," "I was going to play there, but you blocked me," "He's going to win again," "What did I tell you?" became more frequent. I've reminded her many times that it's just a game. Whether we win or lose, we won't wake up the next morning any younger, richer, or better looking. When we said it was time to quit, she said, "So y'all are just going to leave me out?" We agreed to play one more …win, lose, or draw, that was going to be it. Happily, Mom won, so we got to quit. Hallelujah!

FRIDAY, DECEMBER 9TH

Pop and I saved the dirtiest job for last – cleaning out the valley and gutters on the west side of the house. Those gutters form a wide U and catch a load of pecan leaves and twigs. In a good year, they might catch a bunch of pecan hulls, but this was NOT a good year. Some weird disease swept through all of Mom's and Dad's pecan trees in the yard and wiped out the entire crop. In all Pop's nearly 100 years, he's never seen anything like it.

I really didn't want him on that ladder, so I scrambled up first and raked everything off the first valley, then used my gloved hands to sweep the gunk out of that long gutter. My pretty new work gloves were a soggy, sorry mess in just a few minutes. I dragged the hose around and flushed out the muddy stuff with the power nozzle. Went in to check on Mom and returned to find Pop on the ladder cleaning the short middle section. Hobo the cat has to be right up in our business, so she had climbed the ladder and was perched on the rung just below where Pop was standing.

After we finished, we were both filthy. Then we had to haul all that roof and gutter junk down the slope into the dirt road. However, these leaves were not as dry as the ones yesterday and did not want to burn. Pop had the brilliant idea of using the leaf blower as a giant bellows to fan the flame. That did the trick - those Seabees and their "Can Do" spirit!

I had thought that we might finish this job early enough for me to drive to Tyler and do some Christmas shopping, but nope. I would have had to clean up, and by then it would be time for snacks and meds. Instead, I wandered to the edge of the yard and gathered cedar, pine, and holly to put in a red vase on the dining table – very festive. Pop is not feeling very festive – he has developed a cold, and I have the early symptoms as well. Ho, Ho, Ho.

SATURDAY, DECEMBER 10TH

Pop coughed a lot last night and didn't get up until nearly 8:00. I sure hate that he had to get sick. I was up by 5:30 and had coffee by the lights of the Christmas tree – that hot coffee felt so good on my sore throat. After all the usual morning chores and visiting with Tam and then with Shaun about his trip to Branson, I headed for Nac.

Grandson Cooper's swim meet is today in Birmingham... Ben and Shelley sent a video of one of his races. He beat all of his previous times in each of several types of strokes! Sure wish we could see one of his meets in person.

Found out that Stu and Ashley had already made plans for the first day and a half that Ben and his family will be here. Ben didn't tell Stu when they were coming, and I didn't mention it to Stu in time either. I feel terrible about it since we don't get to see Ben and family very often nor for very long. "What we have here is a failure to communicate." They need to talk to each other and not depend on me – I can't remember well on my best days, and certainly not now when I'm trying to keep up two different households. I'm tired, I'm stressed, I'm disappointed, and I want a Silent Night, a Holy Night, and 12 Days of Christmas with nothing to do except what I want! Waaaaaaa ...

SUNDAY, DECEMBER 11TH

Well, I got an Un-Silent Night of coughing … feel way worse today. Had to call my Sunday School sub and ask her to teach this morning. I'm not going to church and spread germs over the congregation. Hope Pop doesn't feel worse. I dragged myself around and got some chores done – would rather have stayed in bed, but I don't have that luxury. Ben and family will be here next Saturday, with Christmas hard on their heels.

MONDAY, DECEMBER 12TH

Not feeling quite as crummy today, thank the Lord. The plumber came out to fix the toilet in the room Ben and family will stay in – wonderful to get that very necessary item repaired. Found out that Pop had another intestinal wash-out in addition to his cold. Poor Pop.

FRIDAY, DECEMBER 16TH

This entire week has been a flat-out run … cleaning, tire replacement for my Jeep, Christmas gift shopping and wrapping, making millionaires (Mom's favorite candy) for part of her gift, finishing Christmas cards, laundry, etc. Melanie is at Mom's and Dad's this week, and she's worried about Dad's not drinking enough water, about keeping Mom up and going, and about a cow that they think ate a boatload of acorns. That can kill a cow.

SATURDAY, DECEMBER 17TH

All day of final readying for Ben and family's arrival. Around 4:15 the back door opened and a skinny young giant walked in! I had to reach **up** to hug my grandson Cooper who is only twelve! And his voice is deeper! Noooo … He just can't be growing up so fast. Parker is taller also, but he's just seven, so he hasn't hit that amazing growth spurt of the preteen years yet. Hugs all around … wonderful to have them under our roof for a few nights.

MONDAY, DECEMBER 19TH

A cold rain today, but this was the best time (really the *only* time) for Ben and family to visit Mom and Dad; unfortunately, it wasn't the best time for Dad. His eye shot was scheduled for this morning, and he absolutely can't miss one – those shots are keeping his macular degeneration at bay. After a shot, he usually just stays in his recliner with his eyes shut for most of the day. But, Ben and his family only get to come this way once or twice a year, and at Mom's and Dad's age, waiting for "next time" isn't realistic. We had as good a visit as possible under the circumstances.

Melanie made her incomparable yeast rolls – bless her heart! Parker wanted to serve everyone, so he took each person a hot buttered roll on a saucer; he loved being the waiter. Pop got the first one, of course, and by the time everyone else had been served, he had eaten his, and asked Parker to bring him another one. That Pop doesn't miss a trick! We try to watch Pop's sugar, and of course, bread basically turns to sugar after you eat it, but If you can't have a second homemade roll at 99, when can you?

TUESDAY, DECEMBER 20TH

Had a little time with Cooper early … we sat on the love seat and talked and looked at my Christmas tree. I treasure these very special times with him. He's twelve now, so those times are probably winding down … most teenage boys aren't too interested in talks with grandma! Fixed a big breakfast and boy, did Coop eat! He needs a lot of fuel for that tall body. After they loaded their car, we all got a group photo in the kitchen.

Thankfully, the rain had stopped by the time they pulled out, heading to Shelley's folks in Mississippi. I didn't have time to sit on the couch and be sad about my very-empty-feeling house because this is actually **my** week at Mom's and Dad's – Melanie just stayed over so I could be here with my kids. So, after Bill left for work, I flung everything into the car: Christmas Eve exchange gifts, extra food for the holiday meal, etc.

Had to cover the lemon tree in the front yard before I left – we're supposed to get really cold weather in a couple of days, and I didn't want Bill to have to do that. Drove to J'ville with my head in a whirl remembering the wonderful time I had just enjoyed and thinking ahead to what needed to be done at Mom and Dad's before Saturday.

When I arrived, Melanie was packed to leave but was nearly doubled over with stomach pains! She thought it was one of the supplements she takes. I had brought some gingerbread cookies and offered her some of those. I'd read that ginger can soothe the stomach – worth a shot. After she'd been on the road toward Marshall for a while, she called and told me that her stomach was better.

One chore Melanie and I had talked about was locating the underpinning boards for the east side of Pop's Homeplace house and getting those screwed in. When the weather turns really cold, Pop has to put those on to keep the plumbing under the old house from freezing, and he just hadn't done it yet. Neither Melanie nor I want Pop to get out in the cold and do that. Shaun came over to check on the folks, and he helped me find the boards in the little barn and load them up along with the right screws to use. Tomorrow is supposed to be a warmer day, so I'll tackle the job then. Very busy day, and so odd to be at my house with the kids this morning and then with Mom and Dad in a completely different situation this afternoon. Tried to write in my journal, but just too sleepy … the past several days (weeks?) have been nonstop. Hope my little brain can keep up.

WEDNESDAY, DECEMBER 21ST

Pop didn't get up until a little after 8:00 – he had that watery intestinal issue again. I wondered if it could be caused by one of those supplements he takes at night. I Googled those, and magnesium was on the list. It's **so** hard to fix things! What works for one ailment isn't good for another; two good supplements can't be used together; some are taken on an empty stomach, others with food, on and on. It's like a juggling act.

Went to town for things Mom and Dad need, plus some last minute Christmas gifts. Fixed lunch, then went to the hay barn to get some hay for her to put in her dog's house to keep him cozy, and some extra firewood for her, but first I put antifreeze in the barn toilet. Shaun drove up to get on the tractor and hay the cows, so I opened the gates for him. Tam drove up – she's had a cold and can still barely talk, but she wanted to help get the firewood and hay. We loaded that stuff on the truck and drove it to her house.

Back to Mom's and Dad's. I stuffed some extra hay in the buckets Shaun had put over the outdoor faucets so they won't freeze. When I went around the back of the house, I saw one faucet we'd forgotten. Shaun came back from haying and said he had a "cozy" he could put over it. I put Hobo in the garage and set up a kitty litter box for her – she will be warm since the back of the fireplace is part of the garage wall, and that throws a little extra heat in there. I guess we've battened every hatch. Sure hope so.

THURSDAY, DECEMBER 22ND

Pop said his innards are about the same. He must get so tired of fighting that, in addition to the loss of a lot of his hearing and sight, dizzy spells, swollen leg and foot… He's a trooper for sure, rarely complains and does the best he can. We are doing all we know to help him and Mom stay in the upright and locked position. Lord, bless our efforts and please give them good days until You call them home. After I got breakfast and meds for them, I moved Mom's car over in the garage so I could park in there too. Also moved Hobo's house into the garage ahead of the really cold weather. If she doesn't like being in the big space of the garage, she can curl up in the house Pop built for her.

Finally had a chance to do that shopping in Tyler. Talk about last minute! Back to the house and wrapped gifts in front of the cozy fire. Mom and Dad both fell asleep – welcome to the Land of Nod! I miss other years when they would keep me company while I was wrapping, since very often I was wrapping for them, not for myself. But this time was a silent one except for the rustle of paper and the sound of the scissors and tape.

Mom says there's a draft around her bathroom window, so I covered the whole thing with a towel and taped the edges down, same with the kitchen window, except just on the bottom half so we can still see out.

After that, I finished up that 2022 agricultural census for Pop … incredibly detailed! I'm surprised they didn't ask him to estimate how often his cows pooped. Pop slept a lot this afternoon – I guess that intestinal disorder, along with last week's cold, is taking its toll. This Christmas may not be so "Holly Jolly." But when I asked him if he'd rather we'd tell everyone to just stay home, he said No, that if he needed to, he'd just go to his room and quarantine himself. He should be over his cold by now – I caught mine from him, and I'm already over it. He may also be feeling the effects of all that wood splitting, leaf blowing, and so forth. Already 16 degrees out. Bill called and said that wild wind had blown my lemon tree cover loose and he'd had to put it back. Hopefully, we won't lose power and those heat lamps will keep the tree warm enough.

FRIDAY, DECEMBER 23RD

Holy Moly! Got down to 9 degrees last night! When I went to the kitchen, I saw a two-inch wide band of ice above that towel over the window … on the Inside! Yikes. So thankful we didn't lose power. And, Pop feels better this morning – Yay! Mom stayed warm, too. After breakfast I started cleaning for tomorrow's gathering… thought I'd start vacuuming in the sunroom … we'll need **all** our space since it will be too cold for folks to eat outside as we often do. Pop closes that room off during the winter, so when I went in there, I had to wear a coat – ice on the inside of each window. Before people get here tomorrow, I'll roll Pop's electric fireplace in there and warm it up. Vacuumed the whole house; set up the dessert table and got out the paper goods.

Melanie arrived, then Rita and the kids. They were excited about opening the gifts I'd bought them… such fun to watch little ones at Christmas. Fixed a centerpiece for the table and helped Melanie chop onions and celery. Bill called and told me that indeed we had lost power for two hours this morning, so my lemon tree is probably toast. I'm glad that Bill just stayed in bed for those two hours instead of getting up to do stuff and freezing.

Hobo is not too pleased about being in the garage – she is a "people" cat and likes to be around folks, but we can't risk her jumping on the counters where the food is. If she doesn't stop yowling, I'll toss her furry behind out in this 20 degree weather for a few minutes and see how fast she straightens up! I'm going to sleep on the couch tonight in the big room.

Oh goody, Mom has a movie on with lots of yelling and squalling; she's getting hard of hearing now, so it's **loud**.

SATURDAY, DECEMBER 24TH

Got some sleep in spite of the melancholy squawks. Melanie and I both got up early and enjoyed a brief time in front of the fire. After about 45 minutes, though, the pressures of the meal prep could no longer be ignored and we launched into serious cooking mode: chicken and dressing, ham, salad, green beans, candied sweet potatoes, yeast rolls, and so forth. Melanie is the queen of the feast! If we had to do without her dressing and rolls, we would be sad indeed. Of course we also had casseroles of all sorts and desserts galore as people arrived with their contributions.

The day is always a blur of activity leading up to the meal around 1:00. Everyone gathers around and Pop says the prayer, always a heartfelt one of gratitude for each other and all the blessings we have. This is Pop's 100th Christmas! I'm sure that when he was a very little child standing outside in the night watching their house burn up, his mama crying and his dad trying to comfort her, he could not have dreamed of having such a nice house as now, large enough so that all the family can gather comfortably. We only had about 25 people here this time since some were sick or having the holiday with in-laws.

After the wonderful dinner, Tam set out the supplies for the cookie decorating contest – always a fun event. She makes the cookies and the frosting, and supplies sprinkles in every color, edible glitter, and little sugar decorations of all sorts. The winners don't actually get a prize, just bragging rights, but they enjoy it as much as if money was on the line. After the winners were announced, we started the gift exchange game, a bit early this year so that people could get home before too late since the weather is so cold. Not everyone participated in the gift exchange, so it wasn't quite as much fun as in years past.

Things change, though, and people get busy or older or just out of the notion. That's one of the challenges of the march of time – many of our fondest memories, we suddenly realize, are just that, memories. They won't be coming back. We can waste a lot of time trying to recreate the past, or we can just reframe our new reality and enjoy the present.

Anyway, after everyone left, Mom and Pop rested while Melanie and I cleaned up the kitchen, put the leftovers away, and got things mostly back to rights. Finally we relaxed in front of the fire with Pop … for about ten minutes. Then he picked up a piece of firewood without using his leather gloves and somehow knocked some skin off his fingers! The blood thinner he's taking made it bleed worse, but we finally got it stopped and bandaged. Poor Pop … he was really aggravated with himself.

SUNDAY, DECEMBER 25TH

Ordinarily, Bill and I leave Mom and Dad's on Christmas Eve so we can be home for *our* gifts on Christmas morning, but Bill urged me to stay with the folks this time because, as we find ourselves saying (or at least thinking) more and more, this could be the last one. It was thoughtful of him to encourage me to stay over, and such a relaxing early morning by the fire with Melanie and Pop. Mom didn't want to get up early – she was still tired from yesterday. I made some pancakes for breakfast and got a photo of Pop flipping one.

A treasured memory from my childhood is of Sunday mornings with Dad in the kitchen making pancakes and sometimes singing a snatch of a church hymn. Aunt Jemima pancake mix and Blackburn syrup were staples in our house. And that syrup was the thick, extra sweet kind – no light syrup in the 60s. We had a carb overload that lasted all the way through church. It's a wonder we stayed awake during preaching.

Pop was too tired to go to church today, but Tam and Shaun did after they dropped by to say Good Morning. After breakfast, I made a batch of buttery shortbread cookies; Pop loves to have one or two with coffee.

Lunch was a delicious repeat of yesterday, only with fresh yeast rolls. Tam and Shaun both came to eat, along with Tam's husband Marc. Pop had said earlier that this would be the first time in years that he and Mom would have all us kids around the Christmas dinner table. But Mom didn't come to the table; she wanted to stay in her room. I wish I had pressed a little harder for her to at least come and sit with us, even if she wasn't ready to eat yet. It would have been more like old times for everyone. Later, she got ready and came in the big room so that we could get a photo of all of us (Mom is all about pictures), but I wish she had come to the table. Again, that thought intruded: What if this was the last time?

Melanie

NOVEMBER 28TH – DECEMBER 3RD

December started off with an eye appointment for Mama, something she has to be cajoled into doing. I told her how pretty the drive will be because the fall colors are at their peak. We had a wonderful drive and oohed and ahhed around each curve of the road. After we arrived, I found a small wheelchair. It is a challenge to get Mama out of the car and into the wheelchair without bumping her legs. Her blood thinner causes any bump to turn into a large purple red bruise. The incline is steep to the door, but we make it to the desk, I write Mama's check, she laboriously signs it, we travel down a long hallway, and find a nice spot at the end of a row of chairs. I rejoice that I can still handle this very physical task! A lady there with her mother pays Mama a compliment about how pretty she is. Mama's spirits lifted with that and her appointment went well, although Mama couldn't see and was feeling nauseous from the shot. Mama's threshold of pain is 0. I finally found the button to recline her seat so she would be more comfortable and we had a pretty good trip home. She lamented on the way that she couldn't see the beautiful leaves. Later, we had a freeze, and those leaves were history, but the memories of that drive are in vivid Technicolor.

As Papa and I sat by the fire the next morning, he told me one of his dreams. He is reading an autobiography of Teddy Roosevelt and that subject played into this dream. Papa and I are looking for a "pony" (Teddy Roosevelt's name for his horses on his ranch.) We spot one pony at a distance on the outside of a fence. There was an old rancher on the other side of the fence who talked to us about the pony. Papa said he couldn't see the pony clearly. He talked about his age and how that affected him. The old gentleman said, "I've got 11 years on you!" He was 110 years old! Daddy couldn't believe it. He was in better shape than Papa. Daddy said, "I better stop talking about my age and ailments since it is affecting my dreams."

The traditional Mom and Dad picture in front of the Christmas tree.

Papa's next dream was the whole process of old time butchering of a hog: how to hang him, the kind of knife to use, barrel of hot water, wash pots to heat the water; the whole thing. He said after all that preparation, he never did get to the killing of that hog.

This dream sent Papa down memory lane to when he was 14 years old. He and his younger brother, Floyd, were supposed to kill a hog and butcher it. No Walmart meat markets back in the day. You had to process your own meat. It was messy and wet in the pen; so, they turned the pig out. They were having a time drawing a bead on that moving pig. Grandpa Bart, Papa's Dad, came down, got the gun, pointed and shot. He dropped that hog in its tracks! He turned around and went back to the house and left them to stick, gut, scald, scrape, and butcher that pig. What you would call in today's vernacular: a hands-on learning experience. In later years, Papa said that Uncle Floyd would call him to come "help" him butcher a hog. Papa would go knowing what would happen: Uncle Floyd would sit in a chair and watch as Papa did the whole job. Shades of Grandpa Bart!

During this month Papa caught a cold. Rounds of Zicam, homemade chicken soup, cough drops, and tissues. This cold seemed to settle somewhat in his ears and left him even harder of hearing. My loud volume had to ramp up a notch. He has hearing aids but those are for church and special company. They are too much trouble for Papa to use daily. (This is Papa's opinion.) I hope I don't get laryngitis. I might have to teach Papa sign language!

I am quilting a beautiful Flower of the Month quilt that Mama embroidered years ago. She is too shaky to quilt anymore. It will be an heirloom quilt from Mama and me to Angela. JoAnna will have an embroidered State Flower quilt that Mama did both the embroidering and the quilting on. The Flower of the Month quilt travels back and forth from my house to the folks. I can usually manage to get *some* quilting here and there, but sometimes that quilt just takes a ride.

DECEMBER 12TH - 19TH

Shaun and I had an episode with one of Papa's cows. She got down for whatever reason and couldn't get up! We gave her penicillin, water, and hay. Then, we decided to borrow a contraption called a hip lock that you use to lift a cow to her feet. We got it on; but she was too far gone. It is so sad to lose a cow or a calf.

Papa and I enjoy watching NFL football. We especially enjoy the Kansas City Chiefs; because Patrick Mahomes, the quarterback, is from Whitehouse, not very far from Papa's place.

DECEMBER 24TH - 30TH

We gather on Christmas Eve, eat an early supper, do the cookie decorating contest (kids and adults), read the Christmas story, and do a gift game. Angela and her family were not here; but Andy and his family were over Covid and got to be here! No holiday would be complete without a trip to the pole barn and a fun climb around on the hay rolls. That is one activity that the grands and great grands do not miss out on.

We forgot to get our family photo, so Sherry propped her phone on the table and we got one on Christmas Day.

After everyone else left, Sherry and I finished the clean-up and enjoyed some rest and fire sitting time. Holiday meals are a lot of work for the cooks and dishwashers, but they are always the maker of many great memories. We reflected on the past, enjoyed thinking about today's events, and have a sweet hope for next year.

I stayed through the weekend since my week starts on Monday; it makes sense to stay and not travel home for just 2 nights and a day.

We had a really cold spell around Christmas. The ponds glazed completely over with ice which made for some pretty pictures. We enjoyed this cozy time with extra sister conversations, and more great food that blesses the heart if not the hips. Daddy's 100th Christmas and Mama's 96th…even though they were only babies on those first Christmases.

The week after Christmas was a collage of bowl games and Papa's sweet dream of Josh, my brother who died over 35 years ago. In the dream, Mama, Daddy, and Josh were in the sunroom looking out. Daddy noticed the yard was full of pig weeds. Daddy said he better get the tractor and mow them down. He didn't want Josh to volunteer to do it because the weeds were too close to the house and fence. Josh said that he had burned some undergrowth near a big oak tree close to the house. Daddy said it was still smoking.

We continued to talk about dreams. I had told Daddy before, when he dreamed of folks long gone, that it was like a little visit with them even though it was a dream. He agreed. Tam came by on her way to WMA and asked if Daddy remembered it was Josh's birthday. He smiled – the dream became even more special!

Tamra

SUNDAY, DECEMBER 4TH

Today was our annual Thanksgiving/Christmas dinner at church and I didn't even get any photos. I was so put out with myself. Dad and Lurlene, who is 100 years old, were both there, plus Rita and Caleb and their kids. I was so busy getting the food out, heating stuff up and making coffee, etc. I just plumb forgot. I fixed Mom a plate to take home and some stuff for Dad to have tomorrow.

FRIDAY, DECEMBER 9TH

Took Marc to his eye appointment in Tyler and after all he went through this past summer, now he has a retinal tear. Good grief…I don't know what is going to happen to him next. After we got back from the doctor, Rita and I went Christmas shopping. It was one of the only days we could go between now and the celebration, so we squeezed it in somehow.

SATURDAY, DECEMBER 10TH

Shaun and I went to hay and found a cow down with a bulge in her backside. It was bitter cold and getting colder, but we went back to the house to get several shots of penicillin. She wasn't moving, so I was able to just walk up to her and give her the shots. We watched her for a bit and she finally got up and walked a ways, then went down again. I don't think she is going to last the night.

SUNDAY, DECEMBER 11TH

Poor Dad is fighting a cold. I've felt bad for a couple of days, but I am trying to stave off whatever is trying to take me down…again. Dad doesn't feel like going to church, but I decide to go ahead since I don't have a fever or any symptoms, except just feeling weird. It is strange when our routine is interrupted; it throws the entire week off. I felt some better this evening, so I'm hoping I have managed to win the battle and stay well. Shaun and his son Christopher got back from their Branson trip late Friday and he came up yesterday to tell us about it. He was anxious to show Mom and Dad his pictures and recount their adventures, but he didn't have enough time, so he came by this morning. He was excited to show them the video of one of the shows because he was chosen from the audience to participate on stage. It was hilarious, but neither Mom nor Dad laughed. I think he was a little disappointed. I felt sorry for him. The jokes they told had modern references they didn't understand. Plus, Dad couldn't hear half of it and Mom seemed irritated that her regular schedule had been usurped by an unplanned gathering in her room. I tried to help by getting Dad's hearing aid, but he couldn't understand the jokes anyway, so that didn't work. A singing part came on and Mom started frowning, so Shaun offered to fast forward through it, even though it was beautiful. Then, several more jokes they couldn't understand and Dad kept asking what they said and poor Shaun was shouting over the still running video trying to explain, but Dad couldn't make heads or tails of it, so he just stared at the TV. I guess he was trying to be interested, but it was frustrating for him. When you feel left out of a conversation or situation, it is not a very good feeling.

I apologized to Shaun because I had to leave for Sunday school. I am the secretary, so I needed to go early. Marc came by to pick me up and as I rode to church, I thought about this exchange and other incidents with Mom and Dad where shared jokes and conversations were lost on them. It made me sad to realize that the world we live in daily is leaving them further and further behind. They still inhabit a world where things like Metaverse, YouTube, gamers, and bitcoin don't exist or even make any sense. It's not that our world is all that great; I just wish they weren't left out of the conversation. Their world, in my opinion, *was* better.

I tried to enjoy the beautiful scenery along the way, the dark pines against the smooth browned pastures of early winter, but all I could see was a swirl of memories…Dad driving us to church in our white 4-door '66 Buick Electra, Mom smelling like Avon's newest perfumed lotion mixing with the whiff of Dad's Wild Root hair tonic. My sisters still fussing with their Dippity-Do and brush curler hair do's plastered in place with White Rain hairspray in a can. My brother Josh squirming in the front seat between Mom and Dad while Mom tries to give him a spit bath with her handkerchief, scrubbing off the remnants of Dad's Sunday morning Aunt Jemima pancakes and Brer Rabbit or Blackburn's syrup.

"Anything coming?" Marc asks, breaking my reverie, as we come to a crossroad. "Nope. All clear." He resumed his silence as he pulled onto the road. He knows better than to question me when I'm in one of my "moods" and I am grateful for that. Forty-four years have taught him that when I'm ready, I will talk, but not before. And I did talk…on the way home. "It's just not fair. Mom and Dad are smart, capable, and still pretty active for their ages, especially Dad, but their hearing loss limits them. Everything is changing so fast even I have a hard time keeping up – I can't imagine how hard it must be on them. I can see them getting further and further behind and I want to pull them along, but I don't think they are that interested in going. Dad enjoys reading about new things, but they don't "stick" like his memories of the past.

I am ashamed to admit it, but sometimes I get so frustrated with them because I want to share some everyday stuff that happens, like I always have, but now, more times than not, I get a blank stare or a confused look. I don't even share my writing anymore. I know they are proud of me, but they really don't understand what I do; after all, it's not a "real job." Maybe I shouldn't need it after all these years, but even old kids need to hear a "good job or I'm proud of you" every once in a while.

Now, all the encouragement and affirmations are going the other way. They were always the cheerleaders and we were the receivers…now it's our turn to be the givers. I never realized how hard it would be to have the roles reversed, to be the caregiver instead of the cared for – to be the parent to your own parents. You fret and worry and try to get them to do what's best for them, but often they stubbornly refuse or go behind your back and do what they want.

Wow…I am paying for my teenage years, in a way I never expected. I guess they are getting the last laugh…lol. Parents…you can't send them to their rooms or spank them, you just have to try and keep your sanity and not become angry or bitter towards them. I don't have many moments like that, thank goodness. The hardest times are when I am feeling unwell, like today, or when they are sick.

As Marc pulled into their driveway to drop me off, I unloaded one last thought. "I just feel so sad for them, feeling left behind. To be in the world, but not feeling a part of it anymore, more a spectator than a participant, safe inside their own space, where things are familiar and they know how to function. Maybe I will be the same way, if I reach their age. Maybe I'll be one of those old people that are always griping about how terrible everything is and nothing is like it used to be and I wish things were like they were when I was growing up."

I looked at Marc as I reached for the door handle. He had a funny half-smirk on his face that instantly irritated me. Then, it dawned on me. "Who am I kidding?! I am that person **now**. The more I see of this world, the more I realize I need to show Mom and Dad some empathy. They may be out of the loop and not understand technology and stuff, but in reality, they don't miss much." I grinned at him as I opened the door to get out. "Thanks for letting me vent." He just smiled and said, "I love you too." I watch him drive over the hill towards home before turning around to head inside.

Unlocking the door, I am immediately assaulted with the roar of Sunday night football coming from Dad's room and some Hallmark Christmas movie blasting from Mom's room…it's going to be a long night.

WEDNESDAY, DECEMBER 14TH

Can't talk at all now, I open my mouth, but nothing comes out. I did manage to get the Thomas the Tank Engine train set up around the tree. Crawling around on the concrete floors is rough on the knees, but you will do anything for your grandkids. They are coming over on Friday to decorate the tree and make cookies. Even though I have been feeling like I've been pulled through a knothole backwards, I am looking forward to having them over and carrying on the tradition.

FRIDAY, DECEMBER 16TH

Well, even though everything didn't go exactly as planned, (What does?) we had a fun day of making sugar cookies, decorating, and eating too much. The look on Raylan's face when he saw the Thomas the Tank engine going round the tree was worth all the bruises and creaks I suffered in my knees. He was so happy, I'd do it all again in a heartbeat! Rachel and Addie were also able to join us, so it was even more memorable. It is a rare treat when we can all be together and do something fun. I took lots of photos. I want to remember this for a long, long time.

WEEKEND OF DECEMBER 18TH & 19TH

I felt so bad by Saturday morning that Mel stayed through the weekend for me. It was cold and getting colder. Mel and Shaun brought over a load of firewood for me so I didn't have to get out. Poor Mel had been trying to keep that sick cow alive, but we finally figured out she had acorn poisoning; there was nothing more anyone could do. Shaun finally had to put her out of her misery today. It was 22 degrees this morning. Stayed home from church since I didn't feel any better; it is weird not seeing Mom and Dad. Didn't do much but read and rest and take care of my critters – that has to happen no matter how bad I feel.

WEDNESDAY, DECEMBER 21ST

Winter Solstice, my favorite day of the year, next to New Year's Eve, I don't feel 100 percent yet, but I have to go to town and get stuff to make my Christmas Eve dishes and some extra groceries and supplies in case the power goes out. The Siberian Express, they are calling it, is supposed to hit tomorrow about noon and is expected to drop temperatures to 10 degrees or below by Friday morning. They say it won't get above freezing till Christmas Day. Mercy! I spent the rest of the day getting more hay for Eula Mae's dog house and for my chickens' nests, extra wood, and preparing all the outdoor faucets, etc. for the deep freeze. Hope we don't have any pipes burst and we keep power.

THURSDAY, DECEMBER 22ND

It got down to 8 degrees last night! So far everything is holding out. The ponds are beginning to freeze over and so is the swimming pool. Crazy Texas weather.

SATURDAY, CHRISTMAS EVE 2022

It was 22 degrees this morning, a warm-up from the 18 degrees yesterday, so there's hope we will thaw out eventually. I spent the last few days working on my final article for TWA magazine and on my column. It will be strange not having that outlet anymore; I really enjoyed writing for them. I made the squash casserole, and sweet and sour beans to take to Mom and Dad's. I also brought the sugar cookies for decorating and all the stuff to put on them. Everyone seems to enjoy that activity. By this morning both ponds were completely frozen over. That doesn't happen very often, but when it does, it is quite a sight. The cows aren't sure what to make of it.

We have a tradition of saying "Christmas Eve Gift" to our family on the 24th. The first one to say it is the "winner" and the other person is *supposed* to give them a gift, but we never have, it's just a fun tradition. Everyone always tries to get Dad because he is so good at it. We almost never do, but this year, I got him! Then, Dad quipped, "I thought you had moved." It had been about twelve days since I had been over to see them. It felt like two years. We had a good day, eating, catching up with everyone, decorating cookies, exchanging gifts, and hearing the Christmas story from the Bible, all the things that make this holiday so special. Sherry asked Dad what his favorite Christmas was in all the 100 Christmases he celebrated and he said "the one after I came home from the war." Mom's was "the Christmas she got a little celluloid doll" since she had never had a doll before then. I thought about my favorite Christmas too, but it was too sad to share. We left about 5:00 pm because I had to feed and water everything. Still below freezing so any pans of water left outside freeze solid in just a while. Maybe things will thaw out soon.

SUNDAY, CHRISTMAS DAY 2022

It was weird being home on Sunday morning again. I left early to visit with everyone before church. Sherry stayed the night so she could make pancakes for Dad on Christmas morning. Dad always made pancakes for us every Sunday for breakfast. It was a tradition all through our childhood and beyond. Shaun came up to eat breakfast and to feed the heifers since it is still below freezing and Dad is not completely over his cold. Marc and I went to church. The sanctuary looked so pretty with all the bright poinsettias and wreaths. Marc dropped me off at Mom and Dad's so I could visit before lunch. Mel made a fresh batch of rolls and we had our yummy leftovers from yesterday. Marc came over and ate with us. After we cleaned up from lunch and the messes made yesterday, we all sat around the fire and visited. I put Mom a new puzzle out and she came in and started working on it while we were all in the Big Room.

Dad always made pancakes for us every Sunday morning growing up and since Christmas Day fell on a Sunday this year and we were all at home, Dad revived the tradition.

It was then that Sherry realized we didn't get a picture of all of us with Mom and Dad yesterday, so she rigged up her phone with some books on the side table and finally managed, after numerous attempts, to get one we were all pleased with.

Dad told Melanie the night before that it was "the first time in a long time that all of us kids would be there and we'd be together, just us." I hadn't thought about it, but it has been years, probably fifty, since we were together, just our nuclear family on Christmas Day. I know it must have meant a lot to Dad since he mentioned it.

TUESDAY, DECEMBER 27TH

Today is Josh's birthday; he would have been 61 today. I still miss him terribly, even after thirty-six years. When I stopped by Mom and Dad's on my way to WMA, I mentioned to Dad about it being Josh's birthday. He said he dreamed about him last night. He and Mom were visiting with him in the sunroom. Dad said he looked well. I wish I could see him again. I have only dreamed about him a couple of times in all these years. I told Dad about my favorite Christmas memory, the one I didn't share on Christmas Eve. It was 1984; the last Christmas Josh was healthy. He'd just graduated from college and was coming back home with all his stuff. He asked us to wait for him so he could go get the tree with us.

On the 19th of December, the weather was getting iffy. It started snowing and the roads were getting icy and dangerous. We didn't know if he'd make it home, but he did. Dad let us get the tree together that year, breaking tradition, but as it turned out, it was a divine decision. Josh, my then three-year-old daughter Rachel, and I retrieved our old wooden homemade sled from the barn and took off to the woods at the back of our place, across the creek. By then, the snow was really coming down and had covered the ground, allowing the sled to glide across the pasture, except when we hit a frozen cow patty. We found the perfect eastern red cedar for our tree and strapped it to the sled, putting Rachel on the front so she didn't have to struggle through the deepening snow. After a few minutes, she decided she wanted Josh to carry her instead, so he laughed and put her on his still strong shoulders and carried her the rest of the way home. (She told me she still remembers crossing the creek on his shoulders and the happy snowy trip back to the house.) It started snowing harder than ever as we walked merrily home, singing Christmas carols and laughing. Josh said, "It's just like a Christmas card – the perfect Christmas – just like I've always dreamed of." I truly believe that God gave us that gift – of that perfect Christmas. It was the last one we celebrated and it is one of my best memories.

SATURDAY, DECEMBER 31ST

Today is one of my favorite days, not because of a midnight celebration, but because it gives me the feeling that I get a second chance, a do-over. I love Mondays for the same reason, it's a new workweek to try to get things done and make better choices than I did last week. Starting a new year is the best feeling, a whole calendar of Mondays! I took down Josh's wreath at Mom and Dad's today, packed up the angel centerpiece, and put up the manger. I think it's hilarious that no one noticed that I put a tiny Bigfoot in the manger scene. Addie finally saw it, after I'd pointed out that something was amiss. She thought it was so funny. She laughed and said, "Oh my Mammy! Bigfoot and baby Jesus, you're killing me!" Next year, I think I'll stick a baby Yoda or maybe a tiny Boba Fett in it and see if anyone notices. Ha-ha

After I finished with the Christmas decorations, I washed and changed sheets, Mom's gowns, towels, etc., fed Mom and Dad, and then worked on my 2023 list while Mom and Dad slept in front of the fire. It was a quiet evening, just the kind I think we all needed. C'mon 2023…

DON'T NEGLECT YOUR OWN *Family* IT IS DIFFICULT TO FIND TIME, BUT YOU HAVE LOVED ONES WHO NEED *You*.

JANUARY

January in the South is a welcome pause to most. We can breathe a sigh of relief that the frenzied holiday activity is behind us and settle into a comfortable season of cool, sometimes cold temperatures with fewer bothersome insects like fire ants, wasps, mosquitoes, and flies. I love January! The weather, the absence of pesky bugs, warm fires to enjoy and read by, no yard to mow or weeds to pull…a quiet month devoid of weed whackers, mowers, and blowers. It is a lovely month; one I wish could last much longer.

Dad doesn't care for January, but it hasn't always been that way. I sometimes wonder if his dislike of January stems from that six-week interminable LST trip he took across the Pacific during WW II. Or it could be that at his age, the cold seeps into his bones, making it uncomfortable; whatever the reason, he is definitely ***not*** *a fan now.*

When he was younger, he relished the "blue northers" as he called them, working outside right through a cold spell. Haying the cows in that kind of weather was always fun back then, especially if the chance for a rare Texas snow was in the air.

Now, Dad gets chilled if the thermometer dips below seventy degrees. The colder it gets, the more it bothers him – and the more I like it. We go back and forth – he declares his impatience for spring – I say a perpetual January would suit me just fine. The thermostat is a matter of contention at times…me burning up, while he says he's freezing. Mom can be one or the other in the space of five minutes. It is a constant battle to try and keep them comfortable and keep me from running screaming to the hills for relief from the "greenhouse" they call home.

I miss the days when we would bundle up and sit out on the patio drinking our coffee and reminiscing about our travels to the mountains out west. There, we enjoyed our coffee in the brisk mountain air every morning while watching the sunrise. Those memories are so close in January. I can imagine us sitting by a campfire with the clean citrusy scent of the firs and pines surrounding us. It is so real sometimes I can almost smell it.

Dad and I used to enjoy taking walks in the occasional snows we get during January, but the last time we took a walk in the snow was almost six years ago. I didn't know it then, but that walk would become one of my favorite memories. Dad and I walking side by side across the familiar hills and meadows bundled against the cold, our breath puffing white with every step.

That is the thought that follows me through every day now…will this be the last time? Every conversation, trip to town, to the doctor, every good night and good morning, I wonder…it flits through my mind, but I don't dwell on it. I try to stay in the moment and soak it all in, just in case.

I guess that is the most important lesson I've learned in the last few years – don't take anything for granted – be present with the people you love because you can never get these moments back. Once you've spent your allotment of time, you and your loved ones become just a collection of memories.

Every day I tell myself this, especially on the days when I get aggravated or discouraged. Sometimes it helps. Sometimes…honestly, it doesn't, but I will keep trying.

Sherry

SUNDAY, JANUARY 1ST, 2023

Happy New Year! Short service at church today followed by a lunch at home of black-eyed peas, cabbage, and baked sweet potatoes – that ought to set us up for a good new year. Bill and I took down some of the outdoor Christmas lights. Nothing is as over as Christmas is on the first of January.

MONDAY, JANUARY 2ND

Now we are into Pop's least favorite month – January seems to begin right after the Christmas dinner and lasts at least eight weeks! Short days, long nights, with spring green-up a very distant prospect. I hope we'll have enough tasks for Pop to keep him busy during the daylight hours. In the early morning and evening, we can enjoy sitting in front of a cozy fire in the Big Room.

When I arrived, poor Tam was on her cell phone with Verizon and had been for nearly two hours, trying to get Mom and Dad's phones back on – they've been not working since last Friday. The cell phone service here isn't great, so sometimes her call would drop, and when she got back with Verizon, she had to start all over with a different person who wanted to get her to unplug and replug, turn off and back on, etc. that she'd already done with the previous person. When her call dropped once again, she just gave up … so very frustrated over spending all that valuable time for nothing. I told her that I would try later.

Put new batteries in the blood pressure monitor and checked pressures to see how the folks are motivating – pretty good readings. Shaun came by to get Pop so they could feed the heifers and check the gopher traps … they've caught five so far. Those critters dig tunnels downhill, then a hard rain turns the tunnels into mini-flumes (like the old Log Ride at Six Flags). They wash out and fall in, starting gullies – bad news for pastures. So, the gophers gotta go! On cold, windy days, Pop doesn't get out of the side-by-side; Shaun does it all, but both of them love doing things like that together. Shaun and Pop are really close, one time at church on Father's Day, Shaun stood up to say how much he appreciated Pop and said, "He's my best friend."

While they were gone, I adjusted the straps on the little floor cycle I got for Pop so that he can get more exercise this winter. Hope he uses it. Fixed lunch. Washed dishes after we ate. Tam called to apologize for being grumpy when I arrived, but I assured her that anyone would be grumpy after all that jazz with the phone company. Things like that should be easier than they are … so much for technology making life a breeze, like on the Jetsons cartoon. And Tam had also taken down the porch Christmas lights, cleaned the floors, and other things, so she deserved a pass.

TUESDAY, JANUARY 3RD

Realized this morning that I gave Mom her morning meds last night instead of her evening meds! It took me awhile to figure out why. I guess Tam gave Mom her morning meds yesterday, then filled the pill pack for the whole week. Normally on Monday night, the morning section is empty, but they were both still full, so I just opened the AM side. This every-other-week duty makes it hard to stay in sync.

We're having company today. Melanie's grandson Brandon is home on leave from the Navy, so he, his mom, and two brothers are coming for a visit before he has to report back. Pop was in the Navy in WWII, so I'll bet talking to Brandon will be a special treat for both of them. When they arrived, I asked what they wanted on their burgers, and drove to town to pick those up while they all visited Mom and Dad.

Pop loves fries, but we're trying to watch his sugar/fat/salt intake, so instead of getting him fries with his burger, I decided to "procure" a few fries from each of the boys' orders – I figured they wouldn't miss a few. As everyone gathered around the table, I was busy getting everything organized and didn't notice Pop's plate for a bit. When I did glance over, his fries were gone. When I asked if he'd already eaten them, he said, "You didn't give me any fries." Just as I began second-guessing myself, I saw that smile … he was trying to con me out of some more!

As young people will do, the guys were finding funny stuff on their phones and laughing about it, but Pop can't really see phone screens well enough to enjoy that, and of course, 20-something humor is not the same as 90-something humor. Tam suggested that I encourage them to put their phones away and talk to Dad about something he could relate to, and they did. Brandon also put on his Navy uniform so Pop could see him in it … just about the same as the one Pop wore back in WWII, except they aren't made of wool any more, and the 19 buttons around the pants' front are just decorations – they don't actually button the way his did.

We all had a great visit until they left around 3:30. I got teary eyed as I watched Brandon hug Pop and say goodbye … could this be their last goodbye? At Pop's age, that's always in the back of my mind on such occasions. I wonder if that thought occurred to them?

Mom hadn't felt like joining us, and stayed in her room. When I checked on her again, she said her heart hurt. She wanted two baby aspirin, so I gave her those. I did mention that maybe gas was the culprit, but she didn't think so, and wanted more after a short while. Mom tends to expect immediate relief from any medicine she takes. I checked the bottle and saw that two more would be okay, but that was all I was comfortable giving her since she's on a blood thinner.

I called the doctor's office and told them the situation. They said we could try Tums or go to the ER. Mom nixed the ER, of course, and took some Tums. When Pop got back from the heifer and gopher run, he went in to see her and prayed for her. Melanie had also prayed when she had called earlier – that always makes Mom feel better. As it turned out, it *was* gas, not her heart. But afterward, both Mom's and Dad's blood pressures were high – Mom's because of her pain, and Dad's because Mom was hurting.

WEDNESDAY, JANUARY 4TH

Pop had his appointment today to check if the blood thinner is helping the blood flow in his swollen leg and foot. I had high hopes as we drove up there. The technician checked the flow at his big toe, ankle, and so forth, but the flow was still only 30%, a real disappointment. Dr. J said he could do an angiogram and put in stents, but Pop said, "The Lord may call me home before I need that!" Doc told us that if either of two things happened, that would trigger the surgery: If his foot started bothering him all the time or if he got a wound on it since it probably wouldn't heal due to insufficient blood flow. For now, Pop is content to use pain cream when he needs to and elevate his foot while he's sitting. The idea of surgery bothers

Dad was cleaning the gutters and Hobo thought we were being awfully neglectful letting Dad up on a ladder by himself.

him – he hasn't been in the hospital since his stomach surgery in 1965.

Had a nice sunny drive back home, then Pop got coffee and hinted that a slice of my cranberry orange cake would sure go good with it! What the heck … I gave him a nice hunk of it. Found out that Mom had taken two Dulcolax tablets already and still felt stopped up. She thinks they should work more or less instantly, so she wanted more. I warned her that she could have a blowout, but she was desperate, so I gave her one. Then I started paying their bills and making plans over the phone with Tam about taking Melanie out to lunch on her birthday. Then I called Melanie to tell her so that she wouldn't schedule something else on that day. While still on the phone, I heard Mom calling me and walked toward the Big Room. Mom was standing in the doorway with a mad look on her face and loudly announced, "I don't want to be here anymore!" (as in, on Earth) I asked, "Mom, what do you want me to do? Hit you in the head with a stick?" Of course Melanie heard the whole thing and cracked up. Mom said she wanted another Dulcolax. Mel said, "Give her one." Oh well … sure enough, about an hour later the trotting to the potty commenced. She probably may not have to "go" again until sometime in February.

When Tam and I had talked earlier, we also figured out that part of Mom's blood pressure issues the last couple of days may have been because she didn't just miss **one** Metoprolol, she missed three! Melanie had only had enough of those pills to go through last Friday. When she called the pharmacy to ask for a refill, they said they'd already filled it. Melanie looked everywhere and couldn't find it a new bottle, so she called again later and spoke to a different person who said they would fill it. But Melanie didn't go get it; Tam picked it up Tuesday. By then, Tam had already put the pills in Mom's pill case for the week, and it didn't "click" with Tam that the Metoprolol wasn't in there for Saturday, Sunday, or Monday. Sometimes, it takes a village to really mess up!

THURSDAY, JANUARY 5TH

Pop and I love to enjoy our first cup in front of a cozy fire, and when the Christmas tree is up, we usually have only those lights on. Today is the last day for that since the tree is coming down. I bought three matching green storage boxes to put the tree parts and lights in – the original box was getting worn, and with the entire tree inside was way too heavy to tote anyway. I took the tree down and put different sections into the three boxes, labeled each one, and stacked them in the garage. Organization is my happy place. (My sisters might call it obsessive/compulsive!) I like to fold towels and shirts in a particular way, stack the measuring cups in order, and so forth. I'm no Marie Kondo, but I do like less clutter.

I called Verizon and got a "remedy ticket" after nearly an hour and a quarter. The rep started off wanting me to unplug this and reset that, but I told her about Tam's futile two hour effort on Monday and that I didn't want to do all that yet again. She understood, and gave me the remedy ticket … I guess they will try to figure something out on their end. If we weren't here to handle stuff like this, what would Mom and Dad do? Without, I guess. Pop couldn't see to do any of it, or even hear what they wanted him to do, and Mom wouldn't even make the attempt.

Mom didn't want to eat her cereal this morning, but I told her that if she didn't eat and began to lose weight, we'd have to put the Shady Rest Old Folks Home on speed dial. She knew I was kidding, but she ate. Later, she asked me to fix her hair – always a sign that she feels better. Then she and Pop watched me change out the mantel decorations from Christmas to Valentine's Day. I love doing that and they enjoy seeing new decorations. Later, lunch, puzzles, reading, meds, snacks, etc. Overall, a good day.

FRIDAY, JANUARY 6TH

After breakfast, I worked on Pop's feet; he has hard spots on the bottom that hurt if I don't keep them "sanded" off as much as possible. I also gave him a manicure, and he fell asleep while I was clipping and filing … I don't see how he does that! He even dreamed that he and Melanie had gone to see Mrs. Killion (long ago deceased) and looked at her garden. She had put rocks around every single plant. He'd told her that if she ran short, he had a rock she could have. Funny … he has a big blue tub of rocks we picked up out of the pasture – the aftermath of a crummy chicken litter application

– a very sore spot for all of us. People who cheat old folks will get a serious judgment someday.

Mom came in to work on her puzzle, and I asked her to walk a few rounds in the room while I turned over the rest of the pieces for her. She needs to keep moving as much as she can. Later, Pop and I went to town, and he wanted to go by Shaun's job and look it over. Shaun is very good at what he does – I know Pop is pleased that he taught him well. One of the best things he did was encourage Shaun to figure the bids on jobs separately from Pop and then compare notes. Pop was surprised at how fast Shaun got good at it, and that Shaun just walked through and figured the whole job in his head; whereas, Pop wrote it all down, room by room. This job was the 1950s update that combined retro fixtures with some new ones that complement the look. Pop had never painted that house and enjoyed seeing the inside.

When we got home, Mom wanted me to gather all her special quilts and put them in her room so she can give them to people before she dies. Not exactly a fun assignment. I finally located the box, brought it to her room, and stacked the quilts on the end of her bed. She has slept in the recliner for years, so the twin bed with big drawers underneath is like a giant storage chest. Mom has made some beautiful hand quilted spreads and also bought several quilts her cousin embroidered. However quilts are made, they are a labor of love. I hope whoever gets these will treasure them. A friend of mine made a quilt for a family member and discovered later that it had become a dog blanket!

After getting the quilts for Mom and writing a letter to my grandson Cooper, I raked up five-gallon buckets of acorns on the east side of the house, toted them to the big ditch by the road, and poured them out. Can't take a shorter route and pour them over the fence because the cows will stuff themselves and possibly die. I've never seen such a bumper crop of acorns as this year – too bad they aren't pecans. Pop helped with the acorns after he and Shaun returned from their run to feed the heifers and check the gopher traps … up to 12 now! When we finished shoveling and hauling off acorns, we took a walk down the road – the full moon was beautiful.

SATURDAY, JANUARY 7TH

After driving to my house and launching into my chores, I called Verizon again because I thought the "remedy" would have kicked in by now; no, it could take until January 12!

MONDAY, JANUARY 9TH

Headed to Jacksonville for Melanie's birthday lunch. She and I arrived about the same time and sat with Pop on the side porch, waiting for Tam. Pop said he had something he wanted to "run by us." He began by saying that when Melanie was born, that was really the start of their family and how special that day was. He and Mom had talked about our sister-get-togethers and the fact that they don't happen as often as they once did. They feel it keenly, even though they don't often bring it up. And Pop didn't really voice that part out loud this time – he didn't have to. But he said that he and Mom wanted to pay for our lunch today – that way, they could be there in spirit, if not in body. He got teary-eyed as he talked, and Melanie cried, it was so touching – sweet and sad all at the same time. We hugged him and thanked him and went to Mom's room and did the same. When Tam came, we told her what they'd said. Nothing says Happy Birthday like a good cry!

Our lunch at Postmaster's was lovely, but also a bit odd – we haven't all three been away from Mom and Dad for any length of time in several years. One of those changes you don't see coming until it's in the rearview mirror. And what did we mostly talk about? Mom and Dad! It reminded me of new parents who leave their little one with a sitter so they can enjoy a quiet dinner with adult conversation, only to find themselves talking about the baby and unconsciously listening for a cry.

When we got back to the house, we fixed lunch for the folks. Then Mom gave us each a quilt, and we took a picture with her and our heirloom. Mine was one she had bought from her cousin; it had a white background embroidered with purple bows and flowers. So beautiful! Tam received a Dutch Doll quilt – one that Mom and Granny had made together many years ago. Melanie's was a state flower quilt – Mom spent countless hours on that one … there's no telling how much time she spent doing quilting and embroidery through the years. She still has several to give away. For years, Mom has said we could have this or have that, but she wanted us to wait until she was gone to get whatever it was. So when she let these items go, it surprised me, and bothered me a little, too. It's hard to put into words.

SATURDAY, JANUARY 14TH

Back to J'ville a little sooner than usual – I'm taking over for Melanie who has been there since Monday – Tam is at a book club convention in Florida and won't be back until Tuesday. Melanie helped me carry my stuff in, and then we visited for a little while. She was tired and wanted to get home, but she finds it hard to leave as well. We never know when we're saying goodbye if this will be the last one.

Shaun and Pop got two more fat gophers! Mom worked on her puzzle. Pop watched the wildcard football game. I made a trip to town for some groceries and didn't get back until after dark … Pop was watching for me on the porch … pretty special for a 72 year-old woman to have her 99 year-old father worrying when she isn't home early!

SUNDAY, JANUARY 15TH

Pop got a good night's rest but his lower regions are upset again. He takes cinnamon capsules, and those can cause that, but even if it's coincidental, we'll just leave them off for a while and see what happens. I fixed breakfast for us and for Shaun who came up to take Pop on a ride in his buggy. Mom ate most of her breakfast, but later balked at the Boost shake and meds. (Only a few are actual medicines – most are supplements Mom has decided she needs.) I asked her if she wanted to stop taking **everything**. After thinking it over, she said she didn't want us to feel guilty if anything happened to her, so she went ahead and took them. But I think she's afraid to stop taking anything she thinks might be helping her.

After Pop came back, he and Mom watched David Jeremiah preach on TV while I started lunch prep. Drove Pop to Sunday School, but I had to come back to the house to finish cooking and check on Mom. Saw Shaun's buggy in the pasture and heard him talking; I figured Caleb was with him … .found out later that Sancho, Pop's longhorn steer, had gotten both horns inside a hay ring and couldn't get them out! He had dragged that hay ring all the way down

After church, Dad and Shaun enjoy catching up on the latest community news.

the hill toward the pond. Shaun was trying to get him loose, and he was talking to Sancho. It took a while, but he got him out.

Back to church to get Pop, then home for lunch. At 2:00, I saw that Mom hadn't taken her noon pills; one was actual medicine and the other was a supplement – a big honker of a capsule. I asked if she just wanted to take the little one, and she said yes, so I pursued that idea: "Mom, how about you take only the actual medicines and leave all the supplements off, just to see if you feel better?" She decided to try that except for a few. I do hope that she feels better after this change. Trying to see what works for the folks is a constant challenge, but at least we sisters can bounce ideas off each other – some people have the entire burden alone – my heart goes out to them.

MONDAY, JANUARY 16TH

Decided to double check the meds Mom is still taking and saw that her thyroid medicine should be taken on an empty stomach – she's been taking it after breakfast for a long time. Changed it to the noon slot since she would have eaten breakfast a lot earlier than noon and wouldn't eat "lunch" until about 3:00. I also called the cardiologist to double check on that dosage.

Pop wanted to get out of the house, so we took a nice long buggy ride all over the pastures. The cows were huddled under the trees out of the north wind. We enjoyed that outing; time in the winter hangs heavy on Pop's hands ... he wants to get out every day and do something, but the weather doesn't often permit it.

When we parked at the house, we heard a horn honk – Shaun was right behind us! He and Pop went to feed the heifers, unload some scaffolding from Shaun's job, and check the gopher traps. I fixed Mom's hair and took her picture with some completed jigsaw puzzles. Rita and Athena came for a visit. Later Pop watched the Tampa Bay/Dallas game while Mom watched her movies, and I worked on the lesson for a ladies' group Bible study. Pretty good day.

TUESDAY, JANUARY 17TH

In addition to the usual routine, I called Verizon again since the "remedy ticket" didn't remedy anything. The young lady started to launch into the litany of reset this and unplug that, but I stopped her and explained everything we'd done multiple times, to no avail. I simply wanted to know if they would send a technician out and how much it would cost. After reviewing the whole saga, she said they'd send a new base out for 50% off. I requested a reduction in Mom and Pop's regular bill since they've had no phone service since December 30. After being put on hold, listening to that awful, scratchy music recording, their line rang and someone brand new got on the phone and asked how she could help me! I told her that I had been on this call for 55 minutes. Then *my* phone rang, and it was the first lady calling back .... Good Grief. Anyhow, they are supposed to overnight that new base. We'll see.

WEDNESDAY, JANUARY 18TH

No Verizon base came. Also had to call about a hospital bill amount, but the lady said I wasn't on Mom's HIPPA form – I've been on it since last summer. She finally found it in a different computer location. I really miss some things about the days before computers ...

THURSDAY, JANUARY 19TH

Had to get the folks all squared away so I could attend a college board of trustees meeting. Asked Tam to check on the folks at noon since I couldn't call them. The meeting lasted until 2:30; tore home and fixed Pop's lunch, then called Verizon again ... while I was on hold, I had time to prepare Mom's food and greet Nurse C when she came and greet Rita and her kids when **they** came. Pop and Shaun got back from feeding the heifers and running the gopher traps ... still on the phone – one hour and 57 minutes!

Bounced from one person to another, starting over, hearing completely different amounts for the base, and so forth. The first lady I spoke to said they didn't send the base because I hadn't paid for it. I nearly exploded! I told her that I had offered to go ahead and pay for it, but the person I had spoken to on Tuesday had said the charge would just be added to their phone bill! Another person I was bounced to asked if the requested equipment was an "upgrade." I told her, "Yes, if by 'upgrade' you mean going from one that *doesn't* work to one that does." Such a frustrating experience. Aaackk!

FRIDAY, JANUARY 20TH

One would think that I'd have plenty of time while at Mom's and Dad's to do some reading, letter writing, etc. One would be wrong. Here it is Friday, and I haven't finished studying my Sunday School lesson, haven't finished preparing the lesson for my Sunday night ladies' group, didn't write a letter to Cooper … I can't leave Pop to just sit by himself a lot, and Mom needs attention also. Being company for them is an important reason for being here, and I want to do that, but it leaves little time for anything else. And when I get back home, chores there have piled up, but I will "presevere" as Aunt Babe used to say. She was so funny … SAS shoes were ASAs, an LTD sedan was an LDT, an afghan was an african, and if you feared confined spaces, you had close-a-phobia. We loved hearing her talk.

Before I left, Athena got peeved at her younger brother and cousin (both 3) because they wouldn't do what she wanted. Athena stomped past us adults and exclaimed in a disgusted tone, "Kids!" We burst out laughing and agreed heartily, although I'm sure she completely missed the irony.

WEDNESDAY, JANUARY 25TH

Tam called today with good news: the Verizon base arrived at Mom and Dad's. Bad news: they could not get it to activate, and after an hour on the phone, Tam's call dropped. Hoping that maybe the problem was in the phones themselves, Tam's husband picked up a new set of phones he saw on sale at Walmart, and they worked with the old base! So, now I have to call Verizon for a return label for the new base they sent and try to get that charge off their phone bill. Yay.

MONDAY, JANUARY 30TH

Cold, wet day … good time to sit by the fire. Pop and Tam drove to Tyler for Pop's eye shot. He usually sits in his recliner with his eyes closed for most of the day after one of those, so today will be a fireside day for sure. I showed everyone the baby shower photos … it was so lovely, and they got such an array of nice gifts. I loved the special touch of everyone at the shower having a little storybook for the baby instead of the traditional card. Most of the time, cards get thrown away, but the books with the giver's little note written inside will last for years.

Shaun came by after work. He has a cold and was going home to rest after feeding the heifers. He kept his distance, but those cold germs travel. I do hope Mom and Dad don't get it, or me. Got a call about my daughter-in-law's blood pressure going up … she's had several long work days in a row. I pray that she gets some rest after the softball game tonight and that her pressure goes down.

Got the folks all ready to turn in and heard Hobo yowling, although it didn't exactly sound like her. It wasn't. A stray white cat was sitting in the flower bed, and Hobo's food dish was empty! I chased him off and put Hobo in the garage for the night.

TUESDAY, JANUARY 31ST

Another cold, wet day. Pop and I got a laugh out of Pierce's cows across the road. Pop and I had answered the front door and were talking to a FedEx fellow while I signed for Shaun's package. As the young man left, I noticed Pierce's cows all huddled up in one spot right across the road. When that FedEx truck backed out of our driveway and started off, those cows came pelting along the fence after him! They chased him until a cross fence blocked them. Pop and I laughed and laughed. We figured that Pierce's truck was pretty close in shape, size, and sound to the FedEx truck, and they just knew they were about to get some yummy cow cubes. When Pop used to feed cubes in winter, the cows came running whenever he fired up the truck. It got too dangerous, though; a few of the cows wound get so nutty, we were afraid they'd knock Pop down trying to get to the cubes first.

Went to town and dropped off the Verizon package – Yay! Got the ingredients to make a pumpkin pie – that sounded like a fine treat for a cold winter afternoon. Shaun's face lit up when I told him I was baking today.

I showed Pop the poems I had typed and copied in a really large font, but he still couldn't read them. That was sad – I love poetry and had copied some that I thought he would like: "When the Frost Is on the Punkin;" "The Lake Isle of Innisfree," "Stopping by Woods," and other nature poems. I read them to him, but it isn't the same as reading them yourself. My original plan was to make a poetry scrapbook and share it with Pop, but he wouldn't have been able to read those at all. Maybe I can figure out a way to get them on the Kindle in a really big font. I'm so thankful that there are ways to adapt to Mom and Dad's changing physical limitations … at least so far.

Melanie

MONDAY, JANUARY 9TH

My first day at the folks is also my 74th birthday! I am always startled when I think of my years on this planet. I feel the same on the inside as I did 35 years ago. That makes me reflect on how Mama's and Papa's thoughts are on age. Papa is always quoting Solomon, who warned us of things to come. How true are those words from the wisest man who has ever lived. Papa is very philosophical about age and death. He often says, "Nobody gets out of here alive." No matter how much we wish things were different or lament over things we can't do, Papa's upbeat attitude carries the day. Enjoy each morning, do all you can; rest, and do some more. He inspires me with that keep-on-keeping-on attitude. With hearing going and failing eyesight, he enjoys each day: the flickering of a good fire, sunshine that warms him on the side porch, the smell of cornbread baking, or a homemade yeast roll hot from the oven; these things, great or small, are a joy. He was sitting on the side porch, in the sunshine, when we girls started to leave for the birthday lunch. Papa said he and Mama decided they wanted to pay for the lunch. With tears in his eyes and a tremble in his voice, he said "when you came along, our lives changed forever." I hugged him and told him how much I appreciated those sweet words. He said he and Mama couldn't be there in person, but they would be there in spirit.

We went to the old post office turned coffee shop. It is an impressive, historical building that my Papa worked on as a young man. Sweet talk, lunch, and thoughtful gifts.

Back home we had a quilt session. I had made Mama and Papa a quilt and a wall hanging back in the 1980s. Mama gave Sherry a beautiful quilt that Mama's cousin had made. Tam was given a very old Dutch Doll quilt that Mama and *her* Mama (Granny) had made together.

TUESDAY, JANUARY 10TH

Today Papa and I were sitting in front of a nice fire, and we got to talking about school. Being a former middle school and high school teacher, I found Papa's educational process very interesting. He attended a country school at Enterprise for grades 1 – 8, and then had to transfer to Jacksonville for grades 9 – 11. There were only 11 grades back then. In the town environment he felt he didn't fit in, so he quit school and started working. His sister, Josie, loved school and finished, then went to nursing school and became an RN. Papa's youngest brother, Oscar, joined the army, and finished his college degree after his service to his country. He was a teacher, principal, and headmaster of a private school before he retired.

Papa had another interesting dream. He dreamed he was in a different town visiting with the head of law enforcement that was going down to a funeral home to check on things. They were having a funeral without the proper papers or certificate of death. He stopped the walking funeral procession and told them they couldn't proceed without the proper papers. A guy stepped up between Papa and the officer and agreed. He said, "How do you know he is dead? Look at Stuart McAnally. He is 99 years old and he looks dead! This other fellow looks like him. How can you bury him?" Papa woke up. Now, we will never know the fate of that poor man and his funeral!

Mama is having problems with her stomach. I conferenced with Sherry, and we decided to try switching her breakfast to first place and her Boost and meds second. The hope is, with food on her stomach, the meds will not upset her system.

I dozed off and had a brief, vivid dream of Papa. He was in his gray suit and walking up the front porch steps. He was smiling and had his patriotic tie in his hand. He wasn't bent, but standing tall! Dreams are peculiar things reflecting our stresses, hopes, fears, and outlook to the future, our minds striving to reconcile our lives on so many levels.

The bushels of acorns from the huge oaks around the house have become a walking hazard. Sherry and Papa worked on cleaning them up last week and today, Papa and I worked some more, finally making a dent in the bumpy carpet of nuts.

MONDAY, JANUARY 23RD

Time to head back to Jacksonville for the last week in January. It is a nice drive – about eighty miles. Blue sky; but cold. I got there, unloaded and set up my quilt by the south-facing windows in the Big Room. After dinner, Papa and I went out on the front porch to sit in the sunshine but discovered that flies were everywhere! I went back inside for the fly swatter and killed 103, yes, I counted them! It's the science teacher in me. Mama joined us for a bit and she was a good fly spotter, even with her macular degeneration.

FedEx brought the black box for the phones that the lightning had fried. Tam and Sherry had spent hours trying to fix them because with older folks, things must stay the same. Learning to use a new appliance, phone, or vehicle is challenging for Pop and out of the question for Mom. Shaun, Papa, and I fed the heifers and checked the gopher traps. Now Papa and I are sitting by the fire. He is reading on his Kindle; Mama is watching *Lord of the Rings*. We get the full benefit of all the battles through her wall and door! Daddy can't hear it, and I have developed amazing skills of concentration. I wrote down a new calf – date, kind, and mama cow number in the cow record book.

Mama seems perkier today. She even did 5 or 6 laps around the Big Room and worked on her puzzle several times. Sherry brought some 2 lb. hand weights for Papa. She would like to build up his arm strength for spring work. I use them to try and inspire Papa. So far, I'm doing a good thing for my arms, but Papa is not inspired.

There was a lot of angst this week to try and fix those old phones, thank goodness, Marc went to town and found two phones that were new but, looked and operated just like the old ones. Problem solved.

Something new this week – Papa washed his hair at bedtime and I dried it. In the summer he washes it early and lets the Texas heat and sunshine dry it. He shaved earlier in the day, too. For over seventy years, he shaved every day. These days, twice a week is good. His vision is a handicap; he shaves more by feel than sight.

Details matter to Papa. Awhile back, the large return air vent in the hall was taken off so we could check on a leak. It was put back on upside down. That had been bothering Papa for a while. Due to the lack of light in the hall and his poor vision, he had not taken time to fix it. I got a screwdriver, removed it, took it outside, cleaned the dust off, and put it back on right side up. The next morning Papa had finished his first cup of coffee and was headed back to his room. As he passed that return air vent, he turned around and said how glad he was that I had fixed it. A little time, a little effort, and a pleased Papa!

Rita brought Papa some onion sets. She loves gardening and thinks of ways to help Papa enjoy growing things. He had big gardens all of my growing up years and many after that. Gradually the gardening dropped back to onion, potatoes, watermelons, and tomatoes, then to a row of tomatoes in his 97th year and then containers with tomatoes in his 98th year. I planted those 12 onion sets in the flower bed by the front porch so he can check on them as they grow.

SATURDAY, JANUARY 28TH

This last morning of my week, Papa got up at 3:30 am! I got up at 3:45 am, opened the kitchen door, and asked him if he knew it was 3:45 am. He said he was tired of wallowing around in that bed. I can't blame him. I have done the same thing; only, I don't make coffee, and stir up that water heater! We are convinced that that water heater has a gremlin in it that sets up a howl when the water level changes. The water heater closet is in the hall close to my bedroom door, so I get the full benefit of the gurgles, burps, and rumbles.

We sat in front of a lovely fire and talked through the rest of that long predawn stretch. As usual, the rest of the morning activities tick off like clockwork. Tam has a Bible study date with a friend later this morning, so Shaun will be coming over to hold down the fort till she gets back. Leaving is always hard. Lots of hugs and kisses. I assure Mama that I will call when I get home. Mama used to come out on the front porch to wave as I left, but she can't do that anymore. I miss it. Daddy and Tam wave as I drive away. I roll down my window and wave until I am out of sight down the hill.

Tamra

SUNDAY, JANUARY 1ST, 2023 – NEW YEAR'S DAY

This morning drinking our first cup of coffee by the fire, I said, "Happy New Year, Dad!" He looked at me and said, "It is, isn't it?! Happy New Year to you! I am looking forward to getting some things done this year." I smiled and thought about how much I love that Dad, at ninety-nine, is still making plans and has goals he wants to accomplish. Hopefully, I will still have that same outlook on life as I get older.

The New Year is always a time for reflection and pondering the future. I enjoy the process as it helps me to recalibrate things in my life. Realizing where I am and where I would like to be this time next year has always been an important part of my goal-setting during January. Not that it always works out the way I'd like, but just having a plan helps me feel more settled as I face the uncertainty of the coming months.

This morning I noticed an article folded on the trunk in Josh's room where we stay while at Mom and Dad's, and realized that Sherry had brought another tidbit to entertain Dad. She is good about that.

That started me to thinking of the underlying current that makes up our everyday lives. It is a constant searching, scanning, and procurement of items that will aid, entertain, or make life better for Mom and Dad. Without realizing it, we have given that part of our lives priority. While that is admirable, it is, in some ways, detrimental to our own mental and emotional health. If our "finds" receive the expected level of approval or outcome, we are validated, but if they meet with less than desirable results or disinterest, we feel rejected at some level, even angry at the seeming waste of time and energy.

We would never express these feelings, except at low levels of frustration, because at the same time, we realize we have put our own expectations on both Mom or Dad or the situation we were trying to alleviate. They are completely unaware of our efforts on their behalf a big part of the time and to require validation is unfair.

It is complicated. Family dynamics and emotional situations take finessé and a large degree of self-control. In our case, we get a lot of practice. We are still the children, they are the parents, but those roles can no longer be viewed the same. We have become the caretakers, the ones who sacrifice *our* time, energy, and emotional effort…we have become the reluctant parents.

MONDAY, JANUARY 2ND

Re-stocking the wood rack is an ongoing chore throughout the winter months.

Tried calling Mom's meds in today, but the phone was out. Called and tried to get someone on the phone to get them fixed…. two and a half hours and two disconnections later…still no help. I still managed to get a lot done while on hold, but when Sherry arrived, I had to go. Today I am turning in my last article for the TWA magazine. I am more than a little sad; I have written for them for over eight years. I also had to turn in my column, ahead of the coming storms, in case they knock out our electricity.

WEDNESDAY, JANUARY 4TH

Sherry took Dad to Dr. J appointment today. Since the phones are still not fixed, I went over about 10:00 to check on Mom and give her breakfast and meds. Went down to the church to take down all the Christmas wreaths and decorations and set everything in order for Sunday service. Afterwards, I stopped back by Mom and Dad's to see what the Dr. said and ate a piece of the cranberry walnut bread Sherry had made.

SATURDAY, JANUARY 7TH

Have had Emelia since Thursday evening; we have had so much fun. She went with me to Mom and Dad's for the day and it was interesting. She was a busy bee and followed her Pawpaw everywhere when she wasn't trying to "help" Nannie with her puzzle. She is a good girl and plays well by herself, but at three, you need constant eyes on you, and so I was worn out by the time Caleb came to get her. Keeping up with Mom and Dad is hard enough, but throwing in a tiny person really ups the game!

MONDAY, JANUARY 9TH

Mel's birthday today and we took her to Postmaster's Coffee for brunch. We had a good time. It was so sweet that Dad wanted to pay for our outing. We went by to pick up some stuff for Mom and Dad afterwards and I talked to Kathy M. about our upcoming Amelia Island, Florida trip while Mel and Sherry shopped. I have got a ton to do before we leave on Wednesday.

WEDNESDAY, JANUARY 18TH

Got home late yesterday from my trip to Florida, and I am exhausted, but happy. Needed to get a few things done before going to Mom and Dad's for the weekend, so I went right to work; then about 12:30, I went over to say hello to Mom and Dad and Sherry. When I got there, Sherry was nowhere in sight, but I heard this strange "squeak, squeak, squeak" coming from the Big Room. Dad was going to town on the little pedal exerciser Sherry bought for him to use this winter to keep in shape. When I finally got close enough for him to hear, I yelled, "Hey Dad! Where ya goin'?" He looked up and smiled. "You made it back. How was your trip?" He stopped pedaling and we talked a minute. Sherry came through on her way to Mom's room without saying a word. I knew something was off, so I filled Dad in on the highlights of my trip, and then went to find Sherry, who had disappeared into the other end of the house. She was furiously scrubbing on Dad's tub/shower, but finished shortly, and we retreated to the kitchen table. Her exhaustion and frustration were evident in her voice and her expression. I let her vent about how Mom had been so down and wanting to just "go on" and how it makes her feel. Mel usually prays for her or gets upset and leaves her alone. I try to jolly her out of it by talking about old funny things that happened or all the things she still has to be thankful for, but if that doesn't work, I just tell her, "Well, maybe you'll go on soon." And I leave her to wallow in her self-pity, but poor Sherry, she lets it unsettle her and seems to take that kind of talk the hardest.

Sometimes, I think Sherry feels she carries the brunt of the load for Mom and Dad. Whether or not that is true, it doesn't change your feelings. I wish that she could just slow down some and not feel so driven "to do" all the time. It is almost like she has to look for something to do if she has a free minute, always organizing and cleaning. Maybe I'm too much the other way and don't see what needs to be done…I don't know. I do know that I have to give myself some time each day to think and rest my mind and body or I become a basket-case. Being content to reach a small goal on most days is good enough because I know my limits. Loving people is hard work and if we don't love and care for ourselves, it becomes nigh impossible to love others.

You can give until you run dry and then you're not fit to help either man or beast. Even my cat Maxine doesn't want to be around me when I get in one of my "poor pitiful me" moods. I don't blame her. Maxine is a good barometer of my emotional state. She has a knowing stare she levels at me from her perch on the back of the couch – get a grip on yourself, she seems to say, get over yourself, **you're** not that important – **I** am. Maxine always makes me laugh, and she helps break my indulgent mood and lifts my spirits considerably. We all need a Maxine in our lives – an equalizer – someone who helps you regain your perspective.

When you don't acknowledge your own frustration, whatever the cause, I feel that "keeping it all together" builds up to an almost helpless and incredible sadness which is hard to deal with. There are times when we all feel we do more, and we probably do, for that time, but the way I see it, as Mom used to say, "It will all come out in the wash." In other words, in the end, what we do for good will be known and eventually it all evens out. We all work our buns off doing what we do, maybe we could cut ourselves a little more slack here and there, but we appreciate what we all contribute, maybe not perfectly, but in our own way.

FRIDAY, JANUARY 20TH

Went over early to Mom and Dad's so Sherry could go home and make cupcakes for her son Stu and daughter-in-law Ashley's baby shower. I had Emelia with me, so it made for an interesting day. Rita and her kids had camped out by the pond last night and came up for pancakes, and then she took them all fishing.

SATURDAY, JANUARY 21ST

Busy day keeping up with Emelia, Dad, and Mom…sometimes I felt I was meeting myself going back and forth and in and out all day. Emelia loved following her Pawpaw around outside…she kept up, step for step with him, which isn't easy to do. I really hope she sleeps tonight. Once, when I went to check on them, I heard her talking and saw them disappearing over the hill towards the pond. I could still hear her, even when I could no longer see her.

SUNDAY, JANUARY 22ND

Emelia slept with me tonight, but she didn't stop talking, even in her sleep! She is also a roller and kicker, so I didn't get much rest. She was as good as gold in church today though and really enjoyed singing along with the hymns. She knew a lot of them because at night, she loves to listen to my Alan Jackson CD of old-time hymns.

Dad and Mom gave us a special time together to celebrate Mel's birthday.

When we got back from church, she followed Dad back to his room, chattering away, where he took out his hearing aid. I came in the room just in time to hear him sigh and say, "Peace." I cracked up. If you're not used to little ones and their constant verbal onslaught, it can wear you down, I understood perfectly.

Tonight, I was getting dressed for bed and looked down at my pajama top. A buttonhole was too big and wouldn't stay buttoned. They are my favorite pair, with cats on them, and are getting a little worn. I realized for the first time, I couldn't ask Mom to fix them for me. She can't see to thread a needle any longer and her essential tremors make it impossible for her to sew. I thought back on all the shirts she had rescued for me over the years, most I still wear, and that one small thing hit me with an unexpected jolt of sadness. Bit by bit, I was losing her and it had happened so gradually that I failed to notice the many small things we had both lost along the way.

MONDAY, JANUARY 30TH

Spending an entire day alone at my house is a rare treat, so when Marc had to take his parents to Dallas for the day, I took advantage of the time and had more fun than should be allowed by one person! I built a fire in the woodstove, sang songs loudly and off-key, danced like a nut to my old 60s and 70s albums, drank a ton of Lady Grey tea and Wide-Awake coffee, laughed out loud without having to explain myself, read funny books, wrote funny lines to myself, and generally had a marvelous time. Everyone needs a day like I had today.

TUESDAY, JANUARY 31ST

Last day of my old friend January…I am not ready to say goodbye. Went to WMA meeting at church this morning, as usual, and on my way back, I stopped at Mom and Dad's to see how things were going. Sherry had gone to town and Dad was in the kitchen making a pot of coffee. He asked me if I wanted a cup, but I said no…I'd better get over to the house and get busy. I left him heading for the Big Room and the warm fireplace, a good spot to be on a cold day like today. As I left, though, I couldn't shake the feeling that maybe I should have taken him up on his offer, enjoyed the fire and a cup with him, even for a few minutes. It bothered me the whole way home and even after I got home, I tried to reason with myself, there would be another time, another day to sit and enjoy Dad's company…at least I hoped. Next time, I finally told myself, I would not rush off.

EVERY DAY WON'T BE A *Good* DAY, BUT TRY TO FIND THE GOOD IN *Every* DAY

FEBRUARY

Icicles are everywhere – an appropriate beginning to the typically coldest month of the year in Texas. In February, we have our greatest chances of snow and even though it's usually not much, I look forward to the white stuff. This is another month I enjoy immensely. On the other hand, Dad is always "building the fire up" as he says and keeping it so dang hot in the Big Room that he even runs Mom out, and she is on blood thinners. I tell him that his "regulator" is broken. But he just grins and says, "It worked for many a year," as he throws another log on the already roaring fire. And it did; some of the best memories I have are of going with my Dad and siblings to hay the cows on frosty February days. The excitement and anticipation of finding icicles and frozen puddles are mostly lost to old age, I guess, but I'm not there yet.

It is a good thing that February is a short month and spring is not far behind because I think Mom and Dad start getting a little depressed when it is cloudy and dark for too many days. Twenty-eight days probably feels like fifty to them. February to me is like the lull before the storm, a respite to prepare for the busyness of spring and all the outdoor chores that wait. I find myself hoping that we can make it through the month without any major health events, so Dad can enjoy the spring time when it finally does arrive. Until then, it is challenging to keep them engaged and interested on a day-to-day basis, but we all work to lift their spirits and make the hours more entertaining when we can. A monotonous routine can slowly eat away at your zest for living, at any age. Dad is counting the days till spring…I saw him staring at the calendar the other day. I know he's hoping for an early spring this year. Maybe he will get his wish.

Sherry

WEDNESDAY, FEBRUARY 1ST

Done with January! Pop is glad that interminable month is over … now he can look forward to spring green-up in a few weeks. Not today though – a freezing rain here. Hope it doesn't weigh the trees down too much. Broken limbs usually mean no electricity. Hobo is glad to be in the garage on a cozy mat, and Pop is enjoying the fireside. Taking care of the fire is his main daily chore in the winter: filling the wood box, keeping the fire going, cleaning out the ashes, etc.

Melanie called. She still hadn't found the hummingbird scissors Mom got her years ago. I suggested that she take **every**thing out of her quilting bag instead of just rummaging around in it since those scissors are tiny and could have slipped way down. Sure enough, there they were!

Talked to Bill – we have rain at home, but it isn't freezing. Mom worked on her puzzle, and Pop read on his Kindle but said he could barely read it. Tam had thought it was on the largest font, but I was able to bump it up another notch. Only problem is that there are fewer words on the screen now; I need to get a Kindle with a bigger screen to offset that larger font. Hope he is able to read a long, long while.

Shaun visited and said the pumpkin pie I made yesterday was really good. I'd taken some to him almost straight out of the oven. So yummy! Speaking of warm, the temperature outside got high enough to start melting the ice off the trees, fences, power lines, etc. I looked at the rain gauge to see how much we'd gotten, but it was still too frozen to tell.

Pop gets cold when he leaves the Big Room and goes into the other part of the house. We shut the door to the Big Room to keep the draft from sucking all the fireplace heat up the chimney, and the rest of the house is just on the thermostat, which is set pretty low. When Pop comes back to the Big Room, he usually grabs the round green cushion from the rocker and puts it on the hearth so he can sit right in front of the fire screen and warm up. When his back is nice and warm, he tosses the cushion back on the rocker and goes to his recliner. When he stood up tonight to toss that pillow, he went a little sideways. When I asked, "Pop, what's up with that?" he said, "My money in my pocket shifted, I guess." Ha! He knows we keep an eagle eye out for anything that signals dehydration or blood pressure issues, so he makes light of most things.

THURSDAY, FEBRUARY 2ND

Groundhog Day! – Mrs. Tassie Dean's birthday. She's gone now, but years ago she told me her birthday was Groundhog Day and said I'd never forget it. And I never have. She was a sweet lady – very small with a dowager's hump, which made her even shorter. My boys used to get a kick out of watching her drive out of the church parking lot. All you could see was her knuckles on the top of the steering wheel and a fringe of gray hair. She lived across a busy highway from the church, so she had to wait for an opening in traffic. When one appeared, she shot that sedan across the road!

Yesterday when I was on the love seat, Mom was at her puzzle table in the corner, Pop was reading, and the fire was cheerfully crackling, I told myself to enjoy this peaceful moment when all is well, because the next day could be very different … today, Pop said he was taking a cold. Shaun has had one and has visited the past few days. Even though he stood several yards away, germs travel. Tam and I talked about something to give Pop; she suggested Zicam nasal swabs, so I decided to get some.

Mom didn't want to catch Pop's cold, so she decided to isolate in her room. I moved her puzzle table and chair in there so she could still entertain herself with that. Raced to town to drop bills off at the post office and look for Zicam. Found some at the second store, then home to get Mom's meds. Pop and I ate lunch, then I started on a huge stack of dishes and fixed Mom's plate. Did some laundry. Coffee and pie for Pop. There was only one slice left after that, so I saved it for him to eat tomorrow. Back in the day, I'll bet Mom and Dad saved food for us kids to eat when they would have like to eat it themselves … now it's our turn to do that.

Nurse C came to check Mom's INR level and had to stick her finger three times to get enough blood for a reading. Poor Mom, she lets it be known when she hurts! But three sticks would be unpleasant for anyone. Her reading was 4.0, so I'll have to adjust her warfarin dose, I'm sure.

Later on, Pop wanted to take something to help him rest in spite of his cold; he prefers to take Nyquil, but Tam said that could raise his blood pressure. We checked Tylenol PM, and that seemed to be okay, so he took two of those and was in bed by 8:00. A rather long day of health issues ... still raining.

FRIDAY, FEBRUARY 3RD

What I mentioned yesterday about watching Mom with her puzzle and Dad on his Kindle ... was **that** ever a true sentiment! Enjoy the good moments because you never know what another day will bring.

About 2:00 this morning, I heard a loud thump and raced into Pop's room ... he was in the bathroom with the door almost closed. I asked if he was okay, and he said that he couldn't get up! He wanted to try again, but after a minute I told him I was coming in. He was sitting on the toilet lid in his boxers, leaning way over to the right with his arm resting on the edge of the tub. He couldn't sit up straight. I tried to pull him upright, but he just kept going over farther and farther until his top half was over in the tub and his knees were on the floor. All he could do was rest his head on his arms and groan sporadically ... I was afraid he was having a stroke. I told him to hang on and ran back to my room for my phone, tore back to Pop, and called Shaun. It just rang once and went to voice mail. I called Tam – same thing.

I told Pop that I'd have to call 911 if I couldn't get anyone to answer. He didn't want me to do that. "They'll want to haul me to a nursing home." At least I knew he hadn't had a stroke because by then he could talk clearly. I called Shaun again, then Tam. She answered, thank the Lord! She said she'd yank some clothes on and stop by for Shaun on the way.

I knew Pop had to be cold against that tub with only a pair of boxers on, so I grabbed a big towel and put that under his arms. Tam and Shaun got here in record time. Shaun had to lift Pop onto the toilet, then Tam rolled his desk chair over, and we all got him onto that, then rolled him over to his bed and got him in it. We tried to figure out what had happened. Apparently, he got up to take more Tylenol around midnight and he shouldn't have taken any that soon. He may have thought it was way later since he went to bed so early. We don't really know and Pop couldn't remember. Bottom line – he was weak as branch water.

I told Tam and Shaun that I was going to stay in his room in his recliner and make sure he didn't try to get up again. I put some cough drops in a bowl on his bedside table. He had used all of them by 6:00. I got him another and asked if he wanted to just sleep a bit more. He slept until 8:00. Shaun came over to help him get ready and into the Big Room. I had a fire going. Melanie called after that and sounded so concerned about Dad, so I started telling her how weak he was. Then I asked who had told her about it, and she said, "Told me about what?" Oops, I was going to tell her later when we had some good news to report, but I let the cat out of the bag. I told her about last night and said for her not to walk the floor over it, but to pray for Pop.

I fixed breakfast for all three of us – I'd already given Mom hers since we had such a late start to the day. Washed the dishes and gave Mom her Boost and meds. Shaun left and Pop slept a good bit. Called Dr. B and rescheduled Pop's eye appointment from Monday to Thursday, with the understanding that I might have to put it off even more, depending on how he feels. Dr. D's office called about Mom's INR level and told us to skip her Warfarin dose for tonight, give a 2 mg Saturday and Tuesday, and 4 mg the other days. Went in Mom's room to switch those pills in her pill case and note the change on her med sheet.

Pop needed to go to the bathroom. I finally got him to his feet and holding on to the walker. Seeing him like that broke my heart. He has a cane but rarely uses it, and has never needed a walker …this is an extra one we have for Mom who has used one for years. He opted for the hall bathroom since it's closer to the Big Room than his bathroom is. The walker barely fit through the door. I remembered our uncle falling in that bathroom and hitting his head on the tub, so I left the door cracked in case Pop couldn't get back on his feet. All I could see was Pop's upper half over the cabinet as he struggled and struggled to get up. I wanted to weep. I called Shaun and asked him to come help, and he was here in a flash. I know Pop was embarrassed to need that kind of help, but **so** thankful Shaun could be here for him. Poor Mom is getting less attention today, but you give more to those who need it.

Later Pop said he needed to use the bathroom again, but just the "stand up" kind, so I got him to his feet, finally, and helped him to *his* bathroom this time. The walker could fit over the toilet, and I thought he would be okay. I stood outside the door and in a minute or so, I heard a noise that didn't sound quite right. After an announcement of my intention, I went in, and Pop was bent at the waist sideways with his head down between the toilet tank and the shower! He was still hanging on to the walker, but he could **not** straighten up. I just knew he was going to fall into the tub and break something. I threw my left arm across his chest and grabbed a belt loop with my right hand and pulled back. Daddy couldn't help at all, but I was determined to keep him from falling. I knew he had to have something to land on, so I hooked my foot around the leg of the little bathroom chair to pull it closer, but it tangled in the cord for the electric heater. Finally I got it closer, and prayed out loud for God to help me. I heaved with all my might and got Dad in the chair. Hoping he wouldn't list to one side and fall out, I ran for my phone and called Shaun. He came in just a bit and helped Pop onto the toilet seat so he could use the bathroom, then we both got him in bed. Shaun swapped Pop's khakis for pajama bottoms. Poor Pop was worn out and went to sleep quickly even though the sun hadn't set.

I stayed in his room, sitting at the round table, writing in my journal, watching the sun sink toward the horizon, and going back and forth between Mom and Dad. Later, I saw Pop kick the covers back, and I said, "What are you fixing to do?" He thought it was morning and was going to put his house shoes on and go to the bathroom! I told him it was still night – only two hours or so since he'd had the last ill-fated trip to the toilet. He seemed determined, so I said, "If you can get on your feet with no help, go ahead." I did help a little, and he got to his feet, but sat right down again. He'd have fallen if the bed hadn't been there. Shaun had brought him a urinal, so I handed him that and went out of sight to give him some privacy. Then he wanted a fresh pair of boxers, so I got a big gray towel to hold in front of my face and sashayed over to his chest of drawers, got a pair, and threw them in his direction. He had to get out of the old ones without standing up, and that was tough. Then he struggled to get the new ones on; he said they were around his feet, so I came back from around the corner with my towel shield to look, and they weren't there. So another sashay over to the chest of drawers … I felt like an Arabian princess doing a spastic "dance of the veils." Got another pair of boxers and threw them over to him. This time he got them up – I peeked around when he said they were on, and he was standing! That was encouraging.

He got back in bed, so I checked on Mom again and called Bill to tell him the saga. He told me to do what I needed to do and stay as long as it took. Then I realized that in all the drama, I hadn't given Pop his nighttime blood thinner pill, so I had to wake him up for that. Checked on Mom and took her more water. What a day. But so much to be thankful for. God woke me up just before 2 A.M. or I would not have heard that thump Pop made falling back against the toilet tank. God woke Tam up so that she heard her phone go off. (He kept Shaun from shooting Tam when she pounded on his door in the wee hours!) He sent an angel to help me keep Pop from falling into the tub this afternoon … how else could a 122 pound, less than 5 foot 5 inch woman support her 6 foot 1 inch, 170 pound dad, standing on one foot with the other foot hooked around a chair leg? I want to meet that guardian angel someday and shake his hand.

SATURDAY, FEBRUARY 4TH

Long night, but things are looking up! I was in the recliner in Pop's room again … didn't sleep much, of course, and around 11:20 I saw some skinny legs go by between the "flame" of the fake fireplace and my chair. "Pop, what are you doing?" He said matter-of-factly that he was going to the bathroom. I leaped up, flipped the light on, and put my hands on either side of his back in case he started going down, but he got to the bathroom door okay. I sat and waited in case he couldn't get back up from the toilet since he hadn't been able to do that all day yesterday and even up until 3 hours ago. He came out, though, and got back in bed. Hallelujah! I would definitely call that "turning a corner."

Don't think I actually fell asleep until after 1:30 or so and woke up just after 6:00 when Pop got up again to go to the bathroom. I told him I would make coffee and start a fire, and asked him if he would please use the walker when he headed to the Big Room since that's a long walk. He said he would. I peeked in his room again later and saw him sitting on his bed. I asked if I could help him get dressed, but he said he thought he could handle it. Fed Hobo and let her outside for a bit. Checked on Pop and he was lying down again – getting on his pants and shirt had worn him out. I got a cup of coffee after I checked his temperature, then sat at the round table, writing in my journal:

"I hear Dad's soft breathing – he's sound asleep … such a sweet sound. White frost this morning with a beautiful sunrise. The cows are standing around the hay rings … Shaun will need to put more hay out today. The hay supply is getting low, with this month and March still to go. It's 7:32, should I wake Pop? He needs to eat, but restful sleep is healing … it's a dilemma."

I checked on Hobo, and there was that white cat! I chased him off, and then went to the Big Room to answer Melanie's text – I knew she was anxious to hear how last night went. Bill called to check on us also, and while I was on the phone with him, I heard a noise in the kitchen. Opened the door and saw Pop headed my way with *one* hand on the walker and the other holding his cup of coffee! After he was seated in his recliner, I called Melanie back to tell her about that – I knew it would make her feel just as relieved as it did me. Pop is on the upswing one more time!

Got meds for both the folks, and our breakfast. Shaun came up to check on Pop and feed the heifers, then Tam came over and hauled her stuff in for the weekend. We sat and talked about what happened yesterday afternoon and last night – we had to laugh over my zooming back and forth with the towel in front of my face! Laughter helps a lot, when you can manage it. Shaun came back to bring Mom and Pop a load of firewood and to report that once again, Sancho had gotten his long horns stuck inside a hay ring. When Shaun left to try to get him out of it, Tam and I watched through the binoculars, and cheered and clapped when he succeeded. He could hear us whooping and hollering, and it tickled him.

Loaded up my stuff and headed to Nac. After I unloaded all my goods, I asked Bill if I could help him with anything, hoping the answer would be No, since I was not feeling tiptop, but he wanted to cut back the lantana and bridal wreath bushes out front. I helped, but all the time, I felt worse and worse … I had caught Pop's cold.

SUNDAY, FEBRUARY 5TH

Well, this was a red letter day. Had chills and coughing and a horrible headache during the night. Got up around 11 P.M. and sprayed Lysol everywhere so Bill wouldn't catch this evil. Finally took a Nyquil capsule around 2 A.M. Gradually the headache eased, and I slept some. Before going to church, Bill stuck his head in to ask how I was doing. After he left, I got up to get some coffee and a piece of toast. Fixed both, but got dizzy and leaned against the kitchen counter. The next thing I knew, I was waking up on the floor, coffee all over my pajamas, toast and cup on the floor. The coffee had been hot, but I didn't seem to be burned anywhere. Don't know how long I was out. Had to change into dry pajamas and get back in bed. Later, I discovered a very sore spot on the side of my head – I guess I hit something on my way down. On a positive note, my cup didn't break. It's my favorite one.

MONDAY, FEBRUARY 6TH

Bill looked in to see if I was still alive and to recommend that I get up and move around later so I won't get pneumonia. I did and even managed to get some chores done in the house. **So** thankful that I didn't get this junk earlier, or there's no way I could have kept Pop from falling last week … another blessing. I went outside a few times to get some vitamin D before the clouds thickened up.

Stu called to tell me that Ashley went to her OBGYN with contractions, but he thinks they will stop … the baby isn't due until April 5th. Ashley has decided to stay home from coaching until the baby comes. I'm glad.

Found out that Shaun's back is giving him trouble – I wonder if it's related to lifting Pop out of that tub. He fell years ago on the job, and if he twists just right (or wrong), it gives him a fit again.

TUESDAY, FEBRUARY 7TH

Stu called early this morning and said that he and Ashley had been at the hospital since 3:30. She was having contractions – they gave her something to stop them, but that may or may not work. I got up and dressed. Then Stu called and said that today would be Knoxlynn's birthday! He had gone down to the hospital cafeteria for some breakfast, thinking that he and Ashley would be going home. When he came back to her room with the tray, the doctor gave him the news, and he nearly dropped it.

I couldn't believe it. The first grandchild to be born here in my town, and I have to miss it – all because of this stupid cold! The gloom settled on me, and I called my sisters to whine and cry. They were sweet, but their sympathy didn't remove the sadness. Then a ray of sunshine … my daughter-in-law's mom called and said they wanted me to mask up and come – just in the hall outside, not in the room. She said there were people all over the place anyway, plenty of germs to go around. So I prepared as well as I could and stayed well away from anyone going in and out of the room. I touched nothing, didn't even hug my son when he came out with a victory salute. I only saw my new sweetie from a distance, but at least I got that much – I'm thankful.

FRIDAY, FEBRUARY 10TH

Baby girl has to go back to the hospital, in NICU. She's so little that she isn't maintaining her body temperature. Poor Stu was a mess when he called me. I raced to the hospital so I could lend some support when they arrived. Poor dears! It's a blow, but the staff will take excellent care of her, and Stu and Ashley can be there a lot. Since she's already been "out in the world," she'll have her own separate room from the babies who have not left the hospital. Lord, protect my sweet little family, especially this precious wee baby.

MONDAY, FEBRUARY 13TH

Had a little quiet coffee time, but then had to scurry around and pack for J'ville. Sure wish I could be in two places at once so I could see my new granddaughter and also take care of Mom and Dad. I texted Ashley to ask if she wanted anything to eat – she's at the NICU feeding Little Bit. I went to Walmart first and got Valentine cards for the folks to give each other tomorrow and some flowers for Pop to give Mom. Over to the hospital and visited with Ashley awhile – she looked tired, poor girl.

On to Jacksonville … Rita, Jason, and the kids pulled up about the time I arrived; they were going fishing in one of Pop's ponds. Tam helped me carry my stuff inside and looked at pictures of the baby. Pop came in and asked if I'd gotten over being mad at him because he gave me that cold; then he added, "Of course, I was just the middleman." (Meaning that Shaun gave it to Pop first … Ha!) I assured him that I was *never* mad at him, just disappointed at the situation..

Shaun came to take Pop to the Homeplace to set traps for the beavers that are trying to flood his pasture. They've built an impressive dam across the creek. Cleaned up the kitchen and found two missing puzzle pieces for Mom – they were under her chair. I have actually recreated pieces for puzzles when we could not find them anywhere. It's pretty tedious: tracing the outline of the missing piece, transferring the outline to a piece of cardboard, cutting out the shape, painting it white and letting it dry, painting the piece to blend in, then coating it with a clear coat that has a sheen like the other pieces. I think I've done that for at least four of her puzzles; I enjoyed the challenge, but don't want to make a career of it.

Ashley sent photos of Bill and Stu with Knoxlynn – she's out of NICU and into a regular room. Thank you, Lord!

TUESDAY, FEBRUARY 14TH

Pop got up first today and built the fire. He used his last two pieces of bread for a toast and ham sandwich, so I started a grocery list for later. Ricky R called, wondering if Pop was up for a visit today – just the ticket he needs – company! I swept and straightened up a little. Mom felt terrible and said she would just stay in her room … no Valentine photos today, I guess.

Dad and Mom celebrate Valentine's Day with a card and flowers…

Ricky brought two gentlemen with him; one of them had read the book Tam wrote about Dad's experiences in WWII and wanted the others to hear Pop's stories first hand. I had already put his hearing aid in, (He has two, but only wants to wear one.) made coffee for the guys, and then just sat back out of the way. Tam came by, which was a good thing – one of the guys wanted to buy a copy of her book and get her and Pop to sign it. After that, the guys went to the sunroom with Pop so he could show them some of his mementos from the war. They all seemed to really enjoy the visit. It means a lot when veterans get to share their experiences with others.

After they left, I was about to head to the store. Pop wanted me to use his credit card, but he couldn't find it. The last time he'd used it was at Dr. B's last Thursday. I asked if he'd given it to Melanie afterwards to use at the store, but he couldn't remember. I told him my money was on Melanie having it. I used my card at the store and called Melanie on my way back to ask if she had it … she did. Ha! Dad was relieved that he hadn't lost it.

My little granddaughter got out of the hospital today! I'm so thankful and am looking forward to holding that precious little girl in my arms, something I have not gotten to do yet.

WEDNESDAY, FEBRUARY 15TH

Pop has a special coffee cup, English china with an apple design. Melanie and I bought several of these cups at an estate sale, and all of them had fruit designs, but Pop likes the apple one best, so that's **his** cup. This morning I set mine close to the coffee pot when I went to build a fire. Pop wasn't paying attention and grabbed my cup and poured his coffee. After he had a sip or two, I asked if the coffee tasted any different this morning and pointed at the cup he was holding – one with blueberries on it! We got a laugh out of that.

Fixed Mom's breakfast … she's down to 111 pounds. We really have to encourage her to eat; she just shudders when we mention eggs, and she doesn't want any kind of bread. It's tough. Did a round of cleaning after helping get another load of firewood. The day actually turned out pretty warm – Pop loved it. He even ate lunch outside. Later, I told Mom we needed to fix her up for a picture because Pop had something to give her. She didn't feel up to it yesterday on the official sweethearts day, but better late than never. She wore her red flannel gown, and I fixed her hair.

Rita, Athena, Raylan, Caleb, and Emelia all came to see the folks, and Caleb carried the big vase of flowers in the Big Room for Pop to give Mom, and they had cards for each other. I took some pictures … so glad Mom finally felt well enough to take part! Counting their courting days, that's around 80 Valentine's Days for them.

THURSDAY, FEBRUARY 16TH

Cold, windy day. Pop got a haircut when we drove to the "village for some herbs" as he sometimes puts it. Normal day of cooking, meds, and so forth. The Homeplace beaver is still being Houdini. Mom's INR is up, so I will have to adjust her warfarin dose. My baby granddaughter has gained back to her birth weight – good news for sure. Ben and his family are busy with school and sports. Good day overall.

FRIDAY, FEBRUARY 17TH

Rick Webb had told Pop that he'd come over for breakfast sometime this week, and this morning, Pop said Rick was "running out of week." Another cold, windy day, though, so maybe he's waiting for a better day. The pink and white amaryllis has five giant blooms on that tall stalk – such a pretty sight in the dregs of winter. I let Hobo in the enclosed side porch, and she and Pop wanted the same chair – Pop won. Hobo had to settle for the end of the table. After Pop dozed off, I went to his room to pay a couple of bills, and Hobo took advantage of the situation, winding up in the middle of my bed. That got her a quick trip back outside. A fairly normal day.

SATURDAY, FEBRUARY 18TH

Rick Webb made it this morning at 7:00 – just before running out of week. Tam arrived and we had the information swap before I left. On my way home, I found out that several of my church folks are having severe health issues, so I'll need to check on them, plus get groceries and catch up on the laundry. Also, I'm making supper for the new parents tonight. And I get to see the baby and hold her – can't wait!

MONDAY, FEBRUARY 27TH

Back to J'ville after doing chores here and trying to get some photos done at Walgreens. Pop and Jason are working on that new fence line on the west side of the place and were already hard at it. Pop likes an early start on any project if the weather is good. Checked on Mom and helped her with a butterfly puzzle until the guys came in for lunch. I thought they might call it a day, but after they ate, they headed back out, but "only" worked until 3:30.

TUESDAY, FEBRUARY 28TH

Pop had to get up at midnight and put some of that Nervive cream on his foot, then got up for the day at 5:00. Since Jason wasn't coming until 8:00, I encouraged Pop to rest after he'd had breakfast and his coffee. He did, and even dozed off. Later after he and Jason left and Mom was situated, I drove to town with the grocery list.

Made lunch for the guys, then braided Mom's hair and helped her change into a lighter gown. Checked her BP, then checked Pop's before he went back to the fence work … it was 97/57. Jason said maybe that was why

Pop was a little dizzy this morning. Oh, my goodness! Checked it again, and it was 91/51. "Pop, this isn't going in the right direction! (I thought his lunch would kick in – those cheddar biscuits had 400 mg of sodium each.)

Jason suggested that they call it a day, and Pop agreed. They drove back up to the fence to collect their saw and other tools, then sat on the patio and talked for a long while. I fixed Mom's lunch, then visited with Tam when she came over. I gave her a tray made in Italy that I'd bought at an estate sale. (Love going to those) She recognized the name of the manufacturer and said that a new one cost *several* times what I paid for this one … always nice to find a bargain.

Later, I decided to walk up to the fence and check out the progress. Saw Shaun and Pop in the buggy – he wanted to show Dad how nice the pasture looked where he'd used the drag. I'm so thankful that Shaun is doing the chores that would be difficult or impossible for Pop to do. We all have our special contributions to helping Mom and Dad stay at home.

Melanie

MONDAY, FEBRUARY 6TH

This month started off with concerns for Sherry's health. She developed a bad cold or flu. Passed out Sunday morning after Bill left for church. Came to with coffee spilled all over her and her toast tossed across the floor. She didn't break her cup though. The next day she was feeling better. Ashley, her daughter-in-law is at the hospital having the baby a month early! Sherry was bitterly disappointed at first, but made peace with it. About that time Ashley's Mom and Ashley told her to get a mask and come be present and enjoy the excitement and process of the birth of her first granddaughter. Such a blessing for Sherry! She was super careful and everything went fine. Even got to run a few errands for the new parents.

I went in the kitchen to wash dishes and the sink would not drain. I did the usual drain opener, wait 15 minutes, and pour a quart of boiling water. Heard something, and here came a tsunami of soapy water from under the sink! I quickly put the plug in the sink, then dashed for towels to mop up.. Daddy came in and directed me to keep it from under the stove. Plopped a towel in that direction. Daddy got nice tubs and we put all the stuff under the sink in those. I threw away some items, transferred flower vases to another cabinet, and mopped up under there. When I got Daddy's flashlight and looked at the drain, I saw the problem and sent a picture to Shaun. He said he would get the stuff to fix it after work. Good brother! Daddy said we needed a little heater under there to dry it out. Got that going.

Daddy's ears have some spots on them that interfere with his hearing aids, so I've been applying Neosporin on them for several weeks and they seem to be improving.

The nights are sometimes so hard. I need sleep and yet that is so hard to get on a consistent basis: woke at 12:30 AM – again at 2:00 AM, and by 3:30 AM I know it is hopeless. I figure doing something constructive is a positive attitude, so I studied my SS lesson and read my Bible. At 5:30 AM my stomach is making an uproar, so I fix my peanut butter toast and drink my energy drink. A fire is a fine way to warm a restless spirit. Daddy is up at 6:30 AM. Had his coffee ready for him to put the finishing touches on. After a while it's the usual routine.

Shaun came by with two new metal parts for the bottom of the sink. He will be by tomorrow to put them on. He filled up the wood box before he left.

WEDNESDAY, FEBRUARY 8TH

Last night, Dad and I both slept well. Fire sitting – rain falling – peaceful. Did usual morning things, then fixed Mama's hair, washed and lotioned her arms, hand, legs, and feet. She cleans her face with Ponds and washes it with a hot wash rag. She loves the attention, now for a fresh gown and morning meds. Wednesday is watering day: orchids, poinsettias, etc.

Lots of baby news and pictures from Sherry. She takes the new parents meals. What a great mom-in-law! Shaun is here to replace the sink bottom with new parts. Yea! This "automatic" dishwasher needs both sides of that sink in operation to be happy.

THURSDAY, FEBRUARY 9TH

Took Dad to his eye appointment today, after taking care of Mama. We left around 9:00 AM. Foggy. As we got closer to Tyler, the traffic started backing up. There was a wreck due to the fog. An 18 wheeler was laid over in the right lane. Slow going to get around it. Got to the appointment on time. We were in and out fairly quickly. A beautiful sunshiny day – on the return trip.

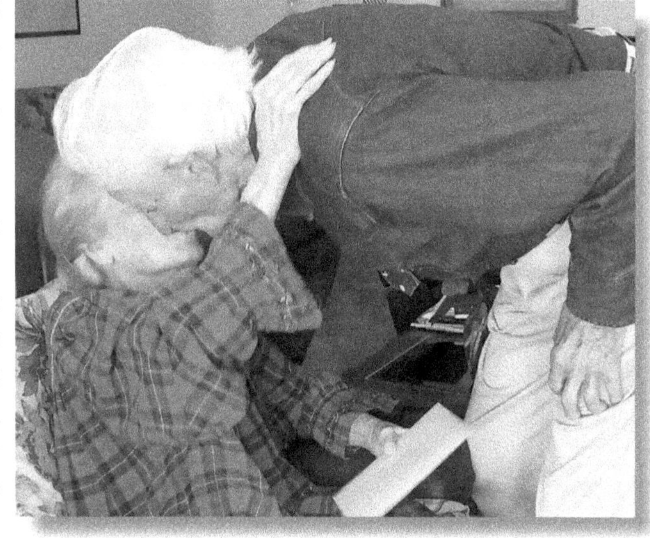

...and a kiss!

Later, me and Daddy were sitting on the front porch in the sunshine, talking about life. I reflected that life was kind of like what we observed yesterday and today. Yesterday was dark, rainy, and cold. Today, after the fog, bright, sunny, and hopeful. Daddy said how darkness and light affected some more than others. He said, "What goes on in your mind determines what your life will be be. You can clutter your mind with so much junk that it doesn't know which way to go. Clutter of the mind will cause you to waste your life – you go through life and accomplish nothing." Daddy's wisdom comes from a lifetime of experiences watching other people and meditating on the Word. "As a man thinks in his heart, so is he." Proverbs 23:7.

FRIDAY, FEBRUARY 10TH

Today was much the same except for the vacuum. I worked on it – belt off – still wouldn't work. Sherry knows the Rainbow Doctor by his first name ... she will get it to him. Ricky R, Daddy's lawyer friend, called and they talked awhile. Nurse C came; Mama's INR is 2.0 – great! Shaun came and fed the heifers. I invited him for morning blueberry pancakes and ham tomorrow. Quilted and have one block left.

SATURDAY, FEBRUARY 11TH

Woke up at 3:40 AM. Not going back to sleep. Got up and dressed, packed my stuff, ate, read devotionals and Bible. Mama coughing some at 5:15. Daddy wanted to clean the ashes out, but I went ahead and did it so I could build a fire. Heard Daddy making his coffee at 6:00. He seemed glad I had that chore done, then reminisced about his Dad's attempt at coffee making when Daddy was 10-11 years old. Got a better picture on paper of the old house they lived in. Love hearing stories of his childhood. So thankful I am writing those down. I made blueberry pancakes with ham. After we ate, Daddy helped me fold and put my quilt into its bag. Did all the meds and stuff and fixed Mama's pizza – yes, for breakfast – she ate it all. Finished loading more stuff and remembered to get the blueberries Sherry shared with me. After Tam came over at 10:00, we went over everything – changing of the guardians. Ate a bite of cake Tam had made. Good. Left at 10:30.

MONDAY, FEBRUARY 20TH

I always forget something when I go to help the folks. You would think I would have it down perfectly by this time. Usual morning things. I planted two hyacinths and watered them, washed dishes, took out the fireplace ashes, braided Mama's hair, turned over the puzzles pieces for her, and fixed lunch. It's an 80° day, wind blowing at 16 mph with gusts up to 26!

Shaun came by and said he got a lot done on Judge D's house and is going to Rusk tomorrow for jury duty in Judge D's courtroom. He asked if that connection with work would get him out of jury duty, but the judge said no. Of course Shaun was just joking. He and I took a ride in the side-by-side and fed the heifers. Shaun had nailed the trough to the light pole because the heifers had turned it over the day before. We found a new calf – a black heifer with white "eyebrows."'

Tam came over to try a hearing aid on Mama – didn't work. I parched Daddy some of the peanuts my daughter Joanna had sent him. Put Neosporin and lotion on Daddy's feet. He shared more about his war experiences, and his visits with two friends whose first names both happen to be Ricky.

TUESDAY, FEBRUARY 21ST

Slept well. Life is sweet after a good night's rest. Wrote more of Daddy's memories. I always hear something I didn't know or had not written down. Love these times of seeing into the life of Papa.

We went to the west fence, hunting markers. There were not any. I hiked a long ways, so did Daddy, fortunately he had his cane. I called Sherry and she called the surveyor. He will send his crew out at 10:00 AM tomorrow to put a line of stakes so we can finish our fence.

We porch sat after lunch. Gave Mama her bath and "beauty treatment" regime, changed her gown and braided her hair.

Shaun came by and told us he was picked for jury duty. He fed the heifers then he and Daddy went to the Homeplace to get the beaver traps. I took the side-by-side and went to get a picture of the new black heifer to show Mama.

When I got back, Tam was here with groceries and piece of blueberry pie for me. Yum! I did mark two blocks on the quilt, but no actual quilting.

WEDNESDAY, FEBRUARY 22ND

Up at 4:21 AM. Read awhile, went back to sleep, and woke up at 7:00. Our usual morning. At 10, we went up to the west side, and the surveyors were just getting started. We went back after lunch and saw that they had put stakes every 150 feet all the way back to our back stake. Now we know where to put the new fence. Daddy is talking about taking off the t-post clips on the old fence so he can roll up the old wire and reuse it when we move the t-posts over … Sigh. I feel work coming on!

Daddy and I were outside in the afternoon – Daddy steadily eating those peanuts and me with binoculars, birdwatching. Saw a small flock of cedar waxwings eating the American holly berries, and a pair of tufted titmice; heard the call of a mourning dove. Daddy said *his* dad would say that it was time to plant corn when you heard the mourning dove.

Shaun on jury duty – didn't get out until 4:30 PM, back tomorrow for closing arguments. Talked to Joanna. My grandson Brandon has his assignment: the air craft carrier USS John F. Kennedy out of Norfolk, VA. So proud of him!

THURSDAY, FEBRUARY 23RD

Usual morning stuff, then on to Walmart. Back home and got a roast on to cook. While I was in town, Daddy had rounded up the tools we would need for that west fence.

Used hand clippers to clear a path so I could work on the bottom wire, then took it loose. Daddy pulled it up the hill by wrapping it around the trailer hitch knob on the truck. We did good! Got both the bottom and second wire pulled out. By then I was thirsty, and we had not brought water, so we went to the house for lunch. Rita, Jason and the kids came up looking for cross ties to make a raised bed for vegetables. We talked until daddy finished eating, and he went with them to get those crossties. Jason volunteered to come help Daddy with the fence in the morning.

Daddy and I went back up and got the next wire undone and pulled. I started on the top wire, then looked up. Daddy was fighting back the heifers at that open gate! Half of them came on in. I ripped through the briars as fast as I could and herded several back out. Daddy honked the truck horn and led the outside bunch to the barn. (They associate that horn with a handout) He put some feed out to keep them up there. Three heifers were still in the area where there was only one top wire to keep them from getting into the neighbor's pasture. I tried to get herd them back, but every time I would get them close to the gate, they turned and ran back. I prayed out loud for the Lord to send some angels to herd them toward the gate. Slowly, that is what happened. The heifers went through the opening, and I had to lean on the gate to catch my breath. I had made three passes toward that gate – high stepping through waist-high briars as fast as my legs would go. Shaun drove up and had a lot to say about shutting gates … sigh.

I went back to our work area and got the bucket of tools, gloves, cap, etc. Shaun got the lawn chair for Daddy and carried it to the side-by-side. After we returned to the house, Shaun stayed awhile and told us they'd wrapped up the trial. I was so tired – chasing heifers can take the starch right out of these 74 year-old legs.

FRIDAY, FEBRUARY 24TH

It rained early this morning, but Dad worked anyway. After I took Mama her breakfast, I finished taking the wire clips off the t-posts, then went back and got her meds and mixed up a batch of yeast rolls and set them out to rise. Went back up on the hill to check on the progress; Daddy and Jason had pulled up all the t-posts with the tractor.

One of the owners of the adjacent property, a man we'd known all our lives, came by to ask a few questions about the new fence line. He seemed good with what was going on. His sister called and wanted to talk. I enjoyed reconnecting with her. Danny went with us to the house and took a couple of pictures of our survey. It will only affect their land less than a half-acre. Daddy is trying to work out all the details of inheritance of the land before he passes.

SATURDAY, FEBRUARY 25TH

Daddy and I made a pasture run after he helped me fold my quilt and put it in its bag. It's a queen-sized quilt and requires help to fold it. We follow the pattern Daddy used when he folded drop cloths back in his painting career … works beautifully. We found the two new calves and determined that they are bulls. We admired Shaun's dragging of the lower pasture. It smoothed out the fire ant mounds, loosened the top layer of the soil, and will help the grass grow come spring.

Loaded up and headed home. Lovely, misty drive with redbuds and gill-over-the-ground in bloom, giving a purple beauty to the spring-like weather.

Tamra

FRIDAY, FEBRUARY 3RD

We all wondered, privately, on whose watch it would happen. Shaun and I were relieved it happened on Sherry's because when it comes to crises, especially involving Dad, Mel doesn't do very well. And so, at 2:00 am, last night, I got the call. Dad had fallen and everything changed.

I had a houseful too. It had been a chaotic day already. First, the ice storm had taken out Rita and Jason's electricity and they needed a warm place to stay, so they came over. Raylan and Athena were delighted to find Emelia and Addie also spending the night. Atlas, Rita's dog, came too.

Every bed and couch was full. Emelia did **not** want to go to sleep. I bet I put her in bed at least twenty times before she finally went out. I was exhausted. When the phone rang, I knew it wasn't good news.

Dad and Hobo take in some sun after raking leaves.

I jumped in my clothes and as quietly as I could, went out the door. Of course, Rita heard me and got up to see what was wrong. I told her what I knew, and then hurried down to Shaun's to pick him up on my way to Mom and Dad's. The house was dark. Banging on the door and yelling, "It's me, Tam! Dad has fallen and we've got to help get him up!" I saw a light come on almost immediately and heard Shaun coming through the house. Not wanting him to mistake me for a crazy person, since it was the middle of the night, I kept talking so he would recognize my voice. I found out that was a good thing, because he was still half asleep and had grabbed his gun on the way to the door. When he answered, I told him what had happened and he put on his shoes and we were at Mom and Dad's in less than five minutes. Poor Sherry met us at the door and filled us in. It took all of us to get Dad up and back into his bed. It was a sad thing to see Dad, always so strong and capable, rendered so helpless. Of course, at the time, we didn't think about it; we just did what we had to do to take care of him, but later that day, the gravity of the situation would sink in.

After I dropped Shaun off at his house, I stopped to get my mail before going to the house. In the chaos of the company arriving earlier, I'd forgotten to get it. I'll bet my neighbors were wondering why I was checking my mailbox at 3:00 am.

SATURDAY, FEBRUARY 4TH

When I got to Mom and Dad's to take over from Sherry, I could see she was beyond exhausted. I had hoped she would be able to take it easy and recover this next week, but once she got home, she started feeling worse and worse. Dad was still feeling the effects of his fall and over-medication, so he didn't do much, except read and sleep. I know Dad doesn't sleep well if he doesn't take a shower before bed, so I asked Shaun if he would come up and help Dad get a shower this evening. He was a little reluctant, I know that kind of thing makes him a bit uncomfortable, but to his credit, he agreed. I was so thankful for his help. It did make Dad feel much better and I think it was good for Shaun to help out that way.

Mom was pretty quiet most of the day, working on her puzzles and in her puzzle book. I helped her some and kept the fire in the fireplace going while Dad read. We stayed in the Big Room till after 10:00 pm reading and enjoying the fire. I was so thankful that Dad was better.

SUNDAY, FEBRUARY 5TH

Grateful for answered prayers; we all slept pretty good last night. Dad was up at 7:45 am and sat on the closed-in porch in the sun all morning. Got a text from Sherry – she is really sick now and even passed out this morning in the kitchen. Dad and I didn't go to church. Shaun came by on his way to check on Dad and then again when church was over. He said there weren't many there because of the flu and Covid. Larry C. dropped by for just a minute to check on Dad and that perked Dad up a bit. Mom shows signs of getting Dad's cold, so I started her on the Zicam and zinc routine I have Dad on. I hope it keeps her from getting too sick. Dad seems to be better.

MONDAY, FEBRUARY 6TH

None of us slept very well. I had asked Dad last night if he could get by without taking a shower since Shaun was visiting his son, Christopher. I didn't know if it would be a good idea for him to try it by himself since he was still not real steady on his feet. He did shave yesterday and that about wore him out. I had to get the stool for him to sit on, something he hasn't had to do in a long time. He didn't shower, but was up at 11:30 pm, 2:30 am, and for good at 5:30 am, I know, because I was up too. He declared this morning that he was taking a shower before bed tonight! Later by the fireside he said, "I went for two months in a foxhole on Iwo Jima, not bathing, not even changing my socks, and now I can't sleep unless I take a shower every night…I've gotten old and soft!" Mel got here about 10:30 and I filled her in on everything. Showed her the cold treatment routine, food, etc. before I left for a dentist appointment.

SATURDAY, FEBRUARY 11TH

My week was spent taking care of Emelia, getting groceries, meds for Mom and Dad, helping Addie with her school work, cleaning, and trying to play catch up with my work. Marc was busy with his Mom and Dad, taking them to doctor appointments in Dallas and staying with them a couple of nights.

This morning, Mel gave me the rundown on Dad's feet treatment, etc. before she left. He is feeling more like his old-self again and I am glad to see it. It was cold and rainy most of the day, so Dad was content to sit by the fire and read. Shaun came by to talk with Dad and check on Mom. She is feeling better too, but is not ready to admit it yet.

I did some washing, cooked lunch, and changed the sheets, and had time to read and write some. It was a nice quiet day. When Shaun came by to visit, Dad had gotten up and was walking through the dining room all hunched over. I said, "Straighten up, Dad!" We had just been talking about people getting all bent over when they get old. Dad went to leaning back, trying to walk straighter and almost got off balance. Shaun was behind him and said, "You'd better look out, bending over too far. One of these days you're gonna walk right out from under your face!" I got tickled and so did Dad.

SUNDAY, FEBRUARY 12TH

The eastern sky this morning was ribboned with purple and rose-colored clouds as the daylight slowly made its way across the horizon…crowding out the night and the bright stars that sparkled when I first went outside. I fed Hobo and checked the temperature – 28 degrees. Looks like Dad might get some porch sitting time later today. Dad said he dreamed about Aunt Eva and Aunt Babe (his older sisters) last night. They were broken down on the side of the road in an old brown car that was smoking. He said he never even got to talk to them before he woke up.

We went to church today and Dad was so glad to see everyone. On the way, we were laughing about what Shaun had said about him straightening up yesterday. When he went into the foyer at church, he stopped and straightened up before heading to his Sunday School room. He had a smile on his face the whole way. He told me later, coming home, that "it sure was good to talk to the boys." When I asked him about his Sunday School lesson on the wanderings of the children of Israel, Dad said, "They drug those poor Jews around something awful."

Before the Super Bowl, Dad and I had a good visit at lunch. We talked about our trips to Mobile, his with military reunions and mine with press trips, and the things we enjoyed and learned about the area. I love talking with Dad, but sometimes it can wear me out. I wish he would wear his hearing aid more, because we have to practically shout to be understood.

Mom was pretty pitiful today; her right knee is giving her trouble. I hope it doesn't cause her to fall. The sun finally came out late this afternoon and Dad wanted to sit out on the porch. I brought a throw to wrap around him and then talked Mom into joining him for a little while. It wasn't real warm, in the sixties, but I wrapped her in some blankets and she was fine.

We couldn't get the Super Bowl on Dad's TV, so I took him over to our house to watch the game with Marc. I fixed him up with his foot elevated and got some snacks for them before I went back over to stay with Mom. I forgot his nightly pill, so I had to run back over with it before I could stay put. I missed most of the game, but it was ok. I did get to see the last few minutes when I went over later to pick Dad up. It was an exciting game they said and we were all happy the Chiefs won with that last minute field goal. When we got back to their house, Dad took a shower and went to bed. After checking on Mom one more time, I retired too. It was a long day, but a good one.

MONDAY, FEBRUARY 13TH

Sherry brought some flowers and a card for Dad to give Mom for Valentine's Day tomorrow. I was helping her arrange them when Dad walked in the kitchen to say hello. He asked Sherry if she was still mad at him for giving her the disease (his cold). She laughed and said no. Mom isn't feeling as perky as she was yesterday…I hope she's better by tomorrow.

TUESDAY, FEBRUARY 14TH

I stopped by after WMA to check on Mom and Dad. Ricky R. and two other guys were there to interview Dad. They all asked about the book, so I went over to the house and brought copies over for all three. Dad seemed to really enjoy their visit. Mom was not doing well; I hope she feels better by tomorrow.

WEDNESDAY, FEBRUARY 15TH

Dad didn't give Mom her flowers and card till today. She seemed pleased with the gift, and Dad was glad to see her feeling better. My world has turned upside down since this past weekend. Caleb needs to find a cheaper place to live; his rent is going up over three hundred dollars a month. So, until he finds a place, I told him he could move in with us. Having your 34 year-old son move back in is a big step, and I was hoping it was the right thing to do. You want to help your kids out, but sometimes you don't know if it is helping or hindering. Hopefully, it will be a positive thing for all of us.

THURSDAY, FEBRUARY 16TH

Spent yesterday and today cleaning out Rita's old room so Caleb could put his stuff in there. He will be moving this weekend. It was a strange feeling, moving out her bed, dresser, and other things – they have been there since she left for college over fifteen years ago. I had entertained the idea of turning that room into my art studio, but thank goodness, I hadn't followed through. Maybe I will do that after Caleb moves out…who knows?

SATURDAY, FEBRUARY 18TH

Wanted to get over to Mom and Dad's early so Sherry could leave and go hold that new grand girl of hers, she hasn't been able to hold her yet because she was sick with that awful cold. I know she is as excited as she can be! I am happy for her. It was a quiet day with the folks, and I am more and more grateful when those days happen.

SUNDAY, FEBRUARY 19TH

The 78th anniversary of the Battle of Iwo Jima is today. I recorded Dad telling a bit about the morning that he went on shore. I posted it on the Instagram account I started about him and the book we are working on. Hopefully, it will get people interested in that part of history. At church, Dad told his Sunday School class about landing on the beach that third morning. Bro. Bert said after church that he "could have listened to him for hours."

Sherry finally gets a granddaughter! Knoxlynn is so tiny and sweet

Dad and I didn't sleep too well last night, so I tried to take a siesta this afternoon, but it didn't work, my phone kept ringing. Shaun and Caleb moved his stuff this afternoon. He brought Leia, his cat, and she was yowling because she didn't like being shut up in his room. She had to stay put until he could bring her litter box and because I didn't want her and Maxine fighting. My poor geriatric cat is not doing well, and I don't think she'd hold up too good in a cat fight.

Dad said this evening while he was sitting on the hearth, "I haven't completely recovered from my sickness. I haven't got my strength back." I suggested that maybe tomorrow, if the weather was good, he could take a stroll outside and maybe blow off the patio with his leaf blower. He said that sounded like a good idea. We could hardly talk, because Mom's TV was so loud. She was watching *Highway to Heaven* and she can't understand what they are saying, even at that extreme decibel. I asked her why she was watching it, if she can't understand what they're saying; she shrugged and said, "It's something to do." Dad has read all the books we had on his Kindle, so I downloaded several more today.

MONDAY, FEBRUARY 20TH

Finally moved Mom's puzzle table back into the Big Room this morning, I had moved it into her room when Dad was sick. She protested, but I said she needed to walk more and keep moving, so she pouted a bit and sounded pitiful. She said, "Well, I guess I have to do what y'all tell me." (Like I was ordering her to the gallows or something.) This evening when I went over to give Shaun the blueberry pie I made him, she was happily working away at the puzzle table.

SATURDAY, FEBRUARY 25TH

I had Emelia all day today and she had a ball. She followed Dad every step he took. It was so cute. She had on one of Josh's old red hoodies and she looked like a little redbird following Dad around over the pasture. Caleb came and picked her up this evening after work. Dad enjoyed her company…said she never stopped chattering the entire time! Emelia and I also made a batch of cookies today, and she told Dad about all the thistles "we" dug up yesterday down in the bottom by the creek. When I put Emelia down for a nap and fixed Mom's lunch, I missed Dad and went looking for him. I found him up in the west woods with his chainsaw. He was cutting some small trees that were on the fence line. He waits until we are busy, then he wanders off to do what he knows we will try to talk him out of doing. He was so tired by the time I got there, I had to literally push him up the hill to the truck. I carried the saw too. I don't know what he would have done if I hadn't showed up…sat down and crawled the rest of the way, I guess.

Dad was in a talkative mood tonight, so after he took a shower and I doctored his feet and dried his hair, he reminisced for about an hour before turning in. I enjoyed listening to him talk about old times, people he worked for over the years and those that worked for him. I am always amazed at his ability to recall the smallest details of events and places. It is a gift. After looking at his feet one more time before he turned in, I told him he is going to have to do something about his right leg and foot; it is not getting better.

SUNDAY, FEBRUARY 26TH

This Sunday was weird because Shaun was gone all day with Ricky and Caleb to a truck show in Conroe. We missed him. Dad was fixing his coffee this morning, when I came into the kitchen. He waved me ahead to the coffee pot and said, "You go ahead and pour yours since you don't put anything in it and I'll decorate mine up when you get through." Later, after breakfast, I asked him if he needed anything and he picked up a tangerine and started peeling it saying, "I'll jerk the hide off this and eat it."

Dad and I went to church, then changed clothes and went up to feed the heifers, since Shaun wasn't there to do it. Lunch, gassed up the truck, and then went by the Homeplace to see if the beaver had thrown the traps. Dad was able to maneuver onto that narrow jetty close to the beaver dam and use the shovel he'd brought to lift up the traps and move them. Pretty amazing balancing act for a fellow nearly one hundred years old!

When we left, Rita, Jason, and the kids were just coming back from the circus in Tyler. The kids were wide-eyed and so excited to tell us about the elephants. When we got home, we settled in for the evening. I checked on Mom, got her lunch and helped her work on a puzzle. I doctored Dad's feet again tonight and he stayed up till Shaun came by and told us all about the truck show; sounds like they had fun. Dad was in a talkative mood again after Shaun left, and I would like to have recorded some of what he told me, but Mom's TV was so loud, even with the door shut, that you couldn't have understood anything.

MONDAY, FEBRUARY 27TH

This morning Jason got here at 8:15; Dad was raring to go, with everything already loaded in the truck. They were working on the west fence again. Before I left, I fixed Mom's breakfast and set her meds out so she could take them later. Sherry will be here soon.

IT IS NOT A *Competition*. JUST BECAUSE ONE FAMILY MEMBER SEEMS TO DO MORE, DOESN'T MEAN YOU HAVE TO "UP THE ANTE." *Everyone* CONTRIBUTES IN THEIR OWN WAY.

MARCH

This is a tug-of-war month in East Texas. Spring is hard at work, bringing warmer temperatures and rain, coaxing cheery daffodils and tiny Quaker Ladies out of their winter sleep. On the backside of the calendar, Old Man Winter is pulling back for all he's worth, trying to make us believe it's still February. Honestly, I root for the old guy – I am always sorry to see winter leave, even if it's been a very long one by Texas standards.

When I was a kid, I remember a melancholy would come over me as we marched towards April. I couldn't explain it; I just felt a sense of loss. Spring does have its own beauty and I have fond memories of watching tiny baby leaves sprouting from the bare branches and of finding bluebird or mockingbird nests full of freshly laid eggs.

This month usually brought a different rhythm to our household, one that seemed to lean forward on eager tiptoes to see what is next. Growing up, it was a busy time of plowing, planting, clearing pastures and cleaning barns of winter clutter. It also meant the end of haying the cows and the start of searches for spring calves.

It is still much the same, even though we don't do as much work by hand anymore. It is easier than it used to be, but now that we are older, even easy isn't as easy anymore.

Dad still supervises the daily operations, but he is turning over more and more responsibilities to us. He, of course, always has the final say. Looking back, I remember how we all looked to Dad for the direction our family would take in all that we did. He was and is the undisputed leader. This is as it should be.

I hope we have a long spring this year and it stays somewhat cool until after Memorial Day – usually wishful thinking in Texas. Sweating is not something I enjoy doing. Some years we go straight from winter to summer in about three weeks, so I guess I'd better 'gird my loins' just in case.

Sherry

WEDNESDAY, MARCH 1ST

68° - too warm for a fire, even by Pop's and Mom's standards. After getting everyone situated, I drove to Tyler and bought some preemie clothes for my granddaughter (they look **so** tiny) and a few items to use when I change out the mantel decorations for spring. When I got back, Pop and Jason had finished fence work for the day. I'm glad they're only working until noon – that's more than enough for Pop.

Dad gives Hobo a scratch while working on Parker's Flat Stanley project.

After lunch, Shaun came by and visited before going up to drag the pasture – spreading out that free fertilizer produced by the cows. After he'd been gone awhile, Pop realized he'd forgotten to tell Shaun about some lengths of barbed wire on the ground near the west fence. I tore up there in the truck to warn him. Too late! That drag had caught two of the wires, and they were snaking behind it for thirty yards. Didn't hurt the tractor or the drag, but it sure didn't do that wire any good.

Tam came over to gather some daffodils from the cemetery, but first she decided to close the two air circulation hatches under the house – it's supposed to rain tonight. When she walked around back, she could hear Mom hollering for someone. Pop and I had been sitting on the patio and couldn't hear her. Tam and I both raced in Mom's room and found her in the bathroom. She hadn't fallen or anything, but she needed help. She said she'd been hollering for an hour. (I'm sure it felt that way, but Pop and I had not been outside that long.) She'd taken some laxative pills, and they had worked in a spectacular fashion. So, we had to take care of the aftermath … poor Mom kept apologizing for our having to do that for her, but she cleaned *us* up plenty of times when we were small.

THURSDAY, MARCH 2ND

Just a bit of rain in the wee hours, but the weather prophets predict more for later. Pop helped me get the spring mantel scarf situated, then watched as I gathered some items to put on it: two green glass baskets, a clear one, and two of Mom's glass bells with porcelain birds on them. I put the fake Easter eggs in the baskets, then added green candles in clear holders, also the small cross with "He Is Risen" on it. A pretty spring-like display. Mom and Dad both enjoy having something different to look at for each season of the year.

The mesh fireplace screen had come loose at the bottom, so I found a roll of thin black wire in the shop and basically "whip stitched" it back in place. Then Pop and I worked on the fence line, cutting back those awful briars and vines. Very little breeze in the woods, and humid to boot, creating sweaty work. Stopped at noon. When I put the food on the table and prayed over it, we tore into it like we'd been working in the field all day.

Cleaned up the kitchen, talked to Melanie, and was helping Mom with a jigsaw puzzle when Pop walked in and announced that he was going back to "piddle around" in the woods (his code phrase for working without us fussing about it). I replied," Not without me!" We worked until about 5:00 – poor Pop barely made it to the truck. He had been using the chain saw on the bigger brush, while I used the clippers. He'd worked his way down the hill and had to walk back up carrying that saw. When he got back to where I was, I traded him the light clippers for the chain saw and carried it to the truck … he was about used up by then. Back at the house, I figured we needed some coffee and a snack to bring us back to life. Checked on Mom and took care of other chores up until midnight. A thunderstorm came through about 11:00 – enjoyed hearing that rain.

FRIDAY, MARCH 3RD

Groan … Pop got up at 5:15 … sure wish I could get some of last night back. Ran through the morning chores, well, more like *dragged* through them. We're supposed to pen the cows late this afternoon, so I went ahead and dressed in my work clothes. Asked Mom and Pop to guess how much rain we got last night before I went out to check the gauge. Mom got it right on the money, and Pop quipped, "If you'd told me how much, I would have guessed it right." Ha!

Jason arrived and put the chain back on Pop's saw; then they headed to the fence work. There is a brisk, cold wind, but it won't bother them much down in the woods. After lunch a lunch of beans and cornbread, Pop said he was going to lie down and "straighten out his frame." He slept for two hours.

Mom tried out Pop's Kindle – I wanted to make sure she could use it without getting frustrated. Now that she likes it, I will order a bigger one for Pop, and Mom can use this one. She doesn't need as large a font as Pop, so it should be perfect for her. She's a fast reader, so she'll burn through books quickly. We'll have to remind her that these Kindle books aren't all free like library books.

After Pop woke up, he asked if I was ready to "cowboy," and here we went. The first chore was getting the heifers into the hay barn enclosure; that was pretty easy since we had cubes to entice them. Next was getting Sancho into the cemetery pasture – those 6 foot-plus horns are dangerous. He may not intend any harm, but if he swings his head around, and you happen to be in the "sweep," it could be bad. He was happy to go in that pasture, but a cow was hard on his heels, and we barely kept her from going in as well. Last, we had to get the rest of the herd into the largest pen and cut out the smaller bull and a cow and some calves Pop wants to haul to the sale tomorrow. We got that done fairly quickly, with neither of us getting hurt – always a plus.

Just as we finished and got in the truck, Shaun arrived and was surprised that we were through. He was going to put out some hay for the cows, and Pop asked me to tell him to check the gate on the west side when he finished haying (There are two). I asked, "Which one? The one into the woods?" (He and Jason had been in and out of that gate all week, and with part of the fence on the other side of it taken down, cows could get out.) Pop answered in an exasperated tone, "No, Sherry, the one up by the road." I got a little annoyed and said, "Well, Pop, there are gates all over this place!" He could tell I was a bit miffed because he said something about my not being able to read his mind. I told him I'd had plenty of practice, but it hasn't helped.

Anyway, it just irked me because I was the one helping him get all that cattle moving done … I didn't need a medal or anything; it just would have been nice not to be spoken to as if I were dimwitted. But, nobody is perfect. That's where grace and mercy come in. I love the verse, "And be ye kind one to another, tender-hearted, forgiving one another, even as God for Christ's sake has forgiven you," Ephesians 4:32.

SATURDAY, MARCH 4TH

As soon as Tam arrived this morning, Pop started putting his coat on, but Tam said she needed another cup of coffee before we faced the cattle, and we also needed to wait for Shaun to arrive. He came shortly but set up the power washer first so he could clean the cattle trailer as soon as they got back from the sale barn. It doesn't do to let all that cow manure stay on your equipment.

Up at the cow lot, we had to do-si-do different groups. While Shaun was airing up the trailer tires, Tam and I had to cut two runty heifers out to join the sale-barn group and then move two other calves into a pen to feed out for future hamburgers. One gate chain had broken, and we'd tied it shut earlier. Before we even started working the heifers, Pop instructed us to untie the gate first. Really? Tam and I looked at each other and burst out laughing. I told Tam, "I thought we'd just let them smack into the gate and see if they could jump it." I guess in Pop's mind, we're still seven or eight instead of 63 and 72. (I probably do that to my grown sons from time to time.) I remember years ago when Mom was supervising us "girls" in the kitchen – we were in our 40s and 50s at the time. Whatever we were cooking required a two minute boil, and Mom pointed to the giant pocket-watch style clock above the refrigerator and said, "Now when the second hand goes around two times, that will be two minutes." We nearly fell in the floor laughing. It's been a favorite story for years.

After the cattle were loaded and Pop and Shaun headed to the sale barn, Tam and I went to the house so I could load up and leave. Looking forward to seeing Little Sprout!

SATURDAY, MARCH 11TH

Pop's new Kindle arrived. I charged it up, and downloaded some books for Mom. (Apparently, they show up on both Kindles.) This new one is a bit different, but I think Pop will adjust to it easily.

MONDAY, MARCH 13TH

Before I left for J'ville, Melanie called. She was a little upset with Tam and Shaun. Pop had been talking about the work he wanted to get done this week when I would be there. Tam was afraid I would have to work too hard the whole time, so she was talking to Pop about that when Shaun drove up and chimed in. Poor Pop – hope he didn't feel ganged up on. Melanie is also feeling anxious about that boundary fence and any fallout from that, plus the writing we are doing for the book idea Tam has and the typing it entails – both fairly time consuming. As Christians, we aren't supposed to be anxious for anything, but easier said than done at times.

When I did arrive, Pop and I went to town: feed store, pharmacy, and grocery store. We also stopped by Shaun's job downtown – an old building that is getting rescued for a new life as an upscale antique store. It will be something special when completed. Back to the house and the usual routines. I brought a book with me to read to Dad, even though the target audience is younger folks. He loves history and has read a lot about Texas, but he also likes the personal touch of diaries. This one, *The Alamo Diary of Lucinda Lawrence*, is a work of historical fiction that puts a human face on the time leading up to the fight for Texas's independence. Because he's a bit deaf and doesn't want to wear his hearing aid except for church on Sunday, I sit right beside him to read. That way, I can also see when his eyes slam shut, and it's time to quit.

TUESDAY, MARCH 14TH

Saw Pop's light on at 5:30, so I fixed the coffee and made a fire, but found out he had gotten back in bed, so I had a long, relaxing fireside time. Good thing because we are about out of firewood, which means a trek up on the hill for more. When we did go later on, I took some "Flat Stanley" photos for Parker's school project. (This idea came from a children's book about a kid who becomes a paper version of himself and has lots of adventures. The students each make their own Flat Stanley, send him to a grandparent who takes pictures with him, and sends the pictures back so the child can do a "Show and Tell." I did one last year, but this one is supposed to be just about Pop because of his upcoming 100th birthday.) There is a cold wind blowing out of the northeast, so no other outside projects for us today.

Made some maple pecan cupcakes and gave Shaun some when he came over to feed the heifers. Pop rode up with him, and they discovered that the bull had gone through the fence and was in the west pasture with the heifers – that gives us our project for tomorrow. I'd texted Tam that I had cupcakes. When she came over, she didn't seem her usual cheerful self – it turns out that I had hurt her feelings by not telling her promptly that I was indeed going to be able to keep my new grandbaby when her mom has to return to work. I really wanted to keep the baby, but I knew my being gone would create more work for Melanie and Tam. They had both assured me that they would love to give me that special time with baby girl, but I wasn't sure how it would play out for a while since they were also on a daycare waiting list.

Also, I hadn't talked too much about it because I was afraid it had been so long since I'd kept a little one, I'd forgotten how. The "what ifs" kept trying to get in my head. When it finally became clear that I was going to get to keep Little Bit until the end of school, I told Melanie, but neglected to tell Tam. She had wanted to share in the joy as soon as possible. I apologized to her for dropping the ball, and we talked it out. I have to try harder to make sure I communicate with both my sisters, and that we include brother in our info as well.

WEDNESDAY, MARCH 15TH

Doozy of a day. After a bunch of routine inside chores, Pop and I bundled up for outside jobs. He spread the dirt around in the front yard where he'd dug up that althea tree that had split. I gathered the household trash and burned it. Then we headed up to the woods where he and Jason had been working to get our fence fixing supplies. I waded through a sea of briars to the post pile and handed several over to Dad so he wouldn't have to stumble through that stuff. Then we cut some wire from what they'd taken off the old fence and headed to the stretch behind the equipment shed. When we got there, Pop said it looked as if the bull had been sticking his head between the wires to reach some grass and just walked on through since the posts were pretty far apart. The wires were loose, but not broken, so we just drove in two extra posts and clipped the barbed wires to them to snug up the sag.

The next trouble spot was way over behind the pond. A short section was leaning way to the north and three metal posts were bent to flinders – Shaun had gotten a little too close with that drag. Made the repairs, then drove down the line and found several broken wires. Pop stretched those tight and pieced them together. Then I walked down toward the corner to check the rest of the fence while Pop lay flat out on the ground in the sun to rest. I had brought Flat Stanley along, so I got a photo of him and Pop resting. (He is such a good sport!) I told him the top wire had come off the corner tree, but he said we'd take care of it later.

Back to the house for lunch. Around 3:30, he mentioned getting some trees and limbs off the hog wire fences down near the creek. The last storm had made a real mess. We headed down, cleared the fences, drove back up to the fence we'd worked on earlier and fixed the last wire, then up to the barn to feed the heifers. Pop was worn out! I made coffee, closed the hatches against the forecast rain, emptied the ash bucket, and finally sat down with coffee and a cupcake. When Shaun, Caleb, and Emelia came by, I took her on a short walk. Usual nightly meds and so forth. Read to Pop. What a day … Beware the ides of March.

THURSDAY, MARCH 16TH

I woke up needing a nap, but dove into the routine chores plus fence fixing. Got a nice rain late in the day. Weird to think that this is my last week here for a couple of months! I'm looking forward to keeping my grandbaby, but also feeling bad for my sisters who will have to take my days as well as theirs. They are so very sweet for doing this, but willingness doesn't trump the fact that it's an extra burden on them. And Tam found out today that she will need surgery to repair her eye. I know she is concerned about that. I will try to make this time up to them somehow. What a blessing to have siblings to help.

FRIDAY, MARCH 17TH

Pop's light came on at 5:00 this St, Patrick's Day morning. Scurried to get the coffee started, a fire built, and Hobo fed; then saw that Pop's light was off again … he'd gotten back in bed! Sheesh, I could have slept in. But I did enjoy having time to read some Psalms and drink coffee in front of the fire.

After we had launched into the day, Shaun came to get Pop to pick up an excavator they rented so they can tear up that beaver dam at the Homeplace before the entire lower pasture becomes a lake. Awhile after they left, Shaun called to ask me to drive to the rental place and get a part he needed – the previous renter had broken a pin on the excavator and hadn't told anyone when he returned it – he'd just put a wire in its place. . So far, the wire was holding, but Shaun didn't have much confidence that it would last. When I got there, the fellow at the desk appeared very uninterested in helping me, but I finally got two pins and drove to the Homeplace. Neither fit.

Back to the rental place for another. Back to Shaun who had found a huge nail that had held while he worked on the sides of the creek, or what *should* be the creek if it weren't dammed up.

When I'd left earlier, Pop had been in the truck out of the cold wind, but he couldn't see what Shaun was doing, so he crossed the creek on the pipe bridge and was sheltering beside a cedar tree. I grabbed a folding chair out of my Jeep and toted it to him so he could sit down in the sun. He was bundled up pretty well, including his "fur trapper's hat," and was determined to see the show of that water gushing into the creek bed, and gush it did … a torrent of red, muddy water pouring out of the break in the dam. The water that had backed up into the surrounding pasture land began to recede toward the main channel, so it took a while before the torrent slowed. Shaun hollered for me to get their traps off the T-post before he tore that part of the dam up. It took several good yanks to release them from the debris.

Pop was tired and cold, so I drove my Jeep to the bridge to pick him up, then to the top of the hill so he could get in the truck and ride back home with Shaun. They brought the excavator to the house and unloaded it near the north pond. Pop and I went with Shaun to hay, but just sat in the side by side. When he drove by us on his second trip, he said he'd left the big barn doors open, and the heifers were probably in there – calves are notoriously curious. Shaun was right, when Pop and I drove around the corner to the barn, the ones inside took off. One turned the corner too fast and slid down on her behind … too funny!

SATURDAY, MARCH 18TH

Tried to take care of a lot of the household chores before Tam arrives later – her eyes still haven't returned to normal from being dilated yesterday, and she's still wearing sunglasses inside. Pop wanted me to help him get a different horizontal bar on the big tractor … the bar where the bucket and hay forks attach. When Pop and Jason were working in the woods, it got bent and fell off. (Pop is fearless on the tractor, but the machine is sometimes the worse for it.) Pop thought he had one in the barn that he'd previously straightened. The bar we found wasn't exactly straight, but he thought he could fix it. His idea was pretty good: lay the bar (bend up) in the trough where the huge barn door slides open, and hit it with a sledgehammer. Of course we had to brace it so that it wouldn't move. After sliding one board in, Pop told me to get another. He just glanced at the one I chose, and told me to get a ¾ inch board. Well, I brought *both* back because I knew the board he wanted was too thick. Sure enough, it was. I just bent down and put in the thinner board I had picked earlier – a perfect fit. Pop just grunted.

He grabbed the sledgehammer and whacked the bar, but was also whacking the concrete edges of the door trough. I know it bothers him constantly that he can't see well enough to do chores that would have been child's play for him only a few years ago. But platitudes are no use, so I just have to stand silently by and pray for small victories. He did get the bar somewhat straighter, and put it on the tractor, using Pop's know-how and my eyesight.

There is no way Pop could have done all that by himself, and I was pleased to be able to help him. Of course, he wasn't finished. He wanted to get a bucket of dirt to fill in some holes in the barn road, which meant changing from the hay forks to the bucket. It's pretty interesting when Pop is driving the tractor straight at you so you can motion to him where the tabs are he has to hook on. I think about his not being able to tell who someone is until they get pretty close and remember when he straddled the tractor over a stump he didn't see. Saints preserve us.

MONDAY, MARCH 20TH

Tam asked for Dr. J's number – Pop has a suspicious spot under the little toe on his bad foot. Tam said it looked the same way her husband's foot problem started out, and he had a bad time getting over that. Later she said she'd gotten Pop an appointment for Wednesday. I'm glad it's getting a look early on. This may be the jump start for surgery.

WEDNESDAY, MARCH 22ND

Sure enough, Pop has run out of options on his foot. He has a surgery date on April 12. I can't believe I won't be there, but I'm keeping Knoxlynn for

Stu and Ashley. Oh, to be in two places at once. But God will be there, and He's watched over Daddy for nearly a hundred years, and He isn't going to stop now. Tam still doesn't have the surgery date for her eyes – I know she's dreading that. I pray that she has an excellent result from it.

MARCH 27TH - 31ST

On my first full day of keeping baby girl, I thought I was going to have to turn in my Grandma card. The afternoon was especially tough – don't know if she had acid reflux or gas or both. By the time Stu arrived, I was pretty frazzled. They'd had a tough time last night themselves, and had been worried about what kind of day I'd have. But things got better and better during the week, so thankful! This was Stu's and Bill's birthday week, back-to-back on the 28th and 29th – kind of low key celebrations since everyone's working. On Friday, I headed to Jacksonville so I could help with the heifer round up the next day.

Melanie

MONDAY, MARCH 6TH

Leaving my house to go to the folks' is a race to get everything done in order to be gone for almost 6 days. Before I left, the grandsons come by for ice for their fishing trip.

Beautiful drive. Spring is bursting out so early this year. Arrived around 10:00 a.m. Went up to check the progress in the fence. Jason and Daddy are at the furthest point they are going. The rest of the fence will stay where is has always been.

Came on to the house and fixed lunch, then Tam came over and blew off the carport, and I braided her hair. After lunch, I grabbed the binoculars, pen, and paper and walked over the pasture to look at the new calves (eight now) to determine their sex. I heard a cow bawling below the hill and headed that way. Turned out, #12 had a calf, but something had happened; it was dead. Couldn't figure it out. It was a pretty charcoal gray calf and perfectly formed. Sad. Shaun and I fed the heifers and put out salt and mineral. Headed to get the dead calf so we could dispose of it, but the cow was ready to fight me, so we decided to wait until she went for water or hay and sneak it away.

Laundry and bills. Mama puzzling. Jason is coming back in the morning with his chainsaw to cut a small red oak that is leaning over the new fence and might later damage it by falling across it.

TUESDAY, MARCH 7TH

Daddy and I were up at 5:00 a.m. Coffee, fed the cat, breakfast. Shaun arrived at 7:15 a.m. The cow bawling over the dead calf had kept him up most of the night. He was tense, so I massaged his shoulder and neck. That helped. After he left for his job, Daddy got ready for fence and tree cutting. Jason arrived with his chainsaw and a pretty bouquet of flowers and card from Rita and the kids for Mama and Daddy. Did all my Mama things: breakfast, meds, weight, blood pressure.

Sancho gives Dad and Flat Stanley a once-over.

I set up my quilt, tools, and threads, got lunch going, washed up and took pictures of Daddy and Jason. When they came in for lunch, Daddy said his eyes went dark for a bit. Scary! We ate lunch, then he stretched out on his bed and slept for two hours.

When Daddy woke up and got coffee, I made a cup of tea, and we sat outside and enjoyed the beauty of the day. Shaun arrived and we went up and checked on #8 and her new calf; it's a heifer.

Got back to the house and I parched the last of the JoAnna peanuts. Dad ate a bowl full. He drank about four glasses of water today, a victory on the water front! Usual night routine except Mama had to put on a lighter gown. The winter one was too hot. Got to quilt a little before I began to nod off.

Rita texted me late and said Jason was sick and would not be able to help Pawpaw. I texted Tam, "Looks like I will be Papa's "Girl Friday" on Wednesday. Lol."

WEDNESDAY, MARCH 8TH

Got morning meal made and dishes done before we took off to the west forest. Daddy and I pounded in 7 T-posts and put the top wire on. Started to piece the 2nd wire but needed some extra, so we had to pull the wire from the pasture. It was a tangled mess because brother ran over it with the pasture drag. We got 2 strands attached to the truck hitch and pulled all of it down through the gate. Finally got enough to do the 2nd wire on the fence. Green briars tangled our feet and made for a long morning.

We went to the house at 11:00 so I could fix our stew, cornbread, and salad. Dad and I sat outside a while and rested. Another warm, misty, sun in-and-out spring day. After the dishes were done, I asked Mom about washing her hair. When we were all done, I got her outside on the front porch and air dried it as I combed it. Mom called Aunt Aline; it is snowing in Iowa. Mama told her their yard was covered in little white flowers, wisteria blooming, and warm breezes blowing.

Later, Daddy and I take off to town to run some errands and got to wave as we passed Shaun coming home from work. When we got back, Tam was arranging a big bouquet of yellow tulips she'd picked at the cemetery.

Shaun got back from looking at jobs in Tyler and stopped to talk to Daddy. I was so tired I didn't move from my spot at the kitchen table, writing in my journal. Shaun came back through and spotted the chocolate cake Tam had brought me and asked about it, so I gave it to him. Nightly rituals done. Daddy read to me from his book on Bob Hope. I dozed off here and there, and finally went to bed.

THURSDAY, MARCH 9TH

Woke up around 2:40 a.m. There was a fluttering amongst the sacks in the corner of the room. Turned on the lamp, and saw that a crane fly had found his way into the room and was caught in the plastic sacks. I dispatched the little critter and climbed back in bed, but no going to sleep. Sigh. Got my devotional books and Bible, read awhile, then tried again. Woke up to the sound of Daddy making coffee. I started to the porch fridge to get my energy drink, but Hobo would not let me pass without notice. She jumped on the window screen with both front paws and claws. Okay! I swerved around to feed her first. What was I thinking?

I got Mama all set before we left for Daddy's eye appointment. I drove slowly so we could enjoy the misty muted spring beauty. Yellows, whites, and purple in the mist like a Monet painting. I let Daddy out in front of the eye clinic and went to park the car. Got inside and couldn't find Daddy anywhere. The lady at the receiving desk said, "Mrs. McAnally, they were ready for him, and he is back there getting his shot." I didn't correct her on the Mrs. McAnally. I just sat and waited.

Back at home, I did some cleaning. Pam, my friend and neighbor in our younger years, may come to visit tomorrow. She wants to ask what Daddy can tell her about her dad and grandfather. They were lifelong friends and neighbors of Mama and Daddy's. I started making Daddy a pineapple cream pie, one of his favorites. Rita texted that they all have COVID. That's terrible. Sure hope we don't come down with it. Jason was here two days helping Daddy with the west line fence, but he and Dad were out in the open most of the time. Shaun and I fed the heifer and took a short ride. A weather change is coming—blue cloud in the north.

Dad and I sat in the sunroom and heard the low rumble of thunder. At 8:35 p.m., the electricity went off. I carefully went to my bedroom, got that small flashlight, took care of the meds, and made sure the light switches were off in case the electricity came on during the night. Used the flashlight to work on my Sunday school lesson and read a while.

FRIDAY, MARCH 10TH

We were up around 6:00 a.m. after a wild night. It seemed like it rained all night and might have hailed. Tam confirmed that it hailed big time – she thought it would break her living room windows. Checked the rain gauge and it held 2 8/10" of rain. Daddy was reminiscing about Raydean and Rufus, Pam's parents, since she is coming at 10:00 a.m. Got Mama ready for company. Braided her hair, put a pretty denim dress on her and some makeup. Pam got here and we had a delightful 2.5 hour visit. Talked of the past, what she and husband Vernon were doing, their farm, and so forth. She asked about my kids and grandkids. Tam had come over to put Daddy's hearing aids in, and Pam told her how much she liked her book: *A Blessed Life*.

I fixed our lunch, took three puzzle pictures of Mama, and cleaned up the dishes, I'm having more chest pains. Need to get an appointment with my doctor; I think it is stress.

Later, Daddy and I went back up to the west fence for a while. Shaun drove up and helped for a bit before feeding the heifers, moving some tin, and haying the cows. I took pictures of the black jack oak that blew over in the pasture close to the mineral trough. It seems a bit odd to lose these icons of our skyline. They have been our old friends for a lifetime. The large althea in the front yard was felled by the same storm.

Dad stacks wood...with a little help from Flat Stanley.

Up at 5:30 the next morning. Usual flurry of activity before heading home. On the way, I made contact with my other life and heard the latest: new baby chicks, "new" old truck for grandson to drive to school, etc.

MONDAY, MARCH 20TH

The first day of spring, and it 28 degrees. Had to make a fast trip by the Ford place before heading to the folks' – my key fob is not working right. Beautiful drive. Spring started the last of February. Now, many trees have leaves on them. Dogwood and red buds were already at their peak the first week of March. Daddy is in his sunny spot on the side porch. Shaun is finishing spraying off the flatbed trailer after returning the dump trailer and excavator. He took Papa and me on a tour of all he had accomplished with those two machines. He filled eroded places all over the ranch. Erosion is the constant enemy on rolling hills. He also broke apart two beaver dams at the Homeplace to release water down stream and prevent flooding of the lower area.

Back at the house Dad put the last sticks of wood in the fire, so we headed up to the woodshed and loaded a good bit of firewood, speculating and hoping this would be the last load for this spring cool snap. Tam came by with a fresh quiche she had made. Yum.

Rita and the kids came by. It is always a lively time when they are here. Raylan played sweetly after he dumped out his box of toys. I brushed the tangles out of Athena's hair, then braided it—so cute. Tam had walked the fence at the Homeplace this afternoon and marked what areas needed fixing before we take the heifers down there. They will be there from spring until fall.

TUESDAY, MARCH 21ST

Second day of spring and we are hit with another freeze. 28 degrees F. The fire is being stubborn about flaming up to put out some heat. Sitting on the old rocker cushion, huddled close to its weak flame, I feel like Cinderella on a cold day. Finally got it going. Daddy and I talk over what we need in the way of cow working supplies. I put on the roast and potatoes to bake, and we take off to Farm and Ranch for tags and needles; then visit Shaun who is working on remodeling a vintage store downtown. Two more stops, then home where I tear in to make rolls for lunch and check on the roast. Tam came in with a great map to show what fences need fixing. Athena was with her and she had a question about when the rolls were coming out of the oven. I assured her it would be soon. So glad she loves them!

Daddy and I headed to the Homeplace to fix the problem areas. On cloudy days like today, he has more trouble seeing, so the work didn't go very well, increasing his frustration. Some of the work involved driving over the pipe bridge. Ever since Daddy got too close to the edge and wound up with the truck in the creek, I **walk** across. Maybe Jason will go with him to finish those spots.

WEDNESDAY, MARCH 22ND

Daddy slept "fair to middlin." I think mine was only fair. After breakfast, Daddy shaved and showered for his doctor appointment. Tam is driving him there. After they got back, she filled me in on what Dr. J said about Daddy's feet and that Daddy had agreed to the surgery, much to her surprise. It is scheduled for Wednesday, April 12th, so we will do the cattle working on the 8th of April, the same day we are celebrating Mom and Dad's 76th wedding anniversary.

I weed eat a while. Daddy sawed up the large limb from the red oak that had fallen several months ago. It had been down long enough to have a fire ant town all along the bottom of it. Daddy and I danced around a bit getting them off our gloves and pants legs as we carried pieces to the burn pile. Lunch, and a little resting time, then back down to the Homeplace to tackle a bit more fence fixing. This should be a much happier experience. The sun is shining, and it's 80 degrees. Daddy will be able to see better and feel comfortable. He cut a tree that had fallen on the fence in the southeast corner, then we drove two T-posts in and put the ties on. We eyed the water gap and left two posts for a later repair. Found a broken post up close to the corner and put in a T-post and ties. Great work for one and a half hours.

Back home for coffee, hot tea, hot roll with honey, and sun room sitting. Bright, beautiful spring scene that makes you smile and feel mighty joyful.

THURSDAY, MARCH 23RD

Daddy didn't sleep well. He woke up at 5:00 a.m. His eye appointment is for 9:00. We got there at 8:30 and by 9:20 were on our way home. JoAnna texted me pictures of my grandson, Brandon's graduation from Naval Nuclear engineering school. He is sporting a handsome mustache and his brothers are ribbing him about it. Daddy said it makes him look distinguished.

Back home, while Daddy napped, I got my quilt stencil and marking pens and got all five of the remaining blocks marked. I decided to leave it here since I will not have time to work on it at home. After lunch, I needed to get that weed eating done because Shaun plans to mow this afternoon. Worked through two batteries, then the twine jammed. Shaun came up to mow, but first he stopped and fixed the weed eater for me. When he finished mowing, he and Dad went up to the barn to feed the heifers and put out four rolls of hay. Before going home, Brother came in to visit with Mama.

Got Mama's nightly things done. Daddy had his shower and as I "doctor" his right leg and foot, I am so hopeful and prayerful that this surgery on April 12th will be just what that leg and foot need.

FRIDAY, MARCH 24TH

I was awake at 2:30 a.m., worked on the cow book and studied my Sunday school lesson. Prayed for Papa—he seemed so weak yesterday. Turned out my light and napped until I heard Daddy coming through the library room and my heart was so thankful.

As we sat sipping in the sunroom, Daddy said he had a dream that he was the headliner in the newspaper. Headline read: Stuart McAnally optimistic about the future of the city. He said he can see that headline plainly. In the article below it, he caught his name here and there. He kind of chuckled: "as if what I think or say matters." I told him it matters to many people. He started thinking about how the downtown area had changed and reminisced, describing the streets of Jacksonville: how they looked, where the old time businesses were located. I wrote quickly to gather every scrap of information. More memories for Daddy's book.

I need to finish weed eating at the cemetery, so I invited Papa to go with me. Several years ago, I had put a wooden swing on a metal stand up there under a pine tree. The wind through a pine makes a peaceful sighing sound. He sat in the sun while I did both sides of the fence, gingerly dodging the daffodil and tulip greenery. I looked up to see Papa navigating to the truck; the March wind is too strong. He is content to sit and watch from there. Next, I trim the little persimmon "valley" (twelve persimmon trees) and the fence line, load up, and head home.

I need to update the cow book: write down the list of cows that do not have calves and how they are looking. I love strolling through the pastures, using the binoculars to get the cows' ear tag numbers and any distinguishing marks. Many are black, but have some white markings. Six more of the cows look like they are "springing" (looking heavy with calf). Two have lost ear tags. Glad we have the April 8th date so lots of folks will be here for the cow roundup.

After lunch, Mama and I look through her picture album of her puzzles she has worked. Then I get out three puzzles for her to choose from. Earlier she had her spa treatment. Her skin is really pretty for a 95 year old.

SATURDAY, MARCH 25TH

Daddy slept pretty good. 51 degrees this morning. Breakfast, meds, etc. As I loaded the car my eyes drifted over the pasture, and there was a cow and new calf. Went up to the barn and got the cow working supplies lined up, then back to the house for paper, pen, and binoculars. Went down to the north pond and discovered it was number 24 with a gray bull calf. I had felt like she would be next. Shaun arrived and wanted to take us on a long ride. Daddy is always up for a side-by-side ride on a wonderful day like today .Cypress trees at the ponds are putting out tiny green needles. Drove through the western side woods—full of Mayapples blooming, and dogwoods.

Back at the house, I gave Mama a spa treatment. Left just after noon.

TUESDAY, MARCH 28TH

This week Tam and I start taking on Sherry's usual time with Mama and Daddy in addition to ours. This is going to take getting used to. As I drove over, Tam called and told me about the meds and that Daddy had hit his head on the tractor fork and also had a scratch on his leg. After I got there and he showered, I put some Neosporin on his head and leg, then we visited until he went to bed at 10:00, then got Mama tucked in for the night, too.

WEDNESDAY, MARCH 29TH

Daddy and I both slept great. Our usual morning. Loved the pretty hydrangea that cousin Deborah sent to the folks. Took a picture of Daddy enjoying the sunshine on the porch with the hydrangea in the background. Sent it as my thank you for such a lovely gift. She replied immediately, "You are so welcome. Every time I see him, it's like a small piece of Dad is around and my heart smiles." Such precious words.

Working on a stew for lunch. Braided Mama's hair. Tam's grandgirls are involved in the County Livestock Show and are entered in several events. After Daddy got his haircut, we went out to the Livestock Show Barn and got some cute pictures of Daddy and his great-grands.

Later, Shaun texted and asked me to help him hay. He didn't know Daddy had bumped his head on the tractor hay fork. After I told him and he'd put out the hay, he took the rear hay fork off. He didn't want Daddy bumping his head again.

Tonight when Daddy was heading to bed, he half turned at the top of the steps and said his legs felt like he had walked a long ways today.

After he was asleep, I went in there and stood a while. He made a noise as if dreaming. I stood a while longer. Decided to check on him later. Didn't settle down until midnight.

THURSDAY, MARCH 30TH

I thought it was 6:30 a.m.—not. It was 5:30 a.m. I saw Papa's light on. In a few minutes, I heard that sweet sound of Papa's house shoes whispering across the library room floor. Praise God for one more day of Papa's presence on this planet. A fine day today. We love that extra fireplace warmth and lively flame as day breaks.

Mama has a doctor visit. I help her get dressed and braid her hair. Mama tells me, every time, that it needs to "poof" up in front. I patiently try to get it to "poof." I tried about three times, then told Mama this wasn't a poofing day. "Mama, just be glad it is beautiful and don't fret about it." She agreed. The back country roads to the clinic are a beautiful reminder of how roads used to be, so Mama enjoyed that. Had a good visit with the nurse about Mama's meds. Had to call Dr. Tam about what we had cut out for Mama's stomach's sake. Dr. Mc was kindness itself and took the time to ask Mama questions and listen to her. He checked her over, talked diet—what she ate, how often, and appreciated our modifications. He did prescribe an insoluble fiber for Mama that will work better for her colon health. He asked questions to check her mental health as well. Mama got a compliment on how pretty she looked in pink. Mama can sail on a happy cloud for a long ways on such compliments.

Daddy wants to round up the last load of red oak he and Jason had cut up earlier as well as a piece of rich lighter (fire starter wood) that he discovered. I helped him swing it up into the bucket on the tractor. After we dropped those off and salvaged some fence wire, we put up the tractor, ate lunch, then naptime, washing dishes, and journaling.

At 3:00 p.m., we head to the Homeplace, pick up Jason, and cross that ubiquitous pipe bridge. We put in T-post and wires at the water gap, then dropped Jason off and visited with him and the family. They all waved as we left. That is just sweet. When people stand and send you off with a friendly wave, it says you are important to us—come again.

When we got back we unloaded our tools, then watered and fed the heifers and the bull. I was finishing up a block of quilting. Got down to the last leaf and couldn't sew another stitch. Decided to try and write the final part in my journal. Ended up with mysterious squiggly lines down the page when I nodded off. Gave it up and went to bed.

LAST DAY OF MARCH—31ST

Up at 6:30 a.m. Too warm for a fire. We wanted to burn the overflow of feed sacks in the barn, but the wind is too high—17 mph with gusts 20-40 mph. Lots of cleaning in the house, though. Blue-black cloud in the north. Grandson Garrett has a baseball game, but they may not get to play.

Sure enough, Andy called and said he, Kara, and Garrett were ducking and covering in the gym at Arp. Sirens going off. Later, he called and said the folks might get high wind and hail. When I drove off, Daddy came out to wave. They always ask me to call when I get home. Hated to leave with bad weather looming. Called Shaun. He was home and said he would check on them.

Got home and unloaded. Lightening and thundering. No bad weather either here or there, thank the Lord!

Tamra

WEEK OF MARCH 1ST - 4TH

Had a big week of grands, WMA, errands, homeschool, and still managed to take the kids to see Mrs. Lee's Daffodil Farm near Gladewater. We had a blast and my dear friend Kathy Murphy was able to meet us there and join us on the tour. We got some great photos. I happened to stop by Mom and Dad's to check on them after our outing and was shutting the lids to the foundation vents when I heard Mom calling. Sherry and Dad were on the patio drinking coffee and couldn't hear her. She definitely needed assistance! She had an epic blowout that took us a while to clean up. Poor Mom…I know that embarrassed her, but I tried to make light of it and reassure her that it happens to everybody at some time. It has happened to me and at some of the worst possible times. I told her at least she was at home in her own bathroom.

This morning, I was over at Mom and Dad's early, 7:30, so I could visit with Sherry a bit before Shaun got there at 8:00. Dad hopped up when I came in and started putting his cap on. I asked him what he was doing and he said, "Me and you can separate and load the calves and the bull," but Sherry said, "No Dad, Tam came over to drink coffee and visit." I added, "We need to wait on Shaun, he has to hook up the trailer anyway." I could tell it peeved Dad to have to wait on somebody and when a McAnally gets ready to move, they become a force all their own. He was ready to go, but I have been on the wrong end of the cow loading one too many times. I'm getting too old to risk getting stomped again. He milled around a minute then finally went out on the porch to get his hat, and then wandered back into the kitchen when he saw I wasn't moving. Sherry and I visited while she finished getting Mom's breakfast and her meds ready. Apparently, Dad has been on a tear – Mom too. Sherry looked exhausted.

When Shaun showed up, we all went to the corral and got the cattle sorted and loaded, and then Dad and Shaun took them to the sale barn. We always guess the sale price and sometimes the weight. Mel got closest on the total price and I got closest on the bull's weight. I guessed 1675 and he weighed 1650. Dad was still miffed about having to wait this morning because he let me know that he would "just have the check mailed since I was too busy to take him over to get it this afternoon." I didn't let it go by. I said, "Dad you know that is not true, I have always taken you over to get the check, with very few exceptions, for the last several years." He didn't say anything. We went over around 4:30 to pick it up. The drive over was pretty, lots of redbuds and pear trees blooming and the grass was greening everywhere. When we got back, Shaun was there and he called Mel and told her she "won," she was so tickled. This evening I made homemade strawberry shortcake for a treat.

I went to check on the tulips Addie and I had planted at the cemetery, they were just starting to bloom. When I got back, I went over to feed my critters. Mom and Dad were out on the front porch when I returned and we enjoyed the 70 degree evening. I heard and saw some Sandhill cranes flying over and tried to help Mom and Dad see them, but they were too high and small for their eyes. The sun set soon afterwards and Mom and Dad went back inside. Mom worked at her puzzle table a while before retiring to her room to watch movies. Dad read a bit, took his shower, I doctored his feet and he went to bed pretty early. I didn't sleep well last night, so I am pooped. If I don't get some rest soon, I will fold up like a cheap tent.

SUNDAY, MARCH 5TH

Dad was up at 5:00 am. I woke up when the hot water heater popped like a gunshot. It makes the most awful sounds when it gets going. I expect one of these days for it to take off into the stratosphere. No going back to sleep at that point, so we sat and drank coffee till after 8:00 am. He had built a fire and even though it will be too warm by this afternoon, it was nice this morning. After breakfast, we were sitting at the table talking when Dad made the comment that he felt fortunate to be able to enjoy his time on vacation, even though he was a bit of a workaholic. (Ya think?!) He said he could forget about work and just enjoy being wherever he was and be in the moment. I am glad I have inherited that trait because I am able to set aside all of my worries when I am on a trip and that makes a big difference in how much I enjoy it.

We went to church today and Dad was glad that Shaun was there to sit by him.

MONDAY, MARCH 6TH

This morning, over coffee, I asked Dad what his favorite part of the weekend was…he said it was "getting the calves out of the pasture and sorted and getting them and the bull to the sale…it all worked like clockwork."

SATURDAY, MARCH 11TH

I'm so exhausted from keeping Emelia since Thursday evening and doing all day homeschool with Addie, plus the cooking, cleaning, etc. Emelia is good, but a busy bee and always on the move. Mom doesn't like loud noises so I try to keep her outside while I am over here. We went on two walks in the pasture and she played on the patio until time for her nap. I was back and forth tending to Mom and trying to keep Emelia entertained, so when she finally fell asleep, I thought I would take a short nap too. I had just lain down on the couch and relaxed enough to drift off when I heard the truck start up. My eyes squeezed shut harder and I groaned. Noooo, why now, just when I had a brief respite, one I've needed for days! I wanted to cry. Why does Dad always pick the worst time to do things? Because he thinks he can do it all by himself, even though he can't, and he will give out, push too hard, and possibly hurt himself or end up damaging something. I threw off the blanket I had so hopefully snuggled under just moments before, pulled on my boots, and went outside to see what he was up to. An althea tree had split in the storm and Dad decided to pull it up. What he thought would be a "quick job" turned into an ordeal. He hacked, sawed, pulled, and dug for over an hour before he finally had success.

In the meantime, Emelia woke up from her nap. Mom needed me to put out another puzzle...and I still had to cook for tomorrow. After I finished getting everything done, the rest of the evening wasn't too bad. I really hope I rest tonight...otherwise this tent might be on permanent fold.

When I think about the change of seasons, I think about the things I will miss: the condensation and frost on the kitchen window over the sink, Dad's winter caps and coat on the porch bench, the smell of freshly chopped kindling, the crackling and popping of the fire in the fireplace, sitting and drinking my first cup of coffee in front of the fire before anyone else is up, the angle of the sun coming through the big picture window by the kitchen table, the bare limbs of the trees, and the calm quietness of a winter evening at sunset. I asked Dad what he will miss and he said: sitting in front of the fire on cold days and the holidays and family get-togethers. He said, "There's not any way to describe the comfort of sitting in front of a warm fireplace, out of the wind and the cold." Coming from one who has marched into blizzards and spent many uncomfortable nights in a foxhole, I imagine it is a comfort he appreciates more than most of us.

WEEK OF MARCH 13TH - 18TH

This week has been a nightmare and it continues. A misunderstanding has me upset, I am facing eye surgery, my eyes are still dilated so I can't see to read or write, I am behind on my column, and this is the last week of our regular schedule before Mel and I start splitting every week so Sherry can stay with her new grand girl. I am glad we can do it; I just hope not every week is as hard as this last one or I might go screaming into the woods by the end of May.

Sherry was so sweet and left me one of my favorite cupcakes, and one for Dad without the frosting because he's not supposed to have that much sugar. I looked forward to it all weekend, but waited until Sunday night to enjoy it because I was too upset on Saturday to eat. When I got back from church Sunday night, I went out to the porch fridge to get my cupcake and they were BOTH gone! I marched into the Big Room where Dad was sitting on the hearth warming his back and with my hands on my hips I said, "OK, it's confession time. What happened to the cupcakes?" Dad made a face and said, "There was this big rat…" I shot back, "I know! And I'm looking at him!" The look on Dad's face was so funny, I had to laugh, but I *was* disappointed…I love those maple pecan cupcakes.

SUNDAY, MARCH 19TH

Tonight when I was doctoring Dad's foot, I noticed a bad place under his little toe that seems to be getting worse rather quickly. That is just the way Marc's infection ordeal last year started out, so I told Dad I thought it would be a good idea to get Dr. J to look at it ASAP. He surprised me when he agreed. Maybe he will finally agree to have the surgery he's been putting off. His foot is looking much worse and the swelling is not getting better either.

WEDNESDAY, MARCH 22ND

I picked Dad up at 7:45 this morning for his foot appointment. We didn't have to wait long, thank goodness. Dr. J looked at his foot and told Dad "Your daughter did a great job of catching this early. You need to have the surgery." Dad was all for it, which surprised me, but I guess he's getting tired of dealing with it. The surgery is set for April 12. I'll be taking him since it is an all-day thing and I can use the time to do a little work while I wait. The next few weeks will be busy, so I will try to get ahead with my columns. I don't want to worry about meeting deadlines.

SATURDAY, MARCH 25TH

Mel said she was leaving about noon, so I got my stuff together and drove over to Mom and Dad's about 11:00 so we could catch up on Mom's meds, food, etc. before she took off. This is the first week of our new schedule and in a way, I am a little anxious about how it is going to work, because I don't want to short-change Addie on her homeschooling. Rita and the kids came over and went fishing. After they left, I went down to the church and picked up some bluebonnets and hydrangeas that Deborah had for Mom and Dad. There were enough bluebonnets to plant some at the cemetery too.

SUNDAY, MARCH 26TH

Dad and I went to church as usual. I was glad I had put a roast in the slow cooker before we left because I wasn't feeling too great when we got home. Lots of drama…I don't do well with drama. I made some banana bread Sunday afternoon because I didn't want to waste the bananas; they were about gone, but good for bread. Dad didn't sleep very well last night, so I think he has slept through most of the afternoon. Mom was busy puzzling, she had a pretty good day.

After all the tractor-riding, wood-stacking, fence-building, and chain-saw work…Dad and Flat Stanley decided to take a break.

MONDAY, MARCH 27TH

Jason came up to help Dad with the west fence. Dad was ready to go before 8:00 and was waiting on the porch when he got here. He likes to get an early start, before he runs out of steam. I needed to go to town to get groceries, Mom's meds, and go by the post office and the bank. I called Sherry later today to see how things went her first day of babysitting. She said she "might be too old for this." I am sure she will get into the swing of things after the first week or two.

TUESDAY, MARCH 28TH

Addie arrived about 8:30 and after I fixed Mom's breakfast and meds, we got ready for WMA. Dad and Jason were already at work on the fence. After WMA, I made lunch; we worked on Addie's school lessons until time to take her to piano. It was hard, because while I was trying to explain a concept to Addie, Mom was yelling at me about nothing ("Can you turn off my light, close my blind, has the mail run yet?") We got through the day, but I was worn out. I had also gathered all the trash, cleaned the table and counters, and washed dishes, all of Mom's gowns and other clothes. By the time I got to my house this evening, I was done. Mom and Dad were in their chairs in the Big Room right where I left them when Mel got there about 7:30.

WEDNESDAY, MARCH 29TH

Today is the Cherokee County Livestock Show and the grandkids are so excited. I remember how much my kids looked forward to it every year. I went up there to see the grandkids projects and take some pictures. Mel took Dad out there too and got some good pictures. I worked the rest of the day at home.

THURSDAY, MARCH 30TH

Marc got a call from his Mom that his Dad was on his way to Tyler hospital, so he went up there and stayed till late. I worked on my art project, the book, and got everything ready for tomorrow. We had a tornado warning this afternoon, but it bypassed us, thank the Lord. Marc's Dad will be in the hospital for another day or two looks like, so Marc is staying with his Mom.

Communication IS VITAL. SHARING INFORMATION WITH OTHER FAMILY MEMBERS AND CAREGIVERS WILL HELP PREVENT *hurt feelings.*

Mom and Dad after they married in 1947 – quite the handsome couple, don't you think?

APRIL

"April…come she will…" The Simon and Garfunkel song always comes to mind when April rolls arounds. I miss those hauntingly beautiful tunes on the airwaves, making me glad I kept an old turntable. When I'm in a nostalgic mood, I put on one of my old 60s or 70s albums and I am right back there in that moment in time.

The struggle between spring and winter is usually over by mid-April, but we have been surprised before by one final winter blast before the heat of summer starts to creep in. I miss the cold weather, but I don't want a late frost or freeze. The resulting blackened leaves and ruined flowers and fruit crops make for a sad start to a new season. Every year when we have an early spring, farmers and cattlemen here hold their collective breaths until past mid-April, when we are mostly safe.

As the pastures turn green and the trees don their leafy crowns, our thoughts turn to Easter and the festivities of the first full month of spring. We always enjoyed our Easter traditions: the big family egg hunt at my grandmother's house, new outfits for church, and a special Easter Sunday meal. I miss those things more as I get older, realizing what blessings we enjoyed as a close-knit family growing up in the 50s, 60s and 70s.

On Mom and Dad's anniversary, April 5th, we commemorated their special day without much fanfare growing up, not realizing at the time just how wonderful it was to grow up in an intact family unit. Now, we make a big deal out of each milestone, with cards, flowers, and a special meal. Dad and Mom don't expect gifts on the occasion, but Mom definitely expects a card from each of us. If you don't have one, she will call you out…in front of everybody. "Where's **your** *card?" she'll say, as she fixes you with "the look." It never fails to crack everyone up! We don't often come empty-handed.*

Ever the optimist, I always hope for a long spring, praying it won't get over eighty-five degrees before Memorial Day. Sometimes, I get what I hope for and enjoy no sweating until June, but some years, it seems to go straight from winter to summer. I hope this year will be kind, at least in the temperature department.

Sherry

SATURDAY, APRIL 1ST

All hands on deck fairly early – not as many hands as we usually have, but we weren't doing a full-meal-deal cattle herd working either; that will be next Saturday. Pop just wants to move eight heifers to his old Homeplace for the summer. Pop, Jason, Tam, and Shaun got the "girls" into the chute area. Tam filled the needles, Pop and Jason gave the shots. Shaun worked the head gate, and put in the ear tags while Jason held each heifer's head steady. I administered the pour-on cattle wormer and wrote descriptions of each heifer along with her ear tag number. All eight are mostly Angus, so I had to really look for any description other than "black." Occasionally they lose their ear tags, and we need some identifier other than the number.

One heifer lunged and fell sideways in the chute with her head between two bars on one side and a leg through two bars on the opposite side – poor thing! We tried to help her out, but she finally managed to free herself. And wouldn't you know that *her* ear tag was the one that gave Shaun a fit. He worked for several minutes before he finally got it in. Bless her heart. Finally all eight were done, loaded in the trailer, and headed to the Homeplace with Shaun and Tam.

Pop and Jason stayed behind to stack some firewood, and I walked back to the house to drop off the cow notebook, refrigerated medicine, and so forth. Planted the rose bush Melanie and I bought for the folks' anniversary gift, then on the road to Stu and Ashley's to keep grandbaby for a while so Stu could go to the grocery store. Keeping the road hot between J'ville and Nac!

TUESDAY, APRIL 4TH

So sweet to cuddle this baby close, feel her soft puffs of breath on my neck, and breathe in that sweet baby smell. I treasure these days because I know how fleeting they are. And I am so grateful for my sisters being willing to give more of their time so that I can give mine to this little one. I will never forget it.

WEDNESDAY, APRIL 5TH

Mom and Dad's 76th anniversary … Wow! I talked to Melanie and asked her to wish them a happy "official" day for me. She is doing some prep work for our celebration with them this weekend. As usual, the celebration is tied to a cattle working day. Pop doesn't like to "waste all that good help."

THURSDAY, APRIL 6TH

Baby girl's first shots today … oh dear. She had a tough morning. After I arrived, I decided to just hold her as she slept. We cuddled in that recliner until 2:00 when I had to lay her in the "Moses" basket while I fixed her bottle and gas drops – she did not like being put down! That bed isn't nearly as warm and snuggly as Granny B. Tough afternoon for Butter Bean – her chubby little leg hurt from the shots. I pulled out all my granny tricks: singing, swaying, shushing noises, etc. Finally got her back to sleep, poor baby.

Around 11:30 P.M., the phone woke me from a deep sleep – it was Stu saying that they were taking Knoxlynn to the ER because of her breathing. They are afraid of RSV and are taking no chances. I dressed and drove there. Ashley's mom was there also. Since we couldn't go to their ER room, we kept each other company in the waiting room and just texted with them until around 1:30. The test had showed that it wasn't RSV – a definite relief. The congestion is probably from a cold, so they'll just treat that. Back to the house and in the bed by 2, alarm set for 5. Yikes.

SATURDAY, APRIL 8TH

Tough dragging out this morning … Bill and I were all loaded up and leaving for J'ville at 6:30. On the lovely drive, I got a text from Melanie – Hobo is dead! They don't know what happened to her. Early this morning, she was lying on the mat at the side door, as if she tried to get as close as possible to her people before she breathed her last. I was so sad … Hobo was the best cat ever, more like a dog – she'd follow us on walks and wanted to be wherever we were, even if we were making loud noises. I remember using the leaf blower one time when she was lying in one of the patio chairs. As I got closer and closer, she didn't even move. I picked up the chair, cat and all, and set her down where I'd already cleaned. She just lay there like Cleopatra on her barge. One time Melanie was planting some flowers, and Hobo was right there, all up in her business. Every morning when I turned on the kitchen light, she'd jump up on the chair right outside the window and stretch up on the screen as far as she could, just to let me know that she was ready for breakfast, please.

So many memories: her playing in the leaves we were trying to rake, the time she got hurt and we didn't know if she would get over it, leading Pop and me on walks in the evening, the time she jumped onto that chair where I'd laid my soft foam kneeling pad, felt that unfamiliar surface under her paws and shot up like a rocket … and now, she was just gone. She breathed her last with no one to pet her and say how much we'd miss her.

I texted Melanie and asked them not to bury her until I got there. When we arrived, I stroked her fur and told her she had been a good cat. Tam and I buried her near the fence overlooking the pond and hilltop … a good spot. After that, we had to move on to the chore at hand – working the main cattle herd up on the hill. Life is like that sometimes – you don't have time to sit around and be sad because of pressing duties.

Rex, Joanna, and the kids had come to help, along with Jason. Rita didn't come because Athena was sick. For the very first time ever, Pop let Shaun run the cattle working while he, Jason, and Bill split firewood nearby. That was a sea change for us all, though we didn't verbalize it. For a couple of years, Pop has talked about turning all that day-to-day operation over to Shaun and Tam, but he's never been able to really let go. He's forgotten more about cattle, hay, and so forth than all of us kids know put together, but I suppose he thinks it's finally time to let go and see how we manage all this. One thing Shaun found out was that giving those shots in that tough cowhide is no joke. After giving the last shot and steering a few calves (with Rex's help), he commented, "Daddy's a tough old bird!"

After taking some photos, I walked to the house to check on Mom and make tea and some sliders for a snack for everyone since they also had to cut a thick, dying oak near Dad's shop. Ethan cut the tree down, then others grabbed saws to start cutting it apart, one of those being Pop. He just couldn't sit there and watch the others do it all. I went back in the house to work on the anniversary meal. After just a few minutes, I noticed Bill motioning me to come outside – he'd been sharpening one of Pop's chainsaws and had come out of the shop in time to see someone helping Pop up from where he'd fallen, still holding his running chainsaw – Lord have mercy!

I hustled out there to survey the damage. At first I didn't think it was too bad, but then I saw that farther up under his sleeve, he had peeled off two big areas of skin when he'd slid against a rough limb on his way down. It looked awful, but he wouldn't come in right away and get patched up. He wanted to watch the guys finish. Sigh. That McAnally stubbornness has stood him in good stead over the years, but sometimes …

Finally he came in, and Tam and I cleaned up those places, cut the skin off that couldn't be salvaged, and smoothed the other part back over the raw flesh, put on antibiotic ointment, bandaged him up and got him in a clean shirt. He looked intact for the photos anyway! Mom looked pretty in her denim dress with her silver hair braided. Shaun asked the blessing over the meal, and the tired, hungry bunch tied into the food. Later, Mom and Dad opened their cards, and Mom read each one to Dad. When she finished, she asked Shaun, "Where's yours?" We all cracked up – he didn't have one. He'd bought them a beautiful bouquet of flowers instead. A big day for all.

MONDAY, APRIL 10TH

Talked to Tam, and she said Pop had hurt his knee when he fell on Saturday, but it wasn't bothering him too badly. We need to put him in bubble wrap or something.

WEDNESDAY, APRIL 12TH

Pop's leg surgery is today. I can't be there, but I prayed for all to go well. Before Pop and Tam left, Melanie called and put her phone on speaker so I could hear her prayer for them. Sure wish I could be in two places today – here with Little Squash Blossom and there with my daddy.

Melanie called later and was antsy because she wasn't hearing from Tam as much as she wanted. Then Tam sent us a video of Doctor J explaining that God gave us three arteries, two of Pop's were completely blocked, but he was able to open one with stents. Somehow, Melanie heard that he'd opened *all* of them up, but I told her he'd only been able to open one. She had to listen twice more to the video before she heard it correctly. I know she was disappointed to have that happy idea blasted, but we all breathed a sigh of relief that it was over. Tam sent a photo of Pop smiling when it was done – he was relieved, too.

THURSDAY, APRIL 13TH

Melanie told me that Pop hoped the surgery would keep him going awhile longer so he could watch the little ones in the family grow up. I can't wait for him and Mom to meet Knoxlynn in person. Every week brings new discoveries for her. Now, when I burp her on my shoulder, she'll dig her toes in my middle as if she's trying to climb. She's started making cooing noises and focuses on my and face and smiles … such a precious little girl.

SATURDAY, APRIL 15TH

Knoxlynn got to meet her Great Uncle Chuck and Great Aunt Jan yesterday, and today she gets to meet her great grandparents! Stu and I drove to J'ville around 11:00. (Ashley was with her sister who had just become a new mom.) Pop was on the side porch, so he got to see Sweet Pea first. I took a picture of Pop looking at her and thought of the nearly 100 years separating them. What a contrast of time and experiences … Pop looking back over many years and Knoxlynn looking forward to an ocean of all things new.

Melanie was anxious to hold her, of course, and admired her enough to satisfy any grandma's heart. After Tam came over, we all went to the Big Room so that Mom could meet her newest descendant. We put Knoxlynn in her lap and made some sweet photos. Little girl slept away, and Mom was so pleased that she was content in her arms. Pop held her after a while, but he wasn't quite as adept as Mom … I glanced over and saw that Knoxlynn's head was about to disappear under his elbow. Pop said, "I think I'm about to lose her." We rescued Little Bit and had a laugh over that. Shaun sent a text that he wished he could be here to hold the baby, too. Maybe that can happen soon.

MONDAY, APRIL 17TH

Tam told me that Mom did not want to go to her pacemaker checkup since she'd gotten a new one in September; plus, she has a remote monitoring device that constantly sends information to the cardiologist's office. So, I called to cancel it. The first two calls dropped; during the third one, the lady said she'd still need to come in to see her cardiologist, so that appointment was made for June 3rd. When I called Tam to tell her the date so she could write it on Mom and Dad's calendar, she told me that the 3rd was a Saturday – an obvious mistake. Had to call the 4th time to get that fixed for June 7th instead. We all have our jobs to do, and this is one I can do from miles away – make phone calls. Later, I talked to Melanie – she put her phone on speaker so I could hear her and Pop, then hear Tam as she came in from getting groceries, and Melanie's prayer for Tam's eye surgery tomorrow. In addition to taking care of Mom and Dad, we have our own health issues, too. At any point, one of us could be down for the count and unable to help for a while – scary thought.

WEDNESDAY, APRIL 19TH

Tam is in a lot of pain from her eye surgery, but Dr. G said it had gone well. Bless her heart – I pray that she can get some rest tonight.

THURSDAY, APRIL 20TH

Pop is burning the big pile of limbs from the tree cutting … always an interesting time, but at least there's a water hose handy. Tam feels somewhat better today.

FRIDAY, APRIL 21ST

Tam's vision is still not clear – worrisome, and Melanie face planted in the dirt when she turned to run from the burning pile of thistles – she'd put lacquer on them, threw a match on the pile, and it exploded! No telling how many times we girls have gotten hurt trying to help Pop so something or trying to keep *him* from getting hurt.

SATURDAY, APRIL 22ND

Up to J'ville to cover today and part of tomorrow for Tam – giving her a little more time for her eyes to heal up. Mel and I took a walk around the place where she and Dad had worked this past week. Down by the pond we heard some geese! They landed on the pond briefly, but I guess we make them nervous because they took off. Melanie took off shortly too; then I helped Pop change the tractor forks over to the bucket so he could clean up the remains of the old blackjack on the hill.

I went back to the house to dismantle the DISH equipment – I bought that service for Pop several years ago, but since a high speed Internet line came across their place recently, we're switching over to that.

I asked Pop if he'd like a pumpkin pie. (Is it dark at night? Ha!) Got that in the oven, then Pop said he didn't want that DISH post in the yard, so he went to the barn and got the tractor. We wrapped a chain around the post, yanked it out of the ground, and hauled it up to the equipment shed. About that time, Shaun drove up in his side-by-side to take Pop on a ride to see a new baby calf Athena had told him about.

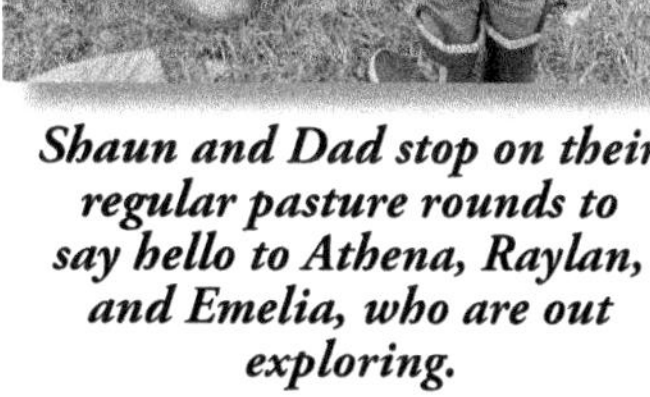

Shaun and Dad stop on their regular pasture rounds to say hello to Athena, Raylan, and Emelia, who are out exploring.

While they were gone, I decided to rearrange Mom's jigsaw puzzles in her closet. Since she'd given Melanie most of her hats, more space was available. While I was working on that, Tam peeped around the corner – she'd brought over an article for me to proofread for her. She still has to wear sunglasses even inside the house. I hope her vision straightens out soon. Pop and Shaun got back for pie, and Melanie called – put my phone on speaker so she could be with us. A fairly lively time until later when the folks were all settled in for the night.

SUNDAY, APRIL 23RD

We still need the occasional fire – like this morning. It's in the lower 50s. Coffee, breakfast and so on, wrote Pop's offering check for church. Good Sunday School time and sermon afterwards. No one lingered to chat since it was raining. Fixed lunch; Tam and Caleb ate with us, then I went over Tam's article with her. She could tell that I was sleepy, so she made coffee, hoping the caffeine jolt would keep me awake on the drive back to Nac. When I got there, I had to gather some food for a dinner honoring one of our high school graduates tonight at church, then Bill and I drove to the dinner. Not exactly "a day of rest", but some Sundays are like that. I guess I can rest when I'm dead.

WEDNESDAY, APRIL 26TH

Tam took Pop for a follow-up visit to Dr. J today – he said Pop's foot will gradually get better, and to keep doing what we're doing. So thankful for the increased circulation.

FRIDAY, APRIL 28TH

Tam did **not** hear what she hoped to hear from Dr. G today. Although the surgery to remove the scar tissue was successful, her vision will not improve without glasses, especially for distance and at night. Glasses are so inconvenient for an outdoor person; they fog up in the winter and slide down your nose in the summer. And, because of Mom's and Dad's eye problems, she's afraid she'll get macular degeneration at some point. Lord, please give her some special blessings to lighten her heart.

SUNDAY, APRIL 30TH

Talked to Melanie awhile to smooth out a misunderstanding. Awhile back, she fell in the bathroom we use at Mom's and Dad's because there was not a proper grab bar, only a towel bar. It gave way, and she fell back between a cabinet and the toilet. It could have been very bad. Her son wanted to do a big bathroom change, which was very nice of him, but that bathroom has looked the same way for decades, and we hate to make it completely different. The more we change, the less like Mom's and Dad's house it will look. Melanie thought we didn't want to change anything at all, in spite of her safety concerns, but Shaun, Tam, and I had talked over several ideas to improve things and had come up with a couple of options. Once Melanie understood that, she was okay.

After Bill and I got home from an afternoon district church meeting, Stu called and said their air conditioner had quit working and the temperature inside their house was climbing. I told them to come on out and spend the night here. After I got off the phone, Bill and I flew around like crazy changing sheets and getting everything company ready. When they arrived, they looked like nomads, toting in all that baby stuff. We loved having them here and getting to kiss Little Bit goodnight. Sweet times.

Melanie

TUESDAY, APRIL 4TH

As I drove to the folks' this afternoon, I got very sleepy. I arrive to my brother's paint job on the carport poles. They are a shiny black and look so good. He had that paint all in his beard, so he left to clean up. Ate the rest of the calzone and blueberry muffin from the retired teachers' luncheon today – not diet friendly. Talked to Sherry. She is really enjoying keeping her grandbaby.

Heard that gnawing in the door frame again. I told Daddy and he tried to listen. Don't know if he heard it or not. He said he would get some rat poison and put it in the attic. I guess I will bathe and go to bed. I'm pretty sleepy after getting up at 5:15 am.

WEDNESDAY, APRIL 5TH

Mama and Daddy's 76th wedding anniversary. Our usual morning routine. About 7:00 a.m. a red truck drove up and Ricky W. got out. He is in Daddy's Sunday school class and had told Daddy he would come by for a visit. While they talked, I got busy and fixed up the porch table for spring, then put on roast and baked a potato for Daddy. It rained most of the morning – ½ inch. Ate lunch. I mixed up rolls, then talked on the phone with Sherry. We ate a snack together as we compared days.

Daddy and I went up to the blown down black jack oak so he could cut some up. I started to go back to the house and noticed buzzards – a lot of them. I walked to the crest of the hill and saw a cow down, and thought I saw a calf. I walked all the way down there and sure enough there was a calf. I scared off the buzzards. Black vultures are aggressive and have been known to peck out the eyes and kill a newborn animal. I walked back up the hill and told Daddy. His saw batteries had died, so we loaded up and came on in. Texted Shaun about the calf. He was at Sam's and asked if we needed anything for the weekend celebration. I said no. He said we would go check on that baby calf when he got home.

Daddy was tired, but when he smelled those rolls, he came into the kitchen and we both ate two with butter and honey.

Shaun came and we all went for a ride. Those buzzards were all around the cow and new calf – very close, but we scared them off. When we got back, Shaun visited with Mama, then left with four rolls. Daddy was tired, showered and laid down. Mama puzzled until 9:00 pm. Got her situated for the night.

THURDDAY, APRIL 6TH

Up around 7:00 am. Raining, windy and cold. Got the morning things done for Daddy and Mama. Dad and I talked a bit about our cattle doings on Saturday and weather issues.

Went to Farm and Ranch and got needles, blackleg med, Ivermectin, and vitamin A&D. Register machine wouldn't work so I got a ticket for the price and I will pay it next time I'm in town.

Got Mama lined up for her appointment – noon meds, denim dress, footies and a pretty coat she had forgotten she had. It was still raining and cold. Neither one of us wanted to go into the teeth of that cold rain and wind. I checked the gas, very low. Will need to get some on the way home.

I conferred with Tam earlier about directions to Dr. Bo's office. Since I get lost in a closet, it is imperative I get a refresher course on where I am headed. Tam says I was born without the iron filings to find true north. I have my directions, Mama is in the car. Daddy literally dashed (pretty fantastic for a 99 year old) to get his credit card off the round oak table in his bedroom, hands it off to me, and I dash back to the car. I hear Mama loudly calling me. "What is it, Mama?!" "I'm cold," she said. "Mama, I was coming right back." The windshield wipers make a horrid sound as I turn them on. Mama shudders and said how awful that is, I agree. We proceed and thankfully the noise subsides with use.

We arrive and I drive up to the covered entrance, dash in to get a wheelchair, help Mama maneuver out and into the chair. It is made more difficult by her lack of shoes. Mama won't wear shoes because her feet are tender due to the shingles back in 2010, and just has her footies on. Somehow Mama manages to haul herself up, turn around and plop down in the wheelchair with mostly dry feet. I get a good grip and push her up the incline. Thank the Lord for whoever invented automatic doors. I leave Mama inside, get back in the car, move it to a parking spot, then splash back to Mama. Good thing I'm wearing rain boots.

I push her up to the counter where we pay for this visit, then off we go down the long hall to await the call. Our 1:30 pm appointment comes and goes. Two hours later, they tease us with time in a room for the eyeball picture. Then back we go to our place at the end of a line of chairs. Phase two of waiting. Mama is now kind of bunched up in a slumping ball with her weary head in her hand. Every once in a while she will say (loudly) "I am so tired!" "I know Mama. I think all God's children in this hall are so tired, too!" I pull out my trusty iPhone and entertain her with pictures of her great grandchildren and some of the outside things Daddy is doing. That does a great job of distraction for both of us.

I check our place in line again. Only one ahead for the next part and 4 ahead for the shot! Mama says, "Mel, I need to go to the bathroom." Sigh. So close and yet so far. I hail the nurse. "Mama's got to go. Does she have time? Remember this is a woman in a wheelchair." "Oh she has time." The closest restroom is occupied, so away we go all the way to the front. We manage to get things done … not much maneuvering room. Holding a door and pushing a wheelchair through at the same time requires finesse and a remarkable use of stomach and left arm muscles. If I did this every day, I would be totally toned for my pickleball game.

Back to assume our positions of hope at the end of our row. At 5:00 pm the call finally comes! Eyechart check and more drops until the eye is numb. More waiting. I notice under-the- sea pictures that are quite lovely and began to tell Mama the names of the creatures as she squints at the screen with her good eye. The Biology teacher in me enjoys this mini teaching event. Before we get very far, Dr. Bo comes in, so I wait in the hall 3 or 4 minutes. Out he comes. Next appointment in 2 months – June, a lovely month. Maybe we will come on a sunny day. It is almost 6:00 pm. I have had no lunch, and there is a slight ache behind my eyes. As we pass a desk of nurses, they ask about the party for Daddy who is turning that 100 year mark in August. They are smiling and wishing him a happy birthday. Sweet.

Get Mama in the car, return the wheelchair, and we are off! I told Mama I felt like a bird out of a cage. She agreed. As we get going, I remember we are running on fumes, so we pull in the station. Our 17 gallon tank held 16.67 gallons!

Back on the road, as we get closer to Whitehouse, Mama started coughing! She needs water and I had none. I remembered Tic Tacs in my purse and told Mama to get those. She began to scrabble through the bag and finally spotted the clear plastic box. She had dumped my phone out in her search, so I glanced at it and saw to my utter astonishment that she had managed to punch in 911! I explained to the 911 operator that my 95 year old Mama was digging in my purse and accidently called them. He was pleasant and said he would cancel the call. A few minutes later, my son called. (He is my emergency contact person.) "Mama what is going on?" When I told him what had happened, I could hear the smile in his voice. He was in Oklahoma on a mini vacation for my granddaughter's 21st birthday. We finally arrived sometime after 6:00 pm. Brother was here with Daddy. They were beginning to wonder about us. Mama headed in with Shaun's assistance. I popped her pizza into the toaster oven and heated myself a couple of homemade yeast rolls, ham and honey. Perfect little sliders to chase off the Hangries.

Later, as I talk first with one sister then the other, we put all things in perspective and we have a good sharing and laughter. But truly, if doctors could get a better scheduling system, the process would be so much easier, especially for those of advanced age. Waiting for hours like that is actually painful for them.

FRIDAY, APRIL 7TH

Daddy reminisced about *his* dad this morning, and how a particular habit of his affected a decision Daddy made as a teenager – he told about grandpa's tobacco patch, and described all the steps in its cultivation. Grandpa was the only one in this part of the country that grew his own tobacco. He dipped, chewed, and smoked a pipe, but Daddy decided that he would never have a tobacco habit. Way to go, Papa!

After breakfast, Daddy got his foul weather gear on to finish his blackjack oak project. Shaun got the tractor and loaded the cut wood into the front bucket to dump at the wood shed – three trips. They turned the cows into the west pasture before Daddy came back to the house to rest. After I finished the pineapple upside-down cake, he wanted to go back to the barn to make sure all cows and calves were in the west pasture and then shut the gate. When we got in the truck to back out, Daddy thought he had a flat, but when I checked, it was a mess of hay bale wrap binding the axle. He intended to crawl under and cut that stuff off with his knife, so I ran out to the shop and found 2 pieces of foam to put under the truck for him to lie down on. After a few minutes he said he thought we needed to move the truck so he could get to the remaining netting. I said, "I'm not moving that truck until you are out of there." He started moving around, but finally said, "Grab my good leg and pull." (Where is someone with a camera when you need it?) I pulled and out he came. I moved the truck a few feet. He crawled back under and finished the job. Then I had to pull on his good leg again to get him out. Then he rolled over, got on his knees, and pulled himself up with the help of the back bumper and my arm. Really? Rolling around on the concrete at 99?!

When we checked on the cows, a few were still in the big pasture, so we tried to head them through the gate. If Shaun hadn't come to help, we'd never have managed it. Glad to get Daddy out of that cold north wind.

Back home, the fireplace draws us to sit and enjoy its comforting warmth. I put away one puzzle and get out another for Mama, then decided to quilt. Mama "hints" about the mail coming, so I stop quilting, put on my coat, Dad's cap and rubber boots and trudge down to the box. Yes, there is mail: 2 more anniversary cards – one from my bird watching buddy and her husband, and one from my sweet Sunday school class. After Mama ate supper, I did her spa treatment in preparation of the festivities tomorrow. I talk with my grandson Wyatt. He tells me about fishing with his little brother Kolt, his 2 gardens, chickens, and new job. He is a dependable young man who enjoys working.

I am writing late – again. Daddy wants to get up by 6:00 am, make coffee and enjoy a couple of cups in front of the fire before the family gets here. He is looking forward to the day – what a blessing for any elderly person, to still look forward to what's next.

SATURDAY, APRIL 8TH

Daddy was still asleep at 6:00 am. I got up, got ready, put Daddy's coffee filter in his pot, then heard him get up. I went out and got my energy drink and wondered why Hobo wasn't stretched up on the outside chair, scratching on the screen for her food. There she was on the mat – dead! I could plainly see that she had died sometime in the night I texted Shaun, Tam and later Sherry. She and Bill were already on their way here. We all loved that cat. She was a faithful companion for Daddy – on a walk, front porch, back patio, even on a ladder as Daddy cleaned out the gutters in the back L of the house. Shaun blamed coyotes, but she wasn't attacked because when Tam came and looked her over, there were no wounds. We believe she died by eating a rat or mouse that had consumed poison. Daddy mentioned that she had started killing moles which is a great asset on the ranch. We were all so sad to lose this furry friend. Tam and Sherry buried her after wrapping her in one of Daddy's old towels.

Ethan, Jared, Brandon (on leave from the Navy), and Hannah, arrived. Rex rode with them. JoAnna drove from a 12 hour shift as a nursery nurse in Longview, straight to PawPaw's house. They all were there early to help work the cattle.

Shaun is the leader of our cattle working this year. He was surprised that Daddy let him be in charge. Daddy was over at the woodshed with Bill and Jason to split the remainder of that blackjack oak.

Shaun had 6 cows in the working chute at a time. Everyone had a job: filling needles, giving shots, putting in ear tags, working the head gate, running cattle into the chute, steering young bulls. Sherry came up to take a few pictures. She was staying with Mama and making some lunch preparations. Team work: Daddy taught us well. We put up all the supplies, then the guys moved over to where Jason and Bill were working on the last huge blocks and helped to split the remaining wood.

Back at the house the next part of Daddy's list began to unfold. A three foot thick red oak was dying, and Daddy wanted to use it to finish filling up the wood shed for next winter. Ethan had brought his big saw with him. Jared got a long extension ladder and attached a 20 foot strap high on the tree. Shaun added a chain and attached that to Daddy's big tractor. Ethan studied the big trunk and got advice on how to make the cut. Finally, the moment of truth, the big saw bites into the wood. First from one side and then the other side – sawdust flies. After cutting it almost two thirds through, Ethan cuts the wedge slice out toward the direction of the fall. Moving to the back away from the notch, he begins the final cut. Jason and Jared are watching the top of the tree to gauge when it begins to fall. Tam, Sherry and I are over by Daddy with phone cameras poised for the fall of this once majestic oak. It begins to sway. Shaun has tension on the tree and pulls the tractor ahead of the mighty crash.

Once it is safely down, many chainsaws come out. Jason, Brandon, Jared, Ethan, and eventually Daddy start the massive job of cutting it up. Brandon measures and marks the length to cut off the trunk, and Shaun positions the tractor bucket to catch that first section. Some do not believe the bucket can hold and lift that huge piece, but amazingly, it does. Shaun takes it up to the wood shed, dumps it and comes back for more. By lunch time, that tree is reduced to some mighty fine firewood.

Sherry made tea and got out the chicken salad while I put the hamburger patties on to cook. During the lunch preparations, Daddy fell outside and skinned his arm pretty badly! Tam and Sherry doctor it and call JoAnna (Great to have a nurse in the family) in for consultation. Eventually, Daddy is patched up and insists he is fine. We gather for the blessing. Daddy asked Shaun to pray, and he did a good job. Rachel, Addie, Gus and Rob had arrived during the tree cutting episode, and joined in the conversations and watching. Not everyone could be here, but it was still a good day.

WEDNESDAY, APRIL 12TH

Surgery day, so no coffee for Daddy. As I looked around the kitchen, I didn't see the coffee pot. Tam had put it on top of the refrigerator so Papa wouldn't forget and make the coffee out of habit. I told him I thought it was cool enough for a fire. He was really happy about that. He needed something to do, so I gladly let him get the fire going. We sat, each with our thoughts to ponder. Mama came in to sit with us. She is concerned about the surgery, too.

Tam came over at 8:35 am. I wave as they leave. My mind is trying to stay positive; but slipping to the "what ifs" unless I pay diligent attention. I will fill the time with Mama's needs and trying to rake up the large area where they cut the red oak behind the shop since Shaun wants to mow tomorrow. I told Mama to call if she needed me - I'm just outside and will have my phone handy.

Tam has Sherry, me and Brother on a group text. She plans to keep us informed all along the process. The first funny was when they wanted Daddy out of all clothes. His comment was "Boy, shorts, too? I should have worn a night gown." The room where they were going to do the surgery was quite a distance. They sent a fellow back to get Daddy. He pulled out a pedometer that showed how many steps he had to take to lead people back and forth. Daddy said, "They may be paying him by the mile." Daddy's blood pressure went up to 205/85, so they gave him some blood pressure medicine. He said it seemed like a half mile back to surgery through three sets of automatic doors. Each door they passed through it got colder. Daddy said it was cold enough for a slaughter house. But when they got there, they covered Daddy with a warm blanket. He said it sure felt good. During the procedure, Dr. J kept asking Daddy how he was doing, and Daddy always said he was fine. He said it didn't seem like long till they were done.

Mom and Dad still hold hands and smooch a bit, even after 76 years together. Mom said it's to "show the grands and great-grands that love can last a lifetime."

He went back to the room and had to lie flat on his back for two hours. They wanted to make sure Daddy didn't "spring a leak." Finally the nurse said Tam could take him home.

From my perspective at home. I was praying continually for Papa. All sorts of things were trying to get the upper hand. I raked a while and got the slope done. Went up and checked on Mama and put another log on the fire. Rita, Raylan and Athena came driving around toward the barn. Rita stopped and said she wanted to get some old hay to go over the ground around her potatoes. Athena stayed and help me pick up sticks, so sweet. After getting the hay, Rita helped too.

All this was right in the middle of Daddy's surgery. After he was done, I still couldn't get a plain picture of how it all turned out. I finally got the video Tam sent - about 3 sentences which could have been texted. I misunderstood what he said anyway! I thought the doctor had been able to open all of the arteries, but after talking to Sherry, I listened again and finally got that only **one** of the tibial arteries was good. The other two were closed off. They had to unstop the good one in two places – it was 90% closed. Tam thought the video would tell the tale, but I felt cut off from the knowledge and felt agitated not knowing. I needed to try and be patient; but, I felt denied my right to know, which in mind, I had sacrificed by not going there in order to stay here with Mama. I just felt left in the dark.

When Daddy got home, he was hungry since he hadn't eaten since yesterday. I fixed him a roll with ham; then he ate another roll and about half of some chicken nuggets Shaun brought. We all visited a while, then Shaun and Tam left, and we got ready for much needed rest.

THURSDAY, APRIL 13TH

In spite of no shower, no foot meds, and late coffee, Daddy rested well. I took out the ashes from the fire place and tried to build a fire since Daddy shouldn't lift the logs. Finally got a nice fire flaming up, and Daddy said, "Well, you aggravated it enough until it just gave up and started to burn." I got a laugh out of that. In a bit, Daddy chuckled, and I asked, "What makes you laugh?" He said, "Me thinking the doctor was tinkering with the wrong leg! He went in on the left side to correct the right leg. For a person without anatomy knowledge, it seemed wrong."

Shaun drove up later and visited a while. He and his friend, Ricky, plan to leave in the morning for a truck show in Oklahoma. Mama came in and asked Daddy how he was doing. He said his foot was burning and tingling like they said it would, due to returning circulation. Tam came over with a card for the staff for their excellent care of Daddy. She checked Daddy's foot and said the toes are amazing. Before, they looked like sticks. This morning they more pliable and the whole foot looks better.

At 1:30 pm Daddy's nurse showed up. She was here over an hour and was very thorough. Even gave him a cognitive test. Another nurse will be coming tomorrow and for the next 2 weeks until Daddy's follow up visit with his surgeon.

FRIDAY, APRIL 14TH

Up at 6:00 am. Good sleep – no foot issues. Shaun came up at 8:00 am to say bye. Lots of house chores, town trip for supplies, yard work, and laundry.

Joseph, a neighbor down the road who also bales Daddy's hay, brought the folks mustard greens and large onions from his garden. Wonderful to have good neighbors!

SATURDAY, APRIL 15TH

The usual race to get things done before heading to my house. Got all packed, then Sherry called. She, Stu and the baby are coming! I decided to make rolls. By the time they got here those rolls were ready to bake. Tam arrived right after they got here. Knoxlynn is so cute! We made pictures of Daddy and Mama holding her. I had fixed Mama's hair and she wore one of her pretty daisy denim dresses. This first visit to see her great-grandparents was so special. I held her a lot until time for them to go. After they left I fixed us some lunch; finally left around 5:00. Got home, walked around checking on my flowers, and made a blueberry smoothie for supper. Time to change gears.

TUESDAY, APRIL 18TH

Time to think of going back to the folks. I'm up before my alarm. Finished journal from yesterday, Bible verses, devotional and prayers. Out to finish what I can on the yard work.

Called and let the folks know I was running late. Got there and put everything away. Daddy had a gut episode after cereal this morning, so he ate a late supper. I fixed Mama's pizza – twice – I burned the first one. Washed dishes Tam and Addie came with groceries. I prayed for her eye surgery tomorrow. I could tell she had that on her mind.

WEDNESDAY, APRIL 19TH

About 12:37 am I heard Daddy going through the library and kitchen headed for the Big Room. His foot was bothering him and he was going after that pain medicine. Tonight, I am going back to our usual routine of lotion and pain medicine. When he got up this morning, he was in a talkative mood, and we spent a lot of time talking about the Depression years and the government programs that were tried to help get the country out of it, like the WPA, CCC, and so forth. Daddy's brother Henry was in the CCC, and later, Daddy had to wear one of those leftover uniforms when he first went to boot camp. Another program that made a big impression on Daddy was the cattle buyback around 1933 or so. The idea was to raise the price of cattle by reducing cattle numbers. He can still see that fellow walking around the pen, shooting the cows with a pistol. Grandpa was pretty salty, and he wouldn't let them shoot any of their stock except one yearling Henry took over there. You weren't even supposed to eat the cows either, just let them rot, but Henry brought that yearling back, and Ma canned it. Daddy has a wonderful memory, such a treasure at his age, and we are amazed at the changes he has witnessed. We want to hear all we can because, as he has said many times, "Each time an older person passes away, a little bit of history is lost."

After the trip through the past, Daddy and I got our gloves and headed to the barn. We loaded a winter's worth of feed sacks, mineral and salt sacks, boxes, and hay roll wraps into the pickup bed, along with some items from the tool room, then drove to the small brush pile by the burn barrel. We had just made a start at unloading when I checked my phone. The home health care nurse had arrived and had a trainee with her.

Mama followed the nurses into the kitchen. I knew what was coming before she said it. "You know how old this floor is?" (Of course they didn't.) "It is 65 years old." Poor nurses. "It looks good," they said. Mama said, "It is rubber and the color goes all the way through." Then she switches gears to the obvious: her age and Daddy's age. Bless her heart, it seems a compelsion, as Barney Fife would say. In her defense, she *did* pick out the flooring. Everything around her has changed including herself. It must be a comfort to look at one choice from the past that has stood the test of time.

The nurses went to Daddy's room to check his incision. I asked him later how he felt about being an "on the job training" subject. He said, "I'll be glad when it is over!" I replied, "It will be – Friday is the last day." We went back to our job and burned that huge load of trash.

Daddy is sleeping in the sunroom with his feet elevated above his heart. Now to start the stew. Hope he will be hungry at 1:30 pm. It is hard for me to adjust from 3 meals at home to two meals a day here, with a long time between and another before bed time. I usually have to eat something at 6 or 7. Because of this odd schedule, it is difficult to maintain my weight and probably not healthy either. Talked to Barbara, Angela, and Wyatt. Sometimes it is hard to keep up with my extended family as I live the life here (the folks') and there (home-children and grandchildren).

Shaun came after work. We went on a ride and I showed him our great cleanup. As we rode around, Shaun pointed out a thistle for *us* to get. He actually admitted he was too lazy to go out and dig them up!

THURDDAY, APRIL 20TH

Daddy came through at 5:15 am to make coffee. At 6:30 we headed out to burn brush and trim the fig trees. I got Mama's breakfast while Daddy went up to the barn for brush wash to start two more fires: old sweetgum stump and brush by the north pond, and the old hickory log and limbs just down the hill from the house. Got those going then came back up the hill and rounded up our first fire. It is looking to be a complete job. Back to Mama. I encourage her to start on a new puzzle.

Papa has elevated his feet and is asleep in his recliner. He has on his denim shirt and jacket. He gets cold so easily now. He loves sitting in the sunshine, such a comforting warmth.

Talked with Andy earlier. He wanted to tell me about the Cedar Waxwings working on his holly berries on the front of his house. We are kindred spirits when it comes to nature.

Texted Tam. Her eyes are still not clearing up. I reminded her that Dr. G said it would take 4-5 days.

While Daddy rested, I eased down the hill and tinkered with the hickory fire. Gathered more limbs to ensure Daddy has a clean field as he mows this summer. Came in and made cornbread, heated stew, out of butter, texted Tam and her 'country pantry' had butter. She also had a few apricot pastries for us. Daddy and I went over. When I ran in for the butter and pastries, she told me how badly her eyes had hurt the first day. She took two Aleve and went to bed. Today they were a little uncomfortable, but seemed to be clearing. Back to the house, then rounded up both fires. I told Daddy there were several big limbs way down the hill close to the east pond, so we went after those. He drove and I loaded; he was surprised at how many there were.

I got Mama situated at the puzzle table; Kleenex, shawl, glass of water and phone with my number so she could call if she needed me. We are expecting stormy weather in an hour; hope our fires will burn down by then. Daddy showers ahead of the storm. I am nodding off trying to study my Sunday school lesson. Storm rolls in – thunder and lightning, heavy rain.

FRIDAY, APRIL 21ST

I slept 8 hours … unheard of! I was so tired last night. Daddy and I sat in the sunroom enjoying a fine spring morning, then headed to the hill top barn. Daddy is interested in getting it cleaned and organized – again. It was really nice two and a half years ago when JoAnna and Rex used it for a wedding venue. The barn sits atop a hill that gives a wonderful view of wooded hills and both ponds. Beautiful!

Daddy cleaned off the cattle working supplies and sorted them. I swept up around the old chrome dining table with a chartreuse green top that Sherry and I remember using when we grew up, and the old feed bin Daddy used to keep hog feed in when he raised them way back in the day. We stopped at noon and came on home with a dash by the burn barrel to dump the paper trash off.

After lunch we went to the Homeplace to check on the beaver dam and the heifers. We were astonished at the red clover covering the hills. We chopped off some thistles before they went to seed, and tossed the tops into the truck bed. Drove to the house and up to the burn pit to dispose of those. After we threw them in the pit, Daddy poured on some lacquer thinner, a highly explosive fire starter. I have the matches. Daddy wanders back to the truck saying something about using a piece of feed sack to toss on the pile to set it afire. I don't think that will work, so I am steadily striking matches and tossing them on the pile, but the wind keeps blowing them out. Then a loud explosion and literal fire ball! I turned, screaming, took two long strides and fell like a ton of bricks, face planting in the spring flowers and (thankfully) soft soil! Daddy, in typical low-key fashion, turned and said, "What are you doing down there? Did you hurt yourself?" I said, "Yep, Daddy, it hurt." I wallowed around and got up. Trying to be positive, I said, "I don't think I broke anything." My little finger on my left hand was bruised and would give me trouble for several weeks, and I did skin the hide a little on my upper lip toward my nose. As we travel back to the house, Daddy said, "You sure you are okay?" I said, "I'm fine." It would be nice if Daddy was quicker with some sympathy; I know he feels it, but he just doesn't verbalize it.

Later, when Tam came over, I related the incident to her and she started to laugh. She could see it play out in typical Daddy fashion. She got me laughing, too. We found our balance in it all. She smiled and said she needed that good laughter. I have more material for her tomorrow: tonight when I reached up and grabbed the towel bar to help me up from the side of the tub, it just folded and I fell backwards, full force, feet flying upward, and strike my head on the base of the commode! I can hear Andy now, "Mama **that** is a towel bar. It isn't meant for you to pull up on!" I sort myself out and realize how blessed I was to fall between the toilet and the vanity. If I had fallen inches either way, I could have broken my neck!

SATURDAY, APRIL 22ND

I woke up at 1:30 am. After reading for a while, I decided to go to the Big Room and quilt. Mama was still watching *Andy Griffith*. She refuses to go by the daylight savings time, so in her realm, it was an hour earlier. She finally turned TV off, and I continued to quilt until 4:30 am. Went back to bed and dozed until I heard Daddy getting another container of coffee out of the hall pantry. Another day beginning. It is around 49 degrees so Daddy made a fire. We get our beverages and sit in front of it. Such a cozy time. At breakfast Daddy always says the morning prayer, asking God's blessing on our loved ones as they work and travel "to and fro"; one of my favorite lines in Daddy's prayers.

Sherry arrived and we took a walk in the pasture. The excuse was to look at the cleaned-up brush pile Daddy and I had burned, but the reality was that it was a beautiful spring day and we had not had the opportunity to walk and talk in a very long time. Down by the north pond we heard honking and here came six Canadian geese that circled the pond and landed. We had never seen that happen before. Back to the house and I left for my home as Sherry was going up to the barn to help Daddy take the hayforks off the tractor and put the bucket on so he can round up the blackjack oak limbs and burn them. Nothing like launching right into the heat of battle! I smile and ask if he could wait on me until next week so I can help. Explosions aside, there is nothing I like better than helping Papa.

Sherry called later. They are discussing changes to the hall bathroom to make it safer for me. I got the word about the bathroom on Sunday. Preservation of the vintage bathroom seems to be the top priority. I think Brother will put up a safer bar that I can pull up on. One side of me understands that, but the other side is feeling that I rate somewhere below the bathroom wallpaper. Sigh.

WEDNESDAY, APRIL 26TH

Back to the folks last night after Garrett's baseball game. It was a wild and stormy night. I noticed that the French drain in the corner of the garage and side porch was stopped up, so I got the hoe and raked out the leaves and such. I discovered that an old license plate had fallen on the drain and was blocking it. Got Mama started on her day. Tam and Daddy went to his follow-up from the leg surgery; that seems to be healing nicely.

After lunch, Tam wanted to go to Steele's in Troup. Daddy was excited to see the bridges on the way to Troup after months of construction, so he came also. We shopped a while – they have so many great items – then the weather sirens went off and the bottom dropped out of a black cloud. It poured. Finally, Tam drove around to the back where could get in the car and stay mostly dry. After we arrived home with our goods, Mama said Shaun had been by and helped her with one of her bird puzzles.

THURSDAY, APRIL 27TH

Checked the rain gauge; we got 4 8/10" of rain the last 2 days! Daddy is reading an autobiography about Hobby Lobby's president. Following a thread of our conversation about that, I went on line to check on the latest developments in manufacturing, 3-D printers, Space X rockets, Artificial Intelligence, and so forth. What does the future hold? From the vantage point of almost 100 years, it seems like science fiction to Daddy. He has observed more change on our planet than any other person alive unless they are his age.

Later when I started lunch, the oven wouldn't come on – had to cook at Tam's. Glad she's close by.

FRIDAY, APRIL 28TH

Tam was over early so I could braid her hair for her eye appointment and she could put Daddy's hearing aids in. Daddy and I had a seminar at the county barn: heifer reproduction, herbicides and weeds, pond management. Had some nice free items and a good lunch. We left before the hover craft demo, but we saw it on the ground.

Stove got fixed, including the drawer for cookie sheets and cooling racks that had been driving us crazy.

Tam came by later very upset. The surgery didn't help her eyes! Later in the day, I saw her walk over the hill and down to the creek. My heart hurts for her. I know she will get over the disappointment – in time. She has weathered so much. I'm so glad her strength will be renewed by her Lord.

SATURDAY, APRIL 29TH

Andy has decided to sell his small longhorn herd. I'm glad I am here and not there. Large beasts with very long and sharp horns being loaded into a trailer is the stuff of nightmares, but my prayers were answered and all went well.

Cloudy and windy. Loaded the car. Gave Mama a spa treatment and braided her hair. Hugs and goodbyes. Mama said she would miss me. As I traveled, I gradually made the transition from my folks' trials and triumphs to my own.

Tamra

SATURDAY, APRIL 1ST

April Fool's Day…I wondered if I could pull one on somebody today? I always enjoyed pranking Marc, he was easy to get…Dad was a little more of a challenge. He can read you like a book…crack a smile and you're done for.

I was up and out the door to Mom and Dad's before 7:30. I wanted some time to visit with Sherry before everyone else arrived for the cattle working. She caught me up on her babysitting adventures and showed me the latest pictures; that little girl is the fattest, cutest baby ever!

After Shaun and Jason showed up, we all headed to the barn. We had good success with working the heifers, even though one got her head twisted between the chute bars and almost passed out before she could get herself extracted. We got the heifers loaded into the trailer, and Shaun and I took them to the Homeplace. If the grass holds out, Dad said we will leave them there until we start haying this fall. We also took some salt and mineral for them.

While we were gone, Dad and Jason stayed and worked on the pile of wood at the shed, splitting and stacking. Sherry went back to the house to check on Mom and found the house locked, so she walked back to the barn and got my keys to open the door…and hung them up on the key board by the door. I didn't discover where they were until after several frantic searches. Sherry left before we got back, so she was blissfully unaware of the entire drama. We all got a laugh out of that.

I went to town to get groceries and meds, and then fixed lunch. Jason and Shaun couldn't stay, so it was just me and Dad. Mom had hers later in the day, as usual. Mom felt pretty perky today. She worked on her jigsaw puzzle most of the afternoon, and then read on the Kindle until almost 9:00 pm.

Mom is single-handedly keeping Puffs tissues in business. I find them everywhere – in her chair, on the floor, the bathroom counter, the pockets of her gowns (which is a mess if I forget to check them before washing). Every surface has a least one box of tissues on it. I must admit, I contribute somewhat to the tissue industry's vitality, as Mom and Dad's carpet kicks up a sneezing frenzy more often than not.

And dang it…I never did get anyone for April Fool's Day!

SUNDAY, APRIL 2ND

Today was a good day, church service especially, and Dad seemed to have recovered from his big day yesterday. Our Easter cool spell, as Dad calls it, is on the way, so today was unseasonably warm ahead of the norther. Rita and the kids came over later, and I took them for a walk in the northwest woods to show them the maypops and dogwoods blooming. We had a good time exploring. On the way back, in the open meadow, Raylan and Athena had fun trying to catch a big yellow Sulphur butterfly. When we got back, they helped me make some cookies for their Pawpaw. Athena was the stirrer; Raylan was the spoon and beater cleaner. After they left, I went home to feed my critters and check on Marc, then went to church. When I got back, I reminded Dad to take his pills, doctored his feet, and then got ready for bed myself. Dad was in a talkative mood, so I stayed up and listened, even though I think I drifted off a time or two before he decided to call it a night.

MONDAY, APRIL 3RD

When Caleb was leaving for work today, he noticed my right rear tire was going flat. So, after I finished feeding and headed back to Mom and Dad's for the day, I called the tire shop. Dad was all ready to go to work on that fallen blackjack on the top of the hill, but I told him I needed to get to town before my tire went completely flat. He said "it wouldn't take long" for him to get that tree cut up. Haha

Dad pulling huge thistles at the Homeplace, it is a constant battle to keep them from taking over the pastures.

He was up there an hour, then went to the barn to get the tractor and start pushing limbs around. I couldn't leave with him out there, so I just kept an eye on him through the binoculars, worked on Mom's stuff and waited. About 10:30, he finally rolled up to take a break and I went to town. Got the tire fixed, a few groceries, and when I got home, I started working on the maple-glazed pork chop recipe I created. I wanted to try it out on Dad to get his opinion. He immediately headed back to his tree work, and I finished cooking lunch. It was quite the feat to keep an eye on Dad, one on the stove, and answer Mom's calls for assistance, but I managed to pull it off. I could see Dad through the kitchen window if I hunkered down and peered through the bottom right corner with the binoculars. I wish I'd had a speeded up video of that episode…would have been ridiculous!

Thank goodness, Mom's curiosity overcame her, and she made her way into the kitchen and sat at the table while I finished dinner. She was still sitting there forty-five minutes later when Dad finally came home to eat. They visited while I set the table and we all ate together, which is a treat these days. Dad gave the recipe his "seal of approval," which means I can add it to my repertoire.

I thought Dad would call it a day, but after he rested, he headed out again. I should have known better…we *both* ended up working on that tree, me chaining and Dad pulling trunk sections and limbs till nearly dark.

THURSDAY, APRIL 6TH

Terrible lightning storm tonight, it hit close by and I heard a crackling sound near the wall by my bed. It hit all five of our phones and the base; they are deader than a hammer. Good grief, another expense. Poor Rita and Jason, the lightning hit one of the pecan trees closest to their bedroom – it knocked pictures off the wall and threw stuff off the windowsills, right on top of them! The kids were in there too because they were afraid of the storm. Rita said it was chaos for a few minutes. It also fried their hot water heater.

Today I had a revelation as I was reading the passage from Luke 12: 7 "But even the very hairs of your head are all numbered." That always bothered me before, because it didn't make sense that God would count the hairs on our heads…and what about bald people? Then, today I realized he was not talking about the number of hairs, but that the hairs had numbers! Of course, God knows us, even down to our DNA number sequence… that is the number He was referring to! Now, it made perfect sense to me. And God just got even bigger than I imagined.

SATURDAY, APRIL 8TH

What was supposed to be a fun day of working the cows and then celebrating Mom and Dad's anniversary started out on a sad note. Mel found Hobo dead outside on the mat this morning. She called me and I came over and moved him to the picnic table till Sherry got here, then we said our goodbyes and buried him. I picked a spot overlooking the ponds and where I knew the sand was easy digging, so I could bury her deep enough and hopefully keep some critter from disturbing her. I am sure going to miss that silly cat! She was always trying to get my attention when I was sitting outside and first thing in the morning, when she wanted fed. She was a handsome cat in her tuxedo coat. I deducted that she might have been poisoned, but it would be hard to tell. People are always poisoning gophers, mice, etc. out here, so she could have gotten ahold of a contaminated pest. I know Dad will miss her; she followed him everywhere, even climbing up on the ladder rungs while he worked. She tolerated us, but she was a one-man cat.

We got the cows worked without too much excitement, which is always good, but the tree cutting that commenced later came with its own heart-stopping moments. After Ethan had cut the huge oak, Dad was running his chainsaw in a big pile of limbs and he stumbled and fell…with the chainsaw running! Fortunately, he didn't damage himself too badly, and after they finished working on the tree, Dad let me and Sherry patch him up.

Mom and Dad read their cards, except Shaun's (haha), and after we ate, everyone visited for a bit, then went their own way. Mel was the last to leave, around 5:00. Dad was tired, so he sat on the porch till it started to "cool off." Even though it was still in the sixties at sundown, he decided he needed a fire. He is going to give me a heat stroke. I would have loved to sit on the loveseat and prop my feet up, I was exhausted, but I'm relegated to the hard kitchen chairs, lest I melt. Dad's 99 year old metabolism is out of whack, so he puts more logs on the fire, fills up the wood box, and sits on the fireplace hearth to "warm his back." How will I survive the summer!

SUNDAY, APRIL 9TH

We had a good crowd for the Easter service today. I took Athena and Raylan some cupcakes and cookies since they couldn't be there for their Nannie and Pawpaw's anniversary yesterday. Hope they get over the strep throat soon, that is no fun.

It was the first time I can remember that we have had no little ones hunting Easter eggs in Mom and Dad's front yard. It was a melancholy afternoon for me, full of memories and the echoes of long ago laughter and front porch conversations.

Shaun came up late this afternoon to take Dad on a ride to see the cows and check for new baby calves. While they were gone, I moved the little house Dad had built for Hobo down to the barn and put her dishes inside, along with her blanket. It looks so bare on the patio now. It will take some getting used to.

This evening, Dad seemed in a rather pensive mood, so we didn't talk much, just sat in comfortable silence and watched the sunset. Thank goodness, it had warmed considerably, so he decided to forgo an evening fire.

WEDNESDAY, APRIL 12TH

Today was Dad's surgery in Tyler. I couldn't find a park, so we circled till I felt part buzzard. Finally, I let Dad off at the front doors and went across the street and down the block where, thank the Lord, I found one parking spot open. We finally got checked in and into the room where Dad was having his surgery. It was my job to keep my siblings and Mom informed. I thought I did a pretty good job, tried sending pictures and updates, but I had a poor signal, so they didn't always go through when I sent them. I think Mel expected a minute by minute account, which I did *not* do. Although I *did* send twenty-six texts, seven photos, and a video, but I guess that wasn't enough…haha. She survived the day though, and Dad did very well. Dr. J was pleased and I made sure the others heard it straight from the doc via the video message. It was a long day of waiting, but I am glad I could be there for Dad. He was in good spirits when we started home late that evening, and he said he was going to "be happy to be in my own bed tonight; that hospital bed was terrible."

MONDAY, APRIL 17TH

I didn't keep up with my journal this past week. No excuses, I just didn't. Glad Sherry and Mel are so thorough… Dad is recovering nicely from his surgery. The home health nurse said he was a great patient. Funny…I don't remember Mom's saying that.

It was a beautiful day today, 45 degrees this morning and up to 78 by this afternoon. Dad piddled all day, did some porch sitting and just enjoyed the sunshine. I cleaned, cooked, tutored after Mom, all the usual things. I also planted the beautiful hydrangeas that cousin Deborah gave Mom and Dad for their anniversary. I helped Mom pick out a thank you card for Deborah and fixed it to mail tomorrow, along with one for Sherry, and a get well to a friend at church. Mom was worn out after that and slept for a couple of hours.

I managed to go over to my house to edit my Mother's Day column and get it sent in, ordered Dad some new sheets too. I am tired of those horrible green ones with the holes in them – time to retire them and give Shaun some more paint rags.

MONDAY, APRIL 24TH

Dad went up to feed the heifers and got some firewood. He also brought the sprayer down for me to clean. After I finished that project, I made some ANZAC Biscuits in honor of ANZAC Day tomorrow. (That has been a tradition with us since we had Bridget, a New Zealander, stay with us as an exchange student. We still keep in touch, even after twenty years.) Dad likes them, so I know they won't last long.

Shaun stopped by early to get the measurements for the new grab bar he is picking up today for the bathroom. Dad's home health nurse is so sweet, they had the best visit. Her Dad was in the service and she wanted to see all of Dad's WW II stuff.

Dad hasn't been reading much lately, so I asked him if he would be interested in a book about David Green, the founder of Hobby Lobby. He said he thought he might like to read that, so I got it downloaded and he started reading right away and read off and on all afternoon. I helped Mom on the new puzzle I got her for Mother's Day. It was a little early, but I thought it might perk her up…and it did. Dad's new sheets came today. I washed them and put them on, happy to send the old holey ones with Shaun. When he came by with the new grab bar to install, I told him about Mom being all grumpy this morning and talking "mean" to me and then when you came by, she was all smiles. Shaun said, "You need to come around less often!" Ha ha, like *that* is possible. He and I both laughed and laughed.

TUESDAY, APRIL 25TH

Crazy day! Fed my critters, etc. early, went back to Mom and Dad's to fix breakfast, meds, etc. Left at 8:30 to pick Addie up at her house, I forgot how long a drive it is. I barely made it back to WMA in time. Afterwards,

I went back to Mom and Dad's to give her the morning meds, checked on Dad, then on to Wally World and Porter's for meds, back home, drop off stuff, head back out to Addie's piano lesson, then back to cook lunch for Mom and Dad. Helped Addie with lessons, and then asked her to talk to her Pawpaw about Japan, since he's been there. She was curious about what it was like during the war and right after. He was there for over six months and has plenty of stories. They talked until Rachel came to pick her up. I thought to myself – how many young people are that lucky, that they can hear first-hand stories from a WW II veteran. I hope she remembers this day. As for me, I am so tired…I can't wait to get home and sleep in my own bed.

WEDNESDAY, APRIL 26TH

I took Dad to his follow-up appointment with Dr. J. The doc said the circulation was much improved and he expected it to continue to get better with time. I hope he's right; Dad has suffered with that foot and leg problem for a long while now.

Late this afternoon, I wanted to go to the local feed store, and check out their gift items and see if they had any new stuff. Mel and Dad wanted to come along, so off we went. We enjoyed browsing while Dad visited with the owners about fertilizer and feed.

While we were there, it got really dark outside and the tornado siren went off. What to do? It started pouring rain and the lightning was awful. Dad didn't look at all concerned. He just found a chair and said, "Well, we'll either get blowed away or we won't, but I'm sitting down." We all laughed because we realized he was right. Where could we go anyway?

We survived the storm and drove the ten miles home in the still pouring rain at a top speed of about 30 mph. Mel was on pins and needles, but Dad and I laughed and joked till we got home. What an adventure for a Wednesday!

THURSDAY, APRIL 27TH

Mom and Dad's oven went out, so Mel had to bring the meat to cook in my oven. I called Leslie B. and he said he could come fix it tomorrow morning. He is a real peach, the best repair man around!

FRIDAY, APRIL 28TH

What a long two weeks it has been…my eye surgery was horrendous, and it took a week of recovery before I was able to see well enough that I didn't have to wear sunglasses *inside*. The light still bothers me some, but only if I am on my computer too long.

I did not get a good report today, so I have had to come to terms with that. Hopefully, time will prove that report wrong.

I am so thankful for my sisters and how they helped me out during this time. Sherry taking part of my "shift" and editing my article for me, Mel by taking part of my time and making sure there was food, etc. at Mom and Dad's when I came back. I am looking forward to getting back into our routine. It is tough sometimes, but I prefer it to what I've dealt with lately.

SATURDAY, APRIL 29TH

I head over to Mom and Dad's to spell Mel off and learned that Dad's only remaining Seabee buddy had called and talked to him this morning. He lives in Pennsylvania and he and Dad correspond and visit by phone often. They are so funny when they get to talking about old times…I love the way Dad's face lights up when he is on the phone with Paul.

SUNDAY, APRIL 30TH

Went to church and after lunch I planted the six poinsettias Mom and Dad had left over from Christmas. They were still in pretty good shape, so Dad hated to toss them. Poinsettias in spring? Who am I to judge?

Rita and the kids came by this afternoon and I got Emelia and brought her over so she could play with the kids. After Rita left, Emelia and I went for a walk in the pasture. She loved rolling around in the tall red clover. She thought it was hilarious when I dropped down on the ground and joined her in the sweet-smelling stuff. We had so much fun rolling around and laughing, we stayed till it was almost dark, and then walked home hand in hand.

Let it go, AS ELSA ADVISED. DON'T HANG ONTO NEGATIVE EMOTIONS, IT WILL *snowball* INTO A MUCH BIGGER PROBLEM IF ALLOWED TO LINGER.

MAY

May is one of the kinder months in Texas, offering an abundance of blooming things, bountiful gardens, and gentler weather. One of the things I remember about past Mays was the busyness of the season – school was winding down for the year, with graduations, end-of-year parties and awards ceremonies, senior trips, but most of all, the anticipation of our family being together again for the upcoming long days of summer… days we would spend working and playing outside, unhurried trips to the library and the Piggly Wiggly, occasional treats at Abell's Drug Store with vanilla shakes and hamburgers from their counter grill, hauling square bales of hay on our truck until the wee hours of the night, time spent fishing in our ponds and wading in the creek.

Blackberry time is in early May and we always looked forward to Mom's delicious blackberry cobblers and blackberry jelly. We would often end the comfortable days of May with a brown stoneware bowl of that cobbler, enjoying the tart dessert on the screened-in porch as we watched night descend on our farm.

Many times, I have wondered what our lives would be like if we had not been raised on that place we call Poverty Ridge. I guess that was the greatest decision Mom and Dad made as a couple, to stay here and make a go of it, instead of chasing their fortunes in the city. That fateful night in Texas City, when Dad told Mom he was taking her home, back to East Texas, changed not only their future, but ours as well…and I am forever grateful.

The security, stability, and comfort of living in one place has given us deep roots and strengthened us as adults. Such old-fashioned notions have grown out of vogue lately – most people think you have to leave where you grew up to "find yourself" and, maybe some do, but for us, staying was, and is, an anchor we grow to appreciate more the older we get. Dad, in his wisdom, saw the value in giving that gift, first to our Mother, then to us. Mom had a mostly wretched childhood. She lost her father at age one, grew up being pulled from "pillar to post" by a stepfather who regularly abandoned his family to go on "walkabouts," as he called them, leaving her Mother with nine children to care for and work in the fields.

Mom grew up as a sharecropper's daughter, never having a place to call home, few material goods, and the overarching fear of never feeling like she was good enough. It was a hard life and affected her deeply. As a result, she never wanted us to do without, but she made sure we appreciated what we did have, even if it was hand-made or hand me downs.

Our parents taught us the value of learning contentment – the wisdom in wanting what you have and enjoying it, and not always looking for the "next" thing.

During this time of year, I find myself reflecting on those long ago decisions, the values that drove them and the contrast to today's families. I wonder what the world would look like now if more parents made choices that valued lasting treasures instead of the temporal…I believe it would be a better place.

Sherry

THURSDAY, MAY 4TH

Love, love, love keeping my sweet baby granddaughter, but there are things I wish I could help with at Mom and Dad's, too. Melanie was trying to handle some financial stuff for Pop today … things I usually do, so I felt guilty for not being there.

FRIDAY, MAY 5TH

Mom and Pop's power went off last night, so Mom came to where Melanie was soundly sleeping and woke her up, wanting her to call the power company. Mom was the only one who noticed it go off because she was up late (as usual) watching her movies. When the power goes off, no entertainment! Poor Melanie, when she is awakened like that, she usually can't go back to sleep … she sounded so tired.

SATURDAY, MAY 6TH

Well, Pop has to deal with some unpleasantness about his fence line – what a shame that he has to deal with such things at nearly 100 instead of just enjoying life. There's still fire under that snowy roof, though; he wants right to prevail. We'll see how it all shakes out.

WEDNESDAY, MAY 10TH

Today is the anniversary of Josh's death in 1986. When I talked to Melanie, she said that she, Tam, and Pop were going up to the family cemetery to spend a little time. I wonder if Pop is thinking that it might not be long before he sees Josh again. That experience had to be the hardest one he and Mom have endured in all their lives. And Tam and Josh were so close. We all lost a brother that day, but Tam also lost her best friend.

FRIDAY, MAY 12TH

My grandson Cooper is 13 today! Oh my, I can't believe how fast he's growing up.

SATURDAY, MAY 13TH

Up to J'ville to celebrate Mother's Day with Mom. I brought a vase of roses from my pitiful, neglected rose garden. There's just no time to do everything with the ten-plus hour days of keeping Baby Girl. Not that I'm complaining … I'll take caring for my little Peach Blossom over a thousand rose gardens any day.

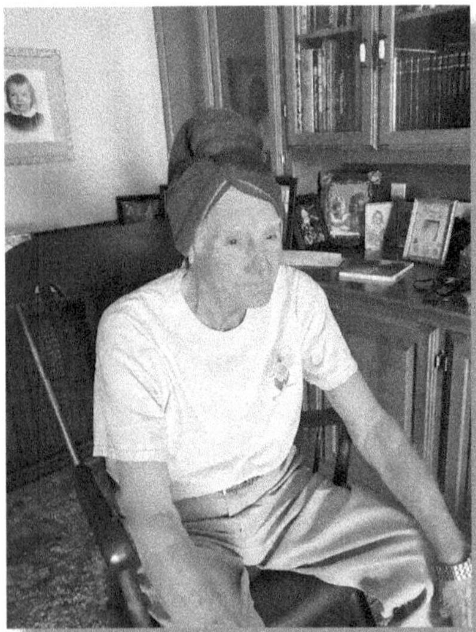

Mel gives Dad a "spa day" and I don't know what he thought about the manicure and the hair treatment…but, I think he enjoyed it.

I gave Pop the new belt to try on – I couldn't believe the sad looking one he had on and that he'd worn to *town* yesterday. A piece of baling twine would've looked about as good. I'd ordered four jigsaw puzzles for Mom from Melanie and me; I let her choose which two she wanted to give Mom. Then she and I went up to the cemetery to water the flowers. After we got back to the house, Mel saw my card for Mom and showed me hers – the exact same card. This is the fourth or fifth time we've gotten the same card for either Mom or Dad. How do we manage that?

Tam arrived, and she and Melanie got Mom all fixed up, then took her picture with two puzzles she'd put together. We wanted to get those taken apart so she'd be able to start one of her new ones today. I gave Pop a manicure then set the dining table. We girls headed out to pick up lunch.

Sometimes you just need to take the easy road instead of wearing yourself out cooking. Shaun was at the house when we got back. After I heated the fries in the air fryer, I piled them on a plate and took them into the dining room. When Pop saw them, he tapped the table top next to his plate and said, "Just put those fries down here." Pop loves his fries! We all had a great time – lots of laughter and talking.

Had to leave at 3:30 because Bill and I had a neighborhood potluck to attend. When Bill reached in his closet to grab a shirt, it was wet! We have a roof leak. Stu came over and found a hole where a limb punched through during one of our spring storms. While the guys worked on a temporary patch, Ashley and I strolled Little Bit down the street. Glad to see them even if it's for such a reason.

SUNDAY, MAY 14TH

Sent Happy Mother's Day texts to several folks. Ben called to wish me a happy day. While he was on the phone, I opened the gifts he'd sent: a Jane Austin cup and a book about where famous writers liked to sit and compose their manuscripts – I will enjoy both of those.

Knoxlynn's baby dedication was at church today – a precious time. After church Bill and I picked up lunch to take to Stu and Ashley's. Her folks came also. The kids had gotten me a necklace engraved with Knoxlynn on one side and Cooper and Parker on the other side. We all had fun and enjoyed watching the little one.

MONDAY, MAY 15TH

The end of keeping my baby is weighing on me – I'm going to cry next week. Pop has an eye exam and shot today – hope it goes well.

TUESDAY, MAY 16TH

Pop now has wet macular degeneration in addition to the dry … so very discouraging. Poor Pop. The shots are very expensive, but they are checking into some help for those.

Two roofing contractors came by today and left bids for a new roof. Yay.

WEDNESDAY, MAY 17TH

My first baby is 46 today! I called Ben and wished him a happy day, and got to say Hi to Cooper and Parker. They'll be moving to their new place nearTampa soon.

SUNDAY, MAY 21ST

Found out that Ben and family will be here for a visit next Friday and Saturday … such a welcome surprise!

MONDAY, MAY 22ND

Last week to keep my baby girl … I will miss this so much – leaning over her crib and seeing that instant smile, watching her gazing up at the leaves overhead on a stroller ride, the satisfaction of getting her little tummy full, then napping together in the recliner under a cozy blanket, so many special moments.

When I got home, I found a lovely bouquet on the doorstep – an early birthday gift from Ben and family – very thoughtful.

TUESDAY, MAY 23RD

I'm 73 today … Yikes! Hope my health holds out so I can keep Sugar Dumpling and help with the folks, too. Lots of cards/texts/calls. Melanie sent a video of her and Pop singing "Happy Birthday" to me. I loved that.

It's also Stu and Ashley's anniversary, so after a brief time at home to fix supper, I drove back to their house to keep Knoxlynn so her parents could have a relaxing meal somewhere.

THURSDAY, MAY 25TH

My last day to keep Baby Cake, at least on a regular basis. I wanted to savor every moment, but some drama on the home front blew that plan up … that's the way it goes sometime.

FRIDAY, MAY 26TH

A whirl of activity until Ben and family arrived around 2:00. Such a joy to see them all! Cooper is so tall – he has nearly caught up to his dad at only thirteen. The boys enjoyed meeting their new cousin, but since Knoxlynn isn't doing much, Coop's interest waned after a while, but Parker remained intrigued a bit longer. Bill surprised Coop and me with a cookie cake – our birthdays are not far apart. A fun time for all!

SATURDAY, MAY 27TH

A busy morning all around with another visit from Stu and family. Then Bill went to the church to trim hedges while Ben and family and I went to J'ville to see Mom and Dad. Melanie had fresh yeast rolls – she knows Ben loves those! I walked with the boys up to the hay barn. Coop was surprised at how different it looked from last December; it was mostly full of bales then, but now it was mostly empty. I reminded him that those bales were the cows' winter food – they'd eaten most of it already. These were leftover bales, but Pawpaw would have to grow a lot more grass for next winter.

Later, Shaun brought his side-by-side up so Ben and family could drive among the cows for a closer look. Parker especially wanted to see Sancho – he is an impressive sight. Ben let Coop drive back up the hill. It won't be long until he'll be driving for real … time surely marches on.

When we left, with a sack of rolls in hand, the same thought came to mind as when Brandon had said his goodbye a few weeks ago: would this be the last time Ben and family get to see Pop, or Mom? Even though Mom is four years younger than Dad, there's no guarantee that she won't go first … no guarantee of anything at their age.

SUNDAY, MAY 28TH

Up very early since Ben and Shelley want to eat by 6:00 and get on the road. After breakfast, they packed and we got a few photos before they pulled out for Jackson to visit her folks, then on to Montgomery to get squared away for their move to the Tampa area. What a whirlwind they have ahead!

MONDAY, MAY 29TH

Tam and Pop were gone when I arrived; they were at the Tecula cemetery where a lot of Pop's family is buried. They were putting flags on the veterans' graves … a good thing to do this Memorial Day. I checked on Mom and helped her with a puzzle until they got back; then Tam and I talked about available food, who needs what, etc. She told me the sassafras trees are all dying – the one just outside the kitchen window, the two on the west side of the sunroom, all the ones at the Tecula cemetery, all dying – some disease that just came out of nowhere. It seems that a new pestilence emerges every few months now.

After lunch I went over to Tam and Marc's to thank her again for allowing me the time to keep Knoxlynn until Ashley's school year ended. If I had missed that opportunity, there would be no getting it back.

Pop plans for us to go down to the Homeplace in the morning and continue painting. He's been having more problems with his intestines – I hope he'll be okay.

TUESDAY, MAY 30TH

Holy Hannah … what a night! Mom hollered for me around 11:30. I woke up with a start and flew into the Big Room. She was standing at the bottom of the three steps going up to the dining room. When I asked what was wrong, she said she thought she was dying – her heart hurt! I gave her two baby aspirin and tried to calm her down. Of course, she wanted immediate results, but we waited a bit before taking a third, then later a fourth. Mom said she'd never felt this way before, but I told her she actually had … I'd recently read it in my journal. And, it turned out to be gas back then. So, I gave her a Gas-X and some Tums. Then I rubbed lotion on her feet and legs to get her to relax. We also walked around the Big Room several times – that can help if you have gas. Poor Mom – she was praying out loud, asking why, and moaning. Bless her heart, she says she wants to go on, but when she hurts, she wants us to fix it!

After a while, she got easier – I don't think she wanted to admit it was gas. Around 3:30, I lay on the sofa outside her room and drifted off to sleep. Then Mom said she wanted to lie back in her recliner, so I got her all fixed up. I thought it was 4:30 and I could maybe grab an hour of sleep, but right after I lay back down, my 5:30 phone alarm went off. Groan.

Turned on the coffee pot to perk, then went back to bed – woke up to the perking and didn't have a clue how long it had been galloping along. I was afraid it would be a stiff cup to drink, but it was fine. Got into bed with the cup, and Pop's bathroom light came on. We have to get a handle on this gut situation. He'll get so dehydrated and weak that he'll wind up in the hospital.

We didn't get to the Homeplace until a little after 8:30. I scraped loose paint off and dusted down the boards while Pop painted. Rita and the kids came out to say hello before they headed out. Athena has a missing front tooth now, so cute. Pop and I worked until noon and got a lot of the east side done. Since we were doing that, Tam went over and fixed Mom's breakfast and got her meds ready.

After lunch, I had a town run, then fixed Mom's lunch and so on until bedtime. Hope I have some good sleep tonight.

WEDNESDAY, MAY 31ST

Well, I did get good sleep, but not Pop – he was up several times in the night with loose bowels. I told him we needed some answers, and the first step was getting a stool sample checked. He's a private person, and talking about stuff like this is hard for him. It doesn't come easy for me, either, but we girls are the front line of defense for him and Mom, so we just have to jump in with both feet, comfortable or not. Tam told me that watermelon could cause loose bowels, too, and Pop and I happened to eat a big bowl of that yesterday, but this situation has been going on for some time.

Down to the Homeplace to paint, wonky gut notwithstanding, Pop is relentless. We worked on the north porch today – Pop on the outside overhang and me on the inside walls and ceiling. While moving the ladder, Pop found a hen's nest with six eggs in it. Athena made an "apron" out of her shirt tail, gathered the eggs, and took them to Rita. After I got my area scraped and dusted for Pop, I moved back around to the east side to paint some more.

We took a break about 10:00 – Pop was feeling the effects of his rough night. He intended to paint the last wall of the porch near the bottom, but he just couldn't do it. He said he was like those batteries for his chainsaw and blower – when they ran out of juice, they just quit. It makes me sad to see Pop discouraged about being so weak. I try to point out how amazing it is that he can do what he does at his age and with the gut issue, to boot. People just shake their heads when we tell them what Pop is still able to do. But he was used up today – he could hardly get into the truck, and I could tell he was dizzy when we got home, so I gave him a glass of electrolyte water and some potato chips.

Checked on Mom, then made sure Pop made it to the sunroom okay. Made lunch and started washing dishes. While I was doing all that, Mom came to the Big Room steps and asked, "Are you ever going to get time to put out another puzzle for me?" She had just finished one this morning. I don't know where that "ever" came from … it wasn't like I was propped up in bed reading a novel and eating bonbons. Anyhow, a full afternoon and evening of chores … found a bill two months past due, don't know how it got buried, but it's a wonder we keep things as straight as we do with our flying in and out.

Melanie

TUESDAY, MAY 2ND

Glad to see the new towel bar in the hall bathroom – it looks nice and strong. I look forward to trying it out tonight. Jason helped Daddy with another tree yesterday and took one load to the wood shed. The small beef calf got out of the pen again. Daddy and I talked about fertilizer for the meadow on Hwy 135 and about turning the cattle business over to Tam and Shaun, again. He knows he needs to let them start taking care of all this, but it's difficult to let go after being in charge for decades. Now Daddy and Mama are doing Kindle reading. I used that nice bar in the bathroom for the first time – I felt very safe pulling up on it.

WEDNESDAY, MAY 3RD

Daddy wanted to get that bent post oak up to the wood shed, so he went to get the tractor and was gone so long I went to check on him. He was trying to air up a tire, so I helped by reading the pressure gauge.

I rode the tractor with Daddy down to the tree where he used the cant hook to maneuver four sections into the bucket and took those to the shed. Got several more loads and on the last one, we both forgot the cant hook was on top and dumped it, but I retrieved it. Home health care nurse coming at 11:30, so Daddy shaved and changed clothes while I started lunch. After the nurse visit, lunch and rest, then back to work on that tree. Rounded up limbs and set those on fire and also got the blackjack oak pile going, then back to the house.

Brother arrived and we took a ride over the pasture. Shaun was lamented the washing away of a lot of his dirt work of several weeks ago. Later, when we were outside, I trained the binoculars on the fence neck that narrows the flow of cattle toward the corral and saw that our escaped beef was up there. We went to see if we could get him penned. He evaded us twice, but we finally managed to get him into the pen. We felt pretty good about that.

Good day with phone calls back and forth with Sherry, Sunday school ladies, Andy's work on his house: all interwoven in this here-and-there life.

THURSDAY, MAY 4TH

Jason came over to split the post oak while Daddy got on the tractor and brought in the last loads from yesterday. I filled up the calf's watering trough, took the weed eater to the cemetery and trimmed the persimmon valley and around the outside of the fence. When we got back to the house, Joseph had left 5 huge onions, a very large cabbage and a dozen eggs. What a thoughtful neighbor. I called and thanked him. Talked with Sherry several times. Her granddaughter goes to the SFA daycare on June 5th. Our schedule will change after that. Got Mama's hair braided, she fixed up with a touch of makeup and we took two puzzle pictures.

Shaun came early and told us about his day. Daddy asked him about the barn door, and they looked at it. Shaun will need help to repair it. Then he got on the tractor and pushed the old hay off the hill and down into the washed-out areas to stop deep gullies from forming. Daddy has a lot on his mind, and needs to talk it out, many times, until he's easy about it or it gets solved one way or another. Mama's home health care nurse arrived, followed by Rita and family. Raylan handed Mama a small wildflower bouquet. Shaun called Jason and he came over to help with the barn door. Late this afternoon I eased down the hill to round up the fire, heard the truck fire up, and here came Daddy. As he passed he said, "Thought you could sneak off without me." I laughed. We enjoyed the day's end; birds, green hills, sawing and piling, a perfect late afternoon.

FRIDAY, MAY 5TH

It was another wild and stormy night. About 2:00 am here came Mama on her walker with a small flashlight! The electricity was off and she was not happy. I told her someone had already called it in. Sure enough, at 3:18 am, it came back on. I had gotten a really late text and picture from grandson, Garrett. He had gotten a beautiful belt buckle from FFA shooting team. I couldn't go back to sleep for a while. Daddy making coffee at 6:30 woke me up. I dragged myself out of bed. We got 8/10" of rain. We went up after breakfast to see if we could open the barn door. Nope. Couldn't budge it. Plan B – I made a list for a town trip. Shaun came by and was not optimistic about a lift for a tall outside job he had. Got Mama's breakfast. Went to the mailbox and found a check we had been looking for and made out a deposit slip for it – one more stop in addition to 5 different stores. While we were in town, Shaun texted that the lift worked great. That was a relief to Daddy – he still worries when his kids have troubles, in spite of the fact that his "kids" are all over fifty years old!

Daddy and I ate lunch. Rested a while. Tried to write in my journal. Ended in squiggles down the page. Shaun came by and talked a while. He plans to fix the barn door tomorrow morning. I went for a walk and saw # 32 have her baby. Looked over the 10 cows still to calve: 3 on the short list – soon, 6 on the June, July & August list.

After Mama's lunch, I helped Daddy put termite poison in the sprayer for tomorrow. We came in and sat on the front porch and watched the moon rise through the dead branches of the big ditch oak. Heard the first whippoorwill of the spring season. Daddy decided we needed to clean out the fireplace and close it, so I got the 5 gallon bucket and fireplace shovel and scooped all the ashes out. We set the bucket of the odor absorbing briquettes in the fireplace, closed the damper, and placed the weighted cover over it. Cleaned out the wood box and swept up. Goodbye till autumn, fireplace. We'll miss you!

SATURDAY, MAY 6TH

Up on Saturday by 6:30 am. After breakfast and cleaning up, Jason came by on his way to help with the barn door. Daddy sprayed around the foundation of the house while he waited for Jason and Shaun to get something they needed from Shaun's shop. Rita brought me 2 ½ quarts of dewberries they had picked. We walked up to the barn and took two pictures, then told all 'bye'.

Gathered up my stuff and went home. Watched the king's coronation; pomp and circumstance, quite lovely.

WEDNESDAY, MAY 10TH

Shaun arrived before 7:00 am. He and Daddy loaded the 1020 tractor to take it in for repairs. Daddy, Tam and I were at the barn and cemetery for a while. On the way there, Tam and I were going to remember to turn on the water. As we walked past the spigot, we both pivoted with perfect synchronization to the right and said, "Turn on the water." We both laughed. You have to be over 60 to understand the humor.

Tam showed me how to fix Mama's pizza in the air fryer. I braided her hair and she went home. Daddy gathered up 5 gallon buckets that seem to multiply on their own and put them in the barn. I made a dewberry cobbler. Brother has radar when it comes to desserts. He came by and I gave him some for later.

Garrett sent me pictures of his history project; WWII and his great-grandfather's part in all that. He did a fine job.

THURSDAY, MAY 11TH

Had blueberry pancakes this morning. Shaun came up and enjoyed them with us. We talked about saving the Aunt Jemima syrup bottles and put them in the museum. It is so sad how differently an issue can be perceived. Trying to placate everyone is a losing proposition.

I wanted to get outside and walk around to check on cows and calves. Daddy said, "I wish I could go." He looked so forlorn. I said, "Well, let me call Shaun." I asked him if I could borrow his side by side. He said, "Sure." So I walked down to his house and drove the buggy back up. I grabbed the binoculars, cattle papers, pen, and away we went. The herd was lying all down the hill or scattered close by, grazing. We wandered from cow to cow checking numbers and looking for cows that had not had calves yet. We are puzzled by some of our bookkeeping last year, so I am determined to keep better records this year. Daddy can't see to do it, and it grieves him so much. I have to do what I can to assure him that it's all straight. We check off 14 calves and all the cows expecting a calf in the next 2 months. We fed the beef bulls, and drove over to the west pasture fence to see if there was any more wire lying around that Shaun scrambled with the drag. Found none. Coming back we picked up limbs out of the meadow to prevent problems for the hay baling equipment. Great to take our time doing something we both enjoy.

Mama got her spa treatment. She always appreciates it. We girls plan a "just us kids" Mother's day on Saturday. Shaun drops by; he is leaving in the morning for a truck show in Fort Worth. After Shaun left, Daddy and I talked of plants and trees in the Bible. I told Daddy about my muscadine vines that I believe will have their best crop in 8 years.

FRIDAY, MAY 12TH

Daddy and I get ready for an early town run. We leave at 8:00 and went by Farm & Ranch for cattle salt, then Wal-Mart for groceries and garden soil. We were early for his 10:00 haircut appointment, but he went on inside. I sat outside and talked to Andy, then called Sherry and got the flood report. She got 4 inches; but some around Nacogdoches got 9 inches! Flooded SFA. Knoxlynn cooing and smiling a lot at 3 months old.

After getting home and taking care of Mama, we loaded the side by side with the salt and soil; took the salt to the barn, then went down to the cemetery and unloaded the soil. When we got back to the house, Daddy began to clean out the garage. Saw a van drive up – Shaun's Mother's Day bouquet had arrived. Huge and Beautiful!

Daddy fixed the bottoms of two porch posts, then sanded the door and facings of the old barn in preparation for painting. We talked about color: white vs. the brown he used on the picnic table. I thought the white would set off the weathered brown of the barn best; he agreed. White it is.

He sanded and dusted. I got out a six foot ladder for him to work from, then said, "It is lunch time, Papa. We need to eat for energy." He agreed and realized he still had his town clothes on. So we ate, he rested and then changed into his work clothes. By 2:00 pm he was painting. Tam and I went to the plant farm to get flowers for the cemetery: two flats of periwinkles.

When we got back, Daddy had the barn door almost finished. We loaded our stuff in the side by side and drove up to the cemetery. Tam and I dug out the old dirt and replaced it with the garden soil, then planted most of the periwinkles at Joyce's grave (best friend), and some at Josh's grave (brother that died at 24). We loaded up that old dirt and poured it into a deep hole by the barn door Daddy had finished painting.

Shaun arrived and told us about his Fort Worth trip. After I fixed Mama's mid evening meal, Daddy and I sat on the patio and watched the evening unfold, accompanied by the sound of two mourning doves. A Cooper's hawk added some drama as he dove on two hunting trips. The calves playing on the hill and an unexpected flock of cedar wax wings added to the close of a perfect late spring evening.

SATURDAY, MAY 13TH

Up at 6:00 am. Daddy came in and the coffee ritual began. Some things never change and I hope this one never will.

Daddy and I went out on the patio and watched the changing atmosphere, heavy with moisture one minute and sun breaking through the next. Sherry arrived and I helped her unload. The puzzles she ordered are so pretty. I have 2 and she has 2 for Mama's Mother's Day gifts. Sherry sat on the bed in our room and opened up her card to Mama to write some additional words. I smile, turn around and open my card and show it to her. She says, "I can't believe it! Of all the hundreds of Mother's Day cards in towns 80 miles apart, we get the same card!" LOL. It isn't the first time. It has happened on Daddy's cards, too. We are wired so much alike.

Sherry and I went up to the cemetery to see the flowers Tam and I planted, and watered them.

Got Mama all "gussied" up. Tam came over and we went to town to get the lunch. They dropped me off at Domino's to pick up Mama's pizza supreme. Tam and Sherry went to Legends to get burgers for the rest of us. When we returned, Shaun was here. Sherry made the meal special by using dishes from Mama's "company" set. It was a delightful lunch. Mama opened her cards and gifts after we ate, then we gathered in the Big Room for photos. Rachel came by with gifts for her Mama and Nannie. She had a new car for work and we all looked it over. Sherry and I left for home.

TUESDAY, MAY 16TH

Concerns about air conditioning unit, but no time to check it over. That's the way it goes. My problems have to wait until I'm back here next week. I loaded a heavy white clay pot for the Mandevilla vine on the front porch at the folks. The wind keeps blowing their light one over. Played pickleball a while. Watered my orchids, checked the chickens that arrived this weekend from Andy's place. Did all the yard things I could. Headed to the folks.

WEDNESDAY, MAY 17TH

What a beautiful morning. The sun is shining through the misty atmosphere. The hills of home are wrapped in a velvet green that defies description. Cool, not a twig moving. A perfect May morning. Papa is sipping his second cup of coffee as the sun eases higher. Such a peace permeates the fabric of this day.

Gave Mama a head's up that we were going to the Homeplace. We mixed up a gallon of fly spray, then went to the barn for salt, mineral, and range cubes, and away we went. As soon as the heifers saw us, they hustled over and started eating the cubes we had poured out. That gave me a good chance to spray them for flies. I spotted people in the pasture as we drove on to the salt/mineral trough. Rita, Raylan, and Athena were looking for dewberries. Darryl, my first cousin, was enjoying the day with them. He has the place next to Daddy's Homeplace. He is a retired surveyor and grows chestnut trees.

The kids want to ride with me and PawPaw, so they hop in. We put out the salt and mineral, then continue to the creek and check the west water gap then the east one. Both look great despite the large amount of rain this spring. Back at their house Athena showed me three new kittens, and we looked at the lightning struck pecan tree and toured Rita's flowers and vegetables growing in raised beds everywhere.

Porch sitting, then up to feed the beef bulls. Just as we finished, Shaun showed up. We loaded the fly spray, some cubes, mineral and salt, and found the cows just over the hill. I put out piles of cubes as Brother sprayed

Back at the house, Shaun told Mama about all our cattle doings. Daddy and I spent time outside at the close of another wonderful May day.

THURSDAY, MAY 18TH

As Daddy came in the next morning, we talked about the date already being May 18th. Both of us would like to put the brakes on these wonderful days. Papa said, "No wonder people get old, the way these weeks and months flit by!"

After breakfast, we headed down to Shaun's to get the side by side. He'd said we could use it the next few days. Daddy also needed a color wheel to choose the house paint. Shaun said he would pick some up after we decided.

Back at the house, we took the color wheel to the front porch and decided on a color, with the final approval of Shaun since Daddy can't see well enough to be sure. Then he decided to attach a fresh piece of sandpaper to his long handled sander. As we worked to attach it, he told me that years ago on one of his jobs, some floor people threw part of a roll of floor sandpaper away. Daddy can't bear to see anything remotely useable thrown away, so he rescued it and has been using it for years. It's tough stuff and takes both of us to notch the paper and put it on the block. The metal pieces that hold the sandpaper are fastened down by wing nuts. I told Daddy my 7th graders in school didn't know what a wing nut was. During a scientific method lab, I taught them about why they were called that and what they were used for.

Daddy starts sanding the side of the house. Later I call him for lunch: stew, cornbread and fresh onion. Then Daddy puts his feet up and rests while I wash dishes and get Mama's afternoon rolling.

Daddy gets back out there with a high-pressure nozzle on the water hose to wash the dust, spider webs, and pecan catkins off the walls. I grab the 6 foot ladder to get a red mud swallow nest down, then realize the gutters are jammed with pecan catkins and sticks. I'm to going to have to dig out the entire length of the gutter with a putty knife, then use the pressure nozzle to finish the job. By the time I finished, I was covered in gutter slime from head to toe. Daddy steadied the ladder as I worked, kind of a danger zone. I tossed one blob that landed on Daddy's denim shirt. At least I didn't toss it on his head! We finished and washed up.

Shaun shows Dad a big renovation job he is working on in the downtown area.

Shaun had said to park the side by side behind the house since thieves would love to steal it. I did but still worried about it. I checked on that side by side 2 or 3 times during the wee hours. I can't keep it overnight any more. I need my sleep.

FRIDAY, MAY 19TH

I woke up at 4:00 am and got up after a half hour. At 6:00, Daddy found me at the kitchen doing Bible reading and highlighting the rest of my Sunday school lesson.

We got ready for town and headed out to the stores for painting supplies, calf feed, and groceries, and were back by a little after 8:00. Usual morning things. Daddy got everything ready for painting and said he would paint an hour and then rest. He painted 4 hours with a 30 minute rest. Daddy had been concerned about whether he could still paint, but he was moving right along. He said, "Well, I haven't lost my touch." He was using a 4" brush (I can't use one that wide.) and was on a 6 foot ladder for the high parts. He had made the comment yesterday that he really enjoyed the transformation of a fresh coat of paint on a home. I feel the same way.

Tam came by to see if we had buttermilk. I just needed a cup for cornbread and gave her the rest. She came over later with a new-fangled strawberry shortcake – delicious. Shaun came by and Daddy wanted him to get the 30 foot extension ladder so he could get high in the eve of the west gable. Shaun said, "No, Daddy. I'll catch that part for you. You don't need to be that high on an extension ladder!" He painted that area and down far enough so Daddy could reach the rest from the ground. Good job, Brother! He also cleaned Daddy's paint brush for him. Daddy was too tired to go with me to check on #44, #46 and #48. Their milk bags were filling out. We should have three more calves by next week.

Later, Papa and I sat on the patio and listened to the bird song and to the first cicadas of summer as they made their shrill calls. Another season rolls around.

SATURDAY, MAY 20TH

Up early. Slept well. Cloudy and cool with a northwest wind. Daddy was anxious to get outside and put that next gallon of paint on. He doesn't see well at all on cloudy days, but he was out there by 7:00. I tried to talk him into waiting until Monday which promised to be fully sunny. He said he had trouble waiting. No surprise there … Papa never has been one to procrastinate. **Now** is always the best time to get the job done. Sometimes, though, that haste puts the rest of us behind the eight ball. His reason for painting the house, or at least starting to paint, was to see if he could do it. He has proved that. Shaun arrived to check on Daddy's progress (after I texted about another high part Daddy had been eyeballing). He told him he would get the high part later.

While Daddy steadily painted, I swiffered the floors, beat the outside rugs, washed up the dishes, cleaned the microwave, washed, dried and put up 2 loads of clothes, mailed the 3 bills I fixed up yesterday, gathered and burned the trash, and kept an eye on Daddy.

Tam came over at 9:00 am. I woke up Mama and told her bye, then went out and said bye to Daddy and Tam. Honked and waved down the driveway and over the hill.

Home to mower fixed. Rooster crowing. Andy said he crows more over here than he did at his house. I find out that my plans for Sherry's birthday will have to come later. Her son Ben and family are coming for a visit!

MONDAY, MAY 22ND

Good trip over. As soon as I got unloaded, I went to town for groceries to make Daddy's favorite holiday meal: chicken and dressing and rolls. Got back, unloaded, then made cornbread for the dressing, made up the rolls, chopped veggies, put out loaf of bread to dry, opened green beans, and watched over Daddy. He is continuing to scrape, dust and paint.

I put lunch on the table at 3:20 pm. Mama ate with us. Now she is doing her word search book. I invited Brother over to give him some rolls. Daddy was very complimentary of the meal. Rita came by and I gave her rolls for the family. She took the kids fishing in PawPaw's pond. Daddy went back out and painted until 7:30 pm.

TUESDAY, MAY 23RD

Watched a beautiful sunrise from the sunroom. Before Daddy got outside to paint (in spite of an intestinal upset), we made Sherry a

Happy Birthday video and sent it to her. When Shaun arrived a bit later, Daddy was painting high up and continued, with Shaun steadily telling him. "That's high enough, Daddy. Stop trying to reach that corner." He finally **did** stop, after a one leg balancing act. When he got down, Shaun grabbed the extension ladder and leaned it against a wall several yards away. I thought, "Brother, do you really think that will keep him off that ladder? This is the same guy that went around the shop and carried it over here in the first place!"

Thank goodness the rest only required the 6 foot and 4 foot ladders. I do recall his putting a 6 foot ladder inside a raised brick flowerbed so he could reach a high part on the patio porch. Sigh! I checked on him regularly as I wrote several cards and letters and mailed them.

Shaun power washed part of the metal roof, sunroom porch, bird bath, patio, carport, brick retaining wall and flower brick bed wall. It looks amazing. He also power washed an old wagon hub that Sherry discovered in the pasture. Daddy said it was from a single horse wagon that his friend L.D. Baham left when he and his wife Muriel (Mama's sister) moved. It never traveled the roads again.

Shaun ate lunch with us. Daddy rested a bit after lunch while Shaun continued the power washing. Just as Shaun finished and went home, Papa came back out to use up that bucket of paint, his third gallon. Amazing that a 99 year old man can put on a gallon of paint throughout a day in spite of being sick.

When Daddy and I were sitting and watching the evening gradually come to a close, he said, "You know, no rich person could look on all this any better than we are. Come to think of it, we are rich and don't even know it!" I smiled and thought, "Oh, Daddy, I have always been a rich man's daughter!"

WEDNESDAY, MAY 24TH

We were up at 5:30 am. Daddy had his 2 cups of coffee and reached for his shoes. He is skipping breakfast until he paints a while. Finally he paused long enough to eat, then rested to let his breakfast settle, then up again. We moved the extension ladder to the west side of Mama's room. She is sick after taking her meds at 8:30. I text Tam and Sherry about it. We have no clue why this is happening, but we tweak her over- the- counter supplements to see if that will help.

Shaun finished painting around and under the gutters. I fixed a repeat of the chicken and dressing meal, along with a fresh batch of rolls. Shaun ate with us and loved it. He saved his second roll for dessert. I opened a jar of the peach jam Daddy and I put up year before last. Brother said that the roll with peach jam was better than cake.

Daddy napped 2 hours then got up and painted the museum door and the outside of the kitchen window screen. He is planning to paint the Homeplace house starting tomorrow, Lord willing. I took Daddy to see Shaun's paint job on a massive kitchen cabinet remodel.

Daddy and I rounded up 3 ladders, hammer, painting supplies, and haggled up two of Daddy's old t-shirts for paint rags. I am to drop Daddy off with all the supplies and go to Wal-Mart for paint. Daddy reminded me, "Be sure and get them to shake it."

THURSDAY, MAY 25TH

Dropped Daddy by the Homeplace along with all our supplies and ladders – including the extension ladder, and took off to town. Daddy and I had changed our minds to Sherwin Williams paint. I went there first and got 4 gallons of white satin latex house paint, properly shaken. Headed for Wal-Mart and rounded up my items, then went back by the Homeplace and gave Daddy the paint. Home to put up the groceries. As I looked out the kitchen window, I noticed a cow down by the north pond. I immediately thought - #44! I ran and got the binoculars. Sure enough she was in the midst of birthing her calf. I went down there to see if the baby was okay. It was alive and well.

Back to the Homeplace. Daddy had made amazing progress. He had sanded and dusted the west side of the house and had painted past the first set of windows. I was the ladder girl – had to make sure it didn't turn over on the uneven ground. Daddy said quitting time would be noon. I doubted it. Quitting time is when Daddy meets his goal for the day. It happened at 1:15. After we loaded up, Athena came around the house and showed us her wiggly tooth in front. Daddy offered to pull it for her, but she said she had to make sure it is "dead" first.

After Daddy and I ate lunch, he went back to the sunroom to prop up his feet while I washed up the dishes, braided Mama's hair, put some makeup on her, and took 4 puzzle pictures for her album. I had her help me disassemble each puzzle and put it back in the boxes. As we finished putting the puzzles away, the home health supervisor came. She took Mama's vitals and was very pleased with her 98% O2 level.

Shaun came and we fed and watered the bulls and checked on #44 and her new calf – a heifer. I went back up to the cemetery at 6:30 pm to weed eat inside and outside the fence and the persimmon valley. Had enough battery power to do it all.

Came back and sat with Daddy on the patio as evening slipped on down. Daddy started to get up and had a hard time – all the days of painting have taken a toll. When I suggested that we might need to take a break tomorrow, he said, "No, I can rest up across the weekend." I thought, "What about me, Daddy? My weekend is just as busy as the week days!"

FRIDAY, MAY 26TH

Woke up at 3:30 am. Sigh. Daddy popped up at his usual time and was eager to get started today with painting the north eave. I told him I would paint the last 3 ½ boards all down the west side. We had a bite of breakfast and were down there by 7:20. After we had painted a while, I went back to tend to Mama; fixed her breakfast, put her meds and shake out, and set the timer. On the way back to the Homeplace, I saw Joann taking a walk. She and her husband Bobby sang at mine and Philip's wedding 48 years ago. I stopped and we talked a few minutes.

Poor Daddy had a gut episode while I was gone. He still finished that north side while I painted the lower boards, but he was shaky. I loaded up quickly, stacked the ladders, and we came home. Ben and Shelley and the boys are coming tomorrow for a visit. I hope Daddy is up for it. After we ate a late lunch, he made noise about going back down to the Homeplace to finish up. I said, "Daddy you need to rest your right arm." We sat a while longer, then Brother arrived on the mower. We watched him mow, then got in the side by side and went up to feed the bulls and put out salt and mineral. We watched Shaun mow the cemetery and checked on the new mama and baby calf – all seemed to be well. Hope we sleep.

SATURDAY, MAY 27TH

Up a little before 6:00 am. Daddy still asleep. He was worn out from yesterday. When Shaun drove up, Daddy was just coming in to make coffee. Shaun had a bad night. His allergies were worse due to mowing yesterday, and he had been up and down all night. I cleaned the house and porches, then got Mom's breakfast, braided her hair, and got her a denim dress for company. Set out the stuff to make rolls. Tam came over. She and Daddy are going to a long-time friend's funeral, "Pug" Lightsey.

When they got back, they said the singing was beautiful. The message was amazing also. Daddy had tears in his eyes over just talking about it. After a while, it was just me and Daddy, and he said a surprising thing – he would like to live as long as Joshua, God's second in command during the Exodus of the children of Israel – 110 years! What a wonderful attitude he has, that in spite of all the health problems he has, he still looks forward.

Mother's Day was a sweet time. Mom received a beautiful picture of her and the newest great-grand Knoxlynn.

Sherry and family got here at 1:15 pm. I had rolls going in the oven; they are Ben's favorite, so I especially wanted him to have some since they don't get to come here very often. They are moving to Tampa, Florida, this next weekend, so no telling when we'll see them next. Cooper is 13 and will be entering 8th grade. Parker is 7 and will be in the 2nd grade. We all had a sweet visit, then Ben and family went on a side by side ride up on the knob and down around the north pond. I think they really enjoyed it. Got Mama outside for pictures before they left. Great seeing them! Afterward, I gave Mama a spa treatment and wrote a letter to Mama's niece, Wanda, before I had to shove off.

Got home, unloaded, watered and wandered around reflecting on the day. Sherry sent me a sweet text about the rolls and pictures I took. Loved doing it all for my dear sister and her family.

TUESDAY, MAY 30TH

Sherry called; Mama had a horrible night. It was gas pressure under her heart, but she thought she was dying! Daddy had another episode, too, but he and Sherry went down to the Homeplace and painted anyway. Can't believe how dedicated Daddy is in spite of feeling bad. Sherry had very little sleep, too, so I hope they survive.

WEDNESDAY, MAY 31ST

Sherry told me all about her and Daddy's painting at the Homeplace. I think they got the front porch and the east side. Called and talked to Mama. She was feeling better.

Tamra

MONDAY, MAY 1ST

Dialed the phone for Dad this morning so he could talk to his old Seabee buddy Paul; they talked for a good while, catching up on the family happenings. While they visited, I changed the calendars, all nine of them, got out the pork chops to fix for lunch, and worked on my column. When I went to the house to do my chores, I made a birthday card for Dad to send to Paul and a grocery list for both households.

After getting Mom settled with her breakfast and meds, I went to town for groceries and meds, a never-ending chore. When I got back, Shaun was putting the grab bar in the bathroom for Mel. We don't want her to take another tumble. He did a good job picking it out…it fits right in with the color scheme.

Dad piddled some today in the shop and read in his Kindle after sunset. It was a beautiful day and he was just happy to be outside. Mom had a mostly good day, but she is still not sleeping well at night.

TUESDAY, MAY 2ND

Finished the last minute cleaning before leaving for WMA; Mel was already on her way. Addie is coming today and I am hoping we get a lot of her lessons finished in the next few weeks, because she will be so busy all summer, we won't have much school time. It is a juggling act at best, to keep everything going.

Talked to Dr. B.'s office about Dad's weird episode with his vision, but they said his meds would not cause it, so that is a relief. I also set up his follow-up appointment with Dr. J for July 5. I hope he gives Dad a good report on his circulation.

Usual stuff this afternoon – piano lessons, town run…again, and helped Dad get Paul's card ready to mail. Caught Mel up on all the doings when she got here…hope she has a good week.

SATURDAY, MAY 6TH

Today is the annual fish fry for the North Cherokee Volunteer Fire Department. Dad always lets them use his pasture across from the family life center for a parking area and landing spot for the hospital helicopter that flies out each year for the fundraiser. It is always a great day, catching up with neighbors and friends. Dad used to enjoy going, but the last couple of years; I have just gone over and picked up "to-go" plates for him and Mom. When I got there, Athena and Raylan were playing in the bounce house. Before I left, I took them over to the pasture to see the helicopter. When I got back with their plates, Mom and Dad both sat at the table and enjoyed their hot fish and hushpuppies. It was a pretty quiet day, which is always a good thing, in my opinion.

SUNDAY, MAY 7TH

Noticed Dad was looking a little "bushy" this morning, so after we enjoyed our coffee on the patio, I got the scissors and trimmed his eyebrows and such. Told him I was "spiffing him up for Sunday School." He laughed and said he didn't think anyone in his class would notice.

We enjoyed services and the drive there and back; everything is so pretty and green. After lunch, we sat at the table and visited for a bit longer.

Miracle of miracles, Mom didn't call me, so we were able to spend some time just talking. Dad was in a reflective mood and one thing he said really stuck with me…he said that after Josh died, he never laughed like he used to…now that I think about it, he hasn't as much. He seemed so sad…then I reminded him of several occasions when he got a pretty good laugh out of the grandkids antics, and he smiled. He agreed there have been more than a few times he's gotten a hoot out of them. That seemed to lift his mood a little and he decided to go out and enjoy some porch time.

Mom and I worked on her puzzles for a good bit this afternoon, after she ate. In fact, we worked right up until dark. We had a good time and she only gave me "the look" a couple of times.

MONDAY, MAY 8TH

This is my grandmother's birthday. Dad still misses his mother; they were very close. He used to go by every day after work to visit with her and drink a cup of coffee. He always makes mention of her special day.

Working on the surveying and getting the place and will in order is a big subject on Dad's mind lately. I do what I can by helping him make phone calls, etc., but the weight of it is ever with him. I am hoping things work out in a way that pleases him. We both agreed that the Lord will handle it; we will just have to wait and see.

TUESDAY, MAY 9TH

Jason came this morning to take Dad to the Homeplace to try and get the panels from around the foundation off for the summer. They were semi-successful. Several wouldn't budge, so they just left them. Addie, WMA, town run, piano lessons, and the usual rest of my Tuesday went without too much fuss. Mel got over here before the rains began, thank goodness.

WEDNESDAY, MAY 10TH

It has been thirty-seven years since Josh died, but I still miss him like it was yesterday. He was my best friend, my sounding board, and my confidante. I usually go to the cemetery alone on this day, but I could tell that for some reason Mel was feeling the loss especially keenly today too, so I asked her to go with me. We then asked Dad and he decided to come along. I think the rainy day was perfect for such an outing. We didn't say much, just tended the flowers, pulled a few spring weeds, and mostly kept our thoughts to ourselves. I did go back later by myself, for a little while, so I could talk to him, like I always do. It seems to help.

THURSDAY, MAY 11TH

Stayed home and helped Addie with lessons, tried to get caught up on my housework and writing. Tonight, I took Addie to the Jacksonville Tops in Texas rodeo. Athena was supposed to do the mutton-busting, but backed out at the last minute. I don't blame her…those big fuzzy sheep are kind of intimidating to a little kid! I enjoyed sharing with Addie and Athena about the first rodeo I went to in this same arena. I was two years old and Michael Landon, Little Joe Cartwright, was the featured performer that year. I had my picture taken with him. So did Mom, Mel, and Sherry…those pictures are a hoot! I also told them about running for rodeo queen and all the play-days and rodeos I did when I was younger. Those were fun days. I pointed out the section near the top in the opposite bleachers where Dad (their Pawpaw) used to sit and watch me and my horse McCloud compete. He never missed a single rodeo. I could always count on him to be in the stands waving as I passed by; that was such an encouragement.

SATURDAY, MAY 13TH

Mother's Day celebration at Mom and Dad's today. I made Mom a card yesterday, after I helped Mel plant fresh flowers at the cemetery. I had a ton of running to do in Tyler, plus getting everything lined out to be at the folks' till next Tuesday. Before I went to the celebration, I ran up town to the grand re-opening of our local feed store. I asked Dad if he wanted to go, but he said he would "sit this one out."

We had a good lunch with Dad and Mom, and she seemed to enjoy the cards, flowers, and puzzles she got. It was nice with just us kids for a change; it almost felt like old times.

SUNDAY, MAY 14TH

Rita came over after church to bring Mom (Nannie), some flowers from her garden, they were beautiful. That girl has a green thumb like her great-grandmother. I took the kids with me to feed the calves, so she could visit with Nannie.

Mom tried calling Aunt Stella, but didn't get an answer. She did catch Aunt Aline though, and wished her a Happy Mother's Day. Later, I put out the new puzzle Sherry got Mom. Boy! It is a tough one…I told Mom I was going to give Sherry forty lashes with a wet noodle next time I see her for getting such a difficult puzzle.

MONDAY, MAY 15TH

Got everything ready before Dad's eye appointment at 9:30 this morning, Mom was pretty pitiful, so I told her to call Marc if she needed something before we got back. We weren't gone much over two hours, so she was alright.

Dad decided to paint the Homeplace house and managed to get all of us involved…especially poor Sherry!

Deborah had given me some beautiful red petunias yesterday at church for Mom's Mother's Day gift. I planted them right before the rain started. Managed to get the calves fed, lids on the foundation shut, and go get some groceries before the bottom fell out.

We got almost two inches of rain and the erosion around the ponds is pretty bad. Mom and I finished that cupcake puzzle Sherry brought, and I put out the coffee and cake one that I got for her. We had a pretty good day, all in all, and even though

Dad couldn't read because of his eye shots, he said he enjoyed watching the rain. The only fly in the ointment was when I tried to turn down the ceiling fan and the pull chain came out. Sigh. Poor Stu, he will have another item to add to his already overloaded agenda.

TUESDAY, MAY 16TH

Dad fell this morning trying to put his pants on. He has been able to do it for ninety-nine years, but I really wish he would start sitting down to pull them on. I am concerned because he seems a little unsteady lately, so I have been pushing his water intake and encouraging him to use his cane, especially when he goes outside. He did blow off the concrete patio and driveway – it was littered with leaves and small twigs after the storm last night. When he and Shaun took a ride around the pasture to check out the damage, they discovered a huge oak limb had fallen and squashed a section of fence, so they got their tools and fixed it.

WEDNESDAY, MAY 17TH

Caleb said his new place is ready and he will be moving in as soon as possible. I know he is glad to have his privacy back, and I will be glad to get the room sorted and cleaned. He is not a stellar housekeeper. Haha

SATURDAY, MAY 20TH

Gloriously cool day and Dad took advantage of it by painting on the house nearly all day. He took a break after lunch, but then went right back at it till around 4:00. Shaun came up and they took a ride in his buggy. Mom finished the puzzle she was working on, so I put out another one and helped her for a little while. I needed to work on three articles I had due, plus my column, so I tried to squeeze in some writing time when I could. Dad and I had a good visit late this evening before I doctored his feet, then he read on his Kindle till nearly 11:00.

SUNDAY, MAY 21ST

Dad was up at 5:30 this morning, so no late Sunday sleeping for me…late is 6:30. He is like the Energizer Bunny – he just keeps going and going!

Addie's piano recital was this afternoon. She did very well, only a slight bobble and she recovered nicely. I am so thankful she is learning to play. Mom and Dad took me to piano lessons for years, and I still enjoy playing.

MONDAY, MAY 22ND

Dad started sanding and scraping on the north side of the house by 8:00. He always started work at 8:00 and worked till 4:30 or 5:00 all the years he was a paint contractor; I guess he is still on that schedule. Found out when I got home later this morning that Caleb's cat had fleas and now I am battling an infestation on top of everything else I have to do…good grief!

TUESDAY, MAY 23RD

Wished Sherry a Happy Birthday and had a full day of running errands, lessons, and vacuuming like a mad woman. Learned that my next door neighbor, John Allen, died early this morning of a heart attack…he was only two and a half years older than me. We grew up together. He was getting ready to retire in just a few months. I am so sad for his sweet family.

Dad painted again all day today. Life is strange. There Dad is, still going strong at nearly one hundred, and there is John, dead at only 66… doesn't make any sense.

Shirley C., my sweet friend, is coming to spend the night here before her surgery tomorrow, got to get her room ready.

WEDNESDAY, MAY 24TH

Dad was finished painting on the house when I stopped by and was working on the "museum" door. I noticed the mimosa tree over the building was blooming, so I picked some and held them out for Dad to smell. He took a big whiff and said, "Smells like old times!"

He told me Mom had not had a good day, so I thought I'd take them in to show her and maybe it would perk her up. Mom couldn't smell them, but she smiled when I brushed the soft feathery flowers against her cheek. She said, "You and Josh used to run in, shouting, 'The fuzzies are blooming! The fuzzies are blooming!'" Mom looked a little brighter for a moment.

Shirley is doing well. She said I could pick her up tomorrow from the hospital, probably after lunch. She will need to spend a couple of days convalescing before she drives home.

THURSDAY, MAY 25TH

Our forty-fourth anniversary, and Marc finally went to the doctor with his foot. It has been bothering him for a week or so. It is broken. So…last May he had surgery on his back, then had two pulmonary embolisms, was in ICU, hospital and rehab all last summer…I asked him, "Are you going to make this type of thing an annual event?" I almost gave myself a headache with the major eye roll I gave him. Mercy! What else? Happy Anniversary.

Picked Shirley up from the hospital; she seems to be doing well. Got her settled, and then I wrote down Addie's lessons for the next week before she went home, worked on my column, and made lunch. Sigh…

SATURDAY, MAY 27TH

Dad and I went to the funeral of one of his oldest friends, "Pug Lightsey," this morning. Dad was really glad we went. He was moved by the service and I saw him tear up several times. He told the pastor afterwards that his Lord would be pleased with his words. On the way home, he talked about it, saying, "He really shelled down the corn!"

It was a beautiful morning, sixty degrees, and a perfect day for Sherry, Ben, and his family to come up for a visit. They got to Mom and Dad's this afternoon, and we sure enjoyed seeing them.

SUNDAY, MAY 28TH

This morning I asked Dad if he would like to go with me tomorrow to the Tecula cemetery for Decoration Day. I told him I would like to put out flags and just sit awhile. He said, "Yeah...that might be nice. You could give me a flag to hold, since I'm about halfway dead anyway." Funny man.

MONDAY, MAY 29TH

Decoration Day or Memorial Day as it is usually called. Dad and I had a real good morning and a good talk last night. We discussed lots of things: the Bible, death, living well, etc. It was one of the best weekends I can remember.

We had a cool morning to put the flags out. It was so peaceful. Dad was able to walk all over the cemetery putting flags near the markers before he sat down to just soak it all in.

Today is the first day Sherry is back on our regular schedule. She has a fish fry at church on Friday, so I will take that night. We try to pinch-hit for one another when needed so that no one misses too much stuff. Sometimes it works well, but sometimes you just miss out. None of us can do everything, even when we *didn't* have this extra responsibility.

After lunch, I picked some Queen Anne's lace and black-eyed Susans for a bouquet. I've wanted to do that for several weeks. I've learned not to wait too long on things like that or the opportunity passes. Guess that is true about most things.

Sherry came over for coffee this afternoon, a rare treat. We enjoyed catching up without being interrupted. My bouquet made a great backdrop.

TUESDAY, MAY 30TH

Dad has started working down at the Homeplace getting it ready to paint. Sherry has been thrown right back into the furnace, because Dad needs her to drive him down there and help him move ladders, etc. So today, on my way to and from WMA, I go by and check on Mom. They are supposed to be back by lunch. I went to John Allen's funeral today...so sad.

Caleb likes his place; I hope it works out well for him. He is really trying to get on his feet...this last year has been rough.

WEDNESDAY, MAY 31ST

Crazy day…took Rita's car to the mechanic because her A/C is out, took Marc to get a cast on his foot, ordered school stuff for Addie, and made a lemon cake because I had "new recipe-itis" which is only cured when you try a new recipe that sounds delicious. I also made a trip to Aldi's, The Granary, and an estate sale that was on the way. Can't believe that May is already over.

NOT EVERYONE WILL UNDERSTAND YOUR *situation*. UNLESS THEY HAVE WALKED THE SAME ROAD, DON'T EXPECT *empathy*.

JUNE

In our family, June is a slower-paced season with only my birthday and Father's Day to interrupt the lazy summer days. Because my birthday usually falls on or around Father's Day, we combined the two into one celebration, which was fine with me. Sometimes, my younger brother Josh would get presents too. His birthday was very close to Christmas, and seemed, at least to him, to get a bit lost in the holiday busyness. Mom and Dad would usually get gifts we could enjoy together: bicycles, board games, bow and arrow sets, etc. For me, it only doubled the fun.

Mom and Dad put up with a lot from us during the summertime. We were always dragging home unexpected house guests, stray critters – both wild and domestic, and other fun stuff. We managed to try Mom's patience on more than one occasion I am sure. When we were small, we would often beg to stay outside long after bedtime or come home as filthy as pigs, causing more work and aggravation for her. I don't remember her fussing at us; instead, she always made us pose for pictures. I think she wanted proof that we were a lot of trouble, so if we complained about our kids one day, she could pull out those pictures.

When I think of summers growing up, I often recall June memories. Somehow those seem the sweetest to me. I guess it's because in June, the summer stretched out ahead, looking like forever. School was just a fuzzy memory and life was good. It was a time for being outside, picking cucumbers and beans in the garden, making frog houses, cloud-watching, chasing butterflies, building tree forts, reading in the shade of the mimosa tree, fishing in the ponds, catching lightning bugs, and listening to the evening sounds of the whippoorwills and brush wolves.

These days, I still look forward to celebrating with Dad on Father's Day, even though my birthday often takes a back seat. I don't mind – that is the way it should be. Every year we have with Dad (and Mom) is an extra blessing for all of us…and that is always something to celebrate.

Sherry

THURSDAY, JUNE 1ST

Lovely cool morning with a little fog in the bottom – very refreshing for an early cup of coffee outdoors. After breakfast, Pop and I drove to the Homeplace. He painted a high spot above the south porch, and I tried to finish the east side – an easy job if not for the pipes and wires running amok. At one point, I had to go around to where Pop was painting and brace my feet against the bottom legs of the extension ladder so it wouldn't slide out from under him on that concrete.

Pop was pretty worn out when we stopped at noon. After we got home I bathed and changed into clean clothes because I *thought* we were done outside for the rest of the day … not. After Pop rested, he wanted to go to town to take care of several errands – first was Sherwin Williams for more paint and some caulk. Pop said, "I wonder what they'll think when I come in with my cane to buy more paint?" Then we swung by the bank, then Legends for a burger and fries. He was trying to cut up a tomato slice with a plastic knife and fork, and it flipped up in the air and landed right back on his plate … such a funny look on his face! On to Walmart after that, then home. Pop was glad to relax in his recliner.

I fixed Mom's food, started a custard pie for my church fish fry tomorrow evening, and told Shaun that I would go up to feed the fattening calves. Checked their water in the trough, and it was very low and nasty, so I poured it out and ran fresh in the tank. Walked to the cemetery and watered the flowers and sat in the swing while I talked to Melanie. Back to the house to finish the pie and take care of things until bedtime.

FRIDAY, JUNE 2ND

Repeat of yesterday morning – hoped for an early square-up. Shaun came by to check out our work just before we finished around 11:00. Headed to the house and did some vacuuming before fixing lunch. Cleaned the hall bathroom and organized some bills before getting ready to drive home for the fish fry. Trying to fit in everything on two fronts can be challenging. I was looking forward to seeing a big grin from Baby Cake, but didn't get one; Stu and Ashley said she'd been fussy all day, but I was afraid she'd already forgotten her Granny B. Stu asked if I'd be able to keep her when they head to a Rangers game, but (of course) that's my week at Mom's and Dad's … like I said about fitting it all in …

THURSDAY, JUNE 8TH

Nurse C called me here in Nac and said she was at Mom's and Dad's and couldn't get in – the door was locked. I told her that Pop and Melanie were painting at the Homeplace, so they had locked the door for Mom's safety, but I'd call Tam to come over and unlock it for her. Glad Tam was home … one of the many juggling acts we do all the time.

FRIDAY, JUNE 9TH

Had to talk Melanie off the ledge about Pop's diarrhea. I'm concerned, too, but I told her it wasn't like he was having chest pains or anything that would indicate an *immediate* threat. I assured her that I would try to do something about it next week. He will just rest this weekend, except for going to church, so he should be okay, God willing.

SUNDAY, JUNE 11TH

Back to J'ville this afternoon to take over early from Tam since she covered Friday night for me. On the drive, I tried to imagine myself on Sanibel Island, watching the surf roll in, the clouds puffing along, and the seagulls wheeling overhead. It didn't work too well, but it was worth a shot. Loved going back to Sanibel, if only in my head.

When I got there, Mom was at the puzzle table, and Pop was reading on the Kindle. Helped Mom a bit, but she wanted to finish the puzzle by herself, so I visited with Pop for a while; then Shaun came up, and Tam dropped by after church. She had her cats with her – they'd gone to church, too. She'd gotten them spayed right before church and couldn't leave them in the car, so she took them in. I asked her if she was trying to make them Christian cats – Ha!

MONDAY, JUNE 12TH

Pop read last night until 11, so I just let him sleep this morning; he got up around 7 – more issues during the night. Sigh. Got breakfast for everyone, then Pop and I left for his eye appointment … a very fast one, as it turned out. Back home for coffee and a snack. Melanie called and said Dad had called *her* and left a message intended for Joseph D – about leaving the west gate open so he could get in and cut the hay. Then Tam came over and said she'd already talked to Joseph; plus, since his guys were cutting the pasture across from Pop's, she left word with some other guys working on the fences to tell the hay folks to come through the corner gate she'd unlocked. Then she went up on the hill to clean out the watering trough and open the gates to the back pasture so the hay cutters could get in there also.

Getting the hay baled and moved is important to Dad and he enjoys seeing a full barn at the end of the summer.

Apparently, the word didn't get to the hay guys because instead of going to the corner gate, they came up the driveway. The only problem there is that an electric line goes from the house down the hill to the little barn, and it sags enough to get in the way of a tall vehicle. Anyway, I told them the areas Pop wanted cut, but I think Joseph had already told him. Then Tam came out to tell him the same thing, plus she didn't think he could get under that line. But he told us that he could lower the cutter and get under it. Then Pop came out and told them again what areas to cut and to turn around and go back up the road to the corner and go through there. They probably thought we were all nuts.

After a while, Pop got worried that they didn't know to steer clear of the septic drain, so Tam flagged the lead guy down to tell him, but he already knew. Meanwhile, I had to go up to the barn to check the water level in the trough – Tam had let it run awhile. It was full and running over a little, so I threw in a mosquito dunk. Went to town for a few items, and when I returned, the truck was gone. I figured Pop had gone up the hill to check on the hay cutting. When he got back, he wanted me to tell Tam to open the gate at her place so they could cut the pasture behind her house. Unfortunately, that gate was blocked by some stuff, so the guys would have to go through *two* gates down at Shaun's house. Since Pop had already told the hay guys to go to Tam's, I had to jump in the truck and drive up to tell them the updated information. It was like Laurel and Hardy. Since they'd just finished with the cemetery pasture, I said I'd go over to open the gates and shut them after they went through. The cows are on this side, so the gates must be closed – that was the benefit of going through Tam's gate, the cows are already shut out of there. Oh well.

On the way to open the gates, I passed Tam and waved and stopped, but she didn't stop. After I finished and went back to the house, she was coming out of the driveway, but stopped to tell me the guys had finished cutting on the hill and were headed to the other pasture, and Pop was afraid I hadn't gotten the word to them yet. Heavenly days … we need walkie-talkies.

Lunch, dishes, proofread article for Tam, fed calves with Pop, checked the water and no mosquito dunk – it either floated over the edge or the calves ate it. Guess *they* won't be bothered by mosquitoes for a while. Later, Pop and I ate a bowl of cereal out on the patio – such a nice evening …then I heard Mom yelling – she wanted to go to her room and needed her pillows from the Big Room. I asked, "Wouldn't it be easier for you to come look for us than to just stand and yell for us?" She had somehow bumped her arm or something, and said using it hurt. Using the arm would probably get the soreness out faster, but anyhow, I got her settled in to watch *Bewitched* episodes.

TUESDAY, JUNE 13TH

Lovely morning: cloudy and a light breeze from the northeast, cows grazing all over the knob. When Pop joined me, he said he didn't have an intestinal issue last night – so glad. Mom said her arm was a *little* better, but still hurt. Pop and I worked on some bills, completed a health care survey, and cleaned off his table, by which I mean "stacked in neater piles." On my way back from checking on Mom at the other end of the house, I saw that same calf out again, right in front of the old barn. We'd had to get it back in the pasture just yesterday! Pop had dozed off in his recliner, but I had to wake him up so we could get that calf back in the pasture. Dad wondered what in the world caused calves to go exploring like that – when it's mealtime, they'll be bawling to get back in to mama.

Since Pop was awake, he decided to repaint a window screen from the Homeplace that had gotten messed up. Then he wanted to paint a long piece of tin that's going around the underside of that house, so I helped him flip that, then started vacuuming. And vacuumed. And vacuumed. There must have been a dust bunny convention here. At some point, I passed by the kitchen window and saw Pop down at the fence where we figured the calf had gotten through – the wires were pretty loose there. So, on with my leather gloves and down to help. 63% humidity and 88°. Holy Toledo, it's drippy.

Pop overused his right arm doing all that painting, so he was running out of steam. Why didn't he get me to help from the beginning? Oh wait, I **know** this one! Because he has always been able to do stuff, and he wants so badly to be independent. We walk a tightrope between letting Pop go ahead and trying to keep him from getting hurt. Sometimes we get hurt, like today – snagged my arm on a barb while trying to get a t-post clip off. We couldn't stretch some of the wires without removing some clips. I had grabbed an aluminum folding chair on my way down to the fence so Pop could rest. He was sitting in it when Melanie called and asked what he was doing. He said, "I'm in my easy chair." I hollered, "Liar, liar, pants on fire!" I ratted him out to Melanie, and we both laughed.

Mom called me on my phone, wanting another glass of water, and I told her I'd bring it ASAP. Right after that, Shaun drove up – I was so glad because we needed just another notch or two in that come-along to make that last wire tight enough, and Pop just didn't have enough oomph to do it. Ran in to get Mom's water, then back out to fetch hammers for them and finish putting the last clips back on. Shaun wanted to take Pop on a buggy ride … perfect! Pop could hardly get into the side-by-side. After they took off, I gathered up the tools and drove the truck back up the hill to the house.

I decided to ask Mom to clean up my arm and put a Band-Aid on it. Although I could have done it myself, I figured that would make her feel useful, small thing though it might be. Everyone needs to feel needed. Her hands were so soft and gentle as she wiped the blood off and put the Band-Aid on. It reminded me of when I was little and she'd clean up my scrapes. She smiled when she finished and I thanked her. I could tell she was pleased to be doing something for someone else.

Later Pop and I ate a bowl of cereal on the patio – it was steamy outside, but I had to get him a flannel over-shirt … golly whoppers. Mom was cold – her thermostat was set on 80° - if our folks get any worse, my sisters and I will just dry up to little petrified knots!

WEDNESDAY, JUNE 14TH

Nothing like starting off with a bang, sort of. Had to get through the stool sample thing for Pop. Oh well. We dropped that off on our way to the feed store. Back to the house with the usual chores, including back and forth to Mom's thermostat: just a little up … just a little down … It's hot in here … I'm freezing …

Pop had a 4:00 appointment with Dr. M. They did blood work and a neuropathy check on Pop's feet, and he didn't feel **any** of it at all. Oh dear. We'll have to keep a close watch on his feet. His A1C was good – 6.8. Dr. M asked about his vein surgery, and Pop referred to Dr. J as his "interior plumber." Overall, Pop just needs to be careful and enjoy his food within reason. Can't eat Blue Bell three times a day, but he really does eat a healthy diet overall. Usual duties back at the house. Went to sleep around 10, but Mom called for me at 10:30 … she needed the thermostat changed.

THURSDAY, JUNE 15TH

Pop had an early visit from the surveyor over a boundary line, so that took a while. I went to town for some items for our Father's Day meal. When I got back, Mom said the Medtronic folks had called, but she couldn't get to the phone in time. Then I saw that her device was unplugged! Don't know when or how that happened, but I'll bet that was the reason for the call. I just plugged it back in, and they didn't call again. Later, Shaun came by on his way to get the tractor from the shop, but Pop wasn't sure about his intestines, so he didn't go along. Poor Pop.

FRIDAY, JUNE 16TH

Woke up just a bit after 4 AM because of the storm rolling through – constant lightning. Then I remembered the open hatches! Grabbed a flashlight, put on my rain boots, and dashed out to close them. Came back to bed and was nearly asleep when my alarm went off. Crumb.

Melanie called later, several times. She'd had a really bad time – the storm was more severe there – no power, the neighbor's mobile home cover was on her fence, and part of the barn tin blew off. And since she has a deep well with an electric pump, no water either. Poor sister. I hope they get her power back on soon.

I got some good news about my brother-in-law, Joe, though. He got the call about his much needed kidney transplant after waiting for months! I pray that goes perfectly. Then Tam called with the results of Pop's bloodwork on Wednesday: Pop's kidney function has dropped since last time. He *has* to stay hydrated and stay out of the heat. That's a battle we'll have to fight until the Second Coming, I guess.

Tried to take a nap later to make up for my short night, but Nurse C came in, then Pop got back from feeding the calves so I got him some water, then Mom wanted something. Gave up on the nap. One thing and another until bedtime. Drifted off to sleep until I heard Mom hollering for me – she wanted me to get the DVD out of the player and put another one in. She was already up and has done that all by herself a thousand times, why holler for me? Maybe she just wanted to see someone else for a minute. While I was taking care of the DVD, she moaned and groaned as if she could barely go, but that loud yell sure showed some zing.

SATURDAY, JUNE 17TH

Busy morning for all, trying to get stuff together for the Father's Day meal tomorrow, and Tam's birthday which is today! Melanie came and put some frozen items in the chest freezer since she is still without power. She had my birthday present and card since she hasn't seen me since my birthday three weeks ago. She was talking to Pop when I got the card out of the sack – it was still wrapped in plastic with nothing written on it. So funny. I asked her if she'd like it back so she could sign it. She snatched it and tore off to another room to write in it, mad at herself for being so distracted. We got a laugh out of it, though. Even funnier, later when I was opening my cards,

Dad decided to repaint the house. Some parts were tricky to reach…so he improvised – much to our dismay.

I told Mom and Dad about what Melanie did and forgot to open her card! I think we're all tired.

We had a good lunch and celebration of Tam's birthday and mine. Shaun had picked up some Chick-fil-A, and Tam brought a lemon cake that was really yummy. Sweet gifts and good company. Later, we discussed Pop's upcoming 100th birthday party and made some initial plans, then Rachel came by and told us about her trip to Kansas City. That evening, we tried to get the cows interested in grazing the cemetery pasture, but they were too full to be impressed. Pop fed the calves. Shaun and Caleb drove up and put the big sliding door back on the tracks. Full day on the home front.

SUNDAY, JUNE 18TH

I had a pretty good night on the couch – that box fan muffled the sound of Mom's *Bewitched* episodes. Sent Father's Day texts to my sons, and called to wish Bill a happy day and told him where his card was. After we had breakfast, I went to give Mom her morning meds, and saw that the compartment for those was empty; neither Melanie nor I had given them to her yet. Tam had come over briefly, so I thought she might have, and told Melanie I'd ask her at church, then call back to let her know. Shaun came up so that Pop could ride to church with him, then I headed out – Melanie had to make up the yeast rolls before she came.

When I got to the Sunday School class, Tam wasn't there. Found out a bit later that she had been looking for the key fob for Marc's truck. Anyway, she hadn't given Mom the meds either, so we decided to take care of that as soon as we got home from church. Our cousin Deborah took photos of us with Pop after the service. Her dad, our Uncle Monroe, has already gone on; this special day has to be difficult for her.

We enjoyed a great meal together – Christopher joined us. Mom stayed at her puzzle table in the next room. Pop opened his cards and gifts: a new flag for the front porch, a new coffee pot, a big can of cashews. When he headed to his recliner to rest, I visited with my sisters a little bit, then headed for Nac. I'm so very thankful that I have the best father anyone could wish for – full of wisdom, integrity, humor, dedication, work ethic, and on and on. What a blessing!

THURSDAY, JUNE 22ND

While the tree service took down a tree out back, and the roofers continued installing a new roof, I called the hospital to set up a payment plan for Dad's leg surgery – one of those things I can do long distance. I also looked up that bath soap Pop likes on Amazon since we can't find it in the stores anymore - $110 for 16 bars! Pop would have a fit if we spend nearly seven dollars a bar for soap.

FRIDAY, JUNE 23RD

Poor Melanie had a crummy day at the folks' today – trouble with a heifer that got out at the Homeplace, forgetting some supplies they needed to fix the fence, Mom getting a bit crossways with her, and so forth. Usually by Friday, Melanie and I have gotten a bit low on our patience and grace. Thankfully, during our "off" week, we bounce back.

I had a nice day – my friends Debbie and Sheryl prepared a lovely meal for my belated birthday celebration, all so delicious, and the cake Deb made was a stunner! Wonderful to have a relaxing time.

While I was fixing supper, Melanie called upset because Tam and Pop had been gone a long time for the appointment with Dr. B, and Melanie couldn't get Tam to answer her cell phone. As it turned out, she didn't have any service there, and on the way home, they were in a bad storm. Then Shaun snagged the electric line that runs from the house to the little barn as he drove the tractor under it. The wire snapped loose, but the bulb was still burning, even with the switch turned off … weird. They weren't sure what to do, and Pop couldn't see because of his eye shot, so Bill and I talked them through it – turn off the breakers one at a time until they locate the one for that line, shut that breaker down, then check to make sure nothing vital was on the same breaker, and label it.

Later, Melanie called again – she'd somehow not given Mom her morning meds. They were still in the pill case. I assured her it would be okay, just be sure she got them tomorrow morning. It's tough to remember everything.

MONDAY, JUNE 26TH

Lots of prep in this desert before heading to the folks' – having to water the world, it seems. I surely was hoping we'd have a decent June before heading into July and August. They've gotten more rain up Pop's way – glad of that. When I got there, his 1020 was parked under the carport, with the mower attached. He'd been mowing weeds near Shaun's house when a shower chased him inside for a while. Tam told me that Pop hadn't had a very good weekend – he had to leave church early yesterday. She thinks he's dehydrated – all that outside painting while having intestinal bouts. She found some stuff called Liquid IV that she's going to order and see if that gets him back on track. And, we're pushing food at Mom because she's losing weight … battles on both fronts.

Pop insisted on going back out to mow, but said he'd just mow about an hour. I helped Mom on her puzzle for a bit, then walked to the barn to get Pop's truck and feed the calves. Tam had told me that Pop had left the truck window down and the seat got wet, but I had forgotten all about it until I sat down and got a wet bottom. Back at the house I grabbed the binoculars so I could walk partway down the hill and get a good look at Pop's face; he looked okay, and when he saw me standing there, he lifted an index finger to indicate one more round, so I walked to the gate and waited for him to come through.

We all sat in the Big Room after that and talked awhile. Then Pop fell asleep, and Mom went to her room. I organized their chart pages where we record weight, blood pressure, etc. Then just did my regular cooking and so forth. Shaun came in the afternoon and mowed the lawn. Pop drove the 1020 to the barn and parked it; I followed in the truck to bring him back. Gave the calves more water and their "supper." Pop went in to lie down until 9:00, then got up to shower and get back in bed. He still needs to bounce back from all his work, which takes a lot longer at his age. Mom is watching

Murder, She Wrote episodes now, and boy, is it loud. Her hearing was great until just the last few months. We may have to see if she can use Pop's extra hearing aids.

TUESDAY, JUNE 27TH

After breakfast, the Energizer Bunny said he was going to mow some more, but needed to grease the mower's tail wheel, so here we went up to the equipment shed. Pop got the grease gun out of the barn while I got a bucket of feed for the calves. When I saw him walking over towards the shed, I just set the bucket down because I knew he would need help. As he slowly backed the tractor and mower out, I watched for that grease fitting to rotate to the top of the tail wheel. Pop got off the tractor and started to pump grease into that fitting, but I told him it looked as if it had a cap over it – this was a brand new tail wheel. Pop didn't think so and went ahead … grease just globbed down the outside – it wasn't going into anything. I told Pop it wasn't working, wiped off the grease, and wiggled that cap back and forth until it came off. Then I helped Pop get the grease gun in place, and it worked. After we got the tractor taken care of, I took the grease gun back to the barn while Pop headed off to mow. Fed the calves – they still had a little left from last night. Pop did **not** want to try to feed them out during the hot summer, but we didn't have any choice because the packing place was booked up until late July.

Drove back to the house and fixed Mom's breakfast – she's down to 107.5. Sigh. She wondered when her word search book would arrive, so I called them to find out. It should be here within a week. While she worked on her jigsaw puzzle, I sat on the patio to keep an eye on Pop, then drove down to check on him and give him some electrolyte water. Fixed Mom some guacamole dip and chips to eat with her morning meds … anything to put some weight on her. Drove down to shoo Pop out of the pasture, but he was headed in anyway. When he tried to get off the tractor, I thought he was going to fall. I was right there in case he did – I guess we'd have both wound up in the dirt, but maybe I would have cushioned his fall. He is so determined to do things, but time is stealing the ability. I know the Lord is taking care of him; I have to keep reminding myself that I am **not** in control.

Once he got in the recliner, he quickly went to sleep. Mom wanted me to help her finish the puzzle so she could get an easier one to work on – this one has more pieces than Mom likes. Afterward, I cleared everything off the mantel, put a new scarf on it, and located some items with a summer look: yellow glass baskets, gold glass nesting hen, glass bells with yellow birds and flowers on the top, lemon yellow candles, and a pocket watch hanging under a glass dome. I can tell where they go back into the shelves later because when I picked them up, there was a clean circle in the dust. Ha! Cleaning all those shelves and whatnots – now there's a chore I'll save for a winter day.

Lunch, town run, down to Shaun's to let the satellite TV guy in if necessary, talked to Shaun about delaying Pop's plan: fuel up the 1020, load it, and drive it to the Homeplace at 4:00 – with a temperature of 97° and heat index of 108°! Pop does *not* need to be in that kind of heat. Shaun agreed and told Pop that he would rather do all that in the morning. After visiting with Shaun, Pop showered and was in bed by 7:00. I think that's a new record for him.

WEDNESDAY, JUNE 28TH

Parker's 8th birthday today! Shelley sent me some birthday photos, then I called and got to talk to him a bit. Those boys are growing up so fast, and I miss them so much.

Shaun came to get Pop and the tractor, drive to the Homeplace, and unload it for him. After fixing Mom's breakfast, grabbing Pop a drink, and talking to Melanie, I drove to the Homeplace, located Pop, and gave him the water. Moved the truck into the shade and sat there reading my Sunday School lesson. As promised, Pop headed up the hill at 10 and parked under the oak. Yay!

Back to the house for a rest and more water, then puzzling with Mom, lunch, meds, etc. Rita and the kids came for a visit – she's going back to Wyoming in August for a wedding and to clear out their storage unit. I'll bet she has forgotten about a lot of items left there … it will be like Christmas. Later, I worked on Pop's fingernails. He said he'd snagged his skin with them a few times. It cannot have been very long since I trimmed them; they must grow like wild weeds. After he'd gone to bed, I remembered that I hadn't given him the blood thinner pill, so I had to wake him. At least he hadn't been asleep very long.

THURSDAY, JUNE 29TH

Pop didn't have a great night – same issue. But when there's mowing to be done, you just get after it regardless. So off we went. I greased the tail wheel for him, then walked to the big pen he wanted to mow first to look for anything that could damage the mower. Found several pieces of wire, a few big rocks, and some limbs. After Pop finished that area, he headed out the gate to the east slope, and I walked back to the truck. Decided to clear away some fallen limbs around the oak he usually parks under. I didn't want him to trip over something as he got off the tractor later. Turns out, it was a good thing that I hung around.

After several minutes, I heard the tractor stop, then heard Pop yell for me to bring the truck. Rita happened to be outside and hollered, "I think Pawpaw's stuck." Oh boy. When I got there, Pop said, "I did a dumb thing; I got too close to that drain and got stuck." Fortunately, we had a chain in the truck. Pop wanted to hook up and work from the south side, but I could tell that was not going to work – we'd be going down into the drain, so I suggested that Pop drive the truck way around to the north side so we could just pull *across* the drain. After he took off, I realized I still had the chain, so I had to wade through waist-high weeks, trying to find a drier place to cross, lugging that chain. Oh well. We got the chain hooked up, Pop climbed on the tractor and started it, and I eased the truck forward. Good thing it's a three-quarter ton truck with 4-wheel drive and heavy duty tires. Easy Peasy. Put the chain back in the truck and Pop was on his way, giving that drain a wide berth.

Drove home and fixed Mom's breakfast. Grabbed a drink for Pop and headed back to the Homeplace. The tractor wasn't behaving very well – Pop said the hydraulic fluid was low, so back to the house and put hydraulic fluid and a funnel in the truck for tomorrow. Chores of one sort or another, a fast estate sale visit with Tam, lunch, dishes, etc. Nurse C came to check Mom's INR level; it's still 1.7, so we'll have to adjust her blood thinner dosage again … a constant balancing act, keeping it between 2 and 3.

FRIDAY, JUNE 30TH

Pop's BP was low this morning, so in addition to breakfast, I gave him some lightly salted nuts and chips – that brought it up somewhat. Shaun took him to the Homeplace so he could take care of putting that fluid in.

I fixed Mom's breakfast, then made a loaf of banana-walnut bread. Texted Rita to ask if she wanted any, and she told me Pop seemed to be having trouble with the tractor. I drove there and found him in a chair under the tree, eating watermelon. Rita had him all fixed up! He'd bumped his elbow somehow and his shirt sleeve was bloody. Plus, a limb had caught his arm and made big purple places like those Mom gets at the slightest bump. I know those blood thinners are vital, but they sure wreak havoc on that tissue-thin skin.

Got him back home and called the clinic to ask if there was any test other than a colonoscopy that would tell us about his intestines. I also called Dr. J's office to ask if one of those blood thinners could be the culprit. He was out, so Pop will have to wait until his appointment next Wednesday. I felt really tired, but I think it was more of an emotional and mental tired. Had to go to town for some things. Tam had suggested an anti-diarrheal medicine, and while I was looking for that, she called me and said her daughter Rachel had suggested a probiotic, which made sense. Pop's gut has been messed up for so long, those essential microbes haven't had a chance. On to the health food store and bought the bottle with the most pro and prebiotics I could find … gazillions of those little helpers! Well, not really, but an awful lot.

Back home and yadda, yadda, yadda … Maybe July will bring better health for the folks!

Melanie

JUNE

So many things vie for attention between my two lives. Here in my neck of the woods, Andy is trying to get his house ready to sell. I help by painting some. Trying to get my own house ready outside and inside for the Roos reunion next month. On June the 4th, a fox or something killed 6-7 of Andy's new chickens. Also, I am always concerned for my (mostly) elderly Sunday School ladies as they face all sorts of troubles for themselves, their children and grandchildren. I know I can leave them in God's capable hands, but concern and prayers filter through my days here and there at the folks. Angela and her family are moving to Missouri in a few days. Change is constant in life. How we process it: flow with it or fight against it, often determines the quality of life we have.

MONDAY, JUNE 5TH

Got to the folks and Tam helped me unload, then we talked about intestinal issues for both Mama and Daddy. Went to town and picked groceries and meds. Mama sick, again. Gave her some ginger ale with noon meds. Tam had left pork chops for lunch and made that easier. Shaun came up to mow. While he was doing that, Aunt Stella called and thanked me for the letter and pictures I had sent.

Prayed with Mama for God's will to be done. She would love to go on to Heaven. Her quality of life is not good. I tell her it is up to Him. Shaun stopped by to tell Daddy about his job and the interesting people he works for. Later, Daddy and I went up to the barn to get a ladder for tomorrow's painting. I took the binoculars and found #48 with a bull calf.

Shaun came back on the side by side. Daddy and I took a big tour with him and saw the new baby. Then Brother took me down to see Daddy's new brush hog mower for the smaller 1020 tractor. Daddy loves to mow. As soon as we get the 1020 out of the shop, I think Daddy will start mowing the Homeplace. Hope to cut and bale hay next week. Shaun went in to tell Mama about the chicken snake (rat snake) that startled him in front of one of his shop doors right at dusk. Daddy plans, Lord willing, to go to the Homeplace tomorrow and start on the west windows.

We sat on the patio and saw a little cat squirrel and a pair of red-headed woodpeckers.

TUESDAY, JUNE 6TH

Woke up at 3:00 am. Didn't go back to sleep. Finished my book. Daddy up at 6:00 am. After we all had breakfast, Daddy and I head for the Homeplace. We worked on the 4 windows on the west side and the kitchen window. These are the original old wooden ones with wood strips between the glass panes. Painting those narrow strips is a pain! (Pun intended.) Before Rita and the kids went to WMA at church, Athena showed me her missing tooth. I guess it was finally "dead" enough. LOL. The one next door is wiggling now. She asked about my yeast rolls, and I told her I would make some before the week was out, probably Friday.

I was trying to help Daddy with the kitchen screen when it slipped and I tore a big two-sided rip in it! I felt so bad. I rounded up all our stuff and Daddy loaded up the screen to be repaired. By noon we were headed home. I put our brushes in water to clean later. Daddy set the screen on the patio and said, "Don't worry about that screen. I'm an expert on rescreening." I smiled and said, "With your expertise and my eyesight, we should be fine." Daddy was worn out and rested in his recliner in the sunroom.

This afternoon I made peanut butter cookies, Daddy and Mama seemed to enjoy them. Shaun took 6 with him for tomorrow. His back was hurting, so no ride today. Daddy and I went up to feed and water the bulls, then put out salt and mineral for the cows and drove to the back of the hill near Tam's cabin. I checked and sure enough, #46 had a pretty heifer calf.

Daddy and I ate our bowl of raisin bran out on the patio and watched the close of another day. After Daddy went in to shower, I stayed outside a little longer, surrounded by the iconic sound of whippoorwills.

Tam is coming to the Homeplace at 9:00 in the morning to catch the high part over the back porch. You have to get up on the metal roof to paint it since it is set back and awkward to get to. Daddy insists that he can do it and faster than Tam, which may be true, but Tam doesn't want Daddy up there. I'm not crazy about it either.

WEDNESDAY, JUNE 7TH

We arrived at the Homeplace and started working. Daddy painted all six windows and 3 screens on the east side. I did touch up green trim on the front west side. Tam arrived, got the extension ladder, and scrambled onto the roof to paint the set back. She didn't like her brush; it was all bristled out, which made cutting in difficult. Athena and Raylan were talking to me as I painted. Athena gave me a piece of watermelon gum. Daddy sat down to rest several times. I had Pedialyte and cookies for him and a granola bar and water for me. I painted the green trim around all six windows and brushed off the screens for Daddy. I was pretty tired. We left about 11:30; Tam had finished earlier.

I didn't start lunch until after 1:00, so it was nearly 2:00 before we ate. Rita came by and visited Mama. She had some pizza for her. Along about 3:00 it started to get dark and looked like it was going to storm. We did get a nice rain. When Daddy and I went up to the barn to feed the bulls, the barn door would only open enough for me to squeeze through. It had been working beautifully. Don't know what happened.

After we came back, I helped Mama do her face cream. Daddy and I sat on the front porch a while, then I checked the mailbox and deadheaded the roses and daylilies. Shaun came by to look at the barn door, then visited with Mama.

THURSDAY, JUNE 8TH

Daddy up at 5:30 am. We were talking about the sunrise and its position. The sun is about as far northeast as it will go – on June 21st - 22nd it will start its journey back toward the southeast. I take care of Mama's breakfast, meds and timer, and make sure her phone is by her side. She tells us to be careful. We will be back by 11:30 or noon. I try to drive a bit slower. Daddy's neck is aggravated by the way this ¾ ton truck rides on rough country roads. Mine, too. When we arrive, Rita and the kids are leaving for a visit and town. Daddy and I tackle the south 2 adjoining windows, the back door and the large decorative posts that hold up the back porch. I can tell he is tired because he sits several times. I try my hand at painting the screens, but I'm not good at it like Daddy, so I stick to dusting them off before setting them on the special ladder that Daddy fixed to hold them as he paints.

The kids and Rita return, and I help her get her groceries in. Then she points to a sonogram on the fridge and tells me she is expecting her 3rd child in January! I told her I was happy for her. By then, Daddy had finished the screens, and Rita helped me load the ladders, assuring me that she was well able to do that. She had made some broccoli and cauliflower soup and gave me a big bowl. I hope Mama and Daddy will eat some. As we were fixing to leave, she went around where Daddy was getting in the truck and told him the good news. He seemed pleased. He told her to take good care of herself. This will be the 17th great grandchild for Mama and Daddy.

Daddy and I went to the sunroom and sat down. Forty-five minutes later I woke up! I quickly heated the soup and gave Daddy a bite to see if he liked it. He did. Mama ate a bowl, too, then I fixed her hair and put a new puzzle out. I washed up the dishes and texted Rita about her successful soup gift. I told her I would reciprocate with rolls tomorrow. She said, "Athena is counting on it." She has asked about Aunt Mel's rolls every day we're down there painting. I told Athena that Friday is baking day.

Shaun came up at 5:00 and talked a bit. Tam came over to talk to Mama about changing from her Dr.Bo to Daddy's Dr.B. Not as long a wait time with Daddy's eye doctor. I think Mama is on board.

FRIDAY, JUNE 9TH

I slept well. Daddy slept 12 hours. After he shaved, we drove to Heath and Heath for screen wire for the Homeplace kitchen window, gassed up the car, then on to the store. Daddy barely made it to the bench just inside the double doors. His lingering intestinal issue is really making him weak. I left him there and hurried to get everything. Back home. Daddy stayed in his sunroom chair all afternoon except when he came to the table for potato soup and rolls.

Rachel popped in, heated her breakfast and ate it since she'd had no time to eat earlier. She brought Daddy some fly meds to mix with mineral and is bringing a fly spray gun for him to try. Rita and kids came. Rita said Athena got up this morning and said, "It's roll day!" I fixed her a bag of 5 rolls and gave her one to eat now. They ate some watermelon, too.

SATURDAY, JUNE 10TH

Up most of the night. Checked on Daddy at 2:00 am and heard him up at 4:00. We were up to stay by 5:20. Sat and watched the sunrise and talked about what to do with this 3 week intestinal issue. I checked Daddy's weight: 166.5 lbs. He usually weighs in the upper 170s. Googled two of the only prescription medicines he takes and both have that side effect. We can tweak his diet to help. That potato soup yesterday was a good choice.

When Shaun came, Daddy declined the ride, which says a lot about how he is feeling. Shaun and I find #43 and her baby – a black heifer. Looks like #30 will be next. When we returned, Daddy was outside working on that screen. Shaun brought his little nail gun, and they got the screen apart and put back together again. It looks good, but will need repainting.

I braided Mama's hair and she wanted me to put lotion on her arms, but Tam said she would do it since I needed to go home.

Came on home. Texted Valerie, to see where they were on their journey to Missouri, and she said Wal-Mart. I asked, "What town?" "Marshall." They'd had to stop for a tire repair and windshield wipers. I hurried to meet them and visited a while. I had been feeling forlorn about not being able to go along on this amazing adventure and God blessed me with a visit and a goodbye wave!

FRIDAY, JUNE 16TH

Big storm at my house! It hit at 1:00 in the morning with 80-100 mph winds and continual lightning. I was walking the floor and praying. There was such a loud humming all around the eaves of the house that I thought the roof would fly off! This went on for an hour, but I finally settled down to sleep. At 6:30 I got up and checked outside. I couldn't believe all the downed limbs, pine cones and trash all over the yard. I rounded the corner of the house and was shocked by the sight of my neighbors' double wide trailer roof on my pool fence and in the north east pasture. I worked on cleanup for a long time; it was hot, but I didn't know *how* hot.

The electricity was off, so no water since my well pump is electric. I took stuff from the refrigerator and freezer to my daughter's house since they have a generator. I couldn't believe the devastation as I drove over to her home. Trees and power lines – poles and all – down. I had a pounding headache and was feeling funny when I got there. Hannah found me an Aleve. I took it and went in to take my cold shower. (Their generator only ran the refrigerators and freezers, so no lights or hot water.) I washed my hair and noticed that my head felt hot; I realized later, when I found out the temperature (100), that I was suffering from heat exhaustion. Knowing I might be without power for a week, I decided to go to the folks tomorrow.

SATURDAY, JUNE 17TH

Tam's birthday. Up at 6:00 am. Tried to do a few things before I headed to Jacksonville. Tam, Sherry and Shaun were there and helped me unload. Shaun took off to town to pick up some lunch. I gave Sherry her birthday bag and card, but when she opened the card, I had forgotten to sign it, so she saved it for later; that will give me time to write in it. I braided Mama's hair and helped her change her gown.

We discussed the upcoming book and traded ideas until Brother came back with lunch, then ate in the dining room – a sweet time. After lunch, Tam got out the lemon cake she had made and some strawberries.

Afterward, we all went to the sunroom to discuss and plan Daddy's 100th birthday celebration. We made a big list – plates, napkins, cups, forks, decorations, cake, Tam's coffee punch (Shaun's suggestion), etc.

Rachel stopped by with the fly gun and meds for her Pawpaw and a cup from Kansas City. Later, Shaun and Caleb drove up and fixed the barn door.

Bill called Sherry about his brother in Canada who finally got a new kidney today! He'd had to wait over a year. Such a wonderful blessing for him.

SUNDAY, JUNE 18TH – FATHER'S DAY

We are up early, sister and I. She starts the coffee, then we sit outside in the morning cool with the sound of thunder to the south. Daddy brings his cup out to sit with us. Later, we got ready for church. I stayed behind so I could mix up rolls and check on Mama, then went to church. Heard a great message.

All of us kids were able to be there with Dad at church on Father's Day...it was a good day.

Hugged Lurlene, the only church member older than Daddy – she is 101 now. Our cousin Deborah took our traditional family picture, then I took one of her with Daddy. Her Daddy and my Daddy were brothers. He passed away 3 years ago.

After church, Brother dashed to town – he'd forgotten to get a card. We set the table and just as the rolls came out of the oven, Brother drove up with Christopher. Good lunch with the lemon cake and strawberries again. Daddy opened his cards; Sherry and I read ours to him. Tam prints hers large enough for him to read. A wonderful time all around.

On the home front, Andy's generator to his shop went out and he lost a freezer full of fish, deer meat etc.

MONDAY, JUNE 19TH

Up at 6:30 am with Papa. Rachel arrived. We compared our storm experiences, with no electricity and water. Since she is headed to Marshall. I told her she better call to be sure the feed stores are open … they might still be without power.

I take Mama her breakfast. She comments with a sorrowful face, "I pray each night to go on home, and I wake up the next morning to misery." My heart hurts for her lingering when she wants to go. I told her I was praying for her good and God's glory, and encouraged her to be patient and wait on the Lord's timing.

I texted Tam about Mama's fingernails. (Mama likes Tam to trim them.) She came over and cut Mama's nails, and I put lotion on her arms. She had bumped her left arm going into the bathroom, and it was purple with bleeding under the skin, but Tam said it was better than it had been. Her Warfarin level is too high, but Tam is working on adjusting it – a constant battle.

Daddy is reading about a guy who hiked the 1,000 mile Appalachian trail, and he shared some of the highlights with me, then got outside and cut the vines (Virginia creeper and poison ivy) crawling up the old barn and pulled them down, then cut down several poke bushes. It was already too hot at 11:00 when he came in. We are under a heat advisory – heat index of 112. Texted my daughter in Missouri to check on her renovations. Talked and texted Sherry about my stomach cramps. Googled my joint meds and determined they were associated with that, so I am cutting them out.

Daddy drank 4 glasses of water today. Yea! Shaun came in and visited before he went to the barn to put the front tractor tire on. He brought out the rest of the east pasture hay rolls and put them in the pole barn, then came in to cool off. We made a plan for late tomorrow to get the highway meadow rolls to the barn.

I texted Pam that I was here for the week. She wants me to see the farm she and her husband, Vernon, have. Her friend in Arkansas, a veterans' advocate, sent Daddy a large print Bible that Pam is bringing tomorrow to present to Daddy. What a sweet thing to do for Papa.

Good news from home: my son and daughter have electricity! Mine is still not on.

TUESDAY, JUNE 20TH

Daddy and I are on the patio. Thunder muttering around. Tam texted about closing the air vent hatches. Did that. Daddy and I head up to feed the bulls, Also time to change pastures with the cows, so we open the gate to the eastern hay meadow where they will graze for 3-4 days. Daddy only got 78 rolls of hay due to the cool, wet May. Great weather for people, but not for hay growth.

Tam came by and got my list of grocery items to pick up. Daddy is reading. I take care of Mama – braid hair, change gown, put up puzzle, find new puzzle, etc. After we had lunch, Daddy changed into his Seabee shirt, tan khakis and black tennis shoes. He looked so nice. Pam arrived and I took a picture of the veteran's Bible presentation. We visited a few minutes with Daddy and Mom, then drove to Pam's farm. Beautiful land. On the way home, we stopped by the old Tecula cemetery where some of her people and a lot of Daddy's family are buried. Back at the house, she talked a while with Daddy before leaving.

Shaun came in at 5:30 pm. He had devised a plan to get the 20 bales from the highway meadow to the barn with a minimum of trips, and it worked perfectly. When they were down to the last bale, I drove him and Daddy back over there to get the machines. It was still extremely hot. Daddy drove the tractor back with the last hay roll while Shaun came back in his side by side. Daddy told Shaun that the heater on the tractor worked really well! Brother unloaded the bales, put everything up, and then went home to shower.

After a while, Mama says she can't work her TV, and wanted me to call Shaun to fix it. I told her he needed to rest, but she insisted, "He will come." Sure enough, here he came, and patiently went over what she did wrong and how to avoid doing that – again. Sweet brother.

WEDNESDAY, JUNE 21ST

Up around 6:00 am. Checked the list I made last night, and Daddy and I decide to go with it, although he is still recovering from painting two houses. We get the fly gun that Rachel brought, the repaired kitchen screen, salt and mineral. I tried the fly gun on the bulls when we fed them – It doesn't seem to shoot very far. I am probably not doing something right.

We head down to the Homeplace after I get Mama settled. I hung the kitchen screen and admired Rita's cosmos, morning glories and zinnias. Daddy and I drove back to the mineral trough and put out the mineral and salt. We locate the herd by the creek, but I count only 7; one is still missing. We drive back and tell Rita. She said she saw all 8 yesterday. Such a relief.

Back home, I check on Mama and she has taken her noon meds with the timer reminder. Daddy drinks a cup of coffee and props his feet up. He is either dizzy from the ride or is still dehydrated from his house painting. I check on my friends in Marshall still recovering from the storm. I called Andy and he said, "No Mama, no electricity for you, yet." Then he called just a couple of minutes later and said, "Mama, your cameras are on line! You have electricity!" That makes me happy. At least when I get there, I can clean out my refrigerator and freezer in a cool house. Angela gave me a progress report on the Missouri renovation and texted a picture of the flooring they have ordered.

Rita texted me that the missing #17 is in Cousin Darryl's pasture, so Daddy and I make plans to take range cubes to coax her through the gate and back with the herd, then fix the fence so she won't get out again.

Daddy and I ate a piece of sweet potato pie still warm from the oven, Yum. Rita stopped by with a bouquet of gladiolas, zinnias and sunflowers from her garden. She ate a piece of the pie and left a sweet thank you note.

Coolest evening in a week. I found Venus and the crescent moon, but, couldn't locate Mars, even with binoculars. I saw a firefly as it got darker, Daddy spotted it, too. We lingered on the porch, enjoying the music of the first night of summer.

THURSDAY, JUNE 22ND

I woke up early – 4:45 am. Later I heard Daddy was up and remembered that I had unplugged the coffee pot to plug in the mixer. I leaped up and came to Daddy's assistance. He can't see to punch the "on" button anyway. He said, "I would never have got that coffee going." When I asked how he felt this morning, he said, "Like an old man!" I gave him the weather report from my iPhone. Daddy said he didn't know but what we would be better off *without* extended weather reports. He said as a child they had a battery powered radio, but didn't have time to listen to it. He said his dad was the closest to a weather man they had. He could study the clouds – lightning in the southeast was a sign of dry weather. But if a storm came out of the northwest, it was fixin' to do something.

We gathered all our fencing supplies and drove to the Homeplace. At the pipe bridge, I got out of the truck and walked across, then we drove through the gate into Darryl's place and tried to entice #17 back over with some cubes. Not happening. To keep the other seven from joining her, we started working to block her escape route. After the preliminaries were done, we discovered that the bucket with all the small tools was not in the truck. We each thought the other had loaded it. Daddy was upset and frustrated. When he could see well, things like this didn't happen. Nothing to do but go back to the house where he plopped in his recliner and said, "I'm not fit for anything!" I reminded him of all the chores he'd completed lately, including painting two houses. That helped for a short while. Then he decided to cut the two sassafras trees that have succumbed to the latest beetle/fungus plague. He started on one, but soon put the saw down, saying he would let Shaun finish it. Another defeat, and I have no words of comfort.

He went inside and read for the rest of the afternoon. Tam had found four new books to put on his Kindle. I decided to make rolls to try to cheer him up, along with peach glazed chicken, peas, carrots, new potatoes, and tomatoes. Shaun arrived and I helped him get the cows out of the hay meadow and shut the gate. Then he cut the sassafras trees and used the tractor to haul them to the deep ditch we keep trying to fill. As he went under the barn's electric lines, he snagged one and down it came. What **is** it with this day?

I came in, cleaned up, retrieved Mama's pillow, and adjusted the thermostat for the 7th time today. She is going to her new eye doctor tomorrow and is not happy about it, but Daddy's eye doctor has a new facility and an extra doctor to give eye shots. The wait time is usually less than an hour. So much better for her and for us.

Susan (Iowa first cousin) and I exchange text messages. She is on her third day of painting her house and starting to whine. I sent her pictures of Daddy painting this house and his Homeplace house. After she saw those, she said, "No more whining!"

FRIDAY, JUNE 23RD

This morning, I leave a note for Mama and we head down to the Homeplace to do the fence repairs. This time, with proper supplies in hand. Daddy has to ease down the creek bank, climb over the H brace, secure the wire, and then climb back up. All the time I am helping him, giant mosquitoes are drilling for blood through my shirt, all over my arms and even my ears! One draws a drop of blood to the surface that even Daddy can see! Finally he was satisfied with the repair and said, "Let's go." Sweet words when you are being attacked from every angle. Daddy drove across the culvert, which is tricky because there is a drop off if you drift over too far to the left. I kind of hold my breath, but we make it across and head home.

After Daddy changed clothes and I get Mama's breakfast, away we went to Daddy's 10:00 haircut, then to the store. Daddy uses his cane to walk to the inside bench to wait in the cool. I hurriedly round up our items and check out. I came to the bench – no Daddy! I look back in the store and there he stands eyeing the cantaloupe. He said a lady told him these tasted really good, so he picked one out. We hit the wall of hot air outside and hurry to the car. I push the button and it wouldn't unlock, tried again. Two young black men came up and said I was trying to get into **their** car! I looked up and sure enough ours was straight across from this one. I said, "They look the same!" One said, with a smile, "No, yours is a lot newer." We get in the right car and head home.

I help Mama get ready for her 1:15 eye appointment, then Tam picked her up. Shaun texted me from work that Daddy's 1020 tractor is ready. After Shaun and Daddy left, I decided to sit in the swing on the front porch and watch a thunderstorm approaching. It got cooler and the wind picked up. Before long, here came Brother, Daddy, trailer and tractor. They hurried up to the barn, unloaded the tractor, and hustled back. The storm was bearing down. Shaun barely had time to dash home and get the trailer and truck put up before the wind started blowing the rain sideways. Checked the rain gauge later and an inch and a half had fallen.

Finally Tam and Mama pulled in; they had been driving home in rain and hail. Mama was exhausted but had done very well. She got 5 or 6 different tests and evaluations and even got a shot in less than half the time of the other place. I got her lunch and a Tylenol.

Another storm kicked up and the lights went off. Daddy decided to shower while it was still light enough to see, and was in bed by 8:30. Mama can't do anything except rest her eyes. I got her evening meds and saw that her morning meds were still in their compartment! I can't call Tam because her phones are out. I called Sherry and she reassured me that a skip now and then isn't the end of the world. Mama even piped up, "I'm not going to die over a few pills missed." I said, "You better not!" She laughed.

SATURDAY, JUNE 24TH

I woke up when the electricity came back on at 5:00 am. Went in to Daddy's room because his light and the sunroom light were on. He was sound asleep. Checked on Mama; she was asleep with the light on and the TV glowing, too, so I turned her light off and read my devotionals.

After we were all up, Brother drove over before his Saturday outing and promised Daddy, several times, that he would fix the broken electric line and hook up the new mower to the 1020 tractor so Daddy could mow Monday. After Shaun left, I fixed Mama's breakfast. When she saw the tray, she gave the usual response, "Oh NO!" She would hardly eat at all if we let her decide. I gave her a mini lecture on a good attitude and being thankful for the effort we make to have a tempting breakfast for her. As I left, she thanked me for fixing it for her.

Tam came over about 9:00, on her way to the Verizon store to straighten out the mess about her phone service. She had no phone service during the storm last night and the power was off 10 hours. I asked Daddy if it would be okay if I went on home. I had fixed Mama's meds and the timer. He said, "Sure, you go on home and be careful." I told him I would call when I got home. Went in to say bye to Mama. She always says, "Thank you for all you do." I gave Daddy an extra hug and a kiss. He said, "Don't forget your purse, phone and sunglasses." Such a thoughtful Daddy. He knows my track record and wants to prevent a trip back for any of those.

Tamra

THURSDAY, JUNE 1ST

Rita told us that she is expecting baby number three! We are happy for her and Jason. Athena and Raylan are excited about a new brother or sister. Mom and Dad will have great-grand number seventeen...wow.

FRIDAY, JUNE 2ND

Covering for Sherry this evening so she can attend her church's annual fish fry. Mom and Dad seem pretty content to puzzle and read. I was wishing I could zap some of that delicious fish up here for us, but even with a drone it would be cold after a fifty mile trip.

SATURDAY, JUNE 3RD

Well, the contentment was good while it lasted…Mom has kept me hopping all day and into the evening. First she's cold, then she's hot… over and over. I am meeting myself coming and going, up and down these stairs, back and forth, I'll bet I've walked five miles today, just in the house! At least I'll stay in shape. Tonight, while I was doctoring Dad's foot, that small rough spot that had been so slow to heal finally came off. It looks so much better.

SUNDAY, JUNE 4TH

Mom has been sick at her stomach for five days, so I decided to switch her routine to see if that will help. Took her off the cereal, went back to eggs and fruit; it seemed to work. She was able to take her other meds without a problem. I sat with her after I got ready for church and tried to take her mind off her situation by talking about old times. She perked up a bit. Then, after Dad got dressed, I asked him to see if **he** could cheer her up. He sat in there and they chatted until time to leave for services. She was feeling well enough that she asked about a new puzzle. I promised I would set one out for her when we got back from church. Shaun stopped by and checked on her about an hour later and said she was working in her Wheel of Fortune book, so all's right with the world…at least for a few hours.

MONDAY, JUNE 5TH

It stormed last night from 9:30 till after 1:00 am, so not much sleep. Mom doesn't like storms, so she called several times. I think she just wanted some company. Dad wasn't feeling well this morning, so he decided not to paint today, which was ok by me. I would have probably fallen asleep and rolled off the roof. Mom is balking again today about eating. So much for the new routine; it lasted all of twenty-four hours. Finally, I managed to find something she would try – pizza. If it weren't for DiGiorno, Mom would probably starve to death. I filled Mel in on everything when she got here and headed home. I was so exhausted I didn't even unpack. I just took a nap.

TUESDAY, JUNE 6TH

Still tired, but I managed to do my usual routine – WMA then errands. Athena went with me today; we had fun, until Mom called while we were in Atwoods and started telling me that she wasn't going to any more doctors' appointments, ***ever***! She went on and on until I finally got a word in and told her we'd talk about it later. She was definitely on a tear.

WEDNESDAY, JUNE 7TH

Went to the Homeplace to paint that high spot on the south end; it is difficult to reach and pretty steep. I had to lie on my back to do most of it, scooting along and trying to keep my paint bucket from overturning. The brush I had was horrible. Dad must have had it for fifty years. If I had known what a sorry brush I'd have to use, I would have brought my own. He said I was slow…I told him I could paint much faster with a better brush. I also said I would be ashamed to have such a terrible brush. It didn't seem to faze him…he said I was too picky, but I saw the traces of a smile, and I knew he was getting a kick out of my fussing. Finally finished about two hours later *and was I glad to get off that roof!*

THURSDAY, JUNE 8TH

Went over to talk to Mom about her appointments; I couldn't face it yesterday. She finally agreed to go to her next appointment, but she let me know she didn't like it one little bit! I'll probably have to convince her many more times before the actual appointment…sigh. I spent a big part of the day on the phone trying to get her records moved and line everything up. She'll go, if I have to carry her. Sherry called me and told me Nurse C. was locked out – Mel and Dad had locked the door when they went to the Homeplace, so I ran over and unlocked the door for her. Good thing I'm close by.

FRIDAY, JUNE 9TH

Still back and forth with the doctors, signing forms, etc. It takes an act of Congress to change doctors. Sometimes, I wonder if it is all worth it. You try to do things to make it easier on Mom and Dad, and sometimes they seem to think you are just annoying them. Believe me, I'd rather spend time writing, reading, or going on a walk than be tethered to the phone trying to answer a million doctor/medical questions, filling out forms, and running papers all over creation. I was feeling kind of sorry for myself when it hit me… Mom always took care of that kind of thing for us as kids. Now our roles have swapped, and we are doing those things for her and Dad. Wow…I stopped my pity party, took a deep breath, and made a fresh pot of coffee…I was going to need it.

SATURDAY & SUNDAY, JUNE 10TH & 11TH

Shaun came up today to show Dad his plans for his house addition. I could tell Dad really enjoyed talking it over with him. Shaun and Dad are especially close. He runs everything by Dad, not that he always agrees with Dad's advice, but at least he listens.

It stormed tonight and one lightning bolt hit so close, Mom and I both jumped and screamed. After the storm, it was nice and cool, so I opened the windows to enjoy the fresh air. Mom was happily working on a puzzle, and Dad was reading a book I found for him about a WW II pilot. It was a wonderfully quiet evening.

Turned off hot again on Sunday – took my cats to get spayed today; it is the only day the clinic is open in our area. Waited for over two hours this morning and barely made it to church. When I picked them up, it was another hour wait. By then, it was so close to evening service time, I just brought them to church with me and set the carrier in the foyer. No one even knew they were there until afterwards. Everybody thought it was funny. When I dropped by to check on Mom and Dad, Sherry asked me if I was trying to turn those cats into Christians. One of them maybe, the other one is definitely a little devil!

SATURDAY & SUNDAY, JUNE 17TH & 18TH

It was an altogether lovely birthday and Father's Day, a relaxed time of visiting with my sisters and brother. Just being in the same room was a treat, instead of being scattered all across East Texas like we usually are. All of us kids were at church with Dad for Father's Day. We took pictures afterwards and visited with everyone. Christopher joined us for lunch since he was spending the day with Shaun. We had entertained the idea of lunch out somewhere, but decided it would be more fun to stay at Mom and Dad's. It felt like old times, even if it was for just a few hours. I think we all needed the break. We celebrated not only my birthday, but Sherry's too, making our time extra special. We gave Dad his cards and gifts after finishing lunch.

Then we joined Dad in the sunroom and began making plans for his 100th birthday celebration. Dad listened, but after answering a few questions, he started drifting off to sleep. He had already told us that whatever we planned was ok by him, so we brainstormed while he snoozed.

Rachel dropped by later with a new fly dope gun for her Pawpaw's Father's Day present. She had just returned from a work trip to Kansas City and regaled us with her latest adventure. We all enjoyed her saga and photos of KC.

It was a good day.

FRIDAY, JUNE 23RD

Such a busy week, I haven't had time to catch my breath. Finished my art project, wrote several articles and my column, and ran back and forth to Mom and Dad's a dozen times or more, plus a hundred other things. Today is shaping up to be a real doozy as well. I took Marc to his doctor appointment this morning, worked in the yard, signed Dad up for a new service at the clinic, went to the phone store to get service changed (my phone stopped working as a result), then I had to take Mom to her new eye doctor appointment at 1:00. We made it, but poor Mom was so pitiful, I felt bad for her.

Dad wanted to see if he could repair and paint our old barn...he did it and in just under a week!

She looked so small and bent in that wheelchair. Every once in a while, she would raise her head and turn to look at me – her once clear, dark brown eyes are now glazed with age. She gives me the slightest half-smile and I pat her arm. "I'm sorry Mom. I know waiting wears you out. Maybe it won't be much longer." She tilts her head to look at the door "Maybe" she mouths, not making a sound. As her head droops again, I feel her weariness begin to creep into me as I sit with her. I can't help but think about how she "used to be." Head held high, eyes bright, moving with confident strides, that's how I like to think about my Mom, not the stooped, frail figure in this wheelchair. This is not my Mama, but only a shadow of who she once was…these sad eyes, wrinkled brow, always asking "why." It's just not her. Time can be cruel, but it keeps ticking…for all of us. When we check off the squares on our calendars, day by day, month by month, year by year, old age just keeps moving closer, whether we consider it or not.

Now, more than ever, I realize that caregiving is the hardest on your emotional and mental state; at least it is for me. It is the constant strain of being privy to the day-to-day decline and drifting away that inevitably comes with old age or illness. Caregiving for me is like losing someone you love, bit by bit, and realizing there is nothing you can do to slow it down or stop it.

SATURDAY, JUNE 24TH

Athena came over to spend the night at Nannie and Pawpaw's with me. She was a spark of joy in our weekend. She helped Nannie with her jigsaw puzzle and they watched movies until late. I taught her how to play "Go Fish" too. She caught on right away; Athena is a smart cookie.

SUNDAY, JUNE 25TH

Dad and Athena had coffee and an early breakfast before Rita came to get her. They are celebrating Jason's birthday today, and Athena didn't want to miss a thing. Dad and I went to church and we all had a pretty good day. I am always thankful for routine Sundays…don't know how many more of these we'll be privileged to enjoy.

MONDAY, JUNE 26TH

Dad was mowing early, but got rained out. After changing into some dry clothes, he went in to visit with Mom and tell her about his encounter with the downpour. She was pretty upbeat, and I overheard her laughing at Dad's description of "trying to out run the rain."

THURSDAY, JUNE 29TH

Called and asked the doctor about prescribing some B-12 shots for Dad; he thought it would be a good idea and called some in. I will be the one giving them; Mel and Sherry can't bring themselves to do it. Since I've worked with animals for years and done plenty of "critter doctoring," giving shots doesn't bother me in the least.

EXPECT CHARACTERISTIC ATTITUDES AND TRAITS TO BE EXACERBATED, ESPECIALLY WHEN SOMEONE IS ILL. DON'T EXPECT A 'SOURPUSS' TO BECOME A 'SWEETIE' JUST BY VIRTUE OF AGING. *Not* EVERY ELDERLY PERSON IS A 'DEAR OLD SAINT' – IF THEY WERE A "*firecracker*" BEFORE, THEY WILL STILL BE CRACKLING AND POPPING.

JULY

Watching thunderheads build up in the southeast, the lightning dancing among the dark billowing clouds...this is what I recall when I think of July. This was one of our favorite family activities in the heat of mid-summer. From our vantage point on our screened-in porch, we would watch the "light-show" mosquito-free. It was usually way more entertaining than anything on our old black and white television.

Dad would often spend that porch time telling stories from his boyhood or funny family antidotes about neighbors and friends he knew long ago. Sometimes, if it was an extra dark night, the air so unsettled that even the night creatures were hushed, he'd tell us a spooky story of unexplained happenings, usually with a surprising ending that would make us jump. Dad is a consummate story-teller, weaving pictures from words, with turns of phrase that are all his own.

Sitting together on that dark porch, surrounded by the summer's smothery humid blackness and the sounds of a thousand Southern creatures, we were mesmerized by those tales of other times and places.

Whenever I am inundated with the buzz of cicadas and the ker-umps of the bullfrogs at our ponds, my mind goes right back to that small screened-in porch and those long ago nights. I let myself wax nostalgic for a moment, but then hurry back into the air-conditioning I have become accustomed to, shutting out the noisy night and reluctantly closing the door on those memories.

Now, we often find it hard to linger, to savor the moment. I wish that I could turn back the calendar more than a few years, and once again enjoy that slower pace for a bit…but, then again, I don't want to give up my a/c. At least, not this July…it is hotter than the hinges.

As he gets older, Dad seems to thrive on the heat. I am the opposite. Let the battle of the thermostats begin…

Sherry

SATURDAY, JULY 1ST

Rounded up to go home, but first needed to go to the Homeplace to get Pop. Shaun and he had gone there earlier with more hydraulic fluid and a spare pin or two in case one had sheared off. As it turned out, the pin *wasn't* sheared, so Shaun poured the hydraulic fluid in, then drove it around a bit to see how it handled. When he got off and looked underneath, the fluid was leaking right back out – hole in the line. He had to just park it until Monday when he can load it and take it to the tractor doctor.

I brought Pop back home since Shaun was going straight to work, then on to my house in Nac to start on chores there.

TUESDAY, JULY 4TH

Had a nice Fourth of July with Stu, Ashley, her parents, and Little Bit. The fireworks didn't seem to bother her much, but Stu didn't get anything really loud. Apparently, it was a low-key time at the folks' in Jacksonville – just Pop, Melanie, and Tam. They shot off some of the fireworks I've bought for several occasions but hadn't used. Mom didn't come out of her room, and Shaun was resting at his place.

WEDNESDAY, JULY 5TH

Pop got a good report from Dr. J, and won't have to go back for a year. I know that made him feel good, that Dr. J is confident that Pop will still be here in 2024!

FRIDAY, JULY 7TH

Had a special board meeting for Jacksonville College at 10:00 this morning, so headed to that. When it ended, I drove out to the folks' and visited awhile. Mel and Tam were both there. Nurse C came by and talked to us about that new medicine Dr. M prescribed for Mom to increase her appetite. She suggested starting with a very small dose a few days after finishing the antibiotic for her UTI. Another suggestion was to add milk to the Boost in her shake since that stuff is fairly thick, and Mom shudders when she has to drink it.

Melanie had fresh yeast rolls ready to go with some smothered steak, peas, cantaloupe, and tomatoes. Such a great meal and good visit with everyone, even if most of our conversation tends to revolve around parent care.

MONDAY, JULY 10TH

Back up to J'ville … Pop was on the side porch. He said I'd caught him sitting down, but he'd only been there ten minutes – he had just cut some boards to replace some rotted ones along the bridge rafters of the little barn. He'd also primed some of the barn trim. Tam was flying around getting stuff done so she could go to her house to post a column and feed her chickens. After she left, Pop said he was just going to prime the boards he'd cut, so I went to help Mom with her puzzle. Later, I decided to check on him, and he was way up on the extension ladder, painting! Changed into my work clothes and started scraping and dusting down the parts he hadn't gotten to yet. I had to wear vinyl gloves since part of what I was scraping off was poison ivy vines that had attached to the walls. Pop had pulled the vines off last week, but those little tendrils had stuck to the boards. I'm allergic and wasn't taking any chances.

That big bunch of poison ivy and Virginia creeper was underfoot, so I decided to rake it out of the way, then climbed on a short ladder and kept cleaning. One board was so rotten that I just pulled it off and about 70 years of junk showered all over me! Yuck. When Pop got tuckered out, we quit that job. Of course then he decided to prime the other side of the new boards. When we got back to the house, Tam was there and saw that Pop was scattering barn debris all over the kitchen floor. I told Tam I'd just take my outer layer off in the laundry room and dash to the bathroom to clean up, and then Pop could do the same. That way, we wouldn't dirty up the floors. Boy, did that cleanup feel great!

TUESDAY, JULY 11TH

A very nice morning, weather wise. Pop wasn't quite as peppy today, though. He let me finish some of the painting after he'd primed the upper part. Another chore was to drill holes in the replacement boards and put them in place, but that meant working at the peak of the barn. I told Pop that since it was such a nice day, he could mow in the pasture and save that other work for when he's rested. He thought that was a good idea, so after I fixed Mom's breakfast, we drove up the hill. After Pop took off on the tractor, I fed the calves and checked their water. On my way back to the house, I saw Pop mowing close to the septic drain. Don't get stuck, Pop!

With the weather heating up, Dad decided mowing was the only activity he could pursue without giving us girls a heart attack.

After he headed back out into the bigger pasture, I got Mom her shake and meds, then started watering the flowers out front. Took Pop a drink, and he said he'd stop at noon. I drove back to the house and gave the big wisteria a good haircut with the clippers, then sat on the picnic table, watching Pop. At one point, he hit something with the mover and I hollered, "Tear it up, Mac!" Of course he couldn't hear me.

Coaxed Mom into making some rounds in the Big Room with her walker before sitting at the puzzle table. Pop came back and sat out in the driveway to rest. Too nice to go inside. A cloudy, cool day like this isn't to be wasted. Melanie called, all wound up in getting ready for the big reunion at her house. Glad she's getting a lot done. After lunch and the cleanup, I tried to write in my journal, but kept getting sleepy. Just as I drifted off, Melanie called again, and while we were talking, Mom called out that she needed her cover – she was cold. Then Mel said her insurance guy was calling and she had to hang up with me. Fifteen seconds later, she called back and said it was a telemarketer. After we finished that call, I leaned back again, but realized it was time to get Mom's lunch.

Pop told me to try my nap again, but shortly after I sat in the recliner, Mom announced that she was finished and I could get her tray. Did that, sat back down, then Mom asked if her puzzle was ready to work on. I finished turning the pieces over for her and sat down after telling her it was ready. In a few seconds, she said she'd need her pillow. When I went in her room to get it, I was laughing. She asked me what was funny, and I told her I must have an alarm on my behind because every time it hit a chair, somebody needed something.

WEDNESDAY, JULY 12TH

Back to the barn project. Our first chore was getting the drill bit box open! What a dumb design. Had to YouTube it. Anyhow Pop got holes drilled in the replacement boards so that he could nail them in more easily. The boards had to go in just so, and on one board, I saw that Pop had drilled the holes in the wrong part. He didn't think so, but sure enough, they were, so he had to redrill those. Putting the boards on the barn was tough, too, since some of "anchor" wood has rotted. He plans to get some tin later to hold the pieces in place; maybe a storm won't blow them off before then.

He needed to drink water when he came back inside, but he mentioned drinking that last cup of coffee after lunch. He went to rest, and I started washing dishes and just automatically poured that coffee out. Not long after, Pop came in looking for it. He had the funniest look on his face and said, "You did that on purpose!" I was laughing, but I honestly forgot.

Of course Pop couldn't stay inside the rest of the day; he got back on the tractor to mow some more. Tam brought pound cake over – yay! Heard from Melanie – she still doesn't have water and is getting a bit nervous. She can't host upwards of 75 people with no running water! When Pop got done bouncing around on that tractor, I started lunch prep and so on until the day wound down.

THURSDAY, JULY 13TH

Finished painting the barn trim this morning – I didn't clean Pop's brush well enough yesterday, so he had to get a different one. I know how to clean brushes, but I just got in a hurry, feel bummed about that. After the barn work, we got ready to go to town: feed store, pharmacy, and groceries. Back home to fix lunch, then dishes, Nurse C came to check on Mom, Shaun came and started taking down the broken electric line between the house and barn. So hot! 96° with a heat index of 108° - I don't like this at all.

I thought I'd do a little of the puzzle for Mom – the more difficult parts. She came in and said, "You're working on my puzzle?" I just got up and said, "Here you go." Tam came in and asked how it was going. I just looked at her and said, "It's Thursday." She started laughing. Melanie and I do pretty well until about Thursday, then the stress cracks start to show – Ha!

FRIDAY, JULY 14TH

After Tam took Pop's picture in front of his latest project, the finished barn trim, Shaun and Pop went after the 1020 from the repair guy, then by the Homeplace to retrieve the mower and bring it home. No mowing today.

Pop said he thought he could get me to the furniture repair guy's place so I could leave a chair to be fixed. He has an amazing memory! We only made one little wrong turn, then smooth sailing to the shop. From there, we went to J'ville so we could check out Guinn's Produce Stand; we like to support local folks. We bought a cantaloupe, some new potatoes, green beans, and fresh peas. Looking forward to getting those on the table.

After we got back to the house, I helped Mom get a bath and into a fresh gown. Then I started trying to make Melanie's rolls, with her on the phone to clarify the steps. She's the roll queen, so I know mine won't match up to hers but at least I can eat my mistakes.

After lunch, Tam came over with chocolate sugar cookies, delish. Since Shaun was here, too, we decided to try the bottle of Sweet Corn Soda that my friend Sheryl gave me. We couldn't believe it – tasted and smelled *exactly* like sweet corn! I don't think I could drink an entire bottle since it *is* very sweet, but it was certainly interesting.

SATURDAY, JULY 15TH

Hustled to my own home after Pop went out to mow and Tam arrived… I'll be coming back on Monday so Melanie can have next week at home to finish up for her reunion starting Friday.

MONDAY, JULY 17TH

Dropped by Guinn's Produce on my way through Jacksonville to get some more new potatoes and yellow squash, then the donut shop for a few treats in case Ricky R wanted something – he's visiting Pop this morning. No question about **Pop** wanting a donut … Is the Pope Catholic? When I peeped into the sunroom, I realized that the visit was being recorded for a podcast, so I didn't interrupt. Went to work on a puzzle with Mom.

Late in the day, Pop and I fed the calves, and I discovered that both blue water tubs were turned over and empty, and the big metal trough was nearly empty. Yikes! If they'd run out of water in this heat, they'd have been in trouble quickly.

TUESDAY, JULY 18TH

Pleasant morning outside – we enjoyed our breakfast alfresco. Shaun came up in his side-by-side to take Pop to feed the calves and then ride around the pasture. I mentioned that he might try going more slowly since Pop seemed to be dizzy most of the time when they returned from a ride. They found a new calf in the pasture, a little black one with a white face. When they got back, Shaun lowered the pressure in the truck tires to make it ride easier, and then they headed to the Homeplace to put out salt and mineral … always something to do either here or there.

While they were gone, I talked to Melanie, all the while cleaning the refrigerator. I usually find some unidentifiable item that needs to be thrown out. My goal each week is to use up every prepared food so that we don't accumulate stuff that sits until it molds and we can throw it out with a clear conscience.

Mom is down to 104. After researching the medicine Mom was supposed to start, Tam thought the fall risk outweighed the benefit of increased appetite, so we did not start it. I decided to go back to that Boost shake, thin it with milk, and put more ice cream in it. If we don't stop this weight loss, Mom will get weaker. As usual, she didn't want it, but when I pointed out that she could wind up unable to do anything, she drank it.

After Shaun dropped Pop off at the house, he got his mower and mowed his yard, then Mom and Dad's. Poor guy stirred up a cloud of dust between the house and barn … it is getting really dry. He'll be coated in dust by the time he's through … When he came in to visit with Mom, she was drinking her Boost shake, and he told her about this green kale stuff he's trying to drink every morning. After he described *his* drink, Mom decided her shake wasn't so bad after all.

WEDNESDAY, JULY 19TH

We have a plague of gnats. I've never seen so many. I keep smacking them dead, but I don't seem to be reducing the number. I even put the bananas in the refrigerator yesterday, but that didn't make any difference. Annoying.

Pop and I drove to Tyler for his podiatrist appointment with Dr. C, a fairly young man, and very nice. Before he came in the exam room, I looked at his framed diplomas on the wall and told Pop, "He was the valedictorian in his class! … Good to know that you're seeing the top guy." (Somebody has to be at the bottom of the class, even in med school.) Dr. C was amazed at how alert and active Pop still is and said that what I had been doing to remove that thickened skin on Pop's foot was right and to just continue. He also said the red splotches on his foot and ankle would not go away, but he could send us to a guy who could make inserts for Pop's shoes to make walking more comfortable. The fat pads on the bottom of Pop's feet are gone – it's just skin over bone, so he needs external padding.

Drove back to the house, Pop rested while I watered the orchids on the porch and fixed lunch. Tam came over for a visit, and we joined Pop in the sunroom. He kept swatting at something and said, "I've got my own personal gnat. My nose draws them like a banana." We cracked up and Tam quipped, "Maybe it's the shape."

After the evening chores, I read Pop some articles in his *Drovers* magazine since he can't see to read that size print at all. One article was about the impact of the drought on cattle numbers and meat prices. Tough times for ranchers.

THURSDAY, JULY 20TH

Dad loves Mel's fresh homemade rolls. I think he would eat the entire basket if he could!

Pop and I were the first ones at the shoe insert place – Mr. C seemed like a nice person, second generation in that line of work. He showed Pop a sample insert and explained what each layer was for, then he brought out a box-like scan device. Pop put his foot on it, and a scanner went up and down in the box, measuring; and then the same for the other foot. When the inserts are ready, Mr. C will give us a call so we can come back. He wants to put them in Pop's shoes and make sure they fit just right. I paid for them before Pop knew what I was doing and said, "Happy Early Birthday!" I can't think of anything I could get him that would be better than more comfortable feet.

After we got home, I tried making the yeast rolls again; these looked better, but were still not as fluffy as Melanie's. Tam came over to eat one, and Pop told her about that scanner, "I've never seen anything like that before. That machine waltzed all around over my foot." After lunch, Rita and her kids came over to visit while Nurse C was here. She had to stick Mom's finger to check her blood. Of course Mom hollered, and Athena was so concerned and went over to see her finger. From Mom's yell, I think she expected to see part of her finger missing.

FRIDAY, JULY 21ST

If a job doesn't present itself, Pop will think one up – this morning he decided to take the 1020 over to Tam's and mow the big area between her house and the road. When I called Tam to give her a heads-up, she said she really would rather he didn't – she's afraid he'll poke his eye with a low limb, but since he was determined, she asked me to get him safety glasses, so I did. While he was doing that, I took care of the calves, then fixed Mom's breakfast, put on a load of towels, and fixed the webbing in one of the aluminum chairs.

When Pop got back, he burned the big roll of poison ivy and Virginia creeper I'd left near the burn barrel. Tam came over and said Mom needed a special cushion to sit on at the puzzle table – she sits there a lot, and we don't want her to develop a pressure sore. She'd also scratched her arm somehow and bled on her sleeve, so she needed a fresh gown and her hair fixed. Tam and I did "Rock, Paper, Scissors" to see who would wash the gown and who would fix Mom's hair.

Later, I went to look for something in the porch fridge, and there was a horrible smell on the porch, like a rotten potato. When I checked the potatoes, they were fine, but then I checked the onions and found the culprit … a big purple onion had become a pile of purple mush. Maybe that's where all these gnats are coming from.

When the evening cooled a bit, I fed the calves and started running water in the buckets. I sat on the pipe fence while they filled up and watched the cows graze down the slope – a peaceful scene I never tire of, but we need rain badly.

SATURDAY, JULY 22ND

Melanie is in full reunion mode today – I hope she holds up in all the activity. Fifty people came last night, and she'll probably have seventy-five total today. I scurried around trying to get a lot done so Tam wouldn't have too much to do over the weekend. After she arrived and we debriefed on food/meds/chores, I left for mi casa.

THURSDAY, JULY 27TH

Ordered the cupcake liners and boxes for Pop's birthday celebration on August 26th – can't believe we're getting so close!

SATURDAY, JULY 29TH

Ben and Shelley's anniversary … hope they have a lovely day. We will get to see them when Ben has his next promotion ceremony – the week after Pop's birthday celebration. What a whirlwind August will be!

MONDAY, JULY 31ST

Watering by flashlight – this can't be good. Such a long time with no rain, and the heat is relentless. If I don't water some of these things before I leave, they'll be dead when I get back. I finally headed out to the folks.' When I arrived, I saw the biggest watermelon **ever** on side porch. Tam said Joseph D had brought it over, and it weighed 65 pounds. I believe it.

Later on, Pop was reading in the sunroom, and I went in to tell him I was fixing lunch. He asked, "About when will it be ready?"

"About 40 minutes," I said.

"Four minutes?"

"No, 40 minutes."

"Oh, 30 minutes … I've got some time then."

I just left, chuckling. Put out a puzzle for Mom, but after a few minutes of trying to put the edge pieces together, she gave up on it and asked for a different one. Got that ready, finished lunch, made a peach cobbler. Shaun came to visit and took some cobbler with him for later. He does love those sweets! Found out that Pop only got 20 round bales off the highway meadow – he needed 30, at least. That field had looked so promising – he'd had it fertilized, then got a nice rain on it, but then the rain shut off like turning off a faucet.

MONDAY, JULY 3RD

My morning explodes with a long list of things to do before I leave for the folks.' I called Sherry and we talked about how hard it is to have two lives and keep both households going. Just because you **want** to do something doesn't mean it's easy to do. Only God can give us the strength and courage to carry on and not be "weary in well doing."

When I arrived, I showed Mama the flowers I picked for them. She isn't doing well and has the beginning of a UTI. Tam brought Daddy back from mowing at the Homeplace. He was wet with sweat and barely able to move. She got him some Pedialyte, and he went to his sunroom recliner. Dr. J is removing one medicine for Daddy, and we're adding a super probiotic and some powdered IV to mix in his water – a new arsenal against this intestinal issue that has plagued Papa for so long. Praying that it works.

Before Tam left, she told me to keep an eye on Mama; if she seems confused or talks out of her head, it is definitely a bladder infection, so I vibrate between Mama and Daddy. Mama keeps praying out loud for the Lord to take her home. I decided to get a urine sample and take it to the clinic. Later, she seemed in better spirits.

Shaun came over to visit, telling Daddy that it might rain on Thursday, so naturally Daddy decided to mow again in the morning. Later, Daddy and I sat outside until sunset – beautiful orange, ruffled clouds, and doves calling above the hum of night critters. Mom is a night owl, so I brought her out on the porch around 11:30 so she could see the full Buck super moon.

TUESDAY, JULY 4TH

Daddy is better than an iPhone alarm. He is already outside sipping coffee and enjoying the coming daylight. I hurry to prepare breakfast, and Daddy is ready when Shaun pulls up in his work truck and off they go. I fed the bulls, put out salt and mineral, watered the flowers, fixed Mama's breakfast, then grabbed the list for town and made that run before stopping by the Homeplace to collect Daddy.

I opened the gate and drove out to where Daddy could see me. He waved and kept mowing one more round, then came on in and measured the diesel level. We drove back to the house where Daddy headed to his recliner while I made up a batch of rolls, then an apple pie. Daddy came in the kitchen and looked around on the counter, then paused and said, "Sometimes a certain person pours out the leftover coffee. What they ought to do is check my vital signs, and if I'm still alive, don't pour out the leftover coffee. I'll pour me a cup and enjoy it." Okay, Papa.

After I cleaned up the kitchen and was trying to write in my journal, I caught myself listing to the right. – almost ended up in Mama's dish cabinet. I smooth went to sleep, so I went to bed and took a nap.

Tam arrived at 8:30 pm. We talk a while about life and opportunities the Lord puts in our way. How the pathways of adventure, with lives touched and blessed, lie in accepting those opportunities, and how fear sometimes blocks that flow and keeps us where we feel safe, which results in no growth, no good changes, nor blessings.

At 9:00 we head out to the patio for fireworks. Tam runs back and forth lighting fuses and dashing to safety. Reminds me of my fateful dash and crash away from the brush explosion! The fireworks are pretty; we can even see some in the distance toward Troup and Tyler. I took a picture of me and Daddy and sent it to Ethan wishing him a happy 24th birthday. I feel conflicted over missing his party, but I need to be here, so I remind myself of my nephew's advice: "Keep your mind where your feet are." So, I adjust my thoughts and wish them well. I am here and God is in both places.

WEDNESDAY, JULY 5TH

We enjoyed a cooler morning temperature, and Daddy heard the pileated woodpecker call. Many times he misses sounds due to failing hearing. We begin our breakfast with his prayer of thanksgiving and patience for others. After we started eating, I was looking out the big window toward the lovely morning when Daddy said, "I must have cut myself shaving." I looked around and blood was dripping off his chin and onto his pants! I ran to get a tissue and apply pressure on the cut and was still doing that when Tam arrived. The flow had slowed down a lot, so we put a band aid on it, and he changed pants so they could leave for his appointment.

After they left, I thought about what Daddy had said earlier before Tam got here, He was sitting at the table, when I saw a reflective look in his eyes and asked him what he was thinking. He said, "about getting old." It made me sad. He tries so hard to keep moving and stay positive, but it must be such a struggle. I pray God's strength and courage each day for Mama and Daddy. It takes true faith and courage to face old age. It is certainly not for the faint of heart.

I texted Brother about the trimmer, and when he brought it up, he said he'd started to come up for the fireworks last night, but was comfortable and a bit lazy. Now he regrets not coming on up, taking Daddy on a side by side ride, and watching fireworks with us. Neither of us said it, but I'm sure we both thought it: What if he'd missed the last July 4th with Daddy?

I leave a note for Mama, lock the door, head up to the barn, feed the bulls, and drive on down to the cemetery and got it in good shape. I stand back, talk a little with Josh and Joyce. Hope they are pleased with our efforts to make this haven look pretty and restful. Who will do this when my siblings and I are all gone? I hope the grandkids will take it on, but who knows?

At the house, Mama is awake and I fix breakfast. Talked to Sherry; they had a good 4th of July as well. Knoxlynn is turning over now. I reflect again on the joy my sister is experiencing watching this little one as she grows.

Tam and Daddy got back. Good word on Daddy: 11% increase in blood flow, good oxygen level, blood pressure and pulse. The sore foot is something a podiatrist needs to address. Dr. J recommended a good one. Tam also says the clinic confirmed that Mama does have a bladder infection, so the doctor called in a prescription. Her weight is down to 106.5 lbs. That is worrisome. Daddy shared that sometimes at night, he experiences incontinence and has to get up and change his shorts. I tell him that that is a problem millions deal with as we age. The easy solution was Depends at night. He seemed ok with that. I called Sherry and she will pick up a box for him to try. Sometimes these health concerns seem to come rapid fire; we handle one, and three others take its place.

THURSDAY, JULY 6TH

Up at 5:22 am. Got ready and met Daddy as he was coming through the library doorway. He proceeded to make coffee, but asked again what Tam did with his old coffee pot. This new one is different, and I can tell Daddy doesn't like it. He said, reluctantly, "Maybe I'll get used to it."

We sit on the patio and watch fog drift in the creek bottom. Daddy says, "It almost feels like a touch of autumn in the air." It won't feel like autumn by the time you quit mowing, I thought. After breakfast, Shaun and Daddy head up to the barn to feed the bulls and get diesel before heading to the Homeplace. Shaun will drop Daddy off and put the diesel in the tractor for him.

Got Mama ready for her doctor visit, thankfully a local one. After we arrived, I signed Mama up for their new Chronic Care Management program. Daddy was signed up last week and had already received a call about the results of his visit to his vascular surgeon. Impressive! Dr. Mc. came in and did his usual thorough checkup. He prescribed a pill for her appetite and better sleep and ordered a blood test – not fun for anyone, but Mama especially doesn't do well with it. While we were there, I signed several things for her to speed things up, but later when I asked if she minded, she said she would like to sign as long as she is able. That's understandable. We need to remember that she is still an adult, not a child. Being old doesn't equal inept.

FRIDAY, JULY 7TH

Daddy up at 5:45. Very pleasant for patio sitting at 68 degrees. Daddy was just getting his shoes on when Shaun pulled in to take him down to the Homeplace. I waved at them, then grabbed the weed eater and worked around the house, trees, flower beds, shop and museum. Picked up limbs so Brother can mow Saturday. I'll have to wait until late this evening to weed eat the rest. Took care of Mama and told her I was headed to get Daddy.

When I got there, I handed Rita and family some rolls I'd made yesterday. The kids rode with me over the hill to see where PawPaw was. Spotted #17, the heifer that had jumped the fence. I'm so glad she's still where she's supposed to be. I got a call from my cousin, Debra. She and Aunt Stella are coming to Daddy's 100th birthday party! All the way from Los Angeles – easy winners of who traveled the farthest. It will be a surprise for the folks. Daddy made a couple more passes up and down the hill. After he parked, I put the kids up on the tractor with him and got a couple of great pictures.

After Daddy and I got back, I started lunch. Nurse C came, and we discussed what interventions might help with Mama's weight loss. Sherry arrived and joined the discussion; we came up with several strategies and are hopeful. Tam came over, but Brother stayed home to rest before heading back to work. We enjoyed lunch and catching up on all our doings, and seeing Knoxlynn pictures … lots of those! After lunch, Daddy headed to the sunroom while we girls lingered at the kitchen table, talking about the two bulls we've been feeding. I told them I had suggested that we sell the smaller one and use the money to pay for the processing of the bigger bull. Sherry said if that was the decision, we needed to call the processing plant to change our order from two bulls to one. We trooped into the sunroom and asked Papa. He gave the OK sign, so Sherry called and told them what Daddy had decided. They appreciated the call since that changes their time allotment, and they might be able to fill that slot with someone else's calf.

We girls continue to talk about life, our world, and how the world is turning these days and times. Sherry had to leave at 3:00, Tam, too. I was saddened that we didn't have more time. Time … both our enemy and friend.

SATURDAY, JULY 8TH

Daddy up at 5:00 am. I had been sound asleep, but got up to greet the day with Papa. Shaun arrived at 7:00 to find me and Daddy standing in the driveway. He said, "Eager to get going?" and smiled. They took off on the side by side ride. While they were gone, I blew off the patio. Daddy said earlier, "That pileated woodpecker has been through and littered the patio again."

I load all my stuff and throw some towels in the washing machine. Tam said she would clean the floors. When Shaun and Daddy got back, they said the larger bull calf had gotten his head hung between the gate and the corral pole and had been there a while. That could have been disastrous. They got him loose and fed and watered them. Daddy to Mama's room to check on her. I braid Mama's hair, give her a kiss, and leave her busy finishing her puzzle. I give Daddy a hug and kiss. He is out on the patio but gets out of his chair and comes toward the driveway to wave. I leave with my traditional honk. The last thing I see as I go down over the hill is Papa waving. Two long weeks separate me from another time with him and Mama. The Roos reunion looms on the horizon.

TUESDAY, JULY 25TH

Those two weeks flew by. Thankful for Sherry giving me that extra week ahead of the reunion to get everything done: yard, house and food. Had 73 here this year: Friday afternoon and evening, all day Saturday and Sunday. My guys do all the setup of canopies, tables, and chairs, and my girls and I do the desserts for the four catered meals. It is a lot of hard work and a team effort on the part of my family. Monday was a recovery day to give me time to finish the cleanup.

I left at 9:00 am. Got extremely sleepy. Called Sherry and she talked to me all the way to the folks.' Tam had taken Daddy for his eye shot. I unloaded and sat in Mama's rom with a cup of tea, then fixed her hair. She was puzzling when Daddy and Tam returned. I gave her about half of the reunion goodies, then Tam left to get groceries before having to run to Tyler after a prescription of Eliquis for Mama. She also brought us a 50 foot water hose to help us keep things alive in this horrible triple digit heat and drought. Shaun came and told Daddy about his work and that Big Red (Chevrolet truck – Daddy got him as a teenager) is ailing.

That evening, Daddy reminisces about the Depression era. He had no shoes as he started first grade. His feet were tough, but cold ground and rocks were hard to handle. His teacher, a very young lady named Bernice C., sent Ma a note asking if she could give him a pair of tennis shoes she had. Ma sent word that that would be fine. Daddy said tennis shoes were only 49 cents, but they couldn't afford them. Those were the first shoes he ever had. He was old enough the next year to work and buy a pair of what they called Boy Scout shoes – a high-top leather shoe. They would start wearing out before the winter was done, and he would use copper wire from old machinery to hold them together. Those shoes cost $1.49. He said kids today would not understand that level of poverty. Upon reflection, Daddy said, "I thought we were the poorest of the poor, but we always had plenty to eat due to the thrift and hard work of Mama." He carried his meal for the day in his back pocket – a fried pie. Daddy was sure that amongst that number of students, there were bound to be some that went hungry.

WEDNESDAY, JULY 26TH

This morning Daddy is thinking about the highway meadow - drought and blistering heat are drying it up. He said, "I need to call Joseph and see if he can cut the meadow." Joseph said he could get to it this week.

Tam and Shaun arrive and load the big beef bull for the processing plant. Daddy is riding with Tam in Shaun's truck, while Shaun drives the truck and trailer. After delivering the calf, Shaun switches to his truck and drives on to his job below Alto, and Tam and Daddy drive back with the truck and trailer.

Sherry and I discuss Mama's bath schedule. She doesn't want to get in the shower because it's hard for her. I caved and just ran back and forth getting hot, soapy wash cloths and them washing off the soapy water, then deodorant, lotion, clean underwear, clean gown, braided hair. She seems to be visibly brighter after that, but mentioned that now, she is the baby. I said, "Mama, you took care of five babies. Now it's our turn to return the favor."

Daddy got to talk to Paul Marabito, the last remaining Seabee he knows. Daddy didn't have his hearing aid on, but said he only had to ask him to repeat what he said two times. Poor Tam had to make another run to Tyler for Mama's Eliquis; there was a problem with it yesterday.

THURSDAY, JULY 27TH

Lovely morning watching fog drift through the creek bottom. Brother came and we went for a ride, then he left for work. I watered the remaining beef calf, the cemetery flowers, and my cypress tree. Came back and fixed breakfast. When it came time for Mama's meds, I put her malt and meds by the edge of her puzzle, spotted a piece on the floor, reached down to get it, and knocked over the malt! It went over the bottom part of the puzzle. I ran for a spoon and ladled most of it back into the glass, then used paper towels to mop up the rest. Washed up the sticky area with damp paper towels and wiped off the 6-8 pieces that were in the flood. I was amazingly calm, but what a mess!

Mom and I get through the hot summer by working on puzzles... come to think of it, that's how we get through the rest of the year too!

Liz came (nurse supervisor) and checked Mama's vitals. Her INR was 3.2 but changing blood thinners may help. I went to check on Daddy. He was asleep with his coffee cup in his hand, perched on his little side table. He woke up and the cup headed for the edge. I caught it just in time. The planets must be lined up wrong: this day has been full of spills and near misses.

FRIDAY, JULY 28TH

Cool morning. Daddy said it had the feel of a September morning complete with creek bottom fog. Amazing that in a few hours we will be suffering with triple digit heat. Shaun came and we went to the barn and fed the bull. As we looked at the cows, we spotted a coyote in the northwest corner loping toward the creek.

Daddy and I sat a while after Shaun left for work and talked of different pandemics that had affected the people in his life: diptheria, TB, and polio. He had Larry on his mind and was hoping he was better after getting Covid.

Rita and kids came by and enjoyed some watermelon on the picnic table. Rita is taking the kids to Wyoming next week. She has a wedding to attend and many people to visit. She plans to camp with the kids. Brave woman!

SATURDAY, JULY 29TH

Tam and Shaun arrived early. He had already backed the truck and trailer up to the loading chute. The bull loaded without too much trouble. We got him in the front section of the trailer so he wouldn't rock it around. Daddy rode over with Tam to the sale barn.

I went back and got Mama situated and my stuff loaded to go home. Fixed Daddy's breakfast when they got back. I had called to check on Larry, and he seems to be better. Daddy and Tam came out to wave me over the hill – such a friendly custom. I am sad to leave. That wave helps.

Tamra

WEEKEND OF JULY 1ST & 2ND

Addie spent the night with me on Friday, so she went over to Mom and Dad's with me Saturday morning. She visited with them while I did a few chores and made preparations for a late lunch. Rachel came by to pick her up around noon. They had a busy weekend planned. I for one, was glad to have a very un-busy weekend…at least, that's what I was hoping for. Even though I had to make some extra trips to the house to help Marc take the boot off his broken foot and then back on, and give him some medicine/food, it wasn't as hectic as I feared.

For lunch on Sunday, I used poor Dad for a Guinea pig again. This time it was a new pork loin recipe with roasted asparagus and potatoes. Cousin Larry had shared some of his fresh tomatoes at church, so we had a couple of those to round out our meal. After we ate, Dad decided to make some coffee while I took Marc a plate. When I got back, he was adding sugar to the sugar bowl. When I came up beside him, he started dumping a heaping spoonful into his coffee. He looked around and said almost sheepishly, "I thought I'd get through before you got back." We have been trying to get Dad to watch his sugar, but when it comes to his coffee, I guess we'll have to make some concessions. Dad added, "That was a fine dinner you fixed. You know, it's a blessing that at my age I can still eat and enjoy food." It is indeed.

Dad has tried twice today to talk to Mom – third time's the charm – this time, she's not in the bathroom. While I cleaned the kitchen and folded clothes, they visited. He was in there for almost an hour. Dad caught Mom up on all the news from church, what he and Shaun had been doing around the farm, and as always, their conversation eased into talking about old times, then aches and pains, upcoming doctor's appointments, and then back around to what Dad's been reading lately and some interesting things he recalls, then a comfortable silence. There is a rhythm to their easy back and forth that is reassuring, even as an adult child…a serenity in the security that your parents love one another and are devoted to each other.

Later, Mom and I work on her jigsaw puzzle till almost 9:00 pm. We had a good time. I enjoy helping her, especially when she feels like smiling and talking a bit. After Dad got ready for bed, I doctored his foot and helped him find his place in his Kindle book – he lost it, again. Mom wanted me to put her movie in before I went to bed, so we went round and round trying to figure out what she had watched last night – she couldn't remember. Disc in, disc out. Was it this one? Episode Two, Season Three or was it Episode Three, Season Two? Figuring out Mom's movies for the night is an exercise in patience. Finally, the light comes on and she remembers! It was Season Three, Episode *Five*…haha.

Finally got in bed about 10:30, but heard a loud *thump* outside the window, so I went to investigate. Didn't see anything, but I figured it was that pesky armadillo, back to try and dig under the house again. Crawled under the covers and suddenly, something stung me! I jumped up and turned on the light, carefully turning the sheets over and there was the vile offender…a red wasp. I don't know how in the world he managed to get in there, but I dispatched him to the underworld in short order, then went to the kitchen to make a baking soda poultice, so maybe I could sleep. Nasty critters!

When I lay back down, I thought about all the times during our growing up that Dad would get up to check on nighttime noises and then reassure us everything was ok. Now, it's my turn to do the "checking."

TUESDAY, JULY 4TH

It is always a strange feeling to not be on a regular schedule – no mail, no trash pick-up, no town run, no WMA. Today, I get to stay at home with no particular demands on my time, except my writing work and some chores. I got the time I crave when I am running around like a mad woman, but we humans are funny creatures…we get what we want and then wander around lost, like we don't know what to do with the gift.

My thoughts drift back to the July Fourth celebrations we had years ago at Mom and Dad's, hamburgers and hot dogs, fireworks in the pasture, with most of us kids and grandkids there to "ooh and ahh" over the colorful sparkly traces in the night sky. We enjoyed those times, the traditions, the laughter, and the running jokes. I don't remember the last time we were all together on the Fourth, but I have those sweet memories.

Tonight, I went over to Mom and Dad's to set off a few fireworks for Mel and Dad. Mom declined to watch, but Dad was eager to see what kind of show I had in mind. Sherry had bought a few ground display type canisters and we were surprised at how big and

Athena and Raylan can't wait for Pawpaw to cut them a slice of the giant watermelon!

bright some of them were. It was fun, even if it was just us. I would light a fuse and run like mad, which Dad and Mel found amusing. I managed to get them all to work, except one that fell over and showered them with sparks, but no harm done.

We reminisced about Shaun and the kids lighting those big boomers down in the pasture and how they would holler and carry-on every time one went off – they were a show all by themselves.

WEDNESDAY, JULY 5TH

Designed the invitations for Dad's 100th birthday and ran it by the siblings. They approved, so I ordered them today. Also started the guest list, one for mailing and one for text invitations. I realized gathering everyone's address would take a lot of time, and the expense of postage would be prohibitive, so a majority will get their invite via text or email. Today was Dad's follow-up with Dr. J about his foot. He got a pretty good report, so we were relived. His appointment was at 8:30 am and even with the two tests, we made it home before noon. Dad was glad he didn't "waste the whole day."

FRIDAY, JULY 7TH

Went to town early to get Mom's meds and some fresh peas – Dad loves peas, so I dropped some off for Mel to fix for his lunch. Sherry was in J'ville for a board meeting today, so she came out to the house to visit before she headed home to Nac. It's a rare treat when we can all be together for no special reason, other than just enjoying one another's company. We all ate lunch with Dad and visited with Mom. It was a nice break from our regular routine.

WEEKEND OF JULY 8TH & 9TH

Usual busy stuff for a weekend…went over the guest list with Dad and see if I missed anyone, of course I did. His memory is better than mine! Made some cranberry walnut cookies and helped Mom with her puzzles. Found out I have a new deadline for my columns, on Monday instead of Tuesday. Mel informed me that Dad did **not** like the coffee pot I got him for Father's Day. I asked Dad and he reluctantly admitted he couldn't see how to use it.

(The old one was so nasty, even after I cleaned it, that we had to have a new one.) I went straight to town and bought one that was as close in operation to his old one as I could find. He seemed pleased. Lesson: Don't try to get a more expensive, fancy coffeemaker for someone who is used to a cheap-o model. It will *not* be appreciated. Ha!

MONDAY, JUNE 10TH

Dad was doing some repair work today. When he came inside, I told him I had swiffered his bathroom and sunroom. "There sure were a lot of peanut hulls on your sunroom floor." Dad didn't hesitate, "Rats. They've probably been in there after my peanuts!" I laughed. "I believe it was the big rat that sits in that green chair." Dad just smirked.

When I got home tonight, I got a call from Aunt Shirley. The District wide WMA meeting is at our church tomorrow night and **we** are supposed to do the program! How we missed that, I don't know, but I volunteered to do it. A book I was reading would make the perfect basis for a short program, so I made a few notes, scanned the book again, and slept on it.

TUESDAY, JUNE 11TH

Did my usual stuff on Tuesday – went to WMA, town, ran errands, and made a cake for tonight's dinner before the meeting. I finished typing my notes at 4:30 and got to the church to set up for the dinner at 5:00. It all went well and we had a good fellowship, but I hope I don't have to pull another rabbit out of the hat for a long while.

FRIDAY, JUNE 14TH

Flag Day. Worked on the video for Dad's party, took pictures of Dad and his barn painting job, got the room ready for Shirley C. to spend the weekend. She is having surgery early Monday morning. A super busy weekend is ahead, I hope I get some sleep.

SUNDAY, JULY 16TH

Brother Glenn, our former pastor, and his wife, Susan, are down from Illinois for a short visit. They came out to Mom and Dad's to visit today after church. It was so good to see them again. Bro. Glenn sang Mom's favorite hymn to her before they left, "It is Well with My Soul." Nobody can sing it like him…I recorded it on my phone so Mom can listen to it whenever she wants.

MONDAY, JULY 17TH

After leaving Mom and Dad's, I unpacked and got ready to get Shirley C. at the hospital. Marc wanted me to pick up his mom while I was there; she was having an infusion. I said I would, but she was at a different hospital… so, I had to coordinate picking her up, then Shirley, getting them both home, groceries, etc. It was a crazy day, but somehow I managed to get everyone where they were supposed to be *and* with all the things they needed.

FRIDAY, JULY 21ST

I noticed Mom had a bad pressure spot this week, so I went by to let Sherry know and devise a plan of action. Catching things early, before they become a real problem, is always better. I like being proactive, even if it is more work in the short term.

SATURDAY, JULY 22ND

Today was Allie Faye's 90th birthday celebration at church. Dad and I went and we both enjoyed catching up with folks.

MONDAY, JULY 24TH

Did some much needed trimming at the church, ran errands, and then late today stopped by Mom's and helped her with the cupcake puzzle Sherry got her. It is a pretty one, but the edge pieces are *all* alike! We have to figure out a solution for those side pieces before we put it together again.

TUESDAY, JULY 25TH

Took Dad to his eye appointment with Dr. B at 9:15, got meds for Mom, groceries, etc. after I dropped Dad off at home, went back to help Mel unload her stuff. I didn't get home till after 5:00…I was worn to a nub.

WEDNESDAY, JULY 26TH

Butcher day and I was over at Mom and Dad's by 7:00 am to help Shaun load the calf in the trailer. He drove the farm truck and trailer while Dad and I followed him in his paint wagon, so after dropping off the calf, he could go on to work in Alto, just south of the processing place. Dad and I enjoyed the drive home. I took a different way back, so we could see "new territory," as Dad calls it. When I got back I put the trailer up and went home to change, then headed to Tyler to pick up Mom's new prescription at the Specialty Pharmacy. They were supposed to mail it, but somehow it got fouled up and I had to pick it up. The invitations came a couple of weeks ago and I've been steadily getting them addressed, but I'm still working on the telephone numbers and addresses. Tracking down some of these is going to be a job.

WEEKEND OF JULY 29TH & 30TH

Over early to Mom and Dad's Saturday morning to load the other calf and take it to the sale. I didn't have to wait too long in line, thank goodness. Washed the trailer out and put it up when I got back, then went home and finished packing for my weekend at the folks. Took Dad to get the calf check; he was pleased and joked that it was about enough to pay for the milk he had to buy to bottle feed it.

Mom was on a tear this weekend: ringing her bell, hollering for me to turn off the fan, turn on the fan, and adjust the fan this way and that, etc. She got me tickled, though, when she complained about her remote not working…she kept banging it on the side table, trying to get it to work… but it was the batteries. I put new ones in and it worked fine.

DON'T BE SURPRISED IF OTHER FAMILY MEMBERS OR EVEN *Strangers* GET TREATED MORE KINDLY THAN YOU, THE CAREGIVER. IT IS EASIER TO LASH OUT AT THOSE YOU *know* WILL NOT LEAVE YOU. SO DEVELOP SOME 'TEFLON' IN YOUR SKIN AND LET HARSH WORDS SLIDE OFF

Marathon

AUGUST 2023

Oh August! Weary August! And we are even wearier this year than usual – partly because of the extreme heat and drought and partly because of the busyness due to Dad's upcoming celebration.

It is hard to believe we have traversed another year already. Dad is going to see his 100th birthday, Lord willing, and we are so thankful. Time runs on whether we are able to keep up or not and this year, we've felt like we were always running behind, waving frantically for time to slow down and let us catch up.

We are looking forward to Dad's celebration, but are looking forward to the end of August for another reason – a break in this awful weather.

August makes me tired…and irritable. I don't suffer with SAD (Seasonal Affective Disorder) in the winter like most people; it affects me at the height of the sometimes interminable Texas summer. I've never tolerated the heat well, but Dad, he just keeps plugging on. Unless it gets over 105 degrees, Dad doesn't even seem to notice. He can't handle the heat quite as well as he used to, but he still does better than most.

Before air-conditioning, we used to lie on our green linoleum kitchen floor in front of the box fan to escape the heat. It always felt cool, even in the dog days of August. I sometimes wonder how kids today would handle that kind of "air-conditioning?" As far as toughness goes, we were cream-puffs compared to Mom and Dad's generation, The Greatest Generation. Today, I don't think kids would even qualify as marshmallows.

Hopefully, before Mom and Dad's generation completely disappears, they can dispense some of their enduring wisdom and grit to this younger generation. If it is left up to us…I don't know how convincing we will be. After all, we did grow up with electricity and running water – what do we know?

Sherry

TUESDAY, AUGUST 1ST, 2023

Too hot for hydrangeas! At least for these little first-year ones, so I found three umbrellas and set them at a slant over the plants to shield them. Looks a little kooky, but does the job. Had a big town run, then home to take care of meds, food, etc. Shaun picked up the big tractor from the fix-it place and used it to bring in the rest of the hay bales. Tam brought Pop's 100th birthday party invitation over so I could have a copy. It looks great – can't believe it's this month!

WEDNESDAY, AUGUST 2ND

Pop said he had a pretty good night – he "only" got up four or five times. Bless his heart. At least it isn't the intestinal issue anymore – I think the combination of stopping one of his blood thinners and taking a great probiotic supplement has helped turn that corner. I just wish he could turn the clock back on certain other things. He told me that back in his working days, he could paint all day long and never go to the bathroom until he got home … not that way anymore. Time sure takes a toll on the body.

We drove to the Homeplace to check on the heifers; they still have plenty of grass and water … so glad that beaver built a dam across the creek. Even though we had to tear *part* of the dam up, there's still enough of it left to keep all the water from disappearing downstream. Came home and watered a few things, then Tam brought Athena and Raylan over for watermelon. We cut that 50 pounder out on the picnic table and really enjoyed it. Watermelon and August were made for each other.

Later, I made banana pudding, and Shaun came by for a visit. When he left, he took some pudding with him. Helped Mom on her puzzle, then worked on Pop's rough foot. That skin is so thick in places and it needs to come off, but I can't be too aggressive – a foot wound would not heal well.

So, I used an emery board and exfoliating glove to get closer to the normal skin. When I finished, the floor looked like it had snow on it! Thinking of all Pop has to deal with, I'm amazed at his positive outlook. He's always eager to get up in the morning, always enjoys the meals we prepare, and is always thinking about his next project. God grant me the ability to follow his example as I grow older.

THURSDAY, AUGUST 3RD

Accidentally set my alarm for 5:15 instead of 5:30, so I was out with my coffee really early. At least I got to enjoy the full Super Moon. As I sat there by myself, I suddenly thought about someday when I will wait in vain for Pop to join me. Through all the seasons: spring mornings with glad birdsong and dewy flowers, summer dawns heavy with the scent of newly mown hay, crisp autumn mornings with fog drifting through trees ablaze with color, winter mornings with the rising sun glistening on frosty hillsides … I'll sit here, unconsciously waiting for Pop to come shuffling out with his cup of coffee. But I won't hear that familiar "Good morning! How'd you sleep?" Pop will be on the other side. I can't even imagine how that will feel. I hope it will be a long time before I find out. Lord, please let Pop stay awhile longer. But I know that even awhile longer will not be enough, and that God knows best. He will help us through that valley. I breathe a prayer of gratitude for that, and suddenly I hear his footsteps across the patio and turn with a glad smile as he says, "Good morning! How'd you sleep?"

FRIDAY, AUGUST 4TH

After coffee and breakfast, I decided to put the water hose on one of the roses out front. When I walked out on the porch later to check it, I felt something and looked down … fire ants were everywhere! Four thick columns of them going across the porch and around the welcome mat. I stomped my feet and brushed off the ones that were attacking me, then went to check for a can of ant spray. None. Pop reminded me about some spray he had out in the shop, so I mixed some up and let those evil creatures have it! Thankfully, they hadn't gotten into the house; I still can't figure out what they were after unless it was something in that mat. It's made out of coconut fibers, I think. Sheesh.

Mom wanted me to put out another puzzle for her. She'd also gotten blood on her gown where she'd scratched her arm, so I had to get her into a clean one. I'd just washed her other favorite gown yesterday, and it wasn't dry yet, so I had to get a less favored one on her, then tackle that blood stain. Then Mom decided the puzzle she'd started on was too hard, so I put it up and got out a different one.

Rachel came by to see the folks – she's heading to New York City for a short solo vacation next week … hope she's careful and has fun. Rita and her kids are heading to Wyoming tomorrow. That girl has true grit! Melanie and Joanna, Valerie and Hannah are heading back today from Missouri – seems like everyone is on the move.

Pop had company this afternoon – his sister-in-law's granddaughter who wanted to know the history behind a piece of property she and her husband are about to build on near Enterprise Church. Pop could tell her the background all the way to the 30s. His first and second grade teachers rented a room from the people who lived there at that time. It was convenient for walking to the schoolhouse – just down the hill, across the road, and up the next hill. While Pop and she visited, I took Shaun to Whitehouse to pick up his red truck that they've been redoing for quite some time. I sure hope it turns out to his liking.

Later, I was on the side porch, writing, and heard a loud Boom! I ran in to check on Pop, but he was reading, then to see about Mom, and she was asleep. I looked outside on the east side of the house, but nothing was amiss. About two hours later, I walked around the house and saw that a **big** pecan limb had fallen onto the metal roof. If I just dragged it off, it would bring a section of the gutter with it, so I told Shaun about it when he came by to give a report on his day. There's always something for one of us to handle around here.

SATURDAY, AUGUST 5TH

Brother came over early to tackle that pecan limb. The thickest part was stuck in the fork of the tree, so he cut sections off that first – in case anyone wants some for grilling. Then he climbed the ladder and cut sections off the smaller end on the roof while I tossed them on the ground. Pop was supervising. He's forgotten more about cutting trees and limbs than Shaun and I know put together, but these days he's (mostly) content to let us handle it, even if we mess up. After Shaun got all the debris in the big ditch, he left and I started watering. Then I blew ant carcasses off the front porch. Pop and I sat outside awhile after I got Mom all situated. Then a trip to town, and back with lunch. Tam came over with her stuff, thinking that I was going home today as usual, but I told her I intended to stay tonight , then drive straight to church in the morning, so she could have tonight off. (She's staying an extra night and two days later this month when I need to keep Knoxlynn.) We started talking about Pop's 100th birthday party, then Melanie called, so we were able to have a conference and clarify some plans. It's going to be here *so* fast.

SUNDAY, AUGUST 6TH

The usual getting ready for church whirl after Pop and Shaun returned from an early buggy ride. Poor Mom is so pitiful in the mornings because she stays up late and then doesn't want to wake up for breakfast. I told everyone bye, and Pop said to tell Knoxlynn that he is looking forward to seeing her at his birthday party. Sweetie Pie was at church – so cute in a little dress and matching bow. Love seeing my precious girl!

TUESDAY, AUGUST 15TH

A whirlwind this morning! Filled the birdbaths, washed and filled the hummingbird feeders, watered the big driveway flower bed, washed dishes, packed the car, ate breakfast, got ready and still arrived at Stu and Ashley's just a few minutes after 7:00 AM. Had a good day with my sweet girl … got to hold her as she slept. Those days are winding down, so I'm going to treasure each one. After Stu arrived and took over Daddy Duty, I headed out to J'ville. Arrived a little after 7:00 PM – weird to get here on a Tuesday evening.

WEDNESDAY, AUGUST 16TH

64° this morning! Are you kidding me? When does that happen in the middle of August in Texas? I actually put on long sleeves and grabbed a lap blanket as I went out to sit on the patio with that first cup. Got Pop up at 6:30 – I knew he wouldn't want to miss such a glorious morning. Told him he'd need Old Blackie. Shortly after he got out there, Tam drove up, super excited about this unprecedented cool spell. Then Shaun drove up to take Pop on a ride. Tam and I gathered a few antique items to decorate with at the party: tin coffee pot, metal Folger's coffee can, metal Navy meal tray from WW II, and so forth. Of course, Pop is the main antique. Ha! Regular morning routine after that, plus a town run. When I started to give Mom her afternoon meds, she said she had stopped taking the fiber capsules because they made her sick. I called Tam, and she said Mom had balked at taking them last Saturday, so she hasn't taken them since. I hate that because Mom hasn't been stopped up since she started those, but what do we do?

Made a pineapple cream pie between watering outside, trimming the wisteria, helping Mom with a puzzle and so forth. Walked a piece of pie down to Shaun's house. About dusk, Pop and I heard the coyotes cutting loose in the pasture across the road – so glad he could hear them. They have to be fairly close these days for his ears to pick up that high-pitched howling. Later on when I was about to go to bed, Mom asked me to put out another puzzle for her, in case she couldn't sleep, so I got the side pieces out. Maybe that will be enough for her to work on.

THURSDAY, AUGUST 17TH

Woo-Hoo! 60° this morning! Shaun and Tam both came over for a little while. After breakfast, Pop sat on the front porch to enjoy the morning while I watered some more and finished cutting back the wisteria – those runners go all over creation. Gave Pop a manicure while we were out there. Later, Tam came over with some apricot pastries she had made – a favorite treat. I took the opportunity to ask her about staying with Mom and Dad when Bill and I fly to Ben's advancement ceremony the week after Pop's birthday party. That's my week up here, but I sure want to go if I can. Later, Shaun came up to mow this brown grass; at least it will be *neat* brown grass. Poor guy was in a cloud of dust the whole time. After he finished, I gave him some pie and rolls to take home. I washed dishes till the world looked flat, and kept moving water hoses.

This afternoon, Tam came over to show us some pictures of Rita and the kids in Wyoming, and she said she *could* take care of those days for me – yay! Mom, Tam, and I joined Pop in the sunroom and started talking over old times, most of which I don't remember. My brain doesn't hang onto things very well. It never has. Tam mentioned when Mom and Dad gathered us kids together to tell us they were having another child, Shaun, but I don't remember that at all. Then she told about the time I wanted to make taffy and have a taffy pull like in pioneer days. She said Melanie and I had butter all over our hands, and the taffy didn't exactly turn out. Dad mentioned the popcorn balls we made … zero recollection of any of it. Maybe someday the Lord will give me back those good memories. I hope so.

Later, I was working on Pop's feet when I heard a cow bawling over and over. I told Pop I was going to check it out, just in case something had happened to her calf. Back in the day, Pop would have gotten up to come with me or at least *mentioned* coming, but he was content to let me go. I don't know whether he thought I could handle it on my own or didn't feel like making the effort or a bit of both. (If I make it to 100, I probably won't get out of my recliner for anything short of the Rapture.) Anyhow, the cow was on one side of the fence and her baby was on the other side. Instead of going to get her baby, the cow was just bawling at her. So, I drove around to the calf, got out, and started it moving in the right direction. They eventually got together.

FRIDAY, AUGUST 18TH

Our cool is gone. I knew it couldn't last, but sure enjoyed that reprieve. I've been loading up Pop's plate with fruit at breakfast – it's cool and helps with his hydration. He enjoys it, but if we weren't here to fix food for Mom and Dad, I know what they would do because it's what I would do if I didn't have to cook for my husband – grab the easiest thing: a bowl of cereal, peanut butter and crackers, cookies, and so forth. Then they'd dry up and blow away. Folks of any age who live alone can fall into that habit. And for sure, Dad would not get more than a fraction of the water he needs. We've been the water Nazis for so long, it's just routine.

Along with breakfast prep, I watered some more. This drought is unrelenting. Put away some laundry, fixed Mom's breakfast, then started getting ready for Pop's eye appointment. He asked me to find two black socks that matched … what a sad assortment of dress socks! Note to self: buy Dad some better socks. Then I tried to iron a shirt for him, but the iron wouldn't work. Mom said, "It worked the last time I used it." I asked, "Mom, when was that?" She hasn't ironed anything since she had shingles in 2010, and probably awhile before that. Anyway, we finally got ready.

Tam brought Marc over so that he could stay with Mom while we went to Pop's eye appointment.

We enjoyed visiting on the drive and in the clinic, remembering funny things that happened on our trips When Pop's eye exam was all done, Dr. B led him back to a large room where nearly all the staff had assembled. They clapped when he came in, and we saw a birthday cake and balloons – a wonderful celebration for Dad! They sang Happy Birthday and took photos. What a lovely thing for Dr. B to do. Who does stuff like that in this day and age?

Dad was so pleased and said, "This is something special." A young lady asked the secret to his long life, and Pop said, "Get up every day with a purpose … something that you want to accomplish." Many times I've heard him say that he needed to get something done to justify his existence. (I guess that's why we kids tend to keep a running "to do" list.) After some photos, the staff had to get back to business, but what a wonderful display of genuine caring and respect.

While we were on our way home, Marc called and said Mom wanted her laxative, but he didn't know where to look. (Tam and I knew that was coming since she stopped taking that fiber.) I told him where it was. Tam said that as soon as we got home, Mom would want more since she thinks medicines ought to work immediately. Sure enough, she said nothing had happened yet. Tam told her to just wait. I started lunch, and Tam looked for photos for the book. After lunch, I started vacuuming and continued watering outside. Around 8:30, Mom insisted on taking more laxatives even though I told her she would have a blowout … she doesn't seem to remember that the misery of constipation is matched by the misery of the opposite condition.

SATURDAY, AUGUST 19TH

Sure enough, Mom said she was in the bathroom all night. (Probably not the entire night, though I'm sure it felt that way.) If she could just be more patient when she takes medicine … I wish I hadn't given in.

Pop decided to let the cows into the east pasture behind Tam's today – they have eaten everything else up, but at least that pasture, since it's near the creek, still has a decent amount of grass. I rode with Shaun and Pop in the side-by-side to gather up the cows. They seemed to know that something good was in the works – all he did was bang his hand on the driver side door and give a whoop, and they came running. By the time he got the gate open, several were waiting to get in to the food, and the rest were pelting down the hill. Pop enjoys seeing them spread out across the pasture, grazing to their heart's content.

WEDNESDAY, AUGUST 23RD

Melanie has had a rough week. Mom is taking Lasix and is weak and feeling terrible, so Melanie has slept on the couch outside her room. With Mom's *Bewitched* episodes blaring until very late, she has gotten little sleep. She and Tam agreed that from now on, we will not let Mom decide what to stop taking (like the Fibercon) or take more of (like the laxative). She wants relief on the instant, and that's not going to happen in any case. So, we will have to make those decisions from now on … another inevitable step on this journey. We don't like it, but there it is.

THURSDAY, AUGUST 24TH

Pop is officially 100 today! What a milestone. And to be as alert and active as he still is … incredible. After Pop and Shaun got back from the Homeplace, I called to wish him a Happy Birthday, then I had to get cracking on those dozens and dozens of cupcakes for the party on Saturday. I had a glitch on one batch; the timer wasn't set properly. Melanie is making Oreo bon-bons and pecan tassies. I hope she won't wind up face-planting in the mixing bowl due to lack of sleep.

Tam has worked like a demon all week, getting the fellowship hall decorated and as heat proof as possible. The main door is full west, so she changed the entry point to a door farther away so the main party area will stay cooler. I am so tired of this blasting triple digit heat. I saw a Facebook post that said, "Whoever left the door to Hell open, please close it." I heartily concur.

Printed out labels for the drinks and goodies. Got gift cards for Nurse C who is staying with Mom so we can all attend the party – Mom doesn't feel up to going, and this heat would be hard on her anyway.

FRIDAY, AUGUST 25TH

More cupcake issues: some of the liners separated from the cupcakes – had to stick those back with frosting. Then the cupcakes sat too low in the holders, so I had to rig that a different way, but, onward and upward ... our Pop deserves a huge celebration, and he's going to get one, by Crackey!

On to town to buy a few more items for the party. I heard from Stu that Knoxlynn is sick, so she and Ashley won't be coming to the party tomorrow; I know he's terribly disappointed, me too. Ben is flying in from Florida to attend the party, but I haven't told Dad yet. I want it to be a surprise.

Loaded all my goods and headed out. Stopped at the church to unload the food; Tam and Tiff helped me. Everything looks great! Tam has put an incredible amount of time and effort into this event: invitations, banners, video room, tables/chair set up, memorabilia, décor, and more. I would have liked to look around more, but I needed to get to the house to check on Mom and see if Melanie needed help with anything before the California folks arrive. Mom was not doing well at all, but I did get her to the puzzle table, then Melanie fixed her hair – that always makes her feel better.

When Aunt Stella and Debbie arrived a short time later, Mom was completely surprised – we had kept their coming a secret. Aunt Stella, Mom, and Dad visited in the Big Room while we cousins talked in the kitchen – a great time of catching up and relaxation before the storm tomorrow. Later on, everyone settled in for the night – Melanie and I slept in the Big Room. She started out on the love seat, then switched to Mom's recliner, then to Pop's. Hard to sleep anywhere with Mom's TV on, even though she turned it down somewhat. Poor Melanie has had a tough time – hope she can enjoy tomorrow.

SATURDAY, AUGUST 26TH

D-Day. After coffee, Tam came over and we went to the church for some last minute chores. I worked on the fruit trays, then mixed the lemonade. Andy and Garrett brought canopies to put at either end of the sidewalk to shield folks from that harsh sun; then Melanie noticed fire ants running everywhere on the sidewalks! I went back to Mom's and Dad's, mixed up some poison, and went back to spray.

When I got back, Shaun was grilling burgers, and Melanie was anxious about getting the burger fixings all laid out, but I needed to iron

Pop's shirt, so I did that first, and when I finished, the lunch prep was all done. I could tell that Melanie was a little upset with me for not helping her first. I hadn't had time to finish writing in Pop's card either, but then I saw that someone else had gotten the exact same card, so I just put mine away and went in to see Mom. She was all bent over like a droopy little bird, and it made me so sad. I knelt in front of her, took her face in my hands, and told her how much I love her and that I don't want her to go ... I need my mom. I started to cry, and she held me and smoothed my hair. She said she loved me too, but it's all up to God. I asked her to try to eat more and get stronger, and she said she'd try.

The worry about Mom and the stress of the past several days (weeks) are hard to set aside, but very soon, it is time to head to church so that we could get family photos with Dad before everyone else arrived. Ben was already there – wonderful to see him. Pop was really surprised and pleased that he would fly in from Florida. My dad, my husband, and both sons all together – a grand occasion! Lots and lots of guests braved the heat, such a testimony to the kind of man Dad is. He enjoyed seeing everyone and catching up with folks. Later on, after the welcome, Shaun spoke about Pop being not only his dad but also his first boss – he learned the painting trade from Pop beginning in high school. He got a laugh when he said Dad was older than sheetrock and latex paint. Then Dad got the microphone and said how much he appreciated everyone coming. He said he'd outlived most of his friends, and if he'd had any enemies, he'd outlived them, too. He said if he had it to do over, he'd make some younger friends so he wouldn't run out! He has such a funny way of putting things.

Most of the time, I was running around trying to keep food items well supplied, so I didn't have much time to socialize. We had a few snafus: No one got the tea, so we had to send Marc and Wyatt to town for that; the ice for the party got left at Mom and Dad's, stuff like that, but we made it. Finally things wound down, and we started packing up food to take back home, along with the party decorations, tablecloths, and so on. Bill, Tam, and I were the last to leave. Even so, she and I will have to come back early in the morning to finish getting things tidy for Sunday School. Tam needs to sleep for about a week to get over all this.

Since I figured Melanie's nerves were hanging by a thread after her difficult week, I decided to stay tonight to help. Everyone was tired and ready to call it a day by 9:00. A big day for Pop – he made it to his birthday on Thursday and through his big celebration today. Sweet dreams tonight, Pop. I hope you're looking forward to more good times ahead in your 101st year.

Melanie

MONDAY, AUGUST 7TH

A litany of thing to take care of before I leave: pool maintenance, water flowers and grape vines, take out trash, mail bill payment, get the fudge I'd bought in Missouri for Sherry and Tam, load up and leave by 9:00 am with a car full of party items – flowers, table cloths, vintage coffee bean sacks, etc.

Tam helped me unload, then I showed the folks the Missouri pictures. Started lunch then followed our usual routine for the evening. Later, Daddy and I wanted to cut the 65 pound watermelon that Joseph grew, his largest, but we couldn't even pick it up to carry it to the table. Called Tam but she was ready for bed (she does that pretty early). Texted Shaun. He said he would be up in the morning to move it. Daddy and I resigned ourselves to no melon tonight.

TUESDAY, AUGUST 8TH

Woke up at 4:00 am. I knew it was over as far as sleep goes. Got up and started writing; worked steadily until Daddy came in and filled the kitchen with the lovely aroma of coffee. Still dark but you could faintly see the edges of morning. As the light grew, I noticed a small flock of egrets fly up from behind the knob down toward the creek, then more and more – so pretty.

Daddy wanted to check on the heifers at the Homeplace so I left Mama a note of where we were, and when we would be back. Before we left, Tam dropped by and picked up the grocery list. She was going to do her town errands before heading to WMA. Shaun came up and put the melon on the kitchen table for us.

When we got to the Homeplace, I unlocked the gate and Daddy took over the wheel. I have always appreciated the fact that Daddy didn't kick up a fuss or refuse to cooperate when his eyesight couldn't be trusted on the roads. He would like to be independent but has the wisdom to see the truth. He just drives in the pastures and seems content with that.

When we check the heifers, there are only 7. One is missing. Sigh. We just can't figure out where these heifers have an escape route, but it's too hot to find it now. One thing we **do** know, Daddy is going to be short of hay unless we get some rain soon. We need at least 30 more rolls. With this oppressive heat and weeks of no rain, the pastures are turning brown. Daddy has already turned the cows into the pasture behind the pole barn. Tomorrow he will open the gate to the west pasture which should have been cut for hay.

After taking care of Mama, I sat in the sunroom with Daddy, then Tam came over and we enjoyed watching Daddy cut the giant watermelon. It wasn't as sweet as I like, but Daddy said it was sweet enough. Tam put the 2 halves in the porch fridge. They barely fit.

While I was dusting Mama's room, the Pledge can got turned in my hand, and I sprayed the left side of my face and eye! Can't fathom how **that** happened. I washed my eyeball repeatedly and put drops in it. Seems ok.

WEDNESDAY, AUGUST 9TH

It was a lovely, breezy morning, but sadly, no egrets. Those white birds are not only pretty to watch as they wheel against the blue sky, but also they eat lots of grasshoppers. Daddy decided that we would head up to the barn to turn the cows into the west pasture. After we poured out some mineral in the trough, the cows crowded at the gate, anxious for it to open. Despite my best efforts, Sancho and Tam's horse pushed through first, the horse bucking as he ran through, and Sancho trailing behind – quite the pair. The herd slowed down as they came through the gate and went to mowing the grass! No milling around, just got down to business.

Shaun arrived – he had been working in his paint room since 6:30 am. I invited him for lunch. He told us about some hay he had located and might buy. After lunch we headed to the barber shop for Daddy's birthday haircut, then drove to Farm & Ranch for cubes to help round up the cows on Saturday. So hot!! We were glad to get back to the cool house.

Mama meds and meal. Daddy and I sat quietly for a few minutes, then I said, "Daddy, I feel trapped in the house by this oppressive heat." I wished I could think of something to do. Daddy said he would get the clothes out of the dryer. We got them folded and put away. I took some towels to the hall bathroom. When I got back, Daddy was stretched out on his bed. "Daddy, it's a little early for that." He grinned and said, "Well, it looked mighty inviting." I said, "I wish we had a job." Suddenly I remembered - Freezer! "Daddy, we were going to defrost the big freezer in preparation for our new beef." Daddy pulled the few things out of the big freezer and put them in the smaller one. I unplugged the freezer and left the lid up. In this heat, it should defrost in an hour.

I wanted to take a walk but still too hot at 8:30. Maybe I'll take one later … like in September.

THURSDAY, AUGUST 10TH

Temperature range today 81-103 (actual); 87-109 (feels like). Later in the week I see a high of only 93 degrees. We can always hope. Daddy and I went to shut the cows up in the west pasture so they will be easier to corral this weekend. A big flock of egrets gathered among the cows and we noticed three odd birds in the mix. They had cool curved bills; we think they are white-faced Ibis.

Later, I went to refill the big water tank and 2 blue tubs. The tiny pond in the west pasture is so low and nasty that we don't want the cows to drink from it. Fortunately, they had found the big tub – it was 2/3 empty.

Daddy and I mopped up the big freezer, then plugged it back in to get cold. After a bit, we switched the frozen stuff into it from the small freezer, then unplugged *that* one to thaw. Got Mama things done. She isn't feeling good. I smoothed her hair a while after praying for her. Checked on her later and she was asleep. Daddy had his Kindle in his lap and was asleep, too. I mopped up the little freezer and wiped it down inside and out. Looked great. After I plugged it back in, I noticed that the side of the freezer was very hot, but Daddy said it would be ok. Googled it and they said the same thing. Daddy's pretty sharp.

FRIDAY, AUGUST 11TH

I was sound asleep, but still heard Mama hollering! I jumped up – no lights! Found my flashlight and made it to the doorway of the Big Room. Mama was at the bottom of the Big Room steps holding her little flashlight. She was upset because the electricity was off. I assured her that either Tam or Shaun had already called it in and it would be back on after soon. She said she felt smothery, so I went back to my room and grabbed Tam's cooling cube and set that up for her. I went back to bed, but heard Daddy and was concerned about him getting to the bathroom in the dark. I called to him, and he said he was lighting the oil lamp. I told him it would heat things up. He must have blown it out because it was dark in there after a while.

I read by the flashlight until the adrenaline settled out of my system, then slept until the electricity came back on. Had to get up and turn off the lights in Daddy's and Mama's rooms. They slept right through those lights coming back on.

This morning I looked outside and saw Tam's car, then looked toward the barn road and here she came with her lead rope over her shoulder. She had moved CT, her horse, out of the west pasture to make it easier to get the cows rounded up. She expressed concern about waiting until next week to reduce the herd. Selling earlier would save grass. I told her I would talk to Daddy. When I asked him about selling tomorrow, he thought it was a good idea.

Later, we gassed up the truck and got some supplies for cattle working. Back home Daddy wants us to unload that sack of cubes still in the trunk of the car. I suggest waiting until Shaun can get it, but he reminds me that he doesn't like to wait. LOL. I back up the truck to the car, and together we heft the sack into the truck. Now to relax, but not for long – Tam called with a meat crisis: one of the large freezers at the meat processing plant is down. Some of our meat is frozen solid, but some is semi-frozen or just cold! She needs to pick it up ASAP and get it in the freezer. I wrote the check for the processing fee, and she came by and got it, then took off. Addie went along to help her. Daddy and I were so glad we got those freezers ready when we did!

When Tam texted that they were close, I backed Mom's car out of the garage, so she could back in to unload. She had been instructed on how to freeze the meat quickly. We layered the meat in both freezers with box lids between so the cold air could circulate. We got the meat inside in record time. The lids must stay shut for 2 days.

Mama went to the sunroom and Shaun arrived. He was very happy about how much work he had gotten done and said he would be up here at 6:30 am for the cattle doings. He was excited about his September trip with Christopher to the Great Smoky Mountains. Shaun and Daddy reminisced about trips of the past, and Shaun expressed regret that he hadn't been proactive about him and Daddy taking more trips in the last 10 years. Me, Tam and Sherry took Daddy to see the autumn leaves of New Hampshire and Vermont when he was 90 years old. Those long trips are a thing of the past now.

Later, Daddy and I went to water the cypress tree by the small pond in the west pasture. The cows were restless. The water in the small pond was churned up and the water level way down. I refilled the tank and the blue containers. I went back up there at 11:00 pm. Seemed they had gotten their fill.

SATURDAY, AUGUST 12TH

Up at 5:00 am. Rounded up my stuff and put it in the car. Daddy up at 6:10, and Tam and Shaun here by 6:30 am. Daddy and Shaun were going to get the cows and calves in the big corral, but things went amiss. Shaun hollered for us and we zoomed up there in his side by side. After a couple of passes, we got them all in except one lone cow, and we didn't need her. Next, we moved the 12 larger calves into the loading pen, then into the trailer. Tam drove that load to the sale barn while we started phase 2: vaccinating the small calves and banding the bulls. Shaun quickly saw the value of the side gate in the working chute; after we finished with each calf, we just opened that small gate and let them out instead of having to open the head gate – it's much harder to open and close. Since Shaun and Tam are going to be running all this soon, they need to get all the experience they can while Daddy is still here to instruct and correct.

After we were all done, Tam sent us a picture of our truck and trailer in line with a bunch ahead of *and* behind her. Many ranchers are being forced to reduce their herds in the face of this extended heat and drought. By the time Daddy finished his breakfast, Tam drove up and parked the rig so Shaun could power wash it, then went home to clean up. When she got back, we wrote down our predictions of how much those 12 head will bring. It's a family tradition I never tire of.

I give Mama and Daddy a kiss and hug, start to leave and see Daddy coming out the door with his cane. I stopped and took a picture of him and Tam waving bye. Daddy called later and gave the cattle report. He was pleased; it was a little more than he'd guessed.

MONDAY, AUGUST 21ST

5:00 am- spiritual boost- Bible and prayers. Usual round of gathering up: party items, clothes, ice for lunch on Saturday; Andy and Ethan came by and Ethan loaded the ice for me. Almost left my party shoes and makeup bag!

Tam helped me unload and told me Mama fell last night! She had to crawl to open her door and holler so Tam could hear her. Then Tam called Shaun and he came and picked her up. That door will stay open this week, **and** we need to find those monitors we have used in the past. Mama is sick now and has a wet cloth on her head. Later, I got her to the puzzle table, along with a little fan to keep her comfortable. Daddy went in two times to check on her.

Daddy and I eat lunch. Mama is pitiful. Smothery- I know it is fluid build-up. Her weight is going up, daily. Every breath she is saying, "Lord help me." Over and over and over. I've prayed with her several times. I don't know what else to do. I called Tam and she said she has done that for the last 2 days. Tam got very little sleep also. I gave her a Lasix pill. Later, she seemed some better. Her feet are swollen – an indicator also of extra fluid. She staggered on one trip to the bathroom and I caught her.

Sherry called a bit teary eyed about thinking she was the cause of Mama's dilemma. Mama can be very demanding when she is feeling bad. The domino effect started when she wouldn't take her Fibercon which is the wonderful pill that keeps her regular. That precipitated constipation, which led to a laxative which she wants to work instantly. When it didn't, she insisted on more. Sherry gave it to her, protesting that it was going to cause problems. It did! Things went south in a hurry. Well, she is over that. This other is due to congestive heart failure and its accompanying fluid. She is taking her Fibercon now and her regularity seems better.

TUESDAY, AUGUST 22ND

Well, it was an interesting night. After my bath I was determined to make peace with sleeping on the couch outside Mama's bedroom. I grabbed two pillows, my book, the new Reader's Digest, and made the best of it. Mama was watching *Bewitched* and it was loud. I was in and out with cold wash cloths. Still feeling sick at her stomach. I adjusted her fan every little while. It has become the new thermostat. She got her night meds down with water, gagging all the while. Because her intestines are getting back to normal, no dairy or milk products. Those are her main source of calories. That is concerning. Up and down steadily until 3:30 am. Finally, Mama drifts off to sleep about 5:00. I caught snatches of sleep and feel pretty good this morning.

The heat dome which is frying Texas has expanded up toward Iowa – 77 to 102 degrees today (feels like 82 to 106).Shaun and I went on a brief ride to see the cows in the creek bottom. Praise God for such lovely deep grass that will provide plenty to eat for Daddy's herd. As we drove past the north pond, Brother spotted a water moccasin on a limb over the water. He nailed it with a 22 pistol. Good shooting!

Tam and Addie came over to gather decorations and pieces out of the museum for Daddy's celebration on Saturday. Shaun showed me the 2 boxes of Wagyu meat patties the people he is working for gave him to try. Looking forward to having those for lunch before Daddy's party.

Mama very weak today and sick again. We tried several avenues: Pepto-Bismol, later a Pepcid AC. Tam talked to Mama's critical care nurse; we have a few more Lasix to get her fluid off. We think the fluid build-up around her heart is making her feel like she can't breathe. I have a cold wash cloth on her forehead and one around the back of her neck. She feels hot one minute – I move her little fan to put the breeze on her, then the next minute she gets cold and I move the fan off her. She almost collapsed when she went to the bathroom, but I caught her. I will need to be very near tonight.

WEDNESDAY, AUGUST 23RD

I was on the couch last night to assist Mama. The TV was on all night as she tried to distract herself from her sickness. I was glad I brought a book. In between doing for Mama, I could read. I might have slept an hour or two before 2:00 am. Nothing after that.

I heard Daddy begin his coffee ritual, so I got up and dressed. He's sneezing a bit. Man, I hope he isn't coming down with a cold right here on the eve of his birthday. I talked to Sherry yesterday; she has kept her little granddaughter 3 days this week – she can't go to daycare because she has a cold.

Shaun came up and took us for an early morning ride just as the sun peeped up over the horizon. Lots of egrets around the cattle. Then Shaun took Daddy down to the Homeplace to check the level of the creek; it is very low. They plan to take the water tank there and put it close to the house so they can fill it up with a water hose; then they'll have to coax the heifers over to it with cubes so they'll know where the good water is. We will leave them down there because they still have enough grass.

Tam is in and out getting more stuff for decorating the fellowship hall. I helped her load up. It is blazing hot! I killed more red wasps ahead of our family gathering. Hope to have them cleared out by then. Tam and Andy are very allergic to wasp stings.

Bobby, a friend from my high school days came to see Daddy. They had a good visit in the Big Room. He brought Daddy his favorite pie, raisin, a gift from his wife, Lily.

Mama is sick – again. Gave her a Pepcid AC. Later she watched *Ben Hur* and seemed to feel better. She was able to eat her supper. I took a nap from 5 to 6 pm. I think I can make it tonight.

Daddy asked me to make sure he is up at 6:00 am. Tomorrow is the day he turns triple digits! August 24, 1923- August 24, 2023!

THURSDAY- 100 YEARS

My alarm went off at 6:00 am. I got up and as I came through the hall, I met Daddy. I stopped in the doorway and sang Happy 100th Birthday and when I finished, he laughed. I gave him a big hug. As we sat outside, he quoted Psalm 90:10 & 12:

"The days of our lives are 70 years; and if by reason of strength they are eighty years, yet their boast is only labor and sorrow. For it is soon cut off, and we fly away. So teach us to number our days that we may gain a heart of wisdom."

Then he talked about the different patriarchs of the faith and how old they were when they passed.

Shaun arrived with his birthday card. Then he and Daddy got some cubes and the big water tank and drove to the Homeplace. They used the cubes to get the heifers to the tank, seven of them anyway.

I made the Oreo bonbons this morning. When I had them rowed up on wax paper on the counter, Daddy came through and said they sure were pretty.

Mama came in the sunroom with Daddy after Nurse C came. Nurse C and I talked about how Mama was doing. I showed her the powdered IV that we mix for Daddy, and she recommended we give it to Mama too. As she left, she turned around and asked who was staying with Mama during the party – I told her we were working that out, and she said, "Why don't you let me come and stay with her? I just work on paperwork, and I could do that here as well as home." I was blown away by that kind offer. I called Sherry and Tam and they thought that was great! So I called her and said we would take her up on that kind offer! She said she would have to bring her 3 grandchildren along, and I said that wouldn't be a problem.

I helped Tam load the plates, napkins and forks from the library room; she was in and out 4 or 5 times today. On one trip she gave Daddy his card, and I did also. Rita called from Wyoming. Raylan sang happy birthday and then Athena. They will not be back from Wyoming until next week and will miss the party. Charlene, Daddy's niece, called and wished him a happy birthday. She doesn't drive anymore and hopes her grandson will bring her on Saturday.

Shaun came up at the end of the day and moved the Wagyu patties out of the freezer and into the porch fridge to thaw. He had gotten a metal float for the water tank at the Homeplace that will let water flow into the tank until it is full and then shut off. Glad we won't have to go there every day to water those heifers. Since Rita uses that one hose to water her flowers, though, we need to get a Y connector so we can attach two hoses to the spigot.

I made nearly 100 pecan tassies. The last ones are out of the oven and cooling. It is 10:15 pm. Aunt Stella and Debra from Los Angeles will be here tomorrow at 2:00 pm. Lots of house stuff to do before then.

FRIDAY, AUGUST 25TH

Daddy officially started his next century! ☺

I didn't do well at sleeping. Mama up until 1:00 am. Up again at 4:00 am.

Daddy and I were on the patio when Brother came up on his side by side. He is going to hook up the long trailer – he has found Daddy some extra hay and plans to haul it this afternoon. They went down to the Homeplace and filled up the water tank. It was ¾ empty. Daddy and I went to town and got a Y connector for the Homeplace and a 75 foot hose, but when we got there, we couldn't get the old hose off. We were afraid we might break the faucet if we twisted too hard, so we just left it for Shaun. It's leaking pretty badly, too.

At the house, I got Mama changed, breakfast, and Pepcid AC. She is at 104 lbs. Not enough calories. She did eat her egg and small piece of ham earlier.

Shaun is hard at work hauling in that hay.2:00 pm came and went – no relatives. Sherry got here at 2:30, then Aunt Stella and Debra arrived. Daddy was so surprised. Mama didn't know who Debra was at first, but finally realized who she was when she saw Aunt Stella. They visited. Debra, Tam, Sherry and I talked around the kitchen table. Later, Shaun came in from hay hauling and visited a bit and took the patties out of the fridge to finish thawing. Tam had to leave, then we found out that Aunt Stella and Debra were expecting to spend the next two nights with us. Sherry and I sprang into action, grabbed all our stuff out of the bedroom, and piled it in the library room. We stripped the sheets off the bed, washed and dried them, then put them back on after Aunt Stella's nap.

Daddy washed his hair and Sherry dried it. I found out Wyatt, is coming! I wasn't expecting that. So happy. As Sherry and I sat writing, I looked at her and asked, "Did you put the beef patties back in the fridge for Brother?" Her eyes got big and she said, "No!" She jumped up and took care of that. Disaster averted!

SATURDAY, AUGUST 26TH – PARTY

It started well, as far as patio time. I played musical sleep stations this morning. Short couch, Mama Bear chair, Papa Bear chair; all to no avail. Slept a couple of hours; up with Mama some. Sherry was up early and made coffee. Mama ate 2 bites of her egg and ham and was done. At 7:30, Daddy and Shaun take off to the Homeplace to fix the Y and floatation device. We take our baked good down to the church. It looks wonderful! I put my pecan tassies and pedestal dish of Oreo bonbons on their respective spots on the table. Andy and Garrett arrive with canopies to shield people from the heat as they walk toward the door. As they put up the canopies, I look down and the sidewalk is crawling with fire ants. I run and tell Sherry. She knows how to mix the poison and where the sprayer is. She and I head back to the house. Tam and Debra head to town to pick up the cake.

After the ants are dispatched, Sherry returns and starts ironing Daddy's shirt. Shaun and Andy are grilling burgers. Tam is in town getting the cake; therefore, feeling a bit frantic, I try to get everything else on the table and tea made. More of the family arrives with their baked goods that need to go down to the church: gingersnaps, Oreo cake, chocolate chip cookies, and red velvet cake balls. All need to be there at 1:15 pm before family pictures at 1:30. Lunch was delicious – the burgers a hit. Mass exodus to the church.

I stayed behind to await nurse C and her grandchildren to sit with Mama. Sherry has things for the grands to do – sidewalk chalk, bubbles to blow, crayons and coloring book. They arrive and I take off. It is 2:00 pm when I get there. Calie is busy photographing everyone, and we siblings get our picture with Papa. We are so blessed by the turn out. Around 110 folks came. Sherry, Tam, Shaun and I, plus first cousin, Deborah, worked tirelessly: greeting, directing, keeping the food out and drink dispensers full. The table for cards fills to overflowing, Daddy smiling and enjoying seeing old friends and family. It was exhausting yet thrilling to see it all come together is spite of a few hitches. Memorabilia fantastic. Many people were looking that over. Media room with video did a brisk traffic as well.

Sherry gave a welcome and thanked everyone for coming. She mentioned folks coming from the west coast (Los Angeles), east coast (Tampa) and mid country (Missouri). Wherever they came from, they all were huge blessings to Daddy. Shaun spoke about how much it meant to us to have a father like we do. Daddy spoke last and got several laughs – he is still so sharp. Then more visiting and well wishes from everyone.

I left at 4:00 pm to relieve Nurse C so she could take her little people home. Such a joy knowing Mama was in good hands the whole time.

My kids and grandkids come back to visit. Angela and Austin gave PawPaw their card and gift: a Case pocketknife. JoAnna gave PawPaw an overnight mail package from Brandon, who is in the Navy in Norfolk, VA. He paid a hefty sum to ensure PawPaw got it today! It was a beautiful card. JoAnna called him, and he and his PawPaw shared a sweet Facetime together.

All day, as the family arrived, they would go in by 2s and 3s to give Mama a hug and tell her they love her. She was feeling terrible, but she seemed to appreciate each visit.

Now, Debra and Aunt Stella are in their room. Sherry and I are at Mama's puzzle table to repair her puzzle that little fingers had taken apart. We talk over the day as we unwind from a hectic time, sweet sharing. Later, I figured out how to fold my body on that short couch and slept very well. Exhaustion can do that for you. We were only up with Mama at 3:30 am.

As I reflect on the events of the week, I realize that it was hard, but so special. Mama's frailty tendered my heart with patience as her need for care outweighed my need for sleep and rest.

Daddy's party required so much effort from all of us: resources, planning, baking, and coordination. Labors of love for our Daddy, which pours from hearts blessed to call him our own.

SUNDAY, AUGUST 27TH

We were up at 6:00 am. Shaun brought the side by side up so I could take the cousins on a ride later. At 7:00 Sherry and Tam headed back to the church to clear out the final items and make sure everything was in place for Sunday School. When they came back, Sherry got ready to travel to her church in Nacogdoches, but first we took a cousin picture, all of us with Debra and Wanda. Tam fried maple sausage to tempt Mama's appetite. I snagged one of those, and boy was it good!

I got Debra and Wanda in the side by side and away we went. Sancho, the longhorn, was just over the hill and posed for some pictures. I drove to the top of the nob, which gives a panoramic view of Daddy's acres, then down to the north pond, with a stop by the middle cypress tree. Debra had her picture made there two years ago, and I wanted to take her picture there again.

Back at the house, Wanda and her daughter, Lori, went in to tell Mama "Bye." Wanda had tears in her eyes. She didn't know if she would be up to see the folks anytime soon since she lives over 3 hours away and needs someone to drive her. Lori had a special item for Daddy's birthday: a replica of a $100 bill with Daddy's face on it. She had one for all of us. Cute! Debra and Aunt Stella left around 2:30 pm.

After I got Mama to the puzzle table and braided her hair, I left and took some goodies with me. About midway through the town of Henderson, I was waiting at a stop light when I closed my eyes. Suddenly I started awake and realized the light was green, and no one was around me on this 3-lane street. I don't know how long I had sat there. It was a strange feeling. I called Sherry and she talked me to Tatum; by then I knew I could stay awake the rest of the way.

So happy to be home and looking forward to a nice shower. At 8:30 pm the power went off: no lights, no water. Welcome home.

Tamra

FRIDAY, AUGUST 4TH

Managed to get all of the invitations addressed, stamped, and mailed and sent all but four of the text/email invites this week. Hopefully, I can track down the last ones today. Rita and the kids are leaving for Wyoming tomorrow, so I dropped off the map and permits I had printed off for her and a water cooler for her trip. I sure will miss them. Don't think they will make it back for Dad's party…I just have a feeling. Not that I blame her, it has been so horribly hot here. An escape to the mountains sounds like heaven.

SATURDAY, AUGUST 5TH

Went to a neighbor's 80th birthday celebration today and was glad I went – for two reasons. One, I got to see some folks I hadn't seen in ages and two, I was able to observe the party set-up and the proceedings. Seeing what did and did not work as far as people movement, etc. gave me some good ideas on how to arrange Dad's celebration set-up.

I thought I was supposed to take over for Sherry this afternoon, but when I arrived at Mom and Dad's, she said she was staying until tomorrow morning. So…I stayed and visited with her and then we had a three-way confab with Mel on the phone. We hammered out some more details about Dad's party, and then I loaded up my bags and went home. It was weird being home on a Saturday night, but I enjoyed it. Rita let me know they made it to Amarillo and it was raining and cool there…I am jealous.

SUNDAY, AUGUST 6TH

Sherry left about 9:00 for her church in Nac, and Dad and I went to church at our usual time. Shaun and Marc were there, but not many at the service today. Sherry and I had talked about Dad's lack of movement these days. He sits most of the day in that hot sunroom and he is not drinking enough water. While we are glad he is reading and enjoying that pastime, we can't get him to understand that he is becoming more and more dehydrated just by sitting in the heat. So…I talked to him and he agreed to move into the Big Room in the afternoons, where it's cooler. That will help, but the water is another thing. Giving him the replacement drink helps some and I guess it is the best we can do. This afternoon, when I was helping him move his Kindle, etc. to the Big Room, he said, "Y'all sure fuss over me; you'd think I was an old man or something." I laughed because I saw that twinkle in his eye and the corners of his mouth turn up as he passed me in the kitchen.

MONDAY, AUGUST 7TH

Last night, at 3:00 am, I heard something and got up to investigate – it was Mom at her puzzle table working away! When Dad got up around 6:00, we sat outside and drank our coffee since it wasn't too hot…yet. Shaun came up before he started work and took Dad on a morning ride. He is working at home today, so he'll be in and out. Mel got here about 10:30 and I helped her unload the decorations JoAnna had sent for Dad's party. It was a busy day at home and running errands. Rita and the kids made it to Laramie – she sounds so happy.

TUESDAY, AUGUST 8TH

WMA and picking up meds for Mom and Dad, gave them their B-12 shots, and trying to work on some writing projects took up most of my day. Mel texted me and said Shaun was fixing to put the giant watermelon on the table so Dad could cut it. I got there just as he picked it up and was toting it into the kitchen. As he set it down, Shaun said, "That watermelon would knock Dad over." Dad was watching and said, "It would be a terrible thing to be killed by a watermelon!" We all cracked up. After we worked on one half, I covered both halves with some plastic wrap and put them in the porch fridge…they barely fit.

THURSDAY, AUGUST 10TH

My poor cat Maxine is becoming incontinent, and I have to keep her confined to one room of the house to try to minimize the clean-up. If I was home all the time, it wouldn't be such a problem, but she could really create a mess in the days I'm not here. Poor Maxine, she can't help it. I laughed out loud when a thought passed through my mind as I cleaned up her messes…I am taking care of old husband, old parents, and old cat! I've got to find the humor in my situation, otherwise, I might go mad.

Addie came to spend the day and night with me. It was the first time I've seen her since she left for camp in June, so we had a lot of catching up to do. Listening to her camp adventures and the trip to BreyerFest was hilarious. She is almost as good a story-teller as her Mom.

FRIDAY, AUGUST 11TH

What a night! Woke up at 1:30 am and the electricity was off. I was hoping Mom wasn't at her puzzle table when it went off. Mel said she wasn't, but she did come to the stairs with her little light and holler for Mel…haha… like Mel could turn it back on. Thank goodness, I had left one of my portable rechargeable fans over there. Mel said it worked great and kept Mom cool. I didn't go back to sleep until sometime after 4:40, but was up at the crack of dawn because I had to move CT, my horse, into another pasture before we work the cows tomorrow. I wasn't about to wait until this afternoon…it would be 108 degrees by then.

Addie and I had a game day today, what fun! We played Scrabble, Skip-Bo, checkers, and Chronology. Around 11:00 am, we were interrupted by a call from the meat processor. One of his freezers had gone out, and I needed to come and pick up our meat order ASAP. I went over to Dad's to let him know, so I could get a check to pay for the processing. Then Addie and I made the round-trip pronto. Good thing Mel and Dad had already cleaned out the freezers. Mel helped me get the meat into the freezers as soon as we got there, some of it was just cold, not frozen, so we stacked it like the fellow suggested to insure it would freeze quickly.

SATURDAY, AUGUST 13

Shaun hooked up the big trailer and we managed to get the twelve head we wanted to sell into it without any trouble. We also had the smallest calves in the corral, so Dad, Mel, and Shaun could give them all blackleg shots while I took the twelve to the auction barn. Dad asked if I needed him to go with me, but I assured him I would be fine. I reminded him, "Remember, I've done this a few times before." He looked tired, so I think he was glad to go back to the house and rest before they tackled the calves and shots. Before I left for the sale barn, I sprayed the cows for flies. Mel got a funny picture of me running around spraying like a mad woman.

It's a good thing Dad didn't go with me, because when I got to the auction, the line went all the way around the building and out of sight. Lots of cattlemen are downsizing their herds because of the drought; it is getting serious.

When I got back I parked the trailer so Shaun could power-wash it before he put it up. I went home to shower and change, get my bags, and come back to Mom and Dad's so Mel could go home.

This evening about 6:00, Dad and I drove over to pick up the check. He was pleased; it will be enough to help pay for the fertilizer and hay baling. Tonight, I could hear those mama cows bawling for their calves, sounded pretty pitiful.

SUNDAY, AUGUST 13TH

At 4:00 am, I got up to watch the Perseid meteor shower. I was afraid it would be too hot, but there was a slight breeze blowing out of the south and it was pleasant enough. It was so quiet and peaceful, I enjoyed the time alone. All in all, I saw about seventeen meteors before the brush wolves started making a ruckus and I decided to call it a night.

This morning Dad and I were enjoying our coffee out on the patio looking out over the pasture. I asked Dad if he'd heard the mamas bawling for their babies last night. He said he didn't, but it always made him feel bad when he did hear them. Shaun stopped by about then and was sitting with us when a big Charolais cow came right up to the fence by the barn and stared Dad down. We all started laughing. Dad said, "She knows exactly who's responsible for taking her baby." And I believe she did! She stood there and mooed at Dad and stared at him for the longest. I told Dad, "I don't believe I would go wandering out in the pasture for a few days. She looks mad!"

Before we left for church, I put another puzzle out for Mom and promised to help her when we got home. On the way to church, I told Dad that when it finally rained I was going to do a jig, leap in the air, and dance like mad. He got that twinkle in his eye and smiled, "Don't hurt your back." I said, "I might, but it will be worth it!"

After lunch and cleaning up, I took a short siesta before I started watering everything. I really hope we get some rain soon. Since we didn't have church tonight, I helped Mom with her puzzle after making a trip home to feed, etc.

MONDAY, AUGUST 14TH

Up before the daybreak to take water to Mel's cypress tree and stayed long enough to watch the sunrise. On the hill by the corral, you can see the brown landscape stretched out for miles – when the red-orange orb rose shimmering over the horizon, it reminded me of pictures I'd seen of the African plains. I described it to Dad when I got back…he said, "I'll bet it was real pretty." After breakfast and meds, I went to town for groceries, etc. and went by the donut shop to get a treat for Dad's afternoon coffee time. When I got back, I talked Mom into changing her gown, fixing her hair, and putting on some make-up for puzzle pictures. She didn't want to, but I said I wouldn't put out a new one until she got her pictures with these, so she reluctantly agreed. After we did that, she was in a better mood the rest of the day.

Since she was in a better mood, I encouraged Dad later today to go and visit with her. He did and they sat in there a good while – I used that time to put out a new puzzle. I love to hear them in her room talking about old times. It brings back memories of hearing those stories from other relatives, my grandmother, aunts, and uncles. In a way, it makes me sad, because I don't see that same level of fondness for the past in this generation. Maybe one day they will see the value in the "old ways," but I won't hold my breath.

Tonight, Mom had me looking for movies. I stood there pulling DVDs from the shelves and shouting out the titles, because she says "I mumble" She finally decided on a John Wayne night: *Big Jake*, *True Grit*, and *The War Wagon*. I told Mom about an article I read recently where John Wayne said that *Big Jake* was the movie he enjoyed making the most because his son and grandson were in it with him. She thought that was neat. The movie sorting only took about fifteen minutes, but it felt like an hour. I was ready to doctor Dad's feet and then get ready for bed myself.

TUESDAY, AUGUST 15TH

Shaun and I went to Sam's today to get some of the supplies for Dad's party. We enjoyed our trip, but after we got into Sam's, Brother had one of those eye migraine spells like I get. Those are not only annoying, but can mess up your whole day. He was hungry, so we stopped at Juicy's on the way and got some burgers for him and Dad. We made it home and unloaded the stuff, but after he ate, he went on home to rest. I gave Mom and Dad their B-12 shots and did a boat load of stuff around the house, made another trip to town, and helped Mom on her puzzle before I left around 6:30 pm, Sherry got there a few minutes later. As I was leaving, Dad said, "Enjoy your freedom." I laughed and said, "I enjoy being over here." He's right, in a way – I am limited in what I can do while I am here, but in some ways, it is easier. I have quiet time, if Mom is not on a tear, that I can't always get at home. So, I guess it balances out.

WEDNESDAY, AUGUST 16TH

Glorious 64 degrees this morning! I did a happy dance and went over early to have coffee with Dad and Sherry on the patio. Of course, Dad had on Ole Blackie and talked about how cool it was!

Addie came and stayed till her mom could pick her up around noon for a doctor's appointment. When Rachel got here, she showed us pictures from her latest NYC trip and told us all about it, sounds like she had a wonderful time. Caleb and Emelia dropped by on their way to the splash pad, and Marc came in from town with fifty pounds of sausage to put in the freezer. Lord have mercy!

FRIDAY, AUGUST 18TH

Marc stayed with Mom while Sherry and I took Dad to his eye appointment with Dr. B. When we got there, we had to wait longer than expected, but it was worth it. Dad was so surprised and pleased when Dr. B had his entire staff gather in the large open area of the office and give Dad a standing ovation when he walked in. When they stopped clapping, he said, "I've had to live a hundred years to get this attention." Everyone laughed. One of the staffers asked him the secret to his long life...Dad didn't miss a beat. He said, "Wake up with a purpose every morning!" Then, Dr. B started singing "Happy Birthday" and we all joined in. After the song, Dad gave a deep bow and said "thank you." I think it tickled Dr. B because he was grinning from ear to ear. They took several pictures and a video. Sherry even got a picture of Dr. B. taking a picture. They had balloons and a cake for Dad to take home with him. Dad couldn't believe they took the time to do all that just for him. It touched all of us. They are a special group of folks.

When we got home, Sherry fixed a bite to eat, while I looked through old photos trying to find the ones I wanted for the book. I finally gave up and Sherry took me home. I had lots to do and it was already mid-afternoon. Marc and Mom got along fine. He said she only called him a couple of times…lucky.

SATURDAY, AUGUST 19TH

When I got to Mom and Dad's this morning, Sherry caught me up on last night, which actually had its root last weekend when Mom refused to take her FiberCon pills. She had told me in no uncertain terms that she will NOT take any more of those "horse pills." Well, of course, the result was constipation. But, instead of letting me know after a couple of days, she waits all week…well, by then, she is plugged up good. She kept on at Sherry last night till she gave her more laxative than she needed. (Mom never waits long enough for something to work; it should be **instant** in her way of thinking.) And now, poor Sherry feels guilty because Mom spent all night on the pot. I'm sorry. I laughed. When you can't reason with someone, sometimes they have to learn the hard way. Mom is like that. Now, whenever she refuses to take her FiberCon, we can remind her of this incident.

Now, Mom is feeling awful, her feet are swelling again, and she's started back with the "I can't breathe" syndrome. It will be a long weekend. Just one week until Dad's birthday celebration and it doesn't look like Mom will be up for it. The rest of the day and into the night, I was running back and forth for Mom. Dad and I got a chance to read some of the growing stack of birthday cards when Mom dozed off for a spell. He has gotten so many cards already; I think it will pass the one hundred mark by his actual birthday.

I was going to put the lotion on Dad's feet before he went to bed, but he was already asleep by the time I went back in there. Mom's litany of "Oh Lord, help me…Oh me!" has been almost constant since I got here. Sherry texted me after she got home to see how things were going. I told her I was at the kitchen table trying to write my column, but it was mighty hard when your background noise sounds like the Bastille. Haha. The torture continues…

SUNDAY, AUGUST 20TH

Watered Mel's cypress again early this morning and was treated to much the same gorgeous sunrise I'd seen on Monday. What a beautiful way to start the Lord's Day. After church and lunch Dad read most of the afternoon and Mom rested. She had to be worn out after yesterday. I took advantage of the quiet and worked on my column and making lists of stuff to take care of this coming week…I can't believe Dad's party is only a week away!

MONDAY, AUGUST 21ST

Heard something last night about 11:30 and got up to check; it was Mom. She had fallen in the floor and couldn't get up. I tried to help her, but ended up calling Shaun. I didn't want to wake him, so I was relieved when he said he wasn't in bed yet and he'd be right up. Mom didn't seem to be in any pain, so I guess her angel had caught her, that's what I told Mom. She agreed. After Shaun got Mom up, he stayed until she was out of the bathroom and back in her chair, then went on home. I am so thankful he lives close. I moved to the loveseat for the night, and every time Mom moved, I was wide awake. Don't think either one of us slept much. At 4:00 am, she needed to go to the bathroom, so we were up for a while. I made coffee about 5:00 and Dad was up not long after.

Later, Melanie arrived, so I could go home and get started on party chores. I made phone calls all day: Ricky about a sound set-up, the cleaning people about the church, people who I couldn't get in touch with earlier to invite, etc. Also, I made a master list of all the things I needed to do before Saturday. Good grief, what a list!

After we got back from Addie's 4-H meeting, Mel called and said Mom was saying she couldn't breathe, so I took my office fan over for her to use.

TUESDAY, AUGUST 22ND

Addie went with me to WMA. We put together our Christmas shoeboxes today, and I will take them to Cornerstone on Thursday so they can get them to the drop-off point. We love doing that ministry every year, even the kids enjoy it.

After our meeting, Addie and cousin Tiff helped me move some tables and chairs around. I am still trying to figure out the best use of the space and make it "people-flow-friendly." I will figure it out as I go. I have some ideas, but will have to see what it looks like before I make up my mind. It will be a huge task, but if I get started tomorrow, I should finish it by Friday, except for the last minute stuff, like cake, punch, etc. Went to town and ran errands, picked up some stuff for the party and got Mom's meds.

WEDNESDAY, AUGUST 23RD

All this week, I've been battling trying to get our home phone straightened out. It has been out for over a month now. With all the technology we have, you'd think a simple phone would work. I am too busy to worry about it now though. I crammed all of the party stuff I could into my vehicle and went to the church to unload. Then I made another trip to Mom and Dad's to get some memorabilia, photos, and other stuff for the tables. I also tested the video I made last week to see if it would work in the TV I am taking to show it on. Thank goodness, it worked! After I got things sorted, I went to town for more flowers and some ribbon for the tables and arrangements. While I was in town, I ordered the banners and the cake. Then I went back to the church and worked for almost four hours. I called Tiff to come and help me for a couple of hours. She is so sweet to help out. We arranged all the tables and chairs, put on the tablecloths, and she did some cleaning that the regular cleaners had missed, while I worked on the arrangements for the tables. She was a big help.

THURSDAY, AUGUST 24TH

Dad's actual birthdate…I can't believe I have a one hundred year old Dad! I made his card and took it by before I went to work at the church. He was standing in the kitchen when I got there and I peered up into his face and said, "I had to come over and see what a hundred year old man looked like." He laughed and said, "Pretty much the same, I reckon." Dad has protested off and on since we started the preparations for his "ta do" as he calls it, but secretly, I think he's enjoying all the attention. The birthday cards keep streaming in – he has about seventy or eighty by now. Took another load of stuff with me today, hope it will be the last one for setting up.

Mom is getting worse, Mel thinks she might have a UTI, I agree. She took a sample to the clinic today, maybe we will find out before Saturday. Had to make a trip to town, got some stuff for Mel at Wally World and some flowers I needed to finish the tables. Ricky met me at the church and tested his sound system. He got everything set up while Tiff and I continued our work on the backdrop for the photos and space for the banners. I feel like I've made a jillion trips to town and back, and up and down this fellowship hall. Heard late today that Forrest Dyess, a well-loved member of our farming community had passed and we missed his funeral; Dad was sad to hear it.

FRIDAY, AUGUST 25TH

It will be so blistering hot tomorrow, I called Mel to see if Andy could set up some canopies to keep the entry to the church a bit cooler. She said he could. I printed off some 1923 prices sheets for the memorabilia table, took the pruning shears to the church and trimmed some limbs over the drive, plus some stray sprouts on the crepe myrtles, put orange caution tape on the sidewalks where they were buckled, and after two more trips to the house to pick up serving trays, dishes, and cake stands, I finished setting up everything I could think of before going to town to pick up the banners and punch stuff.

The video room was set up in a Sunday school room off the fellowship hall; when I got everything hooked up, I gave Tiff a preview. She said it was really good to see all those old photos. I double-checked everything on the memorabilia table: family heirlooms, photos, and his military display. I sure hope Dad likes it.

Melanie noticed ants were everywhere when she and Sherry had come earlier and asked Sherry to come back and spray for them. When Sherry brought her cupcakes by earlier today, I had expected more of a reaction, but I guess she was too occupied with her "cupcake fiasco," to think about much else. That's all right, I was doing it for Dad, but still, I wanted to please my siblings too.

Tiff helped get the floors vacuumed, checked the bathrooms, and we both dusted. We had a time getting the banners up where they wouldn't sag, but we finally managed. We spent most of the day down at the church, but around 3:00, I declared it "as done as we can get it for now," and we left.

When I got to Mom and Dad's, Cousin Debbie and Aunt Stella from California were there. It was so good to see them again. We had a nice visit before I had to excuse myself and go home so I could make the lemon cake and the punch base for tomorrow. I was plumb wore out.

SATURDAY, AUGUST 26TH

It is here at last! The big day…and I go by Mom and Dad's to see if Cousin Debbie wants to go with me to pick up the cake. She does. The cake turned out great and we hurry to get it into the cool. Shaun and Andy are cooking Wagyu burgers for lunch at Mom and Dad's before the party. I don't have time to eat one, so I grab a small patty and munch on the way to the church. Sherry was a little down because Ashley and Butterbean can't be there and because she's worried about Mom. Mel nearly wigged out about lunch, but I'm sure she's exhausted from Mom's week-long ordeal – even when we get aggravated, we aren't too vocal about it. That way, we can move on instead of getting "all up in the air."

Like I thought, Rita and the kids won't make it, but they are having a great time and I'm glad. Caleb wanted to be there, but couldn't get off work. Rachel, Rob, Gus, and Addie made it, so I won't be alone in my family picture with Dad…haha. Our cousin Wanda and her family came too. We haven't seen them in about seven years. Sherry's son, Ben, flew in from Florida, especially for Dad's celebration, which was doubly nice, because we could all congratulate him in person for his upcoming promotion to full bird Colonel. Sherry and Bill plan to fly down for the ceremony next week. I know they are so proud!

The Lord blessed me with abundant energy, a positive attitude, and Tiff this week, or I don't think I would have made it. Everything went well for the celebration. Dad was able to visit with each guest as they arrived and had their photos taken. I haven't seen him laugh and smile as much as he did today in a long time. It was wonderful.

When it came time for him to say something to the guests gathered to celebrate his milestone birthday, he was witty and charming…it was truly his day to shine!

Unfortunately for Mom, she essentially missed the entire weekend and the out of town company. She did not feel well at all. We will have to call the doctor again on Monday because something is definitely wrong.

SUNDAY, AUGUST 27TH

With a houseful of family and company, Dad and I didn't go to church as usual today. We stayed and visited because the out of town folks all had to leave today around noon or shortly thereafter. It felt weird not going to church, but I am glad we could see our peeps off.

After everyone left, the house seemed awfully empty. Sherry was staying because she was flying to Florida for Ben's promotion mid-week, but then we heard about Hurricane Idalia. Now, it looks like their travel plans may be in jeopardy. Poor Sister, she was really looking forward to going.

MONDAY, AUGUST 28TH

Well, right back into the fray. Porter's Pharmacy called, I called the doctor, the Tyler pharmacy called, I was juggling phones, then Mom's doctor called, she does have a UTI, but it only showed up on the culture. Poor Mom, she missed the entire weekend because of something we should have been able to treat quickly. The Sherry and Bill airline saga has begun…this may go on for days.

THURSDAY, AUGUST 31ST

This month has been a series of highs and lows, like most months, but it seems as if these have been higher and lower than most. Sherry and Bill did **not** get to Florida, Mom is not feeling much better, but Dad had a spectacular time at his birthday celebration, and everything turned out beautifully, and Daddy, Sherry, and I **did** get to watch Ben's ceremony via Zoom. We are all so proud of him and his sweet family.

Wow…a whole year has passed and Dad made it to his 100th birthday, just like we'd hoped and prayed that he would. I am so thankful for another year with my family, spending time in my childhood home, talking with Mom and Dad, and sharing my life with the people who know me best…

my siblings. I don't know what this next year holds, but whatever comes, I will always have this treasured time, a buffer against the unkindness and trouble of this world, a gift of family memories and love that will outlast anything material. After all, as the Good Book says, "If you don't have love, you have nothing."

AND MUCH *Fun* WAS

Had BY ALL

"Love is patient, love is kind. It does not envy, it does not boast, It is not proud. It is not rude, it is not self-seeking, it is not easily angered, it keeps no record of wrongs. Love does not delight in evil, but rejoices with the truth. It always protects, always trusts, always hopes, always perseveres. Love never fails."

I Corinthians 13:4-8a

FIND A *support* NETWORK – OTHER FAMILY MEMBERS, YOUR CHURCH, HOSPICE ORGANIZATIONS, HOME HEALTH NURSES OR SOMEONE WHO IS IN A SIMILAR SITUATION. HAVING A *shoulder* TO LEAN ON AND A LISTENING EAR CAN BE AN ENORMOUS COMFORT.

EPILOGUE

This is not the epilogue I intended to write. I always thought there would be one more Thanksgiving, one more Christmas, another anniversary, maybe even one more birthday…but life doesn't always turn out the way you'd hoped, sometimes it throws you for a loop, and that is just what it did to us on Wednesday, November 8, 2023. It was my brother's fifty-fourth birthday. We were all gathered around Mama when she was escorted into heaven. It was a bittersweet moment, one none of us will ever forget.

The weekend before, I was staying with Mom and Dad as usual, when I noticed some subtle changes in Mom's behavior. Saturday afternoon, we had worked on her latest puzzle for about thirty minutes when Mom said she was tired. Usually, her puzzles lift her spirits and give her a renewed burst of energy, but not that day. I helped her with a bathroom break, then to her chair, reassuring her that we would work on it later, when she felt better. It struck me as odd that she didn't request a temperature or fan adjustment as was her routine, but simply smiled at me and said she was going to rest a bit. Her head went towards her lap and didn't come back up…all night. I stayed outside her room on the couch, but didn't sleep much, checking on her every little while to see if she needed anything. No talking, no sitting up, no fan, no thermostat adjustment…nothing. Having dealt with end of life situations before, I knew what this could possibly mean; I felt it in my gut, but wanted confirmation before I sounded the alarm.

Sunday morning, I called the hospice nurse and told her that my instincts told me I should let my Dad and my siblings know. She agreed. "Always trust your gut," she said. When I called my sisters, they were both getting ready for church, but quickly changed their plans and headed to Mom and Dad's. Shaun, however, was another story…he was in Las Vegas attending SEMA and was two days out with his travel rig. When I talked to him, he was unsure what he should do and I think he had difficulty absorbing the news. I didn't pressure him, but tried to explain the urgency, without alarming him. Two hours later, he called Mel and said he was heading for the Grand Canyon, where he had a reservation, was going to rest, then head home ASAP. Shaun made it home in the early morning hours of Tuesday, November 7th, much to our relief.

In the meantime, on Monday morning, we thought we had lost Mom, but she made a miraculous rally. We all think she was waiting on her boy to make it home. That Monday morning, Mom talked about the beauty of heaven, seeing our brother Joshua (who died in 1986), seeing her Mama and her Papa (he died when she was only one year old), she called Jesus' name, and said she heard trumpets and beautiful music. After talking like this for about an hour, she suddenly sat up (which she hadn't done in days) and her face reflected a peace and joy that was uncanny. She even looked younger! I can only think that her brief glimpse of the heavenly realm had completely changed her countenance. She smiled as if she had just shared a wonderful secret. We were flabbergasted, but relieved. Unfortunately, that respite didn't last long and by that afternoon, Mom had folded back into her lap like before and seemed to be slipping away again. All of us had the same thought…what if Shaun doesn't make it in time? We began praying that God would give him swift and safe passage home. He answered that prayer and early Tuesday morning, Shaun came into the room and called out to Mom. When she heard his voice, she lifted her head and reached out for him…her boy was home.

Mom had another rally on Tuesday afternoon, and even though it wasn't as dramatic as the first, we had renewed hope for a brief time. We all stayed close by for the next twenty-four hours. My oldest daughter Rachel came on Monday and fixed meals, did cleaning, and offered much needed support. Mel's daughter, JoAnna, also came over to be with us on Wednesday, helping with meals, and giving her support. We were all grateful for the blessing of their comforting presence.

My brother remembered a request Mom had made a while back…she wanted to "see his face" again. Shaun has had a beard for the last several years and it was quite long, but Mom always liked him clean-shaven, so she asked him to shave it. He put it off time and again, but Wednesday morning, he knelt down beside Mom and told her what he did. She reached up to feel his face…it was such a sweet moment. You could tell it pleased her, and her approval meant the world to Shaun.

That Wednesday, the eighth, was Shaun's birthday, and all of us hoped that Mom would last through that day, but it was not to be. Dad had been at Mom's side almost continually since Sunday evening, but his bad foot was swelling and he needed it propped up. He wouldn't leave Mom's side, so Shaun moved Mom's recliner from the Big Room into her room. They sat together, hand in hand, most of the morning. We three sisters had been on a round-the-clock vigil since Sunday night and needed a break to stretch and eat a bite, so we left Mom and Dad alone around 12:00 that day. About 12:30, I went to see if they were ok and to ask Dad if he wanted some lunch. Dad was still asleep, but when I looked at Mom, I was alarmed. As I knelt down beside her chair, she began gasping for breath and I yelled for my sisters. When they came running, I told them to "Get Shaun!" He was in the front yard on the mower, but jumped off and ran inside. Joanna and Rachel came in from the kitchen and we were all gathered around Mom and held her until the Lord welcomed her into His presence at 1:40 pm.

When it did happen, it was so fast…and even though we knew it was imminent, none of us were prepared for the shock and deep emptiness we all felt at that moment.

I guess that's the way it is…your head knows what is coming, but your heart hopes things will continue as they always have – the people you love will always be there…when you come home, things will be the same…and time will somehow stand still for you…but that is not what happens, no matter how hard we try to fight it.

Life goes on, even when we want to pretend it doesn't. The world doesn't stop because we lost someone we love; it all just keeps going…even when we want it to stop. That's the hard part – figuring out how to continue. What is this "new way" going to look like? Everything changes in that instant, but it seems like forever before we can absorb it and make sense of it.

That is the nature of grief…one minute we are "back to normal," then we hear a song, smell something familiar, or have a memory drift through our mind, and we are right back where we started…angry, sad, hurting, and alone. You never "get over" losing someone you love, you just learn to live with a new hole in your heart. Time does soften the sharp edges of pain, but it never goes away; it just hides in the background until something triggers it.

As caregivers for so many years, my sisters and I felt lost. We had spent so much of our lives taking care of Mom that when she was gone, we really didn't know how to process it.

I still wander through the house and her room thinking I should be doing something…but what? At first, Dad was enveloped in his own grief and we were so busy with arrangements and taking care of details, we didn't have time to grieve. I am still trying to work through it, we all are…the pain is still raw and I am not able to escape from it, at least for now.

Already, it seems the world has moved on…my friends, my church; everyone is getting along just fine without Mom…but not me, not my siblings and certainly not my Dad. How dare people behave as if nothing is wrong? I want to scream at them…don't you know this is all wrong?! The holidays seem out of place, unwanted even. I haven't had time to grasp that Mom isn't coming back. Like my sisters, I feel like she just left the room and should be coming back any minute, wanting us to move her fan, put out a new puzzle, check the mail…It still hasn't sunk in that she will not be here for Thanksgiving or Christmas – not ever again.

This is the hardest part of caregiving – not the sleepless nights, the exhaustion, the worry, or the frustration – but the emptiness that is the end. Caregiving, especially for the elderly, has only one outcome, death.

We all knew it was coming, but nothing prepared us for the empty room, the familiar chair waiting, the number in our phone that we can call but no one will answer, the birthday hug and song you always looked forward to, but now, you won't get that hug or hear that song again because Mom isn't there…there is no more Mom this side of heaven.

I have still not wrapped my mind around it yet…I don't know when that will happen. It feels so unreal – how can the person that has always been there be gone? How do I go forward? I know what the books and the experts say, but no one can walk this path for you. It is as mysterious and uncertain as the weather – every day will be different. Some will be fair and even good, quite a few will be stormy and unsettled, but with the Good Lord's help, I hope to navigate this journey with my faith intact and my courage renewed. I hope to look back on the time I spent with Mom as one that honors her and helps keep her memory alive.

Our family fabric has been torn once again, but like before, God will help mend it and weave it into a beautiful new pattern that will be even stronger and more resilient than the original.

It is my hope that this book and our family's journey will give you encouragement and a refreshed spirit for the path you are traveling.

May God bless you and guide you on your way.

HILDA ESTELLE "*Martina*" MCANALLY

1927-2023

"Who can find a virtuous woman? For her price is far above rubies. The heart of her husband doth safely trust in her, so that he shall have no need of spoil. She will do him good and not evil all the days of her life."

Mom was the love of Daddy's life. Their love story began when she was a skinny fourteen year old girl, walking through the McAnally farm on her way to Bugtussel school – with a sight detour by the sawmill where Daddy was working. Their parting during WW II was just a pause in their romance that saw seventy-six years of marriage, the births of five children, the struggle and joys in creating a home filled with love and laughter – a home that expanded with the addition of grandchildren and great-grandchildren.

Although not an accomplished cook at first (Daddy said he asked for a hacksaw to cut her first pie), she became famous for her cherry pie, fried chicken, and candied sweet potatoes. That love of cooking was passed on to her descendants, although none of us have quite mastered her specialty dishes!

In addition to cooking, reading, and watching movies, Mom also enjoyed embroidering and quilting, creating many one-of-a-kind pieces for her family to treasure. She also left a legacy of thousands of photographs that chronicle decades of family moments. We may have griped about posing for endless photos, but what a treasure they are now…Thank you, Mom.

She not only poured her heart into her home, but also into her church, being a faithful member of Enterprise Baptist Church for over sixty years, the church treasurer for over twenty years, and a member of the Women's Missionary Auxiliary for fifty years. Mom loved studying the Bible, even taking classes at the seminary. She loved discussing the Bible with various ministers who quickly learned that Mom knew her scriptures, so they had better be prepared! Her faith was an active faith; she spent countless hours visiting the elderly in nursing facilities and those confined to home in the community. Mom would often run errands and shop for them as well.

As the years marched on, Mom watched her family grow through marriage and then a parade of grandchildren…nine in all, filling their home with liveliness, sometimes a little *too much* liveliness, at which point, she would invite them to go outside to play. Nannie, as the grands and great-grands call her, always had a stash of goodies. The grands could always find them because they could hear her digging around in her closet or other hiding place for the forbidden treats after they were supposed to be asleep. As the great-grands started coming, seventeen in all, Nannie threw in the towel and started keeping her treats in a bowl by her chair and all the little ones had to do was ask permission and say thank you. She loved to tease them when they asked for a "Kiss" – she would hold out her arms and say, "C'mere, I'll give you a kiss," knowing they wanted a chocolate kiss, not a real Nannie kiss – but, usually, they got both.

In her later years, jigsaw puzzles became a favorite pastime, and she loved doing her Wheel of Fortune word search books, keeping us on our toes by asking if we could solve the latest puzzle question.

Mom loved giving presents, and even after she no longer went shopping, she would order gifts from the mound of catalogs that stacked up beside her recliner. When the gifts arrived, she would hide them until close to Christmas or our birthday; sometimes hiding them so well that she found them the next year.

But, your greatest gift, Mom/Nannie, was always the gift that cost nothing – your love for all of us…a gift you didn't have to order; it was always available in unlimited supply.

And that love will follow us through the years, along with the wonderful memories of you. We promise to surround Daddy/Pawpaw, with all the love we have until God is ready for you to be together again, never to be parted. We love you.

ABOUT *Tamra* BOLTON

Tamra McAnally Bolton is a writer/photographer who loves to travel, be outdoors, find new adventures, and make new memories. She has written numerous articles for magazines, newspapers, and on-line venues. Tamra has authored two books, *When I Was Small*, a children's book about growing up in rural East Texas; and *A Blessed Life: One World War II Seabee's Story*, a bronze-medal award winning tale of her father's experiences leading up to his involvement in the Battle of Iwo Jima. Tamra lives on her family farm and when she's not on the go, she enjoys visiting relatives and listening to their stories.

Contact

You can contact Tamra by email at:
tamrambolton@gmail.com

www.ingramcontent.com/pod-product-compliance
Lightning Source LLC
LaVergne TN
LVHW010556100826
845148LV00014B/2736

* 9 7 8 1 7 3 4 3 4 4 5 3 0 *